Butterflies

A volume in the *New Naturalist* series, a survey of British natural history published by Collins and edited by John Gilmour, Sir Julian Huxley, Margaret Davies, and Kenneth Mellanby. The *New Naturalist* has been described by the *Listener* as 'one of the outstanding feats of publishing since the war', and by *The Times Literary Supplement* as 'a series which has set a new standard in natural history books'. Founded in 1945, it now contains more than 50 volumes, of which the following have already appeared in Fontana:

EDITORS

John Gilmour MA VMH
Sir Julian Huxley MA DSC FRS
Margaret Davies MA PhD
Kenneth Mellanby SCD CBE

PHOTOGRAPHIC EDITOR

Eric Hosking FRPS

Butterflies

E. B. Ford F.R.S

Collins   The Fontana New Naturalist

First published in the New Naturalist Series 1945
Revised edition published in Fontana 1975

Copyright © in the revised edition E. B. Ford 1975

Made and printed in Great Britain by
William Collins Sons & Co Ltd, Glasgow

Contents

Plates

Section 1

Section 2

Section 3

List of Maps

To the memory of my Father
Harold Dodsworth Ford
with whom I collected butterflies
for thirty years

Author's Preface

There are many books on British butterflies but none on their general biology. A few authors have indeed summarized certain aspects of recent research upon insects as a whole, yet it remains true that no book exists which treats of the varied phenomena to be encountered in studying the butterflies of our islands, nor is there one which uses them as a theme upon which to base discussions of the many remarkable problems which they present. This gap in literature I have now attempted to fill.

It has always appeared to me that evolution is the keynote of biological study and research; consequently, while as far as possible avoiding over-emphasis, I have allowed that point of view somewhat to influence the construction of this book. Taking a variety of problems, relating to structure, the senses, classification, habits, distribution, means of dispersal, and genetics, I have, as it were, adjusted them so as to converge upon the last three chapters which are all concerned, directly or indirectly, with evolution. Furthermore, deeply impressed as I am with the importance of the past in interpreting the present, the historical setting of a subject has a value which, so it seems to me, is sometimes under-estimated, at least in science. Thus I have begun this book with a recent history, that of British butterfly collecting, and ended it with a remote one, that of the origin of our butterfly fauna; a subject which it only becomes possible to discuss after building up biological arguments and data throughout the intervening chapters.

I wish to draw attention to certain other features of this work. There are numbers of excellent books describing the adult and early stages of British butterflies, and giving lists of their times of appearance, food-plants, and localities. It has not been my intention to add to these, for to supply such information yet again would be totally unnecessary and a disastrous waste of valuable space. In the Bibliography I have, however, indicated suitable works of reference where such information can be obtained.

The colour plates appearing in the previous editions of this book have had to be omitted in its paperback form. They illustrated all the species of British butterflies as winged insects, some as living, others as set specimens, and they included many local races and varieties.

The black and white plates, like those in colour, were on entirely new lines when this book first appeared in 1945. They showed the early stages of all the principal Families, and of many smaller groups, indicating distinctions used in classification; also the process of pupation and of emergence from the chrysalis. Furthermore, they comprised a selection of pictures demonstrating protective devices and habits, and microphotographs of the eye and of the developing wings during the larval and pupal stages. They also included nine photographs of localities, of which four have been retained here; for these were an innovation, a feature subsequently copied in other works, and one which seemed generally appreciated.

I have written this book in the hope that it may be useful to scientific entomologists and biologists in general but, in addition, I have especially kept before my mind the needs of butterfly collectors and of all those who love the country. Perhaps it may increase their pleasure by widening the scope of their interests. Many would, no doubt, wish to go no further than this, for there must be a large number of collectors and naturalists who have no intention of becoming amateur scientists. Indeed I should not wish all of them to do so; but I hope that some of them may, for they would add to their enjoyment. Accordingly, I have pointed out numerous interesting lines of experiment and observation which could be undertaken by anyone using the simplest means. Nevertheless, if successfully carried out, the information so obtained would be of genuine scientific value.

With these ends in view, I have explained every term on the first occasion that it is used and provided a rather full index, while I have also added a Glossary in which the technical words are defined. The account given here should thus be intelligible to those with no previous knowledge of entomology.

An obvious difficulty which must be faced in a book of this kind is the decision whether to employ scientific or English names. On the one hand, scientific names carry with them a superficial air of difficulty, and many with a genuine interest in natural history are unwilling to master them, though they have notable advantages (p. 73). On the other, there is in entomology, unlike ornithology, so strong a tradition of their use that many expert collectors do not even know the popular names of all our butterflies. Moreover, as these English names exist only for species, not for sub-species, those interested in geographical distribution must master the, really very simple, scientific terminology whether they like it or not. In order to meet these conflicting demands, I have used the English names throughout, but have added the scientific name on the first occasion that each species is mentioned in every chapter except that on History, where scientific names are not used prior to the time of Linnaeus. Also the scientific and English names are given together in the classification on pp. 79-87. I also append, pp. 303-5, a list of both of them, so drawn up that any one can immediately obtain the equivalent in either direction that he needs.

The author of each specific name is given in the classification on pp. 79-87. The authorship of varietal names, and of foreign species introduced into the text incidentally, appears at the place where each is used for the first time, and this can be found from the Index.

My father, Harold Dodsworth Ford, was able to give his opinion on the plan of this book, though he did not live to see it completed. He brought to bear upon natural history the resources of an original and scholarly mind and, possessing exceptional gifts as a writer and public speaker, he had the art of inspiring enthusiasm in others. Beginning our entomology together more than sixty years ago, he and I formed a collection of butterflies and moths arranged to demonstrate geographical variation and a number of other general principles; indeed we always avoided the aimless amassing of varieties, and kept the problems set by the biology of these insects constantly before our minds. The work brought us much happiness, and I am confident that those who make the study of butterflies something more than a mere hunting for curios will find, as we did, that their labours are amply rewarded.

During the preparation of this book I received constant encouragement from my friend the late Mrs John Bright Clark. Her ability as a literary critic and her helpful suggestions have been of great value to me at all stages of the work.

Mr R. F. Bretherton has read the typescript in detail, and I wish to thank him for the large amount of time which he has devoted to it and for his criticism and constructive suggestions. It has been extremely useful to have the benefit of his extensive knowledge both of practical entomology and of the literature of the subject. Professor G. D. Hale Carpenter also most kindly read each chapter as it was written, as well as the proofs, and I greatly appreciate his help: the detailed comments which he made have been of much assistance to me. I am particularly indebted to him also for allowing me to figure any specimen that I required from the collections in the Hope Department of Entomology at Oxford, and from the original collection of J. C. and W. C. Dale, which is preserved there. I had the great advantage of discussing much of this book with the late Sir Richard Fisher, F.R.S., and I was most grateful to him for his valuable suggestions and for his help on a number of special problems.

I am anxious to express my gratitude to those who have made it possible to produce the Plates in this book. Mr S. Beaufoy, who combines the qualifications of expert photographer and accomplished entomologist, took all the photographs of butterflies in their appropriate surroundings. Fourteen of these are carried over into the present Fontana edition, numbered here (but not originally) as 1 to 14. The remaining photographs have been taken for this edition by Mr J. S. Haywood, who is also a photographer of outstanding achievement. They became necessary in order to meet the requirement now arising from the absence of colour plates in the present production, for to these the pictures of imagines had been almost entirely consigned.

The work of Mr Haywood falls into two parts. Five plates (15 to 19) each show a number of separate figures of living insects, and five (20 to 24) reproduce selections of set specimens from the collections in the Hope Department of Entomology at Oxford, with the kind permission of Professor G. C. Varley. Thus it is no longer possible in the present form of this book to illustrate all the species of British butterflies as had been done in the hardback editions, those appearing here being a representative selection only.

The photographs of living insects have posed great difficulties. These have been overcome with remarkable success by Mr Beaufoy and Mr Haywood, and I should like to express my deep appreciation of the skill and untiring care which they have bestowed upon this task.

As time was somewhat pressing, it has not been easy to obtain living butterflies for illustration in the black and white plates of this edition. Consequently, no special attempt has been made to secure perfect examples for each photograph, the desire of the collector rather than the naturalist, but to show the insects adequately as they may appear in the field.

Nearly all the figures are original, but a few have been borrowed from books and periodicals, and I am grateful to the following authors and publishers for permission to reproduce them: Mr F. W. Frohawk, and Messrs. Hutchison & Co (for Plate 12, Fig. 5); the Editor, *Annals of Eugenics*, and the Cambridge Press (for text-figure 9); the Editor, *School Science Review*, and Messrs. John Murray Ltd. (for permission to reproduce my own drawings, as text-figure 1); Messrs. Methuen & Co. (for Plate 6, Fig. 1, also for permission to base text-figures 3-7 upon diagrams in my own *Mendelism and Evolution*).

During the thirty years since this book was written, the distributions of certain British butterflies have altered materially. Moreover, further information, obtained from collecting in new localities or those studied insufficiently in the past, has extended the previously known habitats of others. Some of these facts have been incorporated in the intervening editions and more are included in this one. It should not be supposed, however, that the account given here is brought fully up to date in this respect. That would involve a survey of the literature which I am no longer able to make at all thoroughly, since I have long passed from the study of entomology, as such, in order to develop the science of Ecological Genetics. Nor would it be desirable to add here more than a selection of such new findings: they would overweigh in one direction a work designed to develop principles, and only those calculated to achieve that aim more accurately can be regarded as necessary to this book as it is now to appear.

OXFORD   E.B.F.

Chapter 1

The History of British Butterfly Collecting

Mohammed II captured Constantinople on 29 May 1453, when the Middle Ages, which, it might be said, began on Christmas Day in the year 800, came to an end. The dawn of the new era was, of course, a gradual one: the learning of the ancients, for so long guarded in Byzantium, was brought to the west by a few scholars who had escaped the ruin of their city, and the spread of the Renaissance to which it gave rise was greatly assisted by the almost contemporary invention of printing. Thus it became widely possible to study not only the mythology but also the science of the Greeks, including their works on Natural History. A love for this subject began to revive; fresh ideas were awakened in men's minds, and a new spirit of exploration and inquiry was abroad. The inspired fanaticism of the religion of an earlier age had largely degenerated to an empty formalism or had been directed into a new channel, which led to the Reformation and, as a goal for the adventurous, the 'Spice Islands' replaced Jerusalem.

Before the end of the fifteenth century the period of the great voyages had begun, and for the next hundred and fifty years expeditions were not only discovering new lands but were also returning with samples of their produce and with curios of natural history. Owing to the stimulus provided by the works of the ancients, and the flood of new material which there was an obvious commercial need to study and classify, it became the fashion to collect plants and animals. The first to form a zoological museum seems to have been the great Conrad Gesner, who was born at Zürich in 1516 and died of the plague in 1565. Though England was behind Continental Europe in adopting the new learning, being far from its source, the cultured courts of Henry VIII in his earlier years, and of Elizabeth, were important agents in establishing it firmly during the sixteenth century. Moreover, the success of the English explorers ensured that a rich supply of exotic produce should be available for the curious to examine, so that, in this country also, educated men began to take a general interest in botany and zoology. Before the end of the century there was already some demand for text-books on these subjects; Gerard's *Herbal* was first published in 1597, and a work on insects could hardly have failed to be successful at that period.

The first to supply this need seems to have been Sir Theodore de Mayerne, a physician to Charles I, who in 1634 published a treatise in Latin, known as *Theatrum Insectorum*. It was not of his own writing, though he added an Introduction. Actually its manuscript had for years passed from hand to hand and owed something to Gesner, Wooton, and Penny, as well as to Mouffet, whose name it bears. The book was a great success; nor was this surprising at a time when a man as typical of his class as Lucius Cary, Viscount Falkland, who was killed at the first battle of Newbury fighting on the Royalist side, could say that he 'pitied unlearned gentlemen on a rainy day'.

Theatrum Insectorum, though not confined to our fauna, was, in fact, the first known entomological publication in Great Britain and an English translation of it was published by Edward Topsel in 1658. The section on butterflies, with which moths are included as nocturnal forms, contains a number of florid and obscure descriptions, illustrated by woodcuts of astonishing crudity indented into the text. That of the Peacock will serve as an example: 'The fourth may be said to be the queen or chief of all, for in the uppermost part of the wings, as it were four Adamants glistering in a beazil of Hyacinth, do show wonderful rich, yea almost dazel the Hyacinth and Adamant themselves; for they shine curiously like stars, and do cast about them sparks of the colour of the Rain-bow; by these marks it is so known, that it would be needless to describe the rest of the body though painted with variety of colours.' The British species are thought to include the Speckled Wood, Wall, Dark-green Fritillary, Red Admiral, Painted Lady, Small Tortoise-shell, Large Tortoise-shell, Peacock, Comma, Common Blue, Green-veined White, Orange-tip, Clouded Yellow, Brimstone, Swallow-tail, Silver-spotted Skipper.

In 1666 appeared the first book on Biology in which the species described are exclusively British. It was written by Christopher Merrett and bears the title *Pinax rerum Naturalium Britannicarum, continens Vegetabilia, Animalia et Fossilia, in hac Insula reperta Inchoatus*. This work includes 21 butterflies, which are distinguished by short descriptive sentences instead of names, and some difficulties have arisen in identifying them. Since this list represents the earliest extant account of our butterflies, it is of considerable interest. The species are considered to be: the Speckled Wood, Wall, Marbled White, Meadow Brown, Small Heath, Hedge Brown, Ringlet, Small Pearl-bordered Fritillary, Small Tortoise-shell, Comma, Common Blue, Purple-edged Copper, Green Hairstreak, Wood White, Black-veined White, Large White, Small White, Green-veined White, Brimstone, Dingy Skipper, and Silver Spotted Skipper.

This assortment is a curious one. It can hardly represent all the butterflies that were known to Merrett and recognized by him as distinct. He must have selected in some way, perhaps rejecting some of the more common in favour of certain striking or less usual insects. Thus it is incredible that he should have known the Wood White but not the Orange-tip, or that he could have confused the male of the latter with anything else. The Black-veined White, which has recently become extinct, was not difficult to obtain even within living memory, and it is considered to have been formerly widespread and not uncommon in the southern counties; its appearance in the list of 1666 supports this view. The inclusion in it, however, of the Purple-edged Copper, *Lycaena hippothoe* L., is truly remarkable, if indeed this is correctly determined; yet the words 'externis purpurascentibus' seem applicable to it alone.[1] There is a persistent tradition that this butterfly, now quite unknown in England, once existed here. Indeed since certain species have become extinct in recent times, it is not inconceivable that others did so at a slightly earlier period, though the changes wrought by civilization were then less severe.

We know very little of the methods used by the collectors of the seventeenth century or of the localities where they worked. Certainly those who were then interested in butterflies must have formed collections; it would be virtually impossible to produce such a book as that of Merrett had they not done so. Scarcely any of their specimens survive, but a few are over two hundred and fifty years old.

The first half of the eighteenth century produced several entomological works of importance wholly devoted to British insects, and some exclusively to butterflies. Among these must especially be mentioned John Ray's *Historia Insectorum*,

[1] The phrase certainly cannot apply to the Small Copper, which is omitted from the list.

published in 1710, five years after the author's death. It probably
includes 48 butterflies considered to be British. A few identifica-
tions are in doubt, but most of the descriptions, though un-
illustrated, are remarkably clear and precise. Twenty-nine of the
known British butterflies are first mentioned in this book; among
them is the Scarce Swallowtail, *Graphium podalirius* L., another
of those species regarded as British only by the early collectors,
though a specimen of it was caught in England during the
First Great War. Several ancient, but apparently authentic,
accounts of it survive. One of them is that of its capture at
Netley, Shropshire, by the Rev. F. W. Hope. This insect is
preserved in the Hope Department of Entomology at Oxford,
which he founded, but we do not know which of two specimens
it is! The Scarce Swallowtail is, however, treated by Ray as but
doubtfully British. The species is a fine one. It feeds on black-
thorn and is quite common in some parts of France and Germany. A butterfly now apparently extinct in England is also
among those listed here. This is the Mazarine Blue, *Cyaniris
semiargus*, and it is remarkable that the species, which is somewhat inconspicuous and appears always to have been rare,
should have been noticed at this date.

Ray's book was followed by the *Papilionum Britanniae* of his
friend James Petiver, which is the first work wholly devoted to
British butterflies. It consists of six plates and two folio pages of
text, published in 1717, and describes, as well as figuring in black
and white, 48 British species, three of which – the High Brown
Fritillary, the Brown Argus, and the Large Skipper – have not
been referred to by previous authors. In addition, it includes
something truly strange under the title 'Albin's Hampstead-Eye,
where it was caught by this curious person, and is the only one
I have yet seen.' This insect has been variously interpreted as a
variety of the Speckled Wood and as a South-Pacific butterfly,
Precis villida F., included by some error. It has, at any rate, never
been seen in Britain again. After Petiver's death in 1718, his
collection was bought by Sir Hans Sloane, with whose accumulated treasures it passed to form the basis of the British Museum.
There, in the Natural History Museum at South Kensington, it
still remains, perhaps the earliest collection of butterflies surviving
in its original form.

In 1720 was published the first book giving coloured illustrations of British Butterflies (and other insects). This is the *Natural
History of English Insects* by Eleazar Albin. In it fifteen species

are represented, with their early stages, but none is an addition to those included in earlier works.

At this period many of the English names in common use differed from those generally employed today. Some of them refer to the favourite collecting grounds of a past age, as the Enfield Eye (the Speckled Wood), or the White Dullidge Fritillary, which suggests a locality from which the species intended (the Glanville Fritillary) has long departed, if ever it really occurred there. Others commemorate forgotten collectors, such as Dandridge's Black Fritillary (the Marsh Fritillary) or Handley's Small Brown Butterfly (the Dingy Skipper). Several of the Skippers were strangely called 'Hogs'; the Small and the Large species being respectively the Spotless Hog and the Cloudy Hog. One of Ray's names will especially strike the modern collector as remarkable: the title of 'April Fritillary' employed for the Pearl-bordered Fritillary. This would today be inappropriate, for that insect begins to appear about the end of the first week in May. Its occurrence at the extreme end of April is only recorded as a rare event in especially early years. But it must be remembered that Ray wrote before the change in the calendar, which took place in 1752. Eleven days were omitted from that year, so that in the early eighteenth century the Pearl-bordered Fritillary would normally be seen in the woods at the end of April. Indeed, memories of the unreformed calendar are even yet preserved among us in several ways, for the traditional flowers of May Morning are far more appropriate to a date in the second week of the month than they are to 1 May as now known. The Small Pearl-bordered Fritillary was at this period known as the May Fritillary, for it appears a little later than the larger species. The name would still be reasonable, though not distinctive. Entomologists themselves were in these early days called 'Aurelians'; a name derived from the golden (*aureolus*) chrysalis of some butterflies.

An event now occurred abroad of such importance that it deserves notice here. In 1735 the celebrated Swedish naturalist Linnaeus (Carl Linné) published the first edition of his *Systema Naturae*, in which he introduced the binomial system of scientific nomenclature which is used today; it is described on pp. 72–3. However, he did not adopt it consistently in his writings until he produced his *Species Plantarum* in 1753. Further, the classification developed by Linnaeus was far in advance of any employed by his predecessors. He improved and enlarged the *Systema Naturae* repeatedly, and in consequence of this it has been decided that the tenth edition, published in 1758, should be judged the starting point for all zoological (though not for all botanical) nomenclature. The Linnean methods were first adopted in England by John Berkenhout, in the first volume of his *Outlines of Natural History of Great Britain and Ireland*, published in 1769. This includes 39 species of British butterflies.

Benjamin Wilkes published the most magnificent of the early works on entomology during the years 1747–60. It is entitled *One Hundred and Twenty Copper-plates of English Moths and Butterflies*. These are accompanied by descriptions of the early stages.

The year 1766 is notable to English entomologists as that in which appeared one of those rare works which for generations have served as a guide to students and collectors. This is *The Aurelian* of Moses Harris, a folio volume of most beautiful execution full of accurate and valuable information. Thirty-three British butterflies are included in it, and some moths. Each of the plates is a work of art and separately dedicated to some eminent person, whose coat of arms it very properly bears. The charming frontispiece represents two gallants of the period, beautifully dressed, collecting in a woodland glade. It is especially valuable since they are seen with the collecting apparatus then used.

Copies of *The Aurelian* were treasured and studied with loving care by successive entomologists, who, for at least a century, drew inspiration from them. It would not be fitting therefore to omit from this account a list of butterflies with which the work deals, with the names used in it.[1]

---

[1] The Comma, the Tortoiseshell Fly, the Purple Emperor, the Admirable, the Peacock Fly, the Black-veined White, the Purple Hairstreak, the Painted Lady, the Marmoress or Marbled White, the Grand Surprise or Camberwell Beauty, the Glanvil Frittillaria, the Little Gate-keeper, the Green Fly (*C. rubi*), the Dark Green Frittillaria, the Wall, the Duke of Burgundy Frittillaria, the Dishclout or Greasy Frittillaria, the High Brown Frittillaria, Clouded Yellow, the Wood White, the White Admirable, the Small Pearl Border Frittillaria, the Meadow-Brown, Wood Lady (*A. cardamines*), the Grizzle, Silver Washed Frettillaria, Copper, Dingy Skipper, Ringlet, Swallow-tail, Pearl Border Likeness (*M. athalia*), Pearl Border Frittillaria, Speckled Wood. (The variations in the spelling of 'Frittillaria' are in the original.)

It will be noticed how strange are some of the alternative forms. The word 'Admiral', which appears today in the names of two of our best known butterflies (the Red and White Admirals), is a corruption of 'Admirable', which is still retained for them by Harris.

The Camberwell Beauty, *Nymphalis antiopa*, is an addition to the British list, and the account of it in *The Aurelian* contains the following passage: 'This is one of the scarcest flies of any known in England, nor do we know of above three or four that were ever found here, the first two were taken about the middle of August, 1748, in Cool Arbour Lane near Camberwell; the last in St. George's Fields, near Newington Butts, the beginning of that month; but as these appeared very much faded and otherwise abused, I conclude they appear from the chrysalis, with the Peacock, about the middle of July, and being of that class it is reasonable to suppose that they live thro' the winter in the fly state, and lay the eggs in spring that produce flies in the July following; for in the same manner do all the flies of this class, and as all that have yet been taken were found flying about willow trees, 'tis the common opinion of Aurelians that their caterpillars feed thereon; but their caterpillar and chrysalis, is to us entirely unknown, and the food a mere conjecture. I do intend to make a strict search concerning them and should I make any discoveries worthy of note, I shall find a proper place and repeat it.' We are indeed frequently told that this prized species, which is in reality an immigrant (pp. 153–4), was on a number of occasions, and in different years, captured near the village of Camberwell, where it was attracted by the willows which grew so abundantly there; and that to this circumstance it owes its best known English name.

In 1775, the author of *The Aurelian*, by then famous, produced a second work, the *Aurelian's Pocket Companion*, in which each species is given not only an English name but also that assigned to it in the tenth edition of the *Systema Naturae* of Linnaeus. Several foreign insects were added in error, but three others genuinely found in Britain appear in it for the first time. They are the Adonis Blue, *Lysandra bellargus*, the White-letter Hairstreak, *Strymonidia w-album* (then called the Dark Hairstreak), and the Pale Clouded Yellow, *Colias hyale*.

In 1793 Edward Donovan began to publish his *Natural History of British Insects*, which continued in monthly parts until 1813. Its most interesting contribution to our knowledge of butterflies will, however, be mentioned later (p. 25).

Further additions to the list of British butterflies were made by William Lewin in his *Papilios of Great Britain*, published in 1795. These were the Small Blue, *Cupido minimus*, which must previously have been overlooked, and the Large Heath, *Coeno-*

nympha tullia, which Lewin wrongly calls *C. hero*. This is a northern butterfly first found near Manchester, and the early collecting seems to have been limited to the southern counties. He also includes for the first time two very notable species, the Large Blue, *Maculinea arion*, and the Large Copper.[1] The latter insect soon became the pride of British entomology, for abroad it occurs only as smaller and less magnificent sub-species. However, we retained it for little more than a generation. The first specimens were found in one of the Huntingdonshire fens, apparently not long before Lewin wrote, but the exact date cannot be determined. The butterfly was then discovered in Cambridgeshire by W. and F. Skrimshire, who saw some numbers as they were going to Ely in a gig, but they did not obtain a good view of them; on their return one settled on the road and they then realized that it was something out of the common. This was either in 1797 or 1798. Subsequently the species was detected in Norfolk, also in one locality in Suffolk, and there were occasional records of it from fens in various parts of the country, and to this type of habitat it was strictly confined. By 1835 it had become very rare, and the last captures seem to have been made at Holme Fen in 1847 or 1848. The disappearance of the Large Copper in England will be discussed in a later chapter (pp. 142–3).

Lewin also includes an allied species, *Lycaena virgaureae*, which he calls the Scarce Copper. This, like the Purple-edge Copper and the Scarce Swallow-tail already mentioned, is one of those insects formerly held to be British though unsubstantiated as such and now quite unknown here. Kirby and Spence at a later date (1826) imply that it was found in the fens with the Large Copper, but far more rarely and locally. There may be some truth in this, but confusion of names, errors in identification and actual fraud, are doubtless responsible for some of the records of this insect. Though about a thousand genuine specimens of the Large Copper survive, only one or two of the ancient and supposedly indigenous examples of the Scarce Copper are known.

At the very end of the century one more butterfly was added to the British list, the Chequered Skipper, *Carterocephalus palaemon*. Its discovery was announced to the Linnean Society by Dr Abbott

---

[1] Lewin's figures represent the Large Copper, but he called it *Lycaena hippothoe*. So does Donovan, who described and figured it in his seventh volume (1798). In 1803 Haworth in *Lepidoptera Britannica* showed that it was distinct from *L. hippothoe*, and named it *L. dispar*.

in 1798, and ⸺ ⸺ lished by Donovan in Vol. 8 of his *Natural History of Brit⸺ ⸺ects* (1799).

It is not diffic⸺ to form a general idea of butterfly collecting in the eighteenth century. A number of hunting grounds in the neighbourhood of London were then especially famous. To the north is Epping Forest, to the south Darenth Woods, near Westerham, and at a greater distance Ashdown Forest. In such places the Aurelian might not infrequently be seen with his surprising equipment. This included the clap-net or 'bat-fowling net'; a deep gauze bag five or six feet long, U-shaped in section and hung from rods. These were wielded with both hands and they could be brought together, so closing the net. 'The Bat-folder,' said Harris, 'is made of musketta gause, and is form'd like the batfolding-net made use of to catch birds; these may be had at the fishing tackle shops, by asking for them; they call them butterfly-traps.' The insect, having been engulfed in this contraption, was killed by nipping with the fingers, of course through the net, or sometimes it was only stunned by this means and later killed by being placed in a tin with finely chopped laurel leaves. The specimens were usually pinned into a metal box. This box was usually oval in shape and lined with cork. Thus they were brought home and 'set', sometimes with cardboard braces under the wings in a manner the details of which are somewhat obscure; but the fashion was still remembered by Edward Newman in 1869 as a splendid practice of former days. More usually, however, the insects were simply pinned on a sheet of cork, the wings arranged with needles and held in position by wedge-shaped strips of cardboard, for grooved setting-boards were not in use in this country until well on into last century. Nor were the wings pushed so far forward as is the custom today, indeed often they even sloped backwards.

Apparently the collector sometimes required a choice of nets when in the fields; a ring net, called a 'racket net', of more modern appearance was carried in addition. Or the scissors-net, also called the 'forceps', two small racket nets hinged together like scissors, might suit the needs of the moment better than the egregious clap-net, which was itself surpassed in clumsy ineptitude by some of the tools which the entomologist was advised to employ. These were described with the strange artistic elaboration of the times, their simplification being left to the imagination of the reader. A lion's head cast in bronze, the tongue prolonged and hooked, was to be screwed to a pole; a device recommended for pulling down the higher branches of trees. The collector of this period presumably took a caddy with him. Yet it may be that much of his work was done with homelier instruments less advertised.

Collections were kept in cabinets or boxes much as they are now, but the aim was to display a short series only of each insect. Variety hunting had yet attained no considerable proportions, while the difficulties of studying geographical variation were great, nor was its interest appreciated; for Darwin had not yet come.

One feature of the latter part of the eighteenth century deserves special mention: the rise of entomological societies.[1] The first of these in this, or any other, country was the Aurelian Society, which seems to have existed as early as 1743, if not before. It rented a room in the Swan Tavern, 'Change Alley, and a meeting was in progress there on 25 March 1748 when the great fire of Cornhill destroyed the building, together with the entomological library and collections that were housed in it. The members barely escaped with their lives, and the Society seems thereupon to have come to an end. However, in 1762 a second Aurelian Society was founded, of which nothing is known except that it was to this body that Moses Harris dedicated *The Aurelian* in 1766. The Society of Entomologists of London had but a short life, from 1780 to 1782. This completes what is known of such entomological associations in the eighteenth century, but their progress may briefly be traced further.

The third Aurelian Society was founded in 1801, Haworth (p. 27) being one of its chief promoters. This came to an end in 1806 through natural dissatisfaction with the rule that the members were bound to present to the Society's collection a specimen of any species they possessed which was not represented there. Upon its dissolution, a new body was founded, apparently with the same personnel, called the Entomological Society of London. This issued three parts of Transactions (1807–12), bound together as Vol. 1 in the latter year. They are the first known publication of any entomological society in the world. The later history of this Society is confused and obscure. It seems that after a period of nearly complete inactivity the majority of the members seceded in 1822 and instituted the Entomological Society of Great Britain. In 1824, however, they joined a number of Fellows of the Linnean Society to form the

[1] For the early history of entomological societies see Neave *et al.* (1933).

Zoological Club of the Linnean Society: the predecessor of the present Zoological Society of London.

In 1826 was founded the Entomological Club, which still exists. Though it has long since ceased to perform any active functions but those of a dining club, it is worth noticing as the oldest entomological organization extant.

A document proves that the Entomological Society of 1806 still survived in 1832. The following year the present Entomological Society of London was founded, now one of the foremost entomological societies in the world. The meeting which initiated it was held in the rooms of Mr J. G. Children at the British Museum on 3 May 1833, and he took the chair. The first General Meeting took place on the 22nd of the same month at the Thatched House Tavern, St James's Street, the chair being occupied by J. F. Stevens, though J. G. Children was the first president. The Rev. W. Kirby (p. 28) was elected the Hon. Life President (1833–50), an honour conferred only on two other men, Prof. J. O. Westwood (1883–93) and Sir Edward Poulton (1934– 43). This Society now occupies a fine house of its own in Queen's Gate, South Kensington, to which a magnificent meeting room has been attached. On the completion of its centenary in 1933 it became the Royal Entomological Society of London. Its splendid series of publications date from 1834.

We may now continue the sequence of entomological history. The first publication of the nineteenth century which requires notice is one of great importance. This is the *Lepidoptera Britannica* of A. H. Haworth, the first volume of which appeared in 1803. It has with some degree of justice been called the earliest work on British butterflies produced in a scientific manner. At any rate it is of the first rank, comprehensive and accurate. In it the pale female variety, *helice* Hbn. of the Clouded Yellow (pp. 226–9) appears as a distinct species.

The number of butterflies new to Britain that were discovered during the last century is small. The earliest of them is the Scotch Argus, *Erebia aethiops*, which was first found in the Isle of Arran by Sir Patrick Walker in 1804. This species is now known to be widespread and often abundant in Scotland. It formerly occurred in the north of England in a number of places, but is now apparently extinct in most of them. At the same time Sir Patrick Walker recorded the capture of an allied species which he is said to have found flying with it in the Isle of Arran. This is *Erebia ligea*, the 'Arran Brown', a well-known continental insect, but its inclusion in the British fauna is generally regarded as an error. I shall later (pp. 146–7) give the reasons which lead me to suspect that the original report of its capture is not so fantastic as has sometimes been supposed. The discovery of these insects was made known by J. Sowerby in his *British Miscellany* in 1804 and 1805, in which the figures representing them are transposed. This was corrected, and further information supplied, in Vol. 12 of Donovan's *Natural History of British Insects* (1807), which was then still continuing.

The *Transactions of the Entomological Society*, which was founded in 1806 (p. 27), have an interest for us additional to the fact that they are the first known publications of any entomological society, for in the part issued in 1812 is announced the discovery of our one truly alpine butterfly, the Mountain Ringlet, *Erebia epiphron*. This capture had been made near Ambleside on 11 June 1809 by T. S. Stothard, R.A., but it is wrongly attributed to Scotland by Mr Haworth, who reported it. The species is in reality not uncommon at the higher elevations in Perthshire and some neighbouring counties but this was not known until long afterwards, nor was its wide distribution above 1800 feet in the English Lake District. Indeed, J. F. Stevens, writing in 1828, says that it was for some time considered but a reputed British species, so rare did it appear to be. This was in his valuable *Illustrations of British Entomology*, which he published from 1827 to 1837.

Prior to that work, however, an event of international importance had taken place: the appearance of the far-famed *Introduction to Entomology* in four volumes (1815–26) by W. Kirby and W. Spence, which has had a profound effect upon the science and entitled its authors to a place among the greatest entomologists of history. This, indeed, was a period of notable writings, for the *Introduction to Entomology* is actually contemporary with the great work of John Curtis, *British Entomology*, which appeared in sixteen volumes during the years 1824–39. In it was described the capture of two butterflies new to Britain.

The first of these was the Black Hairstreak in the sense now accepted, *Strymonidia pruni*. The curious circumstances surrounding its discovery are worth recording. A member of the Entomological Club, whose name is not preserved, had in 1828 bought some specimens from their captor, an Ipswich dealer named Seaman, under the impression that they were the Whiteletter Hairstreak, *S. w-album*, the Dark Hairstreak of former days. Seaman accordingly had no scruples in revealing their correct locality, which was Monk's Wood, Huntingdonshire. When, however, the great Edward Newman (p. 30), then in his youth, identified the species correctly, and it became apparent that a Hairstreak new to Britain had been discovered, Seaman decided to keep the true habitat to himself. He therefore announced that the wrong locality had been given: that Yorkshire, not Huntingdonshire, was its home. This error is therefore introduced by Curtis in 1829 (Vol. 6) into his original account of the species as a British butterfly. It was not until 1834 that it was corrected and the true locality divulged by J. F. Stevens in an Appendix to his *Illustrations of British Entomology*.

The second butterfly which appears in *British Entomology* (Vol. 10) as new to our fauna is the Lulworth Skipper, *Thymelicus acteon*. The announcement was made on 2 March 1833 that on 15 August of the previous year J. C. Dale, of Glanville Wootton, an entomologist of high repute, had found this species in numbers at Lulworth Cove and in its neighbourhood. The spot where the first specimen was captured is called Durdle Dore, which is to the west of the Cove. On Plate 14 is a view of Lulworth itself, giving an excellent impression of that locality, in which the species is yet to be found. It is now known that the species is in England almost restricted to the coast of Dorset and South Devon, where in some places it is common.

While John Curtis was producing his *British Entomology*, the first occurrence of a rare vagrant in these islands was made known in the third volume of *Loudon's Magazine of Natural History*, published in 1830. This is Hunter's, or the Scarce, Painted Lady *Vanessa huntera=virginiensis*, an American species which has, in all, been recorded in England about a dozen times. The first capture was made by Captain Bloomer at Withybush, near Haverfordwest, Pembrokeshire, in July or August 1828.

We now reach that turning point in English affairs, the year 1837. 'The History of the Victorian Age will never be written,' said Lytton Strachey, 'we know too much about it. For ignorance is the first requisite of the historian.' This is as true of entomology as of many other activities of the period, so that from now onwards it will be possible only to draw attention to isolated events of special interest to butterfly collectors.

Publications become exceedingly numerous from this date, and I propose to mention but two of the books which appeared after that of Curtis. The earlier of these is the magnificent *British Butterflies* of H. N. Humphreys and J. O. Westwood. It contains 42 most beautifully coloured plates showing larvae, pupae, and adult insects. The plants are charmingly represented, as are some of the butterflies, though others are strangely crude. The work is marred by the ridiculous insertion of numbers of species which have no claim whatever to be British. It was first published in 1841. A second edition appeared in 1849 and in this some of the plates are curiously transposed and altered; when any difference between the two is observable, the later are nearly always the worse. One singular change in the second edition has, I believe, never before been remarked. Plate 1 is among those altered: it is that depicting, among others, the Swallow-tail, *Papilio machaon*. In the earlier edition this is correctly represented from an English specimen, in the later it is from a Continental one. The differences (pp. 285–6) are clearly portrayed. Whether the authors really did not know that the ordinary English race of this species is distinct from any other, or whether they supposed that their readers would not remark the unfortunate substitution which, for some unknown reason, had been effected, does not appear. The note made, no doubt correctly, in the first edition that the Swallow-tail had been drawn from a British example in the collection of H. N. Humphreys remains unaltered in the second, in which it is certainly false.[1] I may add that the two specimens are also perfectly distinct in size, shape, and setting. The second author of this work, Prof. J. O. Westwood, was one of the most distinguished entomologists of the Victorian period and his influence on the science was immense. When the Rev. F. W. Hope founded the Department of Entomology at Oxford in 1849, he appointed Westwood as keeper, and further nominated him first holder of the Professorship which he endowed in 1861.

I cannot omit from this record Edward Newman's *British Butterflies*, published in 1869. It is the most famous work on the subject that appeared in the latter half of the century and one of the best that has ever been produced. The illustrations are fine woodcuts, but they are somewhat blurred in later copies owing to over-use. The text is admirable, a model for all who write on such subjects. Further, Newman had obtained county lists from a large circle of colleagues; these are of great value in themselves, and they will become of much importance as a record of the

---

[1] It is, however, possible that one of the occasional Kentish specimens (p. 286) had been substituted for the example of the normal English fen form shown in the first edition.

distribution of the various species at a former period. Innumerable entomologists have used this work as their principal textbook, as I myself once did; and it has remained for me a lasting source of pleasure.

A special feature of Victorian entomology was the production of journals devoted to the subject. One of these is indeed pre-Victorian, for the *Entomological Magazine* first appeared in 1832. H. T. Stainton established both the *Entomologists' Annual* in 1855, which ran to twenty volumes, and in 1856 the *Entomologist's Weekly Intelligencer*, of which ten volumes were published, ending in 1861. The journal next to be produced is still in existence. This is the *Entomologist*, which had first appeared in 1840, with Edward Newman as Editor, and continued until 1842. This completed the first volume, after which it lapsed for 22 years. It was revived in 1864, the need for an entomological journal having become acute owing to the cessation of the *Entomologist's Weekly Intelligencer*. Newman again took up the position of Editor, making what was virtually a new journal strictly continuous with the old, for it was published as Volume 2 of the *Entomologist*, and from that time onwards it has continued to appear. Two other journals still in existence were also founded during the century: the *Entomologist's Monthly Magazine* in 1864 and the *Entomologist's Record* in 1890.

Four new British butterflies were recorded between 1837 and the end of the century. The earliest of them was the Long-tailed Blue, *Lampides boeticus*, which is a rare immigrant. It was first caught in this country on 4 August 1859 near Christchurch by Mr Latour, and another was taken on the same day by Mr McArthur, who found it on the downs near Brighton, where he actually obtained one more on the day following. Occasional specimens have been captured at intervals since that date.

The next new species to be announced is indeed a remarkable one. It is at once the largest ever found in Britain and our only member of the great family of distasteful butterflies (p. 79), the Danaidae, the majority of which are tropical. This is the Milkweed, Monarch, or Black-veined Brown Butterfly, *Danaus plexippus*. Over a hundred and fifty specimens of it have now been recorded as seen or captured here, and I once had the pleasure of taking it myself in South Cornwall (p. 158). The first specimen was caught by Mr J. Stafford at Neath, South Wales, on 6 September 1876. It was recorded the same year by Mr J. D. Llewelyn in the *Entomologist's Monthly Magazine*, Vol. 13.

No further addition to our list of butterflies was made until 1885. It was then found that two specimens of the Short-tailed Blue, *Everes argiades*, had been taken in 1874, notice of further captures, recorded in the *Entomologist*, having brought the original discovery to light. The butterfly is of excessive rarity here, very few specimens having been obtained; but it could easily be passed over as the Silver-studded Blue, and doubtless this has happened. The original examples, a male and a female, usually but incorrectly stated to be two males, were caught in a small quarry about two miles from Whatley Rectory, Frome, Somerset.

The sequence of this brief survey closes with an extraordinary event: the discovery that an additional species of butterfly existed unsuspected yet commonly in south-east England. This is the Essex Skipper, *Thymelicus lineola*. Up to 1890, when its occurrence was recorded in the *Entomologist* by Mr Hawes, it had been confused with the Small Skipper *T. sylvestris*, which it greatly resembles, though it had long been known abroad. It may be had in plenty along the north coast of Kent and in the Essex marshes, while it is also found in scattered colonies elsewhere (p. 126).

We have now reached the end of the nineteenth century, beyond which it is not proposed to carry this history. Yet a few general features of Victorian collecting may be briefly reviewed. During this time the aim of collections had changed from displaying a short set of each species to the accumulation of varieties and geographical forms. So, too, had its methods; the uncouth paraphernalia of former times had been swept away. The ring net, which might be round or elongated (the kite net), was alone employed, and the use of potassium cyanide for killing became general. Up to the early Victorian period pins were of a construction which at once distinguishes them from the modern type, for the head was made of two turns of fine wire twisted on to the shaft. These will be seen today transfixing all the earlier specimens. Since it was found that common pins caused corrosion, and were unsightly owing to their large heads, small-headed 'entomological pins' were introduced. At first they were usually gilt; subsequently they were made of silver, or some other material not easily corroded, but in later years they were more usually protected with black enamel, which is still the general custom.

In one respect the earlier entomologists undoubtedly deserve censure. It was not until the latter part of last century that it became the general rule to attach a label to each specimen giving its place and date of capture, and the captor's name. That omission robs nearly all early insects of their interest, for upon the existence of such information the value of a specimen naturally depends. Instances of such labelling occur quite early, but they are very rare. Such an omission was as contrary to common sense as to scientific method. It is absurd to say that entomologists cannot be blamed for this folly because the custom of adding these data had not generally been introduced. When my father and I began to collect butterflies, now many years ago, we attached data labels to every specimen from the first, because it was evident that the chief interest of our insects depended on them. Yet at that time we had seen no collection but a very old one, in which the practice was not adopted. What we did others could have done, and they were culpable for their negligence.

The early entomologists are, nevertheless, worthy of the very highest praise. Of the butterflies resident in or normally migrating to this country, all but five[1] had been discovered before the end of the eighteenth century, as well as many of the rare immigrants. Their habits had been studied and the early stages of most of them were familiar. The amount of careful investigation which this entailed was immense. That Merret knew the Wood White as English in 1667 suggests that it was commoner then than now, but the insect would require looking for, and it also suggests that some fairly thorough work had by then already been done.

Moreover, those of us who knew some of the entomologists of, say, the 1850s and 1860s, as it has been my privilege to do, will realize what fine naturalists many of them were. Their knowledge was largely empirical and died with them, but it was great; I rarely find their like today. Indeed, the collectors, and, fortunately, they are in a minority, whose main object is merely to search for varieties, without any real interest in the insects themselves or the countryside which they inhabit, could learn much from the entomology of an earlier age. Yet the history of this subject is of value not merely to such as these but to all who study it; we may look with advantage on the labours of the past whether we seek only to reap the benefit of them or to carry them forward and to extend their scope.

[1] The Scotch Argus, Mountain Ringlet, Black Hairstreak, Lulworth Skipper, Essex Skipper.

Chapter 2

The Structure and Development of Butterflies

The Structure of Insects, The Structure of Butterflies
The Early Stages and Development of Butterflies

THE STRUCTURE OF INSECTS

In order to understand the structure of butterflies and to appreciate both their marvellous adaptations and their imperfections, it is necessary to know something of the great group of animals, the Insects, to which they belong. This is a vast assemblage, for it includes more than half the known species of animals,[1] excepting microscopic forms. All insects possess a number of features in common, but here it is necessary to describe only the more fundamental of them.

The human skeleton is an internal one of bone, and our body is built up round it. Not so with insects, whose skeleton is external, making a hard protective box within which the delicate tissues of the body are housed. It is composed of chitin, a horn-like substance chemically allied to the keratin of which our finger-nails are made. The whole animal is divided into a number of rings or *segments*. In the ancestral forms from which modern insects are derived, the segments were repeated with but little variation down the length of the body. Each consists of a firm chitinous hoop built up of four parts: a large dorsal plate, the *tergum*, and a large ventral one, the *sternum*. These are united on each side by a small and softer lateral region, the *pleuron*. The segments are joined to one another in front and behind by a soft fold which allows of movement, and each bears a pair of jointed walking limbs or *appendages*. Such segmentation is not merely external; it affects also the internal organs, so that the segments have their own muscles and nerve-supply. The body is sub-divided into three main regions, the head, the thorax or chest, and the abdomen, and the structure of the segments has

[1] Hesse estimated that the total number of animal-species known in 1928, excluding Protozoa (the microscopic single-celled forms) lay between three-quarters of a million and slightly over a million, and that between 500,000 and 750,000 of them were Insects.

come to differ widely in these parts; yet they retain their fundamental attributes throughout.

All insects possess three pairs of true jointed legs, and these
are developed on the three segments of which the thorax is
invariably composed, one pair to each. The more anterior
segments have been immensely modified, for they form the head
and there are six (some authorities say seven) of them. The
insect's mouth is merely a round hole at the front of the body,
possessed of no true jaws of its own; it is remarkable that their
place is taken by several of the primitive walking limbs, which
belong to the head segments. These, greatly modified, are held
up round the mouth and form a biting or sucking apparatus as
the case may be: a situation widely different from that found in
ourselves, for our jaws represent part of the skeleton supporting
the gills of our fish-like ancestors.

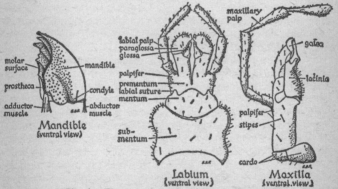

Fig. 1   The mouth-parts of the cockroach.

The mouth-parts of a biting insect, such as a cockroach or a
beetle, are the least modified from the ancestral type; they are
well seen in the cockroach and are four in number. Above is an
unpaired flat plate, the *labrum*, which forms a roof to the mouth.
It is an extension of the tergum at the top of the head and does
not represent modified walking limbs, as do the other mouth-
parts, which are shown in Text Fig. 1. On either side below it are
the main jaws or *mandibles*, worked by strong muscles and
hinged by means of a ball-and-socket joint. Behind them again
is a pair of *maxillae*. These may act as an additional pair of
jaws, the toothed portion (*lacinia*) fitting into a protective sheath
(the *galea*). Attached to them is a jointed structure, the maxillary

palp, which acts as a sensory feeler. The floor of the mouth consists of a flattened structure, the *labium*, which represents a
modified second pair of maxillae partly fused together. In it can
be recognized the remains of a lacinia and a galea, and it also is
provided with a sensory 'labial palp'. The cavity surrounded by
these parts (the buccal cavity) is occupied by a tongue, the
hypopharynx, which is perhaps mainly sensory in function.

A notable feature of insects, well seen in butterflies, is the pair
of sensory feelers or *antennae*. These again have been modified
from primitive walking limbs belonging to the second segment
of the head, in front of those forming the mouth-parts.

The number of segments comprising the abdomen of insects
varies somewhat. In butterflies it is ten. The legs belonging to the
more anterior of them have generally been lost, but those of
the more posterior ones remain, though immensely modified and
put to a new purpose. For they contribute to the formation of
the complex external genital organs, including those by which
the male clasps the female.

Two more striking external features of insects must be mentioned. The eyes will be described in the next chapter, so that it is
now only necessary to notice that they are of remarkable construction, being quite unlike our own. Wings are characteristic
of the vast majority of the species. These are outgrowths of the
terga on the second and third thoracic segments. That is to say,
they have not been modified from walking limbs as have those of
bats or birds; indeed, as already mentioned, the legs belonging
to these segments still remain and serve their original purpose.

When we turn to the internal structure of insects, we find
that its peculiarities are largely due to the nature of the space in
which the organs lie. This 'body-cavity' is, of course, not that of
the gut or alimentary canal through which the food passes; on
the contrary, it is the main space in which are situated the gut,
heart, reproductive system, genital, and other organs. A similar
space, called a 'coelom', is to be found in our own bodies. Yet it
is entirely distinct from that of insects, which, unlike ours, is full
of blood and is therefore called a *haemocoele*, for it represents the
cavities of our own blood-vessels – the arteries, veins, and heart.
A coelom does in fact appear in the embryo insect, as a series of
pouches around which the various segments are built up, and
indeed that is a fundamental feature of their construction. Later
in development this coelom is crowded almost out of existence
by the enlarging blood-spaces which give rise to the haemocoele.

This in the adult is largely occupied by an extensive *fat-body*, in which reserves of food are stored, and it fills up most of the spaces between the other organs.

Insects are profoundly affected by the fact that their main body-cavity is full of blood, and in them this circumstance is a potent factor both for good and ill. It provides an immense simplification in the transport of the products of digestion and in the removal of waste materials, while, on the other hand, it is a great source of danger. The fact that the blood-system of insects is an 'open' one, in which the greater part of the fluid is not confined within tubes, makes any injury particularly dangerous, for most of the creature's blood may gush out through a simple cut.

The heart is a rhythmically contracting pipe or tube running the length of the animal's back just below the terga. As it dilates, blood in the surrounding body-cavity enters it through openings in its sides guarded by valves, a pair to a segment. When it contracts, the valves close, preventing the return of the blood, which is forced forwards along its length and out into the body-cavity again through short vessels at the front end. The action of the heart thus keeps the blood stirred and constantly in motion, like water heated in a kettle.

To familiarize ourselves with the internal anatomy of an insect it is thus necessary to abandon many of our preconceived ideas of what an animal's body should be like, for these are naturally founded upon our own. The central nervous system, instead of being a single hollow tube running along the back, is composed of two solid nerve cords lying side by side ventrally. At the anterior end they part and encircle the gut, forming a brain on either side of it (pp. 54–5). Along the length of the two cords are subsidiary brains called *ganglia*, originally a pair to a segment, but now fused together to an extent which differs in the various groups.

A salivary duct opens into the buccal cavity ventrally and, dividing, runs back to two large salivary glands[1] lying on either side of the front part of the gut. They are modified to form silk-glands in the caterpillars of butterflies and moths. The mouth, which is dorsal to the orifice of the salivary duct, leads into a narrow tube called, as in Man, the gullet or *oesophagus*. This soon

[1] A gland is an organ manufacturing substances of use to the body (secretions) or removing waste products (excretions). The tube which carries away the products of a gland is called its duct.

begins to expand into a region which is variously modified in different species, sometimes comprising a storage sac or *crop* and a muscular *gizzard* provided with horny teeth. Immediately behind this region open a number of short blind tubes, the *hepatic caeca*. These are glandular and pour digestive juices on to the food as it enters the next section of the alimentary canal, which is the *mid-gut*. This is coiled and very short, yet through it alone are the products of digestion absorbed. Beyond it is the long *hind-gut*, also coiled, in which the excrement collects, and this leads to the anus.

The living substance of the body is called *protoplasm*. It is jelly-like material of complex and ever-changing nature, generally divided into microscopic units, known as *cells*. Each of them contains a small spherical region, the *nucleus*, which controls its activity, while the remainder of its protoplasm is called *cytoplasm*. The vital processes give rise to waste products which must be removed or 'excreted', and these are of very varied nature. Excepting carbon dioxide, the elimination of which is one aspect of respiration, the bulk of them consist of nitrogenous compounds. Such substances are excreted by our own kidneys, and insects possess organs having a similar function though a very different origin and structure. These are the Malpighian tubules (named after the great Italian biologist of the seventeenth century, Marcello Malpighi), which are attached at the point where the mid and hind guts join. They may vary from two to over a hundred in number, but they usually look like a mass of exceedingly fine threads. Actually they are hollow tubes ending blindly and, lying in the haemocoele, they are bathed in blood. They excrete nitrogen generally as uric acid, but sometimes as urea or even as ammonia; also the usual inorganic salts, such as chlorides of sodium and potassium, and carbonates of magnesium and calcium. These two latter substances often occur as solid granules in the tubes. Crystals of uric acid may also be present; as may those of calcium oxalate, particularly in the caterpillars of butterflies and moths.

Insects, unlike the Vertebrates, were evolved on land, and only a small proportion of them have been able to adapt themselves to living in fresh water, while extremely few species, out of the half-million or more that are known, have become marine. It is therefore essential for them to eliminate their waste substances with a minimal loss of their restricted water supply. This is achieved, in principle, as in ourselves, by extracting the waste products from the blood and passing them into the excretory organs in solution, and then concentrating them by reabsorbing most of the water again. The details of the process are rather varied, but in butterflies and moths the upper part of the Malpighian tubules contains clear fluid with the excretory products in solution, while solid granules of uric acid, calcium oxalate, and other substances, appear farther down owing to the reabsorbation of water. These products then escape into the intestine and are voided with the faeces. It may be noted that some of the nitrogenous excretory products are used in manufacturing chitin, and even in the production of pigments (pp. 65–8).

The respiratory system of insects is most extraordinary and demonstrates the profound difference between them and Vertebrates such as ourselves. For in the great majority of insects the blood plays no part in respiration. Consequently it does not contain a 'respiratory pigment', like the haemoglobin, which makes our own blood red or purple, depending on whether it is oxygenated or deoxygenated, or even the pale bluish haemocyanin of those relatives of the insects, the Crustacea. These pigments are vehicles actually carrying the oxygen. On the contrary, in insects oxygen is generally brought direct to every cell by minute *tracheal tubes* which ramify through the body in incredible numbers. They arise at openings called *spiracles*, of which there is one pair in most of the segments. These are seen very clearly along the side of the young caterpillar shown on Plate 8, Fig. *b*.

The tracheal tubes have a spiral thickening in their walls, which prevents them collapsing; they branch, and at first interconnect, forming a network. Later they divide repeatedly, becoming thinner and more numerous like the branches of trees, and when they are about one-thousandth of a millimetre in thickness,[1] their structure changes, for their walls are no longer spirally thickened. They are then known as *tracheoles* and they run to the various cells, in which they end blindly. Their thickness along most of their course may be no more than 0·25 μ.

Wigglesworth (1939), who gives an excellent account of respiration in insects, points out that the process has been evolved to meet the conflicting needs of supplying oxygen and

[1] A millimetre is about the thickness of one's thumb-nail, and the measure represented by one-thousandth of it is called a 'micron', and written 1μ.

preventing loss of water. Indeed, the tracheoles usually contain liquid, while the tracheal tubes do not. The capillary pressure of this liquid in a tube no more than one three-thousandth of a millimetre thick is about ten atmospheres. This means that the insect has to exert a force of about this magnitude to prevent the liquid from welling up into the tracheal tubes.[1] When a muscle becomes fatigued the liquid is partly or even wholly withdrawn from the tracheoles supplying it, so improving its oxygen supply.

Though oxygen can to some extent pass through the walls of the tracheal tubes along their length, it is through the tracheoles, and especially the ends of them, that it chiefly reaches the various organs. It may well be asked how the oxygen makes its way down the whole length of the tubules from the spiracles at their entrance to the ends of the tracheoles. It is now known that simple diffusion is adequate for this purpose, though this was long denied. It ceases to be sufficient, however, in very active forms requiring an abundant oxygen supply, and these must ventilate their tracheal tubes by muscular action. The provision of thin-walled air-sacks at intervals along the tubes, which can be compressed and expanded by the action of the body-muscles, makes it possible for them to do so.

The removal of carbon dioxide is achieved in a rather different way from that in which oxygen is supplied. For though it will diffuse outwards along the tracheal tubes nearly as fast as the oxygen does inwards,[2] it diffuses through animal tissues far more rapidly than does oxygen, so that it must chiefly be lost through the cuticle over the surface of the body.

The main water-loss of an insect takes place through the spiracles which are, from that point of view, a source of danger to their possessor. Consequently they are supplied with muscular valves by which they may be closed. Normally these are opened only just enough to keep the animal supplied with oxygen.

One important repercussion of the strange respiratory system of insects is the limit which it places upon their size. Even in those forms which in addition resort to muscular ventilation of the tracheal tubes, oxygen chiefly reaches the ends of the tracheoles by diffusion. In tubes so fine, this can take place with sufficient speed for a distance of about half an inch, but much beyond

[1] Such a force is probably derived from the osmotic pressure of the body fluids, which is of about the same magnitude.

[2] At a rate inversely proportional to the square roots of the densities of the two gases: $0.95 : 0.81$.

that length the process would be very slow. As a consequence of this, no insect has a body much more than one inch in thickness.

A small size has both advantages and drawbacks. The advantages are great and obvious in a flying form, for as an animal grows its area increases proportionately to the square of its length, but its weight increases proportionately to the cube. That is to say, small animals have an immensely greater area relative to their volume than have large ones. If we drop a mouse over a cliff a thousand feet high it will alight at the bottom uninjured, for its great relative area acts like a parachute, so that it soon attains a maximum speed, which is quite a small one, and it may then be said to float gently down. Insects have a greater area relative to their volume than have mice, and in consequence of this the energy which they must expend in flying is minute compared even with a bird the size of a sparrow. Yet a small size carries with it a great danger, to which attention has particularly been directed by J. B. S. Haldane. If a mouse falls into a pond, the film of water which it carries with it when it crawls out approximately doubles its weight, so large is its area. But the film of water on a wet insect, with a much larger area still, becomes a crushing load which may well prove fatal. At the best, it can only drag itself slowly along so that is quite incapable of escaping its enemies. In such unexpected ways as these does the structure of an insect influence its life.

THE STRUCTURE OF BUTTERFLIES

All the general statements made about insects in the previous section of this chapter are applicable to butterflies which, however, possess some characteristics that are peculiarly their own, as well as others that are found only in the forms that are more nearly related to them. The more important of these must now briefly be described, omitting those relating to the sense organs, which are reserved for subsequent treatment (in Chapter 3). It will be convenient first to consider the adult insect and then the early stages.

The mouth-parts of an adult butterfly are highly modified from the fundamental biting type already described, for they are adapted for sucking purposes. The mandibles are practically lost and the maxillae are transformed into the sucking proboscis, which is such a characteristic feature of these insects. The two galeae are immensely elongated and, being channelled along their inner surfaces and held together by hooks, they form a tube through which liquids can be drawn. When not in use this is coiled up under the head like a watch-spring, as can clearly be seen in the beautiful photograph of a Swallowtail Butterfly, *Papilio machaon*, at rest, shown on Plate 1, Fig. *b*. It is uncoiled when the insect feeds, and this is illustrated in Plate 1, Fig. *a*, in which a Wall Butterfly, *Lasiommata megera*, is probing a Michaelmas daisy flower with its proboscis. The palps of the maxillae have degenerated in butterflies, their function as sensory organs having been delegated wholly to those of the lower lip or labium, which is itself reduced to a small plate. In consequence of this, the labial palpi, which are usually well developed, are commonly referred to simply as 'the palpi' in butterflies. In addition, sensory structures on the tarsi of the last pair of walking legs act as taste-organs in some of the species (pp. 55–6).

The legs, when fully formed, consist of nine segments jointed to one another: a very short hip (coxa), a still shorter thigh joint (trochanter), a long thigh (femur), followed by an equally long shin (tibia), and a foot (tarsus) of five joints, the last one ending in two claws. The second and third pairs of legs are always well developed. The first pair may be also, or it may be degenerate; and the variations which it undergoes are of importance in the classification of our butterflies and will be discussed in Chapter 4.

The genital organs are exceedingly complex and their structure has been much used in classification. Portions of the ninth and tenth segments are modified to form the external parts of them in the male. These may be divided into structures by which the male clasps the female and those by which he ejects his sperm. The first of these consist of a pair of *claspers* hinged to the sides of the ninth segment, which is in the form of a narrow ring encircling the body. They are provided with powerful muscles, and often bear spine-like structures (*harpes*) on their inner surfaces. They are prehensile organs and they are especially well developed in the Swallow-tail Butterflies (of the genus *Papilio*). There is no doubt that the claspers represent parts of a pair of limbs immensely modified; probably the coxa of those of the ninth segment. Lying between them dorsally and just above the anus, is a hooked, sometimes forked rod, the uncus. It is median and attached to the ninth segment, the hooked end being free. It seems to be formed from the tergum of the last (tenth) segment, the sternum of which is probably preserved as a ventral plate called the *scaphium*. The two testes are fused into a single median structure, and the sperm-duct runs down from them and emerges between the bases of the claspers, where it is enclosed in a sheath (*aedeagus*), and it ends in an ejaculatory organ.

The last two segments, the ninth and tenth, are fused together in the female, usually forming a tube with the anus at its end, and the opening of the ovipositor, through which the eggs are laid, is just below it in the ninth segment. From this the oviduct leads forwards and divides, running to a pair of ovaries, each consisting of four tubes along which the eggs are developed. Yet the opening of the oviduct is not the one into which the sperms are passed: that is another orifice, the vagina, situated ventrally on the eighth segment. From it runs a very narrow tube ending in a sac (the *bursa copulatrix*), in which the sperms are stored. This is connected with the oviduct by a second narrow tube along which the sperms pass a few at a time, so that fertile eggs can be deposited for a long period after a single copulation.

The two pairs of wings belong to the second and third thoracic segments. They are composed of an upper and lower membrane, which during development are rather widely separated and form a sac. At emergence the two membranes are pulled together by strands connecting them and finally they meet and fuse, except along the course of a number of ribs which support them. These are therefore hollow; they are called *veins* or *nervures*, but neither name is very suitable for them since they are not veins or nerves in the strict sense. The distribution of these nervures is on the whole very constant within the different groups and species, though this constancy has been somewhat overstressed by those who rely too largely upon these structures as a basis for classification. Their general pattern is approximately the same in all butterflies, and it is shown in Text-fig. 2, in which is given the simplest system of notation for them. This is the numerical one, but several others are also in use. In both wings the nervures surround a central space (which may, however, be incomplete on the side away from the body), which is called the 'cell'. From it a number of nervures are given off radially. The main variations in neuration to be found in the different groups of British butterflies are discussed in Chapter 4.

Certain terms are used in describing both pairs of wings. That part nearest to the thorax is called the *base*. The front edge is the *costa* and its extremity is the *apex*. The posterior edge is the *inner margin*, which on the hind wings runs parallel with the body, and it ends at the *tornus*. The edge farthest from the body, connecting

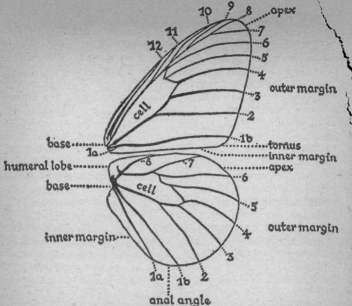

Fig. 2 The wings of a butterfly with the various regions named and the nervures numbered. The costa of the hind-wings runs from the humeral-lobe to the apex, being approximately parallel with the inner margin of the fore-wings. The small nervure supporting the humeral is the *humeral nervure*. Nervure 1 a on the fore-wings is generally small and may be absent. In some species the 'cells' are *open*, owing to the disappearance of the cross-nervure, connecting nervures 4 and 5, at their inner ends.

the apex and tornus, is the *outer margin*. On the hind wings this is often convex and may even be almost semi-circular, when it passes rather indefinitely into the costa without a distinct apex. The point where it meets the inner margin, really the tornus of the hind wings, is often called the *anal angle* since it lies beside the end of the body. These terms are also illustrated in Text-fig. 2.

In the great majority of moths, though not in all, the fore and hind wings are united during flight by a coupling apparatus, the *frenulum*. This mechanism is never found in butterflies, in which the wings are held together only because the front pair overlaps the hind to a considerable extent. The amount of this overlap is increased by the *humeral lobe*, a special projection found only in butterflies, and situated at the basal end of the costa on the hind wings. It is supported by short additional nervures.

The bodies and wings of butterflies and moths are covered with flattened *scales*, each of which has a short stalk fitting into a minute socket. They are arranged in regular rows overlapping one another like slates on a roof. This is well shown in the photomicrograph on Plate 12, Fig. *a*, from the wing of a Silver-washed Fritillary, *Argynnis paphia*. They in no way assist flight, and are simply responsible for the insects' colour (pp. 57–69); and for this purpose they seem to have been evolved. However, in the male some of them are specialized as scent-distributing organs, called *androconia*. These scent-scales are attached to a hollow disc which is connected with gland-cells in the wing-membrane. The volatile scented secretions which these produce pass up the hollow stalk of the scale and are disseminated by the plumes at its distal end. These scent-scales may be scattered, or collected into special patches called 'scent brands'. A selection of various scales, also from the male Silver-washed Fritillary, is shown in the photomicrograph on Plate 12, Fig. *b*. The normal colour-producing type is flattened and more or less racket-shaped, while several of the long plumed scent-scales can also be seen.

THE EARLY STAGES AND DEVELOPMENT OF BUTTERFLIES

Having briefly reviewed the chief characteristics of adult butterflies, we may turn to their early stages. The shape of the eggs is extraordinarily diversified, and the main types found in the British forms will be discussed in Chapter 4. In all of them the shell is of whitish or semi-transparent chitin and at the top there is always a minute opening, the micropyle (a word which signifies 'a little door'), often situated in a slight depression. This can just be seen in the egg of a Painted Lady, *Vanessa cardui*, Plate 7, Fig. *d*. Through it the sperm enters during the passage of the egg down the female's oviduct. This micropyle also allows air to reach the developing embryo. A considerable quantity of yolk is provided inside the egg for food.

When the young caterpillar is ready to hatch, it eats a hole in the egg-shell and crawls forth. The caterpillar or *larva* of a butterfly is a more or less worm-like creature consisting of a head, corresponding with that of the adult, and thirteen segments. The first three of the body-segments represent the thorax of the adult, and each bears a pair of true jointed legs of five parts, ending in a claw. The remaining ten segments correspond to those of the adult abdomen, but the terminal ones are distinct and not modified into complex genital structure. Spiracles are present on the sides of the first thoracic segment and on all those of the abdomen except the last two, nine pairs in all.

The third to the sixth abdominal segments are each provided with a pair of pro-legs or 'false legs', which do not survive in the adult. They are soft and fleshy, unjointed and end in a contractile pad surrounded by a ring of minute hooks. On the last segment is a very similar pair called 'claspers'. It now seems clear that the pro-legs are immensely modified remnants of the jointed appendages with which every segment of an insect must once have been provided. The true legs and pro-legs are well shown on Plate 2, Figs. *a* and *c*. The skin always bears numerous 'hairs', but their structure is entirely different from that of our own hair and they are technically called *setae*. They are present in great numbers even on such an apparently smooth form as the larva of the Brimstone, *Gonepteryx rhamni* (Plate 2, Fig. *a*). In addition, there may be large swellings or tubercles bearing spines, which may also arise from a smooth surface (Plate 8, Fig. *c*).

The head of a caterpillar must be considered separately for, unlike the other parts, it is built up of a number of segments (six in all) intimately fused, as in the adult. It bears microscopic three-jointed antennae followed by mouth-parts very unlike those of a perfect butterfly, for they are designed for biting and resemble more closely the ancestral type. Their most important component is a pair of powerful toothed jaws (mandibles) lost in the perfect insect, while traces remain of the other mouth-parts described on pp. 35-6. Contrary to the statements made in some text-books, the maxillae do not form a second pair of jaws, as they do, for example, in the cockroach. The salivary glands are modified into silk-producing organs and the end of their duct is situated on a median projection, the *spinneret*, formed from the labium. The eyes, here extremely simple, compared with those of the butterfly, are described in Chapter 3.

The fully grown larva differs greatly from its appearance when hatched (see the young and fully grown larva of the Silver-washed Fritillary on Plate 8, Figs. *b* and *c*). The earlier stages of the various groups always resemble one another much more closely than do the later ones, a generalization which is true of all animals. That situation is particularly obvious in the Lepidoptera, with their outstanding metamorphoses during their life before pupation takes place.

Larval development therefore includes not only growth but

also changes in form. However, the creature is encased in a chitinous cuticle, which may be stretched to a limited degree but cannot increase in total area or be modified in its proportions. At intervals therefore the cuticle is shed, disclosing a new one which has formed beneath it; this may be differently shaped, and can grow rapidly for a short time before it hardens. This process of moulting, or *ecdysis*, usually takes place four times during the life of our butterfly larvae.

The occurrence of moulting is determined in a remarkable way, by the production of a *hormone*. This is a special type of secretion which is poured by 'ductless glands' directly into the blood, by which it is disseminated, and very small quantities may suffice to control important processes in the body. Nowadays we are all well acquainted with hormones, owing to the publicity which has been given to some of those produced in our own body, such as *insulin*. This substance, manufactured by ductless gland cells in the pancreas (the Islets of Langerhans), is poured into the blood and enables us to use the sugar which is one of the end-products of digestion. The sugar accumulates, giving rise to diabetes if we do not make sufficient insulin ourselves; in that event it can now be supplied artificially. In a similar way, moulting is controlled by a hormone produced at certain times by glands in the caterpillar's head called *corpora allata*. Thus if the blood of normal caterpillars is injected into those about to moult, the onset of the process is delayed, but not if the blood of moulting caterpillars is used. The production of this hormone must in some way be controlled by growth.

At the end of larval life another moult occurs, giving rise to a much more radical change than those which have gone before it; for this is the metamorphosis, and it produces the well-known chrysalis[1] or *pupa* in which the structure of the adult is strongly foreshadowed. This is a resting stage in which all openings but those of the spiracles are sealed over, and the appendages fused to the cuticle. The chrysalis therefore neither eats, drinks, nor moves from place to place. Nearly all the organs of the adult can be distinguished in it. On either side of the head is a large capsule in which the eyes of the butterfly form, and ventrally the tongue can be seen, and the long antennae. Each of the three thoracic segments bears legs, and the fore wings are about two-thirds the length of the body, extending part of the

[1] From the Greek χρυσός (gold), referring, originally, to the pupae of certain Nymphalidae which are marked with metallic golden spots.

way down the abdomen and concealing all but the tips of the hind pair. All these structures are firmly glued down to the surface. The abdomen has, of course, the usual ten segments, and at the end of it are generally a number of hooks forming a structure called the *cremaster* by which the body is attached to a silken pad spun by the larva.

Three main types of pupae are formed by British butterflies. (1) They may hang head-downwards by the tail without any other support (Plate 2, Fig. *d*), as in the Danaidae, most of the Satyridae, and the Nymphalidae (pp. 79–82). (2) They may be attached by the tail but supported head-upwards by a silken girth (Plate 2, Fig. *b*), as in the Riodinidae, Lycaenidae, Papilionidae and Pieridae (pp. 82–6). (3) They may be enclosed in a cocoon (Plate 9, Fig. *f*), as in the Hesperiidae and in a few Satyridae (Plate 9, Fig. *b*), (pp. 86–8). Thus the great majority of our butterflies have pupae which belong to the first two of these types, and in them pupation is an exceedingly delicate operation, more especially in those which hang head-downwards.

It will be convenient first to describe this process in a form such as the Swallow-tail, in which the pupa is supported by a silken girdle. The larva begins by spinning a small pad of silk upon the stem of its food-plant, and then crawls forward until its claspers can grip this pad. Lying head-upwards, it bends its head and first few segments sideways, and fastens a silk thread to the stem on one side of the body; still bent, it twists round, passing the thread over its back, and fixes it to the stem on the opposite side. This process is repeated, the front of the body swaying it from side to side, until a girdle of sufficient strength encircles it. Then the larva straightens itself, as shown in the Brimstone (Plate 2, Fig. *a*; in Fig. *b* the resulting chrysalis is seen) and the Swallow-tail (Plate 3, Fig. *a*). The remainder of the process is illustrated from the latter species. The larval skin splits behind the head (Plate 3, Fig. *b*), and by a series of alternate swellings and contractions the pupa, which has formed within, bulges out of the rent and pushes the larval skin under the girdle (Fig. *c*) and back to the end of the body (Fig. *d*). Supported by the girdle, the pupa now withdraws its claspers from the shrivelled skin (Fig. *e*), which falls, and with a twist engages its cremaster in the silken pad (Fig. *f*).

This process is still more remarkable in the hanging pupae. The larva spins a pad of silk as before and, crawling forward, hangs head-downwards from it by means of its claspers (Plate 2,

Fig. *c*, which represents the Large Tortoiseshell larva, *Nymphalis polychloros*). The creature has now to perform the extraordinary feat of relinquishing its only support and re-attaching itself elsewhere, while hanging head-downwards in mid-air. The larval skin bursts behind the head and is pushed back to the end of the body, as in the Swallow-tail. A few pupae remain in this condition, supported by the larval skin (e.g., the Brown Hairstreak, *Thecla betulae*, and others, pp. 97–8), though the majority actually get rid of it. This they do by gripping the skin between the last two segments on the underside, which hold it like a pair of forceps. Then the tip of the body pierces through the skin above the point where it is held, and entangles its cremaster in the silken pad spun by the larva. The pupa now relaxes its grip on the skin, which later shrivels and falls, so that it hangs only by the end of its body (Plate 2, Fig. *d*).

After the larval skin is shed, the pupa is at first soft and wet. However, it soon dries and hardens, and the cases containing the legs, wings, and antennae, are firmly sealed to the surface.

It is not difficult to distinguish the sex of a pupa. In the male, the genital opening is always single, and it is situated on the penultimate (ninth) abdominal segment in the mid-ventral line. It takes the form of two narrow oval swellings on either side of a slight depression and much resembles the scars representing the claspers of the larva, which remain above the cremaster on the tenth segment. In the female the margin of the tenth segment forms a pair of blunt lobes lying close together in the middle-line and protruding part of the way across the ninth. The genital apertures form median scars. Usually there are two of these; one on the ninth segment represents the oviduct, the other on the eighth represents the vagina. These may, however, become confluent as a single mark on the eighth segment. In general, it may be said that a mark on the ninth segment and none on the eighth indicate a male pupa. A blurring of the margins between the two last segments (the ninth and tenth) and a ventral scar in the middle of the eighth indicate a female one.

Some of the larval structures become those of the pupa and of the adult insect, or *imago*, without much change, but the majority of them do not. These are destroyed (see p. 150), and the organs of the adult arise from little nests of reserve cells, present throughout larval life, called *imaginal buds*, because they give rise to most of the imago.

Indeed, metamorphosis consists in the death of the larval cells and the release of the imaginal buds from the influence which has held their growth and development in check. This influence is a hormone secreted in the head, though, of course, a different one from that responsible for moulting, but the glands which manufacture it have not certainly been identified. It ceases to be formed at the end of growth, so that the development of the imaginal buds then ensues. Thus decapitation can, in certain circumstances, lead to precocious metamorphosis, an experiment which, however, has never been performed on the larvae of butterflies.

The processes which lead to the destruction of the larval organs are not well understood. The tissues may be attacked by wandering cells present in the blood which can engulf and digest particles as well as produce ferments which act upon the surrounding structures. Such wandering cells or 'phagocytes' therefore possess the same properties as those of our own blood which ingest bacteria and are able to remove cartilage during the formation of bone. However, they are not always the primary agents in bringing about the dissolution of the larval organs, since many of these break down before the phagocytes reach them. It seems that certain types of cells cannot survive the changes brought about by the cessation of the larval hormone. As already mentioned, such changes stimulate the development of the imaginal buds, which represent such organs of the pupa and the imago as are not found in the larva. The formation of one of the typical features of the adult butterfly, the wings, may be taken as an example of this process.

Even a caterpillar has wings, or rather the rudiments of them. These are situated in the second and third thoracic segments, where the adult wings are attached. Here in the larva may be found their imaginal buds. Not long before pupation they consist of little flaps of undifferentiated cells (w) lying in a pocket (p) of the skin (s), the mouth of which is covered over with cuticle (c). In this condition one of them is shown on Plate 4, Fig. a, and it can be seen that it is already divided into two layers which represent the two wing-membranes of the adult. As the wings grow, they stretch open the pocket and so become external, lying between the larval skin (s) and the cuticle (c). They are shown in this state on Plate 4, Fig. b, and they have reached it at the time of pupation. Tracheal tubes, cut across, are visible in this photograph. At an early pupal stage the walls of the wing-membranes are still thick, and in them can be distinguished special cells which secrete the scales (Plate 4, Fig. c). These later grow out as flattened sacs and the wing-membranes come nearer together, but the space between them is still in free connection with the haemocoele. These features are well shown in Plate 4, Fig. *d*, in which tracheal tubes are seen running in the future nervures, which form swellings cut in transverse section.

The colours of butterflies are due to their scales. In the first place, these may be so constructed as to produce 'interference colours', such as give rise to those of a soap bubble or a film of oil. All the shades which change with the angle from which they are seen must be of this type. Much more frequently, however, the colours of these insects are due to pigments inside the scales. The nature of these substances will briefly be discussed in the next chapter. It is here only necessary to mention the ways in which the varied colour-patterns arise.

Different or discontinuous structural colours are produced by the nature of the scales themselves, whose construction varies in different parts of the wing. Pigments or their precursors are, however, manufactured in the body and are carried to the wings in the blood, so it is less easy to understand how their disposition is localized in the required areas. This is due to the interaction of separate processes. It depends primarily on the principle that the scales grow more rapidly in some regions than in others, and that when pigments flood the wings, which they do at various times, they can be deposited only in those scales which are at a particular stage of development. This is a considerable over-simplification of the problem, but it represents the type of mechanism involved. It may be examined a little more fully.

The British butterflies remain as pupae for about three weeks, more or less according to the temperature, except those which pass the winter in that state. Pigment only makes its appearance in the wing towards the end of pupation. But before it does so it can be seen that the scales are developing at different speeds in areas which are related to the pattern of the adult. It is a general rule that the scales develop more slowly in those parts which will be blackish or dark brown than in those which will be paler in colour: red, yellow, or white. This can be demonstrated clearly during a short period in their early development. If a pupal wing is dissected out at this time and dried, the scales which are at a later stage of formation remain erect while those in the future dark areas, being at an earlier one, collapse because they are still soft bags filled with blood. Thus the main features of the pattern become visible in relief. Even at a later stage, however, if the uncoloured pupal wing be dissected out, dried, and viewed in a slanting light, a ghost of the future pattern appears on it as if etched on glass, owing to the varying condition of the scales in different areas. When therefore distinct kinds of pigments are produced one after another, they are taken up by different elements of the pattern, for they can be deposited only in those scales which are at the correct developmental stage. But the formation of some of these pigments is a complex chemical process which occupies a considerable period of time. Thus it may be influenced by environmental changes even in the newly-formed pupa, a fact which we shall encounter in discussing temperature experiments in Chapter 11.

A day or two before the pupal stage ends, the colours begin to appear in the wings and can be seen through the cases in which they are enclosed. From what has just been said, it will be realized that some of them become apparent before others. Finally the colours and pattern of the adult wing are seen perfect but in miniature through the pupal case. The subsequent emergence of this butterfly is illustrated by the series of photographs on Plate 5.

The skin of the pupa splits behind the head and the insect begins to crawl forth, drawing its antennae, legs, and wings carefully out (Fig. 1). Even after it has extricated itself, the empty shell of the pupa retains its form. The butterfly moves to a position close at hand where its wings can hang downwards (Fig. 2). It now begins to expand them (Figs. 3 and 4). They are soft and flabby, and occupy only about one-tenth of their ultimate size because they are thrown into many folds. They are yet bag-like, for the two membranes of which they are composed are still separate. Blood is now forced between these membranes while the strands connecting them shorten, bringing them together. For this reason the wings do not swell into balloons when the blood is pumped into them but flatten out into thin sheets supported by hollow nervures. Having attained their full size they are still damp, and the insect is careful to hold them apart for a time so that they can dry; this can be seen clearly in Fig. 5. They are brought together only when hard (Fig. 6).

About this time a large drop of thick reddish fluid, the *meconium*, is ejected from the anus. It represents the stored-up excretory products of the pupa, from which most of the water has been removed by the action of the Malpighian tubules as already described. The drops of this meconium, produced when great numbers of butterflies have emerged, have given rise to fables of a shower of blood.

The whole process of emergence and expansion of the wings occupies about two hours in the Red Admiral, though it is much shorter in the smaller species, notably in the Hairstreaks. The butterfly is then ready to take its first flight, when it will make its way to the late summer or autumn flowers.

Chapter 3

The Senses and Colours of Butterflies

Senses Other than Sight, The Eyes and Vision, Colour-Vision, The Colours of Butterflies

SENSES OTHER THAN SIGHT

Impressions of the outside world are received by special structures called *sense-organs* situated on the surface of the body in insects as in Man. From them impulses are sent along conducting cells, the *nerves*, to a central organ, the *brain*, where they are classified and interpreted. Nerves are either *sensory*, bringing information into the brain, or *motor*, sending out instructions from it: a single nerve-cell never serves both purposes. In these few generalizations the chief similarities between our own nervous mechanism and that of butterflies are comprised, so different are they in detail. Before discussing the senses of butterflies it will be well therefore to mention one or two of the more peculiar features of their nerves and brain.

The nerves of a man are outgrowths of his nervous system leading to the cells of his sense-organs.[1] Those of an insect are the reverse, being ingrowths from the sense-organs reaching through the body to the nervous system; and when they arrive there they encounter a situation utterly unlike our own. It has already been explained that the central nervous system of an insect, instead of being a single hollow dorsal nerve-tube, is made up of a pair of solid ventral rods or 'nerve-cords'. In the ancestral forms from which modern insects are derived, these had a *ganglion*, consisting of nerve-cells forming a kind of primitive brain, in every segment. But that simple arrangement has become much modified in butterflies. In them a complex brain has been formed, composed of the ganglia belonging to the six segments which comprise the head. The first three of these are united into a mass lying above the gullet, and they form what is called the 'supra-oesophageal ganglion'; the last three, also fused into a

---

[1] Except the olfactory nerve, which, in this respect, is of the insect type, while our own optic nerves are really misnamed, being part of the brain.

mass, the 'sub-oesophageal ganglion,[1] lie below the gullet. Thus the brain is divided into two parts, dorsal and ventral, connected by a nerve-cord on either side of the alimentary canal.

It will be realized that the two parts of the brain are each triple. The front region (the protocerebrum) of the dorsal portion consists of structures called the 'mushroom bodies'. They are the chief centres in which movement and the interpretation of the sensory messages are controlled, and between them lie the ocellar lobes to which run the nerves from the 'simple eyes' (pp. 61-2). Behind these are the great optic lobes connected with the 'compound eyes' (pp. 57–61). The second section (the deuterocerebrum) comprises the antennary lobes which are connected with the sensory and motor nerves of the antennae. The third section (the tritocerebrum) supplies the connections to the sub-oesophageal ganglion, whose three parts innervate the three main mouth-parts, the mandibles, maxillae, and labium. Farther back, the ganglia of the three thoracic segments are partly fused, as are some of those belonging to the abdomen.

The most universal of senses is that of touch. In insects the sense-organs responsible for it are hairs, or 'setae', scattered over the body. These are flexible and non-nervous, but at their base, and stimulated by them, is a sense-cell from which runs a nerve-fibre. Such 'tactile setae' are not only scattered over the bodies of butterflies but are to be found along the nervures of the wings. These, it will be remembered, are hollow struts, and through them nerves often run.

Butterflies have achieved a high degree of discrimination in interpreting such sensations, and this is carried out in the mushroom bodies. Thus they pay little attention when stroked with a blade of grass but are easily startled by an equally light though unfamiliar touch, such as that of a finger or a metal rod. The same sense-cells are probably in part responsible for the perception of temperature changes.

Some butterflies possess sense-organs on the tarsi of the last pair of legs, whose perception is more akin to that of taste than of touch. They have been especially studied in the Nymphalidae (p. 80). When one of these legs is immersed in water to which apple-juice is added the insect invariably uncoils its tongue,

[1] These are unfortunate terms since, as explained, each really consists of three pairs of ganglia fused together.

whereas it does so only once in approximately three trials at the same distance from the liquid when this is not brought into contact with the tarsus, indicating that while the butterfly is capable of perceiving the scent of the juice, it is much more stimulated if it can touch it. A special sense organ must be involved, for immersion of the tarsus of the second leg does not increase the response beyond that produced by scent. It is particularly interesting to notice, however, that something other than a mere tactile sense operates here, since the immersion of the susceptible tarsus in plain water has no effect, even when the insect is allowed to smell the apple-juice as before. That is to say, it is not only the touch but also the quality of the liquid which is perceived. The organs responsible for this peculiar tarsal sense appear to be thin-walled setae having a nerve process which extends to their extremity. Their structure is thus quite different from that of the ordinary tactile setae, which occur freely among them. It is perhaps hardly necessary to add that butterflies also have a more ordinary sense of 'taste' and can distinguish qualities in their food which we should call flavours. They will feed upon a solution of sugar and water but immediately stop if quinine be added.

The sense of smell is undoubtedly located in the antennae. As already mentioned, these have a large nerve supply. They are provided also with numerous sense-organs which are very difficult to study, since they are so closely invested with chitin. This is nearly impossible to soften, as is required for successful section-cutting, without utterly destroying the delicate nerve cells. Scent perception is astonishingly acute in some moths, in which the male will find the female at a distance of a mile or more, or even a box in which one has been. So selective is it, moreover, that he will fly from the country into a town to reach her, and into a room full of tobacco smoke. In these species the antennae of the male, but not of the female, bear long side-branches. Those of butterflies are, however, always rod-like, many jointed, and end in a swollen knob, nor are these insects capable of such surprising olfactory feats. Being day-flying species, the male relies more upon sight in finding his mate (pp. 63–4), though scent may play a small part, and it is by scent that he chiefly stimulates her to perform the sexual act. Numerous experiments have been conducted on amputating the antennae, but chiefly on moths. However, it is at least known that the scent

perception of butterflies also resides in these organs. They seem
in addition to provide the sense of balance and direction: a
butterfly deprived of its antennae usually flies straight up into the
air as though it had lost its powers of orientation.

The ears of many moths are highly elaborate organs, occupying
a considerable space in the body. In general, they consist of a
drum-like structure stretched over a chitinous ring. This is
vibrated by sound waves, like our own tympanic membrane. Its
movements are recorded by a chitinous rod resting upon its
centre internally, the other end of which is in connection with
nerve fibres. Many minor variations of the plan are known, but
no such auditory organ has ever been discovered in butterflies.
Yet these insects certainly perceive vibrations within the range
which we call sound, both as caterpillars and when adult. It has
been shown that caterpillars of several groups (e.g., Nymphalidae
and Pieridae, see pp. 80 and 85) respond to vibrations with
frequencies from 32 to 1024 per second by moving the anterior
part of the body. The organs responsible for this sense are
certainly setae situated in that region, for if these are singed the
reaction is no longer obtained. Adult butterflies undoubtedly
have a faculty at least akin to hearing, as every collector must
know. Nerve endings of a special type are associated with the
tympanic organs of moths and they occur in various positions in
butterflies, but without any accompanying auditory apparatus.
It may be assumed that nerves of this kind are affected by
sound, perhaps through the response of setae, as in caterpillars.

Several sense-organs of unknown function occur in butterflies.
That most thoroughly studied is Jordan's Organ (or the chaeto-
soma). It is paired and lies dorsally behind the antennae near the
eyes in all butterflies and some moths. It consists of two swellings,
representing modified ocelli (p. 61), each provided with long
bristles and having a distinct nerve running direct to the protocerebrum. The organ looks as if it were used for some special
development of the sense of touch, but this is pure conjecture.

THE EYES AND VISION

The eyes of a butterfly must be known to any one who has made
even a casual examination of one of these insects resting on a
flower. For they can be seen at a glance as a pair of almost
hemispherical swellings, shining and transparent, occupying

most of the head. They are called 'Compound Eyes' since they are made up of several thousand separate optical units, each ending on the surface with its own lens. They differ from our own eyes in almost every possible respect, and I am illustrating them in two ways. First by an excellent diagram (Plate 6, Fig. *a*) drawn by that great authority on the subject, Dr H. Eltringham. It is from his work, *The Senses of Insects* (1933). Now it is by no means clear to many people what sort of generalizations are made in preparing a picture such as this: indeed, one is very seldom given the opportunity of comparing a diagram with the structure which it represents so as to assess the extent to which the object may have been simplified for descriptive purposes. Some such opportunity I was anxious to provide, and therefore I illustrate also an actual microscopic section of a butterfly's eye (Plate 6, Fig. *b*), which should be carefully contrasted with the drawing of it. The two obviously agree in their main features, save that the curvature of the section has become somewhat flattened during the complex processes of cutting and staining it. In this respect the preparation is less accurate than the drawing. It will, however, be objected that the latter contains a number of features which could not possibly be made out distinctly from the specimen. This is perfectly true, and there are two reasons for it. First, at the magnification here used, the thickness actually in focus at any one moment is minute, less even than that of the section. The maker of a diagram will therefore focus to different levels, and so study the distribution of the structures in a way that is not possible in a single photograph. Secondly, he will build up his picture from a number of different preparations, each made so as to show some feature particularly well. For these reasons the eye itself shown in Fig. *b* provides, in a sense, rather an unfair criticism of the accuracy of the generalized drawing. Yet the comparison between an actual specimen and a diagram is one which I believe many readers will be glad to make for themselves. In the description of the eye which follows, the various parts that will be mentioned can be found by referring to the labelling provided on Plate 6, Fig. *a*. It would be valuable also to identify them by comparison in the photo-micrograph itself.

The surface of a butterfly's eye when magnified is seen to consist of about six thousand hexagonal facets, each of which is the lens of a distinct optical unit called an *ommatidium*. These ommatidia are complete in themselves, and it will first be convenient to study the structure of a single one of them. The outermost element is continuous with the cuticle and forms the *corneal layer* of the eye. It consists of a rather thick lens (L). This is biconvex and accordingly inverts the light rays, which cross over at its focus. Immediately below it is a transparent layer, the *processus corneae* (K), composed of four cells which have secreted the structure next to be mentioned. This is the *crystalline cone* (J), which is made of clear hard chitin. It has a broad base outwards and its sides converge nearly to a point inwards. Optically its effect is rather complex, for it reinverts the image, since the light-rays cross over again inside it, while their path is so adjusted that they emerge parallel with one another at the inner or pointed end of the cone. This is continued by a long straight transparent rod, the *rhabdome*, extending deep into the eye, and down it the parallel rays of light pass. It is surrounded by six or eight elongated 'retinular cells' or 'retinulae' (H), which run its whole length. These are the actual light-perceiving organs. The bottom of the rhabdome and retinular cells rest upon a small vesicle, called by Eltringham the 'tracheal distributor' (G), from which eight tracheoles extend upwards as far as the crystalline cone. Each retinular cell gives rise to a fibre of the optic nerve. These fibres, in groups of six or eight according to the number of retinular cells surrounding each rhabdome, pass the tracheal distributor and penetrate a basal membrane (F) running continuously below the ommatidia. They emerge round a large cell (E) and then cross a space containing many tracheal tubes, doing so in irregular groups (D), each derived from several ommatidia, and enter a region called the 'periopticon'. This forms the outer part of the optic lobe of the brain. Here the nerves are sorted out into straight bundles of six or eight (C), which seem to consist once more of those from a single set of retinulae. At the base of the periopticon the whole mass of fibres traverses a space where one-half twist across the other, the 'external chiasma' (B), after which they enter an 'epiopticon' (A) in which they undergo a second twist, the 'internal chiasma', and run down to the 'opticon', which is that region of the brain concerned with vision.

One important feature of the ommatidia remains to be mentioned, its pigment cells. These surround the crystalline cones (they are labelled I in the diagram) and prevent rays of light from entering them obliquely. In many forms, pigment cells also isolate the retinulae of one rhabdome from those of another.

In moths, which may fly in the widely different illuminations of the early dusk and of a dark night, a mechanism exists for altering the distribution of the pigment round the cones so as to admit more or less light, as does our own iris. Butterflies, flying in daylight and generally in bright sunshine, do not require or at any rate do not possess such a mechanism, and the distribution of the pigment in their eyes cannot be varied to suit differing intensities of light. A few species tend to fly after the sun is obscured, though the majority do not. Good examples of the two types are provided by the same group, the Satyridae (p. 79). The Scotch Argus, *Erebia aethiops*, seems blind in the absence of sunlight and ceases to fly almost instantly the sun is obscured, while the Meadow Brown, *Maniola jurtina*, and the Small Heath, *Coenonympha pamphilus*, are by no means inactive on dull warm days. It is possible that this is due to a difference in their power of perception, but it may be that the pigment sheath is carried up the cone for a shorter distance in them than in the Scotch Argus. It would be worth while to discover if this is so, also to examine the distribution of pigment in the eyes of the Speckled Wood and Wood White, which are shade-loving butterflies.

(For the technique of making microscope preparations, see Eltringham, 1930.)

I have described the compound eye in some detail in order to demonstrate how extraordinarily intricate it is; for the two eyes of a Small Tortoiseshell Butterfly, *Aglais urticae*, together contain about a hundred thousand sense-cells and tracheoles. It might well be felt that such a structure would not have been evolved unless its complexity carried with it a correspondingly high degree of efficiency. Such an opinion is scarcely justified by the result, for butterflies are extremely short-sighted, and they are probably unable to recognize others as belonging to their own species at a distance of more than three or four feet.

It has already been explained that a real and erect image is formed at the base of each cone in a butterfly's eye[1] and that the rays of light passing down the rhabdome are parallel, so that this image can be perceived at any level within it, while the retinular cells run its whole length. A fair provision thus seems to be made for the perception of the image formed by each facet.

An apparent optical difficulty arises here which, however, is

[1] This is called a 'eucone eye', but an inverted image is formed in a different type of compound eye, the 'pseudocone eye' found in some other insects (e.g., Dragonflies).

eliminated by the construction of the insect's eye. If a transparent rod is surrounded by material having a different refractive index from its own, for instance air, light entering it at one end will emerge only at the other, not through the side. In such circumstances, light-perceiving cells *surrounding* the rod would receive no stimulus. However, the rhabdome is actually secreted by the retinular cells, and it must be in optical continuity with them in the sense that the cells and the rhabdome must have approximately the same refractive index. Consequently no optical barrier to the stimulation of the retinular cells exists.

The clearness of an image formed by a compound eye will depend upon the number of facets engaged in perceiving it, and this will vary inversely with the square of its distance from the object. It is for this reason that butterflies are so short-sighted. Near objects, seen by many facets, are probably very distinct, but they will be rapidly blurred as they recede. Owing to its strange construction, however, the compound eye is very sensitive in detecting small movements, which will affect different facets in succession, and this is its chief advantage.

The 'ocelli', or simple eyes, of insects show great diversity of structure. They are to be found as dorsal ocelli in the adults, in which, when functional at all, they play a very subordinate part to the compound eyes; also as lateral ocelli in larvae, where they are the only visual organs. They possess but a single lens and in all respects are far simpler than the compound eyes.

The dorsal ocelli send their nerves to the ocellar lobes of the protocerebrum. Usually there are three such ocelli set in a triangle, one median and one at each side. Since the nerve of the median ocellus is double, it is presumably composed of two ocelli fused. A very few butterflies possess the median ocellus but, as it is covered by the adjoining scales, it can be of little use. In these insects the ocelli at the sides are always modified into Jordan's Organ (p. 57).

The lateral ocelli of larvae vary from one to about ten on each side; in the caterpillars of butterflies the number is nearly always six. They are innervated from the optic lobes, as are the compound eyes, and occupy the same relative position which these will do in the adult, but the two types are developed quite independently. Each lateral ocellus consists of a single corneal lens below which lie several retinal cells, sometimes in two layers, the ends of which form the fibres of the optic nerve. They are pigmented except in the centre, the pigment extending far down the nerve fibres. Other pigmented cells, variously arranged, are also present in different forms.

These ocelli probably do little more than perceive the difference between light and darkness, and certainly they can have no other use except at extremely close quarters. Caterpillars can smell their food to a limited extent, but their most important sense is certainly that of touch.

COLOUR VISION

There can be no doubt that butterflies perceive some difference between variously coloured objects. In the absence of definite evidence to the contrary it might, however, be maintained that they are chiefly influenced by degrees of luminosity. It is, of course, possible by illuminating a red object more brightly than a yellow one to make the intensity of light which they reflect equal. We still perceive a distinction between them in these circumstances, because we can appreciate differences not only in the total amounts of light emitted by two sources but also in their wave-length. It is this latter faculty which we call colour-vision, and in discussing the ability of butterflies to exercise it we must be careful to eliminate the error due to the fact that different colours reflect different amounts of light when illuminated to an equal degree.

Numerous investigators have studied the colour-vision of bees, but our knowledge of it in butterflies is chiefly due to the work of my friend the late Dr H. Eltringham, also of Dr D. Ilse. I shall here select for discussion a few of Eltringham's simpler and more significant experiments, but a fuller account of them may be obtained from his book, *The Senses of Insects* (1933).

At the outset it should be noticed that the majority of butterflies take less notice of white than of other colours, probably because so much white light is normally reflected from shiny leaves and other objects. Eltringham studied 427 visits made by Small Tortoiseshell Butterflies to a bed of white, pink, and purple asters. About one quarter of the flowers were white, but only 47 visits were made to them. Of the remainder, 135 were to pink flowers and 245 were to purple. The pink flowers were more numerous than the purple in a proportion of about four to three, so that this series of observations suggests that the purple flowers were slightly more than twice as attractive as the pink. In order to determine whether this was due to superior conspicuousness or to colour, Eltringham photographed the flowers, using a screen which gave the effect of relative luminosity only, and found that the purple were not particularly outstanding.

If the eyes of a Small Tortoiseshell Butterfly are covered with transparent dyes, either red, blue, or yellow, the insects seem to be but little inconvenienced, flying and alighting as usual. Were they blind to one of these colours, those specimens whose eyes were stained with it would be totally unable to see, and their behaviour would be markedly affected. For it is hardly necessary to add that butterflies are greatly dependent upon the visual sense. Indeed, if their eyes are coated with a black dye they are wholly unable to fly or to control their movements when thrown into the air. Yet the range of colour-perception is not the same in all species. If the eyes of a White Butterfly are dyed red, the insect can still fly to a window but when liberated its movements are largely uncontrolled. As Eltringham remarks, this is probably related to the fact that these species possess no red pigment themselves. Yet Ilse (1928), who studied the extent to which butterflies visited papers of different colours, found that the genus *Pieris* was most attracted by red and purple, and the Vanessidi by yellow and violet. These results demonstrate that the colour preferences of different species are not necessarily the same.

Eltringham's observation that Small Tortoiseshell Butterflies visit purple asters much more frequently than pink is subject to an obvious criticism when it is used as evidence of colour-vision. It may be that the differently coloured flowers have scents which are distinguishable to a butterfly; by no means an impossibility, since different shades of the same flower occasionally produce scents which are distinct even to our own feeble olfactory powers. This objection is met by another series of experiments. Eltringham made paper models of Pearl-bordered Fritillaries, *Clossiana euphrosyne*, by cutting out photographs and painting them different colours: green, blue, crimson, tawny yellow (the natural one), brown, and a clear pale yellow. The spots were black, as in the real insect. These, together with a few dead and dried specimens, he pinned to grass stems in Bagley Wood, Berkshire, where the butterfly was flying commonly. I give his results in his own words:

'In the first place the superior attraction of the real, but dead and dried, specimens was noticeable. The live Fritillaries dipped to and examined the paper models, but on coming to a real one they touched it and made persistent efforts to elicit some response. The elementary difference seems to indicate acuity of vision and appreciation of form at close quarters. Of the paper models those of the natural colour attracted 27 individuals, red models eighteen, and pale yellow two. The other colours were not noticed at all. It is remarkable that the only colours, other than the correct one, which attracted the live insect were those nearest to the natural one. So far as mere luminosity is concerned, the brown models (a rather pale brown) about equalled the naturally coloured models, whilst the red, though nearer to the natural colour, had much less luminosity.'

Eltringham and I then prepared models by bleaching real specimens, dying them different colours, and replacing the spots with black. The shades used were red, blue, greenish-yellow, buff, and the nearest approach to the natural tawny yellow that we could obtain. Two of each colour were pinned to foliage in Bagley Wood, together with two untreated dried specimens. In half an hour, wild butterflies had paid thirteen visits to the untreated specimens and thirteen to those dyed the natural colour. No visits at all were made to any of the unnaturally coloured models.

There can now be no doubt that these observations on the vision of the Pearl-bordered Fritillary show that this butterfly can detect differences in colour, as apart from those of luminosity, and that they exclude discrimination by scent. Moreover, they demonstrate that it is by sight, and the use of colour-vision, not by scent, that the males find the females in natural conditions.

Such simple experiments as these on colour-perception and mating-habits can easily be carried out. They would furnish a great deal of information which is badly needed, and I should like to recommend them to entomologists. As already mentioned, it is known that the range of colour-vision is not the same in all butterflies. A survey of it, as well as of their colour-preferences, would be most valuable. It may well be asked whether the male finds the female by colour or by scent in the White Butterflies, or in those species in which the female is very dull-coloured, as in the Chalkhill Blue, *Lysandra coridon*, or very inconspicuous, as in the Grayling, *Hipparchia semele*. It would not be at all difficult to answer these and similar questions by the methods adopted by Eltringham, and their interest is considerable (p. 245). Here is a very suitable field for research open to any collector of butterflies.

THE COLOURS OF BUTTERFLIES

We have just seen that the colours of butterflies provide a means by which the males recognize the females, at least in some species. In addition, they are, of course, their chief protection, giving them a resemblance to natural objects by which they may escape their enemies; an aspect of coloration to be discussed in some detail in Chapter 5. Whether present on the wings or on the body, these colours are, as already explained, due either to the structure of the scales or to the pigments carried by them.

Structural colours are usually produced by 'interference' phenomena, as are those of a soap bubble, and they arise when the wall of the scale is built up of a number of excessively fine films separated by material of a slightly different refractive index. They may also be due to diffraction, if the surface of the scales bear very minute ridges, and to other physical conditions. Most of the blues and metallic shades seen in butterflies are structural in origin. However, pigments are responsible for the majority of colours of these insects. Their nature is very varied, but they may conveniently be divided into those manufactured by the animal itself and those directly or ultimately derived from its food. The first group comprises two main types, the uric acid and the melanin pigments.

In 1895 Sir Gowland Hopkins proved that the white and yellow pigments of the Pieridae (or Whites and Sulphur Butterflies, p. 85), are built up from the insect's excretory products, being derived from uric acid, which has the formula $C_5H_4O_3N_4$. He showed that the white pigment of a Large White, *Pieris brassicae*, is a substance called leucopteryn ($C_6H_5O_3N_5$), while the yellow one responsible for the colour of the male Brimstone, *Gonepteryx rhamni*, is similar but contains less oxygen. This is xanthopteryn, $C_6H_5O_2N_5$. These uric acid compounds are soluble in dilute ammonia, from which they may be recovered by subsequent acidification, a fact which any one can verify.

The pigments of the melanin group are related to indigo,[1] the natural colouring matter of Woad, *Isatis tinctoria*: a plant which must have been much commoner in pre-Roman times than now,

[1] They contain the 'indol ring', melanin having the formula:

if we are to believe the history books of our infancy. Typically, the melanins are black, and probably they are always responsible for this and for many of the brown colours in butterflies. For they pass through brownish intermediate compounds in their production; and at an earlier stage a red one, an example of which seems to be provided by the red spot near the anal angle of the wing in the Swallow-tail, *Papilio machaon*. Melanin is extremely resistent to chemical treatment. It is produced by the oxidation of a colourless substance, 'tyrosin' (an amino-acid), through the action of a ferment, 'tyrosinase'. In piebald vertebrates, such as rabbits, tyrosinase is present in the black parts of the skin and absent from those which are white. In butterflies, however, the localization of the black markings is produced by the reverse mechanism, tyrosinase being present in the blood while tyrosin is deposited in certain areas only of the wings and body. The Hon. H. Onslow showed that when the immature pupal wings of the Large White are dissected out, they turn an intense black all over when treated with a solution of tyrosin. When treated with tyrosinase, however, the blackening is confined to those areas in which it will be found in the perfect insect.

Several types of pigment are derived from the larval food, but it is now doubtful whether the green colours of caterpillars are among them. It was formerly held that they were due to the plant pigment chlorophyll. In a number of species it has been demonstrated that this is not so; they are either entirely different compounds manufactured by the insect itself, or those in which the chlorophyll is so altered chemically that its characteristic red fluorescence in ultra-violet light cannot be obtained. I am somewhat handicapped in discussing this subject, since my own studies on the pigments of butterflies have so far included only the flavones (p. 68) and the majority of the red pigments. I have not yet made the detailed analysis of the green that I propose to do. So far, very few of the green pigments have been analysed and it is as yet too early to assert, as has lately been done, that none of those found in larvae is unaltered chorophyll. The absence of this group of substances in some instances in which its occurrence had been presumed seems to have cast too general a doubt upon its existence in others. Gerould (1921) maintains not only that the normal yellowish-green caterpillars of the American Clouded Yellow Butterfly, *Colias philodice* Godt, are pigmented with chlorophyll, but that a bluish-green variety is due to the digestion of one component only of the green colouring matter of plants, the blue-green chlorophyll-A. This example should be studied again from the chemical standpoint.

Green is a rare colour in adult butterflies and in the British species even rarer than it appears. For the green veining on the underside of the Green-veined White (Plate 19) and the green marbling on that of the Orange-tip, *Anthocharis cardamines*, and Bath White, *Pontia daplidice*, are due to an intimate mixture of black and yellow scales, giving the optical effect of green though no scales of that colour are present in these species. The beautiful green on the underside of the Green Hairstreak, *Callophrys rubi*, is structural in origin, and the scales producing it are of uniform type. Accordingly, if they are moistened, the green vanishes. This cannot be done with water, as the scales of a butterfly are slightly greasy, but they are easily damped with a fat-solvent such as chloroform. No green pigment exists in British butterflies, though it does so in the Emerald Moths, *Geometrinae*; also in the Green Silver-lines, in which, however, it is of a different nature.

It has been claimed that the red colours of the Vanessidi (p. 81) are due to substances built up from the chlorophyll absorbed during larval life, though this has been denied. They are at any rate produced by pigments which, though unrelated to uric acid, are rapidly soluble in hot water and dilute ammonia. When exposed to a strong mineral acid (e.g., hydrochloric acid) they become dull and slightly greenish in colour, an effect which is not reversed by subsequent neutralizing (Ford, 1942a). Such compounds arise by normal means in varieties of certain species (for example, the Peacock, *Inachis io*, see p. 204). Some of these pigments are rather unstable, and are of a brighter tint when less oxygenated than when more so; consequently they tend to become dull with long exposure to the air. They can be restored to their original shade or, if fading has not taken place, converted to a brighter one, by the action of chlorine. Attention has, I believe, never before been drawn to this reaction, and I well remember my great surprise on discovering it. When the Painted Lady, *Vanessa cardui*, emerges from the chrysalis it is suffused with a beautiful salmon-pink shade. This is gradually lost, leaving the ground-colour of a rather dull brownish tint. A faded specimen exposed to chlorine recovers all the beauty of youth, for the lovely pink flush associated with the newly emerged butterfly floods back across the wings. The red colours of the other species, such as the Red Admiral, the Peacock, and the Tortoiseshells, are intensified to a truly remarkable degree by similar treatment.

One group of pigments found in adult butterflies is obtained directly from the food-plants of the caterpillar. This comprises the flavones, which are responsible for the colours of flowers ranging from an ivory shade to deep yellow, but they are also present in the leaves of most plants.[1] Flavones occur in the scales of the Wood White, *Leptidea sinapis* (but not in those of other White Butterflies, p. 86), the Marbled White, *Melanargia galathea*, the Large Heath, *Coenonympha tullia*, the Small Heath, the Grizzled Skipper, *Pyrgus malvae*, and the Dingy Skipper, *Erynnis tages* (but in the latter species they are not easy to detect), also in those of the undersides of most of the British Blue Butterflies (Polyommatini), a fact never before reported. It is characteristic of these pigments that they combine with ammonia to produce compounds of a deeper shade of yellow which, in butterflies, are unstable, so that they soon return to their original condition, leaving the specimen undamaged. This explains the surprising result obtained on fuming a Marbled White with ammonia: should any one be ignorant of it, he should experiment for himself! But the same thing can be seen in the other species just mentioned, though, in some of them, in less degree. No effect is produced if we subject a Large White to similar treatment, for it possesses no flavones. This reaction with ammonia is really the most sensitive test for these substances. However, they are soluble in ethyl acetate, which makes it possible to accumulate them from many specimens in each of which they may be present in small quantities only. The wings should be cut from the body

[1] Unlike the white pigment of the Pieridae, the flavones contain no nitrogen. The formulae of the ivory-white flavone apigenin, and of the yellow luteolin, are:

The various types differ by modification of the side phenyl ring. Two allied groups of pigments exist, the flavonols and the chalkones. These respectively substitute a hydroxyl and attach a side chain at position 3 (omitting that at position 2) in the pyrone ring.

and soaked for at least 48 hours. The colourless liquid is then filtered and shaken with an aqueous solution of sodium carbonate, when a deep yellow colour appears if flavones are present. If they are not, the liquid remains colourless (Ford, 1941).

Pigmentary and structural effects may be combined in butterflies, as they are in the male Purple Emperor, *Apatura iris* (Plate 23), in which the iridescent purple colour, changing with the incidence of the light, is produced by structural means on scales containing melanin. The distribution of the various types of pigment is of importance in classification, and this subject will be discussed briefly in the next chapter.

Chapter 4

The Principles of Classification

The Object of Classification, The Classification of Insects, The Position of Butterflies among the Lepidoptera, The Classification of British Butterflies, The Criteria of Classification

THE OBJECT OF CLASSIFICATION

It is necessary to classify any large assemblage which we wish to study so as to reduce it to order and to divide it into a series of groups which may be identified by some logical system. This is true whether it be composed of butterflies, words, or the figures of heraldry. There are usually many ways in which a classification can be made, but that adopted for animals is based upon relationship. It is worth noticing that for certain purposes such a system may not even be the best one. For instance, others may be more suitable for identifying species, and they are not infrequently used for this purpose. Their true nature is then obscured by such titles as 'Keys to the Identification of Genera and Species'. Such keys are logically alternative classifications, used when that normally adopted proves inadequate. Yet one dependent upon affinity is undoubtedly the correct type to employ, save in special circumstances; for it reflects a wider and more important aspect of reality, the course of evolution, than does an arbitrary arrangement made for some particular purpose. Indeed, since it does reflect this wider aspect, it will undoubtedly be, in general, the most satisfactory system. Moreover, when expressed as a diagram, it becomes a genealogical tree and, if it be successful, we can make a generalization of the utmost importance about it: that all the animals included in any group, whether it be a great one like the insects or a small one like our common White Butterflies (the genus *Pieris*), are more closely related to one another by actual descent than they are to any other organisms upon earth.

A few terms used in classification are so important that they must be explained at the outset. Indeed, it is astonishing how seldom writers provide definitions to show what meanings they attach to them, though this might be thought an obvious necessity.

A *primitive* animal may be defined as one which has departed little from the common ancestor of the group which we are discussing; it therefore possesses relatively few characteristics not found in that ancestor. A *specialized* one has, on the other hand, departed widely from the common ancestor of the group which we are discussing; it therefore possesses a relatively large number of characteristics not found in that ancestor. I have been careful to indicate the purely relative nature of these terms. A kangaroo judged as a Vertebrate is highly specialized, judged as a Mammal it is primitive. Similarly the Dingy Skipper is a highly specialized insect but a primitive butterfly. That is to say, whether an organism is primitive or specialized depends upon the point of view from which we regard it. Moreover, an animal which is on the whole primitive may possess one or two highly specialized features.

Analogous organs serve the same purpose, while *homologous* ones are derived from a common ancestral organ. Clearly, two structures may be both, one or the other, or neither. Homologous organs can be recognized in practice by the possession of a common ground-plan, merely analogous ones by its absence. The wings of butterflies and of birds are purely analogous: they perform the same function but have been evolved independently. On the other hand, a bird's wings are homologous with a whale's flippers, but they are not analogous; similarly, in butterflies, Jordan's Organs (p. 57) are homologous, but not analogous, with a pair of ocelli.

A *degenerate organism* is one which has lost specialized structures which its forebears possessed. It might be held that fleas are directly derived from the wingless ancestor of the insects. Yet there are strong grounds for thinking that this is not so and that the ancestors of fleas at one time possessed wings, so that in the loss of them these insects are degenerate. Thus their flightless state is *secondary*, having been reached a second time after a period spent as flying forms. A further and excellent example of a secondary character is provided by the cocoons in which the pupae of some of the Satyridae (The Browns, p. 79) are formed. Such cocoons are usual in moths, but the habit of making them is lost in the more specialized butterflies to which the Satyridae belong. Their occurrence in a few members of that family is an independent and *secondary* character, in this case an acquisition not a survival. In general, primitive and secondary conditions will evidently be analogous only.

An assemblage of animals in which homologous organs are found must have had a common ancestor dating back to the time when such structures were first developed. Those engaged in classification must therefore be on the watch for homologies, though these may sometimes be difficult to detect. They must also guard against being deceived by analogies into thinking that two but distantly related forms should be united; for similarity of function necessarily involves certain, and sometimes close, structural resemblances, though never in the entire structural ground-plan.

When animals are classified, they are placed in groups which are repeatedly sub-divided to represent, as far as possible, the actual course of differentiation during evolution. The more fundamental groups contain large numbers of forms having few but important features in common. The smaller and more numerous sub-divisions, produced by further differentiation, each share larger numbers of more superficial features. We shall here exclude certain of the basic divisions of animals and take the *Phylum* as our initial grouping. This is divided into Classes, and these into Orders; after which the sub-divisions proceed to Families, Tribes, Genera, Species, and Varieties. Further steps of greater or less value may be introduced as required by prefixing super- or sub- to any of the main terms, as super-family or sub-order. Moreover, it is sometimes necessary to discriminate still further, when additional terms are used. The arrangement followed should be one which passes from the more primitive to the more specialized types.

The scope of these groups is necessarily somewhat arbitrary, but the most natural of them is the species. Even this is difficult to define in a way which is satisfactory for all the higher plants and animals. In general, however, it may be said that individuals belong to the same species when they can interbreed and produce fertile offspring, and this statement is entirely adequate for the present purpose (p. 219), though it would require considerable qualification if applied to plants. A variety is an exceptional form of a species, but one which breeds freely with the normal type.

Each species is allotted two scientific names derived from Greek or Latin or at least expressed in a latinized form. The first is that of its genus. This is a group of closely allied species, whose members are all given the same 'generic name'. The second is its own distinguishing title, and this identifies it within the genus. When several species belonging to the same genus are mentioned consecutively, it is necessary only to repeat the initial letter of the generic name on the second and subsequent occasions (for instance, *Lysandra coridon* and *L. bellargus*). The name of the genus should be written with a capital and that of the species with a small letter (even if it is taken from the name of a person or place), and both should be in italics.

The name of a species should be followed by that of the author responsible for its description, as *Colias crocea* Fourcroy. But the author's name is usually abbreviated if it is well known; thus 'L.' stands for Linnaeus (for example, *Colias hyale* L.). The author's name of every British butterfly may be found by reference to the classification on pp. 79–87. In general, it should be given on the first occasion that a species is mentioned in any work, after which it may be omitted. This applies also to the names of varieties, which should follow that of the species, with the prefix 'var.': for example, *Colias croceus* var. *helice* Hübner (which is usually abbreviated to 'Hbn.').

This system of 'binomial nomenclature' was introduced by Linnaeus (p. 21). Its use may be illustrated by two examples. The White-letter Hairstreak and the Black Hairstreak are called *Strymonidia w-album* and *Strymonidia pruni*. They are so similar that they are placed in a single genus and consequently their first, but not their second, name is the same. It at once becomes clear therefore that these two species are more closely related to one another than either is to the Purple Hairstreak, *Quercusia quercus*; a fact which the English names do not suggest. Similarly, it is very well worth noticing that the Large Tortoiseshell, *Nymphalis polychloros*, is more closely related to the Camberwell Beauty, *Nymphalis antiopa*, than to the Small Tortoiseshell, *Aglais urticae*, a fact clearly shown by the scientific names but actually obscured by the English ones. Moreover, the scientific terms are international, and the value of this will be brought home forcibly to any one who has attempted to discover to what species the popular names used in other countries apply. To what British butterflies does a Frenchman refer when he speaks of 'le myrtil' or 'Robert-le-Diable'?

The scale of distinction indicated by the major classificatory groups may be illustrated at the outset with reference to ourselves, our own classification being as follows:

PHYLUM. Chordata. (Animals with a hollow dorsal nervous

system and an unjointed rod in place of a back-bone, etc.)
SUB-PHYLUM. Vertebrata. (Possessing a true jointed 'back-
bone', which, however, is of cartilage in primitive forms.)
CLASS. Mammalia. (Warm-blooded animals with hair and
mammary glands.)
ORDER. Primates (Lemurs, Monkeys, Apes and Men.)
SUB-ORDER. Anthropoidea (which excludes the Lemurs).
FAMILY. Hominidae (fossil and modern Men).
GENUS. *Homo* (includes species, e.g. *H. neanderthalensis*, no
longer surviving).
SPECIES. *sapiens* (all existing Men).

Some species can be divided into sub-species, which are
distinct groups, each occupying a different area. But these will
be discussed on pp. 266–72.

THE CLASSIFICATION OF INSECTS

Insects belong to the phylum Arthropoda and constitute one of
its classes (Insecta); others are the Crustacea (including crabs,
lobsters, wood-lice and barnacles), and the Arachnida (spiders,
mites and scorpions). Some of the characteristics already
mentioned as special attributes of insects are really of wider
distribution, being those of the whole phylum: as are the jointed
segmental appendages, the compound eyes, and the 'open' blood
vascular system. The tracheal respiratory mechanism is, however,
strictly an insect characteristic.

The class Insecta is divided into two sub-classes. First, the
APTERYGOTA: These are wingless forms in which the wingless
condition is primitive. They have no metamorphosis or only a
very slight one, and possess one or more pairs of appendages on
their abdomens (other than genital structures). Classes or, when
they occur, sub-classes, are divided into Orders, of which the
Apterygota contains three. These are the Thysanura (Silver-fish),
the Protura (minute forms much overlooked), and the Collem-
bola (Spring-tails).

The second sub-class of the Insecta is the PTERYGOTA. This
includes winged, or secondarily wingless, forms, nearly always
with some degree of metamorphosis, and with no abdominal
appendages in the adult, save the genital structures. The Orders
comprised within the Pterygota are grouped into two Divisions.
These are (1) the Exopterygota, in which the metamorphosis is
slight, the wings develop externally, and the larvae have many of

the characteristics of the adult; and (2) the Endopterygota with a complex metamorphosis, wings which develop internally, and specialized larvae, very different from the adults.

The Exopterygota are divided into fourteen Orders. Of these the Orthoptera (Cockroaches, Grasshoppers, and allied forms) are the most primitive, while the Hemiptera (including Plant-bugs, Water-boatmen, and Aphides or 'Greenfly') are the most specialized.

The Endopterygota comprise nine Orders, and, since they include that in which the butterflies are placed, they must be tabulated here:

Order Neuroptera (Alder Flies, Lacewings, etc.). About 1700 species are known, many being aquatic in the early stages. There are two pairs of very similar membranous wings, held at an angle like a roof over the body when at rest. The adult mouth-parts are biting, and the larvae are carnivorous.

Order Mecoptera (Scorpion Flies). About 200 species are known. The two pairs of wings are nearly similar, and are carried longitudinally and horizontally at rest. The legs are long and slender. Adults and larvae are both carnivorous, with biting mouth-parts.

Order Trichoptera (Caddis Flies). About 700 species are known. These are moth-like insects. The wings are hairy and unequal, the front pair being longer and more pointed than the hind; they are held over the body in a roof-like manner. The larvae and pupae are aquatic, usually living in cases.

Order Lepidoptera (Butterflies and Moths). Over 80,000 species are known. The body is scaled, as are the wings, the two pairs being nearly always dissimilar. Mandibles are almost invariably absent and there is a suctorial proboscis.

Order Coleoptera (Beetles). This is the largest Order in the Animal Kingdom, about 180,000 species are known. The fore-wings are modified into a horny covering for the hind pair, though these may be reduced or absent. The mouth-parts are of the biting type.

Order Strepsiptera ('Stylops'). Only about 170 species are known. These are internal parasites in other insects, often modifying the sex of their host. The males are free-living, having degenerate fore-wings and large hind-wings, and degenerate biting mouth-parts. The females are larva-like and never leave the host.

Order Hymenoptera (Ants, Bees, Wasps, Ichneumons, Saw-flies, etc.). About 60,000 species are known. The hind-wings are smaller than the fore-wings and interlocked with them by hooks. The mouth-parts are biting or sucking. An ovipositor is always present and modified for piercing or stinging. The larvae are generally without legs.

Order Diptera (Flies). About 50,000 species are known. There is a single pair of wings, for the hind-pair are degenerate. The mouth-parts are of the sucking type, and the larvae are without legs.

Order Aphaniptera (Fleas). About 500 species are known. These insects are wingless and compressed laterally. The adults are external parasites on warm-blooded animals, the larvae are legless.

As is usual, these groups are arranged so as to pass from the more primitive to the more specialized forms, but some of them have evolved upon diverging lines which have reached approximately equal degrees of specialization. These, of course, cannot be correctly represented in a linear series, and their place in it is arbitrary. Thus the Trichoptera are relatively primitive forms and they have actually arisen from the evolutionary line which has led to the succeeding Order, with which we are particularly concerned, the Lepidoptera. But the Orders which follow are independently derived from some remote ancestor common to all but, having departed further from the primitive insect condition, they are placed at a higher level in the classification.

THE POSITION OF BUTTERFLIES AMONG THE
LEPIDOPTERA

The word Lepidoptera means 'scale-wing', which refers to one of the most obvious characteristics of these insects. Various systems have been proposed for the classification of the Order, but it is now generally divided into two sub-orders: (1) the Homoneura, in which the neuration of the fore- and hind-wings is almost identical, and a spiral proboscis is never formed. It includes relatively few primitive moths, such as the Swifts; (2) the Heteroneura, in which the neuration of the fore- and hind-wings is markedly different and a spiral proboscis is present, except in some species in which it has become degenerate. This group contains the great bulk of the Lepidoptera. It is subdivided into eight super-families, of which one, the Papilionina, comprises the Butterflies, while the remainder are Moths. In fact, the usual division of the Lepidoptera into Butterflies (Rhopalocera) and Moths (Heterocera) is hardly justified, for though the butterflies are indeed a natural group they are not, as such a distinction suggests, one whose value is equal to the whole of the other Lepidoptera.

The butterflies then belong to the super-family PAPILIONINA. The main characteristics of the group have been discussed in Chapter 2, but a few features may be mentioned here which especially distinguish it from the remaining, and far more numerous, Lepidoptera, the Moths.

In butterflies, the frenulum, which holds together the fore- and hind-wings of nearly all moths (p. 44), is absent, and its function is performed by a humeral lobe on the hind-wings (p. 44). The antennae end in a club, which is usually abrupt but may be gradually thickened, as in the Swallow-tail (Plates 1 and 23). Clubbed antennae are very rare in other Lepidoptera, and when they do occur a frenulum is always present, so that the two features when considered together are truly diagnostic of butterflies and moths. Nearly all butterflies are diurnal, though a few foreign species are crepuscular. Indeed, our own Peacock and Red Admiral have on several occasions been observed to fly at night, but this is exceptional. The majority of moths are nocturnal, but many fly by day. Nearly all butterflies sit with the wings raised above the back (p. 88); the great majority of moths rest with the wings outspread or wrapped round the body, but some specialized species hold the wings like butterflies.

THE CLASSIFICATION OF BRITISH BUTTERFLIES

Recent writers have classified butterflies in a number of ways, though the differences between their various systems are not very important. Indeed, they chiefly relate to the status to be accorded to groups which are recognized as natural by all. Thus the Danaidae, Satyridae, and the Nymphalidae are usually treated as distinct families, as they are in this work, though some authorities regard the same assemblages as sub-families within a single great family, the Nymphalidae. Moreover, it is sometimes maintained that the Skippers (Hesperiidae) constitute a super-family distinct from the other butterflies and equal in classificatory value to all the rest. There is much to be said for this view, though I have retained them as one of the eight families into which the British butterflies may be grouped. Each of these is in reality divided into a number of sub-families, which, however, I shall not mention unless we possess representatives of two or more of them in Britain.

Numerous and excellent books exist whose chief purpose is to describe the adult and early stages of the different species and the characteristics of the genera in which they are placed. As already explained (p. 11), that is not the aim of this work. Such descriptions may be obtained from any of the handbooks dealing with British butterflies, and references to several of these are given in the Bibliography.

The classification of British butterflies which follows is not identical with any so far published, for it includes some recent information which has not yet found its way into the textbooks. It is the unfortunate custom of entomologists to arrange butterflies in the reverse order to the logical one and to pass from the more specialized downwards to the more primitive forms. As all books and collections seem to adopt this principle, I follow it here. Thus the three families with which the classification begins are the most specialized, though in different directions, while that with which it ends, the Hesperiidae, is undoubtedly the most primitive.

Much confusion has been caused by the fact that the same species may have received several names given to it by different authors who did not know of each other's work. This and other difficulties are overcome by certain international rules of nomenclature, and a few of the principles which they incorporate must be mentioned here. When a genus or a species has received more than one name, the earliest must be adopted. It sometimes happens, therefore, that a well-known name must be displaced, if an earlier one is discovered in some little-known work. When I began to collect, *Colias crocea* Fourcroy (1785) was called *Colias edusa* Fabricius (1787). It was then found that this was incorrect because it was not the earliest available name. Two animals may have the same specific name if placed in different genera; but if the genera were combined, the later of the two would have to be changed, otherwise the names would become wholly identical. Moreover, no two genera may have the same name, however remote from one another they may be in classification. It is sometimes found that the generic name of a butterfly has been preoccupied by that of, for instance, a jelly-fish; the more recent of the two should then give way to the earlier and must be changed.

These and many other rulings have made great alterations in the names of our butterflies since Richard South produced his well-known book, *The Butterflies of the British Isles*, in 1906; they affect the generic names of many species and the specific names of several. Consequently, the Royal Entomological Society issued in 1934 an authoritative *Check List* of the scientific names of British butterflies, which superseded all others. However, the operation of the international rules has necessitated certain further changes even in this 1934 list, and these are incorporated in this book.

FAMILY DANAIDAE

This includes large, mainly tropical species which are protected by a nauseous taste or smell. They are difficult to injure and may recover even after a severe pinch on the thorax. Their colours are therefore conspicuous rather than concealing, and their flight is slow and awkward.

The cells of the wings are closed. The scent-producing organs include two movable pencils of hairs at the end of the body and, on the hind-wings of the male, sac-like pouches filled with androconia are often found which are unique in butterflies. The antennae are delicate and weakly clubbed. The prothoracic legs are degenerate in both sexes and useless for walking, but those of the female end in spiny knobs. The genital organs are complex and the uncus is much reduced.

The eggs are conical and ridged. The larvae are smooth, but may have one or more pairs of soft tentacles, and the pupae are suspended head downwards by tail-hooks alone.

A single North American species finds its way here occasionally. This is *Danaus plexippus* L., Monarch, Milkweed, or Black-veined Brown Butterfly.

FAMILY SATYRIDAE (BROWNS)

These are inconspicuous butterflies whose wings are decorated with eye-like spots. Their flight is on the whole rather jerky and rapid.

One or more of the nervures on the fore-wings are dilated at the base, and this is a distinguishing feature of the family. The cell is always closed, and androconia are usually present in long bands on the fore-wings of the males. The prothoracic legs of both sexes are degenerate and brush-like. Those of the male have one joint only, those of the female have several joints, but they do not end in a spiny knob, as in the Danaidae.

The eggs are generally melon-shaped and grooved (Plate 7, Fig. *a*), but they may be flattened at the top (Plate 7, Fig. *b*). The larvae feed on grass. They are spindle-shaped and covered with a very short down, but are not spined (Plate 8, Fig. *a*). The pupae are suspended head-downwards from plants by the tail-hooks only (Plate 9, Fig. *a*) or else lie in or on the ground, generally in a slight cocoon (Plate 9, Fig. *b*).

There are eleven British species, belonging to seven genera: *Pararge aegeria* L., Speckled Wood; *Lasiommata megera* L., Wall; *Erebia epiphron* Knoch, Mountain Ringlet; *E. aethiops* Esp., Scotch Argus; (*E. ligea* L., Arran Brown); *Melanargia galathea* L., Marbled White; *Hipparchia semele* Hübner, Greyling; *Maniola tithonus* L., Hedge Brown; *M. jurtina* L., Meadow Brown; *Coenonympha pamphilus* L., Small Heath; *C. tullia* Müller, Large Heath; *Aphantopus hyperanthus* L., Ringlet.

FAMILY NYMPHALIDAE

These are brilliantly marked butterflies with a powerful flight. The wings are sometimes sharply angled and indented. The cell of the fore wings is usually closed, but that of the hind wings is open in all but the genus *Argynnis*. The prothoracic legs are in both sexes degenerate and useless for walking. In the male they have two tarsal joints and are brushlike, while in the female they have four joints and the setae upon them are short, giving them a very different appearance from those of the male, so that the sexes may easily be distinguished by these legs.

The eggs are generally ribbed, with a flat area at the top (Plate 7, Figs. *c–e*). The larvae bear spines or tubercles (Plate 6, Fig. *c*). The pupae are always suspended head downwards by the tail hooks only (Plate 2, Fig. *d*).

The family is divided into four tribes:

Tribe Argynnidi (Fritillaries)
These are usually yellowish or reddish-brown insects with black markings. Many of the species are spotted or washed with silver on the under side of the hind-wings. The precostal nervure is

always present. The club of the antennae is flat, the eyes naked, and the wings without projections. Androconia are arranged in longitudinal lines upon the fore-wings. The larvae are spiny (Plate 8, Fig. *c*), and some of the pupae bear gold or silver spots.

The English species are nine, distributed among three genera: *Clossiana selene* Schiff, Small Pearl-bordered Fritillary; *C. euphrosyne* L., Pearl-bordered Fritillary; *Issoria lathonia* L., Queen of Spain Fritillary; *Mesoacidalia aglaia* L., Dark Green Fritillary; *M. adippe* L., High Brown Fritillary; *Argynnis paphia* L., Silver Washed Fritillary; *Euphydryas aurinia* Rott, Marsh Fritillary; *Melitaea cinxia* L., Glanville Fritillary; *Mellicta athalia* Rott, Heath Fritillary.

Tribe Vanessidi (the true Vanessid Butterflies)
These species have a reddish-brown ground colour due to a pigment soluble in hot water and dilute alkalis, the nature of which is discussed on pp. 67–8. The wings are angled, often markedly so, or at least indented, and the cell of the front pair is generally closed. The precostal nervure is present in most genera but absent from *Vanessa*. The antennae have pear-shaped clubs and the eyes are hairy. The larvae are always spined. The pupae have a pointed thoracic tubercle and they are marked with metallic gold or silver, though the adults are not.

We have four genera and seven species:
Vanessa atalanta L., Red Admiral; *V. cardui* L., Painted Lady; *Aglais urticae* L., Small Tortoiseshell; *Nymphalis polychloros* L., Large Tortoiseshell; *Inachis io* L., Peacock; *N. antiopa* L., Camberwell Beauty; *Polygonia c-album* L., Comma. (To this tribe belongs also *Araschnia levana* L., pp. 166–7 and *Vanessa huntera* F., p. 156.)

Tribe Apaturidi (Purple Emperors)
These are large dark insects, usually with an iridescent gloss in the male. They have an excessively powerful flight and delight to soar round the tops of trees. The wings are not angled, in our species the cell is open in both pairs and there is a precostal nervure. The antennae have thick clubs and the palpi are scaled but not hairy. The larva is solitary and remarkable among the Nymphalidae in being smooth, for it is spineless and the only tubercles are on the head (Plate 8, Fig. *d*). The pupa is flattened, leaf-like, and without angles or metallic spots (Plate 9, Fig. *c*).

We have a single species, *Apatura iris* L., Purple Emperor.

Tribe Limenitidi (*White Admirals*)

The wings are rounded. The cell of the front pair is closed by a faint cross-nervure, that of the hind pair is open, and there is a precostal nervure. The club of the antennae is elongated and gradually thickened, and the palpi are hairy. The eggs are most extraordinary and quite unlike those of any other of our butterflies, being honey-combed and spined (Plate 7, Fig. *e*). The larva bears branched spines and spined tubercles, and the pupa has a large dorsal prominence.

We have a single species, *Limenitis camilla* L., White Admiral.

FAMILY RIODINIDAE

This is principally a South American group and in that continent a vast number of species is known, but only one is found in Europe. None is of large size. The family has many of the characteristics of the Lycaenidae, which are placed immediately after it, so that a few only of its features will be mentioned here. It is chiefly distinguished from them by the extraordinary condition of the prothoracic legs. These are degenerate and useless for walking in the male but functional and provided with claws in the female. Thus they are in an intermediate stage between that found in the families which precede and follow this one.

The eggs are small and spherical. The larvae resemble those of the Lycaenidae but are without the honey gland (p. 116). The pupae, which are rather round and stout, are attached to the food plants by tail-hooks and a silken girth.

Our only species is *Hamearis lucina* L., Duke of Burgundy Fritillary.

FAMILY LYCAENIDAE

This family contains an immense number of species; all of them are small and many are brilliantly coloured. Their flight is quick and agile but seldom long sustained, and they often form localized colonies. On the fore-wings the number of nervures is generally reduced to eleven, sometimes to ten; the cell is narrow and closed by a cross-nervure which is often very faint, while that of the hind-wings is open in some genera. The antennae have long clubs. We now reach those families in which the prothoracic legs are in the more primitive condition, being functional in both sexes; but here they are still somewhat less well developed in the male, being smaller than in the female.

The eggs are of a characteristic shape – disc-like, with the edges rounded (Plate 7, Fig. *e*). The larvae are extremely unlike those of any other family except the Riodinidae, being wood-louse-shaped. They have a distinct neck, and the head can be retracted into the prothorax. In many species there is a 'honey gland', situated in the mid-dorsal line of the seventh abdominal segment. This secretes a substance attractive to ants (pp. 116–22). The pupae are extremely stout and rounded, the shape of a trussed chicken, and are nominally attached to the food-plant by tail-hooks and a silken girdle (Plate 9, Fig. *d*); or they may be without girdle or attachment, lying free among leaves (Plate 9, Fig. *e*) or even underground.

Most families of butterflies are divided into sub-families and these into tribes, but in each of those so far described we have in Britain representatives of one sub-family only. It is usually held that our Lycaenidae comprise three tribes of equal status: the Polyommatini (Blues), Lycaenini (Coppers), and Theclini (Hairstreaks). However, I have discussed this subject with Mr N. D. Riley, formerly Keeper of Entomology at the Natural History Museum, London, and he points out to me that these three groups are of very dissimilar rank and that they may best be apportioned between two sub-families, as follows:

[1]Family Lycaenidae
    Sub-family Lycaeninae
        Tribe Polyommatini (Blues)
        Tribe Lycaenini (Coppers)
    Sub-family Theclinae (Hairstreaks)

Sub-family Lycaeninae The scent-scales of the male are very curious, being battledore shaped, not localized into patches but scattered freely over the wings.

Tribe Polyommatini (*Blues*)
Most of the species are of a beautiful blue, either in both sexes or in the male alone (never the reverse). The cell of the hind-wings

[1] Names of families, sub-families and tribes are given distinctive terminations: -idae, -inae, and -i, respectively.

is occasionally open. The larvae possess the honey gland in most species (including all those found in Britain). They feed principally on Leguminosae.

We have ten genera and twelve species: *Lampides boeticus* L., Long-tailed Blue; *Cupido minimus* Fuessl., Small Blue; *Everes argiades* Pall, Short-tailed Blue; *Plebejus argus* L., Silver-studded Blue; *Aricia agestis* Schiff, Brown Argus; *A. artaxerxes* F., Northern Brown Argus; *Polyommatus icarus* Rott, Common Blue; *Lysandra coridon* Poda, Chalkhill Blue; *L. bellargus* Rott, Adonis Blue; *Cyaniris semiargus* Rott, Mazarine Blue; *Maculinea arion* L., Large Blue; *Celastrina argiolus* L., Holly Blue.

Tribe Lycaenini (Coppers)

These species are generally of a brilliant metallic copper shade. The fore-wings are triangular, and the cells are closed by weak cross-nervures. Though some of the larvae have attractive gland-cells scattered over the body, they are never concentrated into a distinct gland. All the species feed on Sorrel (*Rumex* spp).

We have in Britain a single genus and two species: *Lycaena phlaeas* L., Small Copper; *L. dispar* Haworth, Large Copper.

Sub-family Theclinae (Hairstreaks)

The upper-side is usually of a sombre shade, and on the underside of the wings is a distinctly-marked line, or row of small dots, which is responsible for the name Hairstreak. The fore-wings are very broad and the hind-wings provided with tails except in a few forms (e.g., our Green Hairstreak). The cell of both wings is closed with weak cross-nervures, and the scent-scales of the male are concentrated in a patch at the origin of nervures 6 and 7. Some of the larvae possess a honey-gland, and they generally feed on trees and shrubs.

We have three genera and five species: *Callophrys rubi* L., Green Hairstreak; *Thecla betulae* L., Brown Hairstreak; *Quercusia quercus* L., Purple Hairstreak; *Strymonidia w-album* Knoch, White-letter Hairstreak; *S. pruni* L., Black Hairstreak.

FAMILY PAPILIONIDAE

This family is wrongly placed after the Pieridae in several modern classifications purporting to pass from the more specialized to the more primitive forms, though it is certainly the more specialized of the two. It is a very extensive one, for it contains about 508 species, and it includes the largest butterflies in the world. Its various genera differ widely in shape, colour, and habits. None is known to use any uric acid pigments. The majority of the species are tailed, but a considerable number are not. The great majority possess a short transverse nervure between the cell and nervure 1 on the fore-wings. The extraordinary statement is constantly made that this family differs from the Pieridae in the possession of but one anal nervure on the hind-wings. This is quite incorrect. In large numbers of the species, but not in the genus *Papilio*, both anal nervures are clearly visible, and the real distinction lies in a specialization of the inner margin in the Papilionidae, which is modified and upturned. The knob of the antenna is usually curved and the prothoracic legs are fully formed in both sexes.

The eggs are spherical. The larvae are very various, but generally possess on the first segment a forked retractile organ which emits a strong disagreeable scent. The pupa is angular, supported by tail-hooks and a girth.

We have but one genus and species, *Papilio machaon* L., Swallow-tail (see Plate 23).

FAMILY PIERIDAE

The predominant white and yellow colours of this family are produced by uric acid derivatives, as are their red pigments, though these do not occur in any British species. The transverse nervure is absent from the fore-wings, and the inner margin of the hind-wings is not modified and upturned. The knob of the antenna is straight, and the prothoracic legs are fully formed and functional in both sexes.

The eggs are very characteristic, being tall, bottle-shaped and ribbed. The larvae are worm-like without spines or tubercles. The pupae are angular and supported by tail hooks and a girth.

We have representatives of three of the five sub-families of the Pieridae.

Sub-family Pierinae (Whites)

The ground-colour of these butterflies is nearly always white, and they possess no flavone pigments. There is a well-developed precostal nervure.

Four genera and six species are found in Britain: *Aporia*

crataegi L., Black-veined White; *Pieris brassicae* L., Large White; *P. rapae* L., Small White; *P. napi* L., Green-veined White; *Pontia daplidice* L., Bath White; *Anthocharis cardamines* L., Orange Tip.

Sub-family Coliadinae (*Yellows*)

The ground-colour is usually yellow or orange, and flavones are not present. The precostal nervure is greatly reduced or absent. The larvae feed on Leguminosae, our own Brimstone being very exceptional in feeding on Buckthorn.

We have two genera and four species: *Colias hyale* L., Pale Clouded Yellow; *C. australis* Verity, Berger's Clouded Yellow; *C. crocea* Fourcroy, Clouded Yellow; *Gonepteryx rhamni* L., Brimstone.

Sub-family Dismorphiinae

This strange primitive group of 101 known species is almost entirely Central and South American, where 98 of them are found, and only 3 have been discovered outside America. Most of them are exceedingly unlike Pieridae, the wings often being narrow and brilliantly coloured with red, orange, and black. Yet their yellow pigment is a uric acid derivative, as in the normal Pieridae. Three of the four genera, including ours, possess flavones in addition to the uric acid pigments. The cell is extremely small in both wings, and there is a precostal nervure. The few known larvae feed on Leguminosae. I have shown that this sub-family is more primitive than those previously mentioned (Ford, 1941), yet it is placed before them even in the most modern classifications, though these aim at passing downwards from the more specialized forms. This is an error; it should be the last sub-family of the Pieridae.

We have a single species, *Leptidea sinapis* L., Wood White.

FAMILY HESPERIIDAE (SKIPPERS)

As already mentioned (p. 77), this group is sometimes treated as a super-family, equivalent in rank to all other butterflies combined. The species have a distinctive darting and exceedingly rapid flight. In structure they are primitive and approach the moths, and nearly all are dull in colour. They are unique among butterflies in that all the nervures arise direct from the cells, none branching subsequently; also the shape of the head is at once diagnostic of them, for it is wider than the thorax, with the eyes large and protruding. The prothoracic legs are functional in both sexes, while on the hind (metathoracic) pair the tibia is generally, but not always, provided with two pairs of spines, as in many moths.

The eggs are very varied and their form is not characteristic of the family. The larvae taper at both ends; they spin leaves together and live in their shelter. The pupae are long and tapering, often without tail-hooks or girdle, and they are enclosed in a cocoon of silk and grass (Plate 9, Fig. *f*)

Sub-family Pyrginae

Nervure 5 does not arise very near 4. The antenna usually ends in a point. In the male the scent scales are generally enclosed in a fold of the costa on the fore-wings, as in both our species.

We have two genera and species: *Erynnis tages* L., Dingy Skipper; *Pyrgus malvae* L., Grizzled Skipper.

Sub-family Hesperiinae

Nervure 5 arises close to 4. The antennae are not pointed, and the male never has a costal fold but the androconia form a diagonal line across the fore-wings.

In Britain there are four genera and six species: *Carterocephalus palaemon* Pall, Chequered Skipper; *Thymelicus sylvestris* Poda, Small Skipper; *T. lineola* Ochs, Essex Skipper; *T. acteon* Rott, Lulworth Skipper; *Hesperia comma* L., Silver-spotted Skipper; *Ochlodes venatus* Bremer and Grey, Large Skipper.

It must here be noted that two new butterflies have been added to the British list since this book was first published in 1945. It has been discovered that the Pale Clouded Yellow, *Colias hyale*, comprised two species which had previously been confused: the Pale Clouded Yellow, *C. hyale* L., itself, and the recently distinguished Berger's Clouded Yellow, *C. australis* (Plate 22). The latter is slightly smaller than *hyale*, and the outer margin of the fore wings is rounded instead of nearly straight, so making the apex less pointed. Also it is less heavily marked with black. However, the central spot of the fore-wings is large; so also is that of the hind pair, and this is deep orange. The ground colour of the male *australis* is canary yellow, without the greenish tint of *hyale*, and that of the female is white, only occasionally yellowish. The dark shade at the base of the fore-wings is usually restricted to the area between vein 1*b* and the inner margin (Fig. 2, p. 44) instead of spreading across the cell, as in *hyale* (see Higgins and Riley, 1970).

The specimens illustrated in colour on Plate 26 of the hardback edition of this book are true *hyale*. Rather curiously, the male upperside figured by South (1941) on his Plate 21 is *australis*. Yet the two species are variable in all their characteristics and their identification can be very difficult, especially in the females. The larvae, however, are distinct. Both are green, but in their later instars those of *australis* always bear striking black and yellow marks along the sides, absent from *hyale*, and their only food is Horseshoe Vetch, *Hippocrepis comosa*. *C. hyale*, however, feeds on various clovers and trefoils.

C. australis is an insect of chalk downs and limestone hills. It is the wilder and more difficult species to catch, while its spring generation, always disproportionately scarce in *hyale*, is as frequent as the summer one. It is, however, the rarer butterfly of the two. Perhaps about one Pale Clouded Yellow in ten that has been caught in England is, in reality, *australis*, though it is relatively commoner in some seasons than in others.

For the second recently identified British species, see pages 280–1.

Some of the more primitive characteristics of butterflies will have become apparent from the foregoing survey of the British groups, and it will be clear also that certain of their features must be specialized. These indications merit a brief examination.

The most archaic genus of butterflies is *Euschemon* Dbl. from Australia, a continent in which many primitive forms of life are preserved. A frenulum is actually present in the males, and it is now known that the genus belongs to the Hesperiidae. Indeed, the structure of that family is ancestral in several respects. Evidently the prothoracic legs must originally have been functional in both sexes, as they are here. The method of sitting with the wings raised above the back is unknown in the most primitive of the super-families of the Lepidoptera, yet it occurs in nearly all butterflies except some Skippers: our own Dingy Skipper sits 'like a moth' (Plate 10, Fig. *d*), though others have an abnormal, though characteristic method of resting, with the hind-wings held horizontally and the fore-wings partially raised (Plate 10, Fig. *e*). Certain tropical Riodinidae rest with the wings spread out horizontally (as do many Geometridae), but this is a specialization in another direction. It is true that in the Trichoptera, from which the Lepidoptera are derived, almost all the wing nervures run horizontally, but the remarkable unbranched neuration of the Hesperiidae must largely be a secondary condition peculiar to the group. However, the shape of their larvae undoubtedly approaches the ancestral one. The habit of living in hiding within leaves spun together, or under a silken web, is frequent in most groups of the Lepidoptera, but uncommon in the fully grown larvae of butterflies. It is, however, adopted by many young larvae even of the Nymphalidae; and this is probably an example of the general principle that young organisms show more primitive characters, and resemble one another more closely (p. 46) than do the adults.

The pupa is protected by a cocoon in most Lepidoptera, and this is the general condition in the Hesperiidae. It does not, however, exist (save as an occasional specialization) in other butterflies, which adopt very exceptional methods of pupal support. These cocoons are at least partly woven with silk, and it is generally held that the silken girth surrounding the pupa of many butterflies is a relic of them. It is notable therefore that such a girth is found only in those groups which on general grounds are judged the more primitive; and indeed it occurs in many Hesperiidae in addition to a cocoon, though this does not mean that the two structures were distinct in origin, for the girth appears to be merely that portion of the cocoon which holds the pupa in place.

It will be noticed that these primitive features are progressively lost as we pass from the Hesperiidae towards the Danaidae. Attention may briefly be directed to three of the changes encountered on the way. First, the degeneration of the prothoracic legs is a gradual one, the Lycaenidae and the Riodinidae providing intermediate stages between the functional and the aborted states. Secondly, two main types of larvae are found in the Papilionina. The more normal worm-shaped forms are the commoner, and they may be protected in various ways: by the acquisition of nauseous tastes, as in the Danaidae, or of branched spines, as in the Nymphalidae. There is also the entirely distinct woodlouse-like form characteristic of the 'Lycaenid line', the Lycaenidae and the Riodinidae. Evidently, therefore, these families cannot be ancestral to those in which the prothoracic legs are aborted, though in this feature they seem to lead so directly to them. For the evolution of this larval type has preceded the degeneration of the legs, as it is already complete in the Lycaenidae in which the legs are still functional in both sexes. Thirdly, above the Hesperiidae, two main forms of pupae exist. Those, the more primitive, which are attached by the cremaster and supported head upwards by a silken girth, and those which hang head down by the cremaster alone.

It will, I think, now be obvious that the eight families of British butterflies are not equally distinct, but fall into four groups. These may be tabulated as follows, passing down from the more specialized.

Group 1 Danaidae, Satyridae, Nymphalidae.
Group 2 Riodinidae, Lycaenidae.
Group 3 Papilionidae, Pieridae.
Group 4 Hesperiidae.

For generations it has been the custom of entomologists to arrange their collections in a totally unnatural manner: starting with the Papilionidae and following them with the Pieridae, Nymphalidae, Danaidae, Satyridae, Lycaenidae, Riodinidae, and Hesperiidae. Moreover, this sequence has most improperly been adopted in the majority of text-books, except quite recent ones (it is even used in that great work, *The Macrolepidoptera of the World*, edited by A. Seitz, which has been appearing in parts since 1906). This is the more inexcusable since the arrangement followed by Edward Newman in his splendid book, *British Butterflies*, published in 1869, is nearly the correct one (though he makes the astonishing mistake of inserting *Papilio* in the middle of the Pieridae, between the Coliadinae and the Pierinae). I hope that the system of placing the Papilionidae at the head of the butterflies, really only because they are large and showy, will soon disappear from museums and private collections, and that it will no longer be perpetuated in text-books and thus obscure the relationships of butterflies.

THE CRITERIA OF CLASSIFICATION

It is not practicable to discuss here in any detail the evidence upon which the classification of butterflies is based. Yet it is necessary to mention the principle that this classification must rely upon as many distinct kinds of characters as possible. In the past, various systems of classification have been developed based upon some particular feature alone, such as the neuration, the genitalia, or the mode of pupation. Such a procedure is ridiculous, and it should always have appeared logically indefensible. It would never be proposed today. Any classification must take into account as many as possible of the external and internal structures not only of the adult but also of the early stages. In this way alone it is possible to avoid errors due to analogy and to the presence of secondary characters. It does remain true, however, that while paying lip-service to such a principle, undue weight may yet be attached to certain features; a thing hardly possible to avoid. I am myself of the opinion that there is at the present time a tendency to overstress the, quite real, importance of the neuration and of the genitalia in systematic work.

There is one criterion of classification to which I wish to draw special attention: it is that supplied by chemistry, in particular of the pigments. I do so not because it is less fallible than any other, but because until quite recently it has been almost wholly neglected. This gives it an especial interest, since it supplies an entirely independent check on the results reached by other means. It is clearly important to determine whether or not the distribution of different types of pigments tends to support a classification made without any knowledge of it. Such information I have for years past been attempting to supply, and the results so far obtained not only confirm the accepted classification but provide exceptionally strong, because entirely independent, evidence of its correctness.

It is obviously satisfactory that, for example, a special type of red pigment (pp. 67–8) should be found in the Nymphalidae but not elsewhere, and that the distribution of two other red pigments, and of the flavones, should be closely related to the accepted classification of the Papilionidae, though these facts were not known when the groups were composed. A single more detailed instance will serve to indicate the way in which such chemical studies may support the more normal methods used in classification. It had long been realized that our Wood White is a most exceptional species, but it is only in recent years that the step was taken of uniting the little European and Asiatic genus *Leptidea*, to which it belongs, with the otherwise wholly Central and South American sub-family Dismorphiinae, though such an affinity had tentatively been suggested for some time. It was reached on purely structural evidence, derived particularly from neuration. I later found that all the species belonging to two of the three American genera of Dismorphiinae possess flavone pigments and that these do not occur in the Pierinae[1] (while *Leptidea* could not have been placed among the 'Yellows', the Coliadinae or the Teracolinae). It was therefore with some satisfaction that I demonstrated the occurrence of flavones in the genus *Leptidea* (Ford, 1941), including our own Wood White, so confirming, on entirely distinct evidence, the apparently rather bold step of classifying it with that strange group of New World butterflies in which it is now included.

[1] One hundred and twenty-two species distributed among every one of its forty-three genera were tested without finding flavones.

Chapter 5

Habits and Protective Devices

*Habits: The Early Stages, The Adult Insects, Feeding Habits,
Courtship, Hibernation – Protective Devices: The Early Stages,
The Adult Insects*

HABITS

The Early Stages

The eggs of most butterflies are laid singly, generally each on a
different plant. They are attached by a sticky substance which
hardens and glues them firmly in position. This secretion is
lacking in two species only, the Marbled White, *Melanargia
galathea*, and the Ringlet, *Aphantopus hyperanthus*, and these
scatter their eggs broadcast as they fly over meadows and rough
hill slopes, or by the wayside; for their larvae, being grass-
feeders, are certain to find food in such situations. Nine[1] of our
butterflies lay their eggs in large clusters of 100 or more, and on
Plate 11, Fig. *a* is a photograph of the Small Tortoiseshell,
Aglais urticae, doing so, the accumulating mass of eggs being
clearly visible. She is curving her abdomen round so as to lay
them in the usual position on the underside of a leaf, where they
are more protected from excessive rain and sunshine, as well as
from enemies. In addition, five species[2] lay little batches of
perhaps five to fifteen eggs together.

The majority of larvae therefore lead lonely lives, and the
gregarious habit, determined by the method of egg-laying, is
exceptional and carries with it certain noteworthy adaptations.
Two of the nine species in which it occurs become solitary in
their later stages; these are the Small Tortoiseshell (Plate 11,
Fig. *b* young) and the Large White, *Pieris brassicae*. The others
remain in large companies until pupation. The majority of these
gregarious forms are Nymphalidae, whose larvae are beset with
branched spines. Particularly when small, the inconvenience
caused to a predator by eating a single individual might be
negligible, but most animals would avoid a large spiny mouthful
such as the whole batch would provide. Moreover, some of them

---

[1] *E. aurinia, M. cinxia, M. athalia, A. urticae, N. polychloros, I. io,
N. antiopa, A. crataegi, P. brassicae.*

[2] *H. lucina, P. rapae, T. sylvestris, T. lineola, T. acteon.*

(especially the Marsh Fritillary, *Euphydryas aurinia*, and our species of the genera *Melitaea* and *Mellicta*) have developed a curious habit; for when alarmed, the whole brood jerk their heads upwards with strange unanimity, producing a striking effect. Probably it helps to remind any bird which has attempted to eat such larvae in the past of its unpleasant experience. Two of the gregarious species, the Black-veined White, *Aporia crataegi*, and the Large White, are not spined, but these have a disagreeable smell to us and presumably to other Vertebrates. This will be much enhanced when a number of them remain together in close company.

On emerging, many larvae eat their eggshell, which is made of chitin, and this seems to be a necessity to some of them (e.g., the Speckled Wood, *Pararge aegeria*), which die if removed from it. Indeed, it forms the only meal taken in the autumn by the Marbled White and the Small Skipper, *Thymelicus sylvestris*, before they hibernate until the following spring. Having consumed the shell, these larvae proceed to the ordinary food upon which the egg has been laid by the parent. Some (e.g., the Wall, *Lasiommata megera*, the Meadow Brown, *Maniola jurtina*, and the Ringlet) feed only by night, others (e.g., the Marbled White, the Dark Green Fritillary, *Mesoacidalia aglaia*, and the Swallow-tail, *Papilio machaon*) only by day, while many species may be found feeding at any time of the day or night (e.g., the Speckled Wood, the Silver-studded Blue, *Plebejus argus*, and the Black Hairstreak, *Strymonidia pruni*). Moreover, several change their feeding habits as they grow; thus the Scotch Argus, *Erebia aethiops*, will eat only at night in its last larval stage, though it is not so restricted in its earlier life.

The larvae of several butterflies protect themselves by spinning leaves together with silk and feeding under their shelter: the Red Admiral, *Vanessa atalanta*, and the Painted Lady, *V. cardui*, have this habit. Four of the British Skippers[1] live in a similar way, constructing a tent of grass, while the remaining species pass their lives in grass tubes which they form by rolling up the edges of the blades and fastening them with silk. All our Skippers have a valuable adaptation to their life in confined quarters. This consists in a comb-like flap at the anus by which they throw their excreta to a considerable distance, up to three feet, when ejected from the body, so as to keep their dwelling undefiled: a habit found also in many young birds (Huxley, 1942, p. 424).

[1] *C. palaemon T. sylvestris, T. acteon, O. venatus.*

It is not my intention to give lists of the larval food of our butterflies, of the different stages in which they hibernate, or of those which are single- or multiple-brooded, for these facts can be obtained from any of the text-books describing the species (see the Bibliography, pp. 316–7), where indeed this information is usually tabulated. As already explained, such detailed descriptions are not the purpose of this work. On the contrary, during the course of this chapter I shall mention only some more general and significant features connected with these subjects.

A few butterflies are restricted to a single food-plant; for example, the Black Hairstreak, which in nature has no alternative to Sloe, though in captivity it can feed upon garden plum. Others are confined to a single family of plants but not to any one species within it, as is the Green-veined White, *Pieris napi*, which eats Cruciferae only. Some, however, have rather catholic tastes: thus the larvae of the Green Hairstreak, *Callophrys rubi*, may feed upon Rock-rose (*Cistaceae*), Purging Buckthorn (*Rhamnaceae*), Gorse, Broom, and Dyer's Greenwood (*Leguminosae*), Bramble (*Rosaceae*), Dogwood (*Cornaceae*), and Whortleberry (*Ericaceae*). The Large Tortoiseshell, *Nymphalis polychloros*, has similarly a large choice from the botanical point of view but not from that of plant habit, for it is associated only with trees and bushes. It is most usually found upon Elm (*Ulmaceae*), but it will also eat Whitebeam (*Rosaceae*), and Willow (*Salicaceae*) and it has been reported from Birch (*Betulaceae*).

Certain groups are closely associated with particular families of plants. Thus the Satyridae are entirely grass-feeders, as are all our Hesperiinae, though not the Pyrginae (*E. tages* and *P. malvae*), among the British Skippers. Those species of our Argynnidi that are normally marked with silver on the underside of the hind wings are all restricted to the Violaceae, and the 'Blues' (Polyommatini) feed chiefly upon Leguminosae, though by no means all are confined to them. Although a number of butterflies regularly have more than one generation during the year, while others occasionally do so, there is only one species whose food varies with the season. This is the Holly Blue, *Celastrina argiolus*, which in June and July chiefly eats holly, but occasionally buckthorn, gorse and broom. Yet the larvae which result from eggs laid by the second brood of butterflies feed up in the late summer almost entirely upon ivy, though it is said that they occasionally eat bramble at this time.

The pupae of all our butterflies except the Hesperiidae belong fundamentally to one of two types. Either they are attached by the cremaster and held head-upwards by a silken girth, or they hang head-down from the cremaster alone. The latter is the more highly specialized type, and it is found in the Danaidae, Satyridae, and Nymphalidae only. Various simplifications of these two methods occur, and here and there among the groups are instances in which butterflies have resorted secondarily to cocoon-formation. These different modifications must briefly be considered.

Normally, the Satyridae pupate hanging head-downwards, but the secondary tendency to make cocoons is quite strongly developed in this family. The pupae of the Mountain Ringlet, *Erebia epiphron*, the Scotch Argus, the Marbled White, and of the Grayling, *Hipparchia semele*, are all without tail-hooks. That of the Mountain Ringlet simply lies among grass stems, which are loosely fastened together with silk. The Scotch Argus excavates a slight hollow in the ground, covering the opening with a loose web, and pupates head-upwards in the cavity. The Marbled White makes no cocoon at all, and its pupa merely lies among moss and fibres. The Grayling is noteworthy as being our only butterfly which constructs a genuine subterranean cocoon. This is a shell of earth, finished off smoothly within, whose particles are bound together with silk. It is made well below the surface of the soil, and much resembles the type common among moths of the family Agrotidae. Mr S. Beaufoy has, with great skill, succeeded in obtaining a photograph of the chrysalis of the Grayling lying in this underground cocoon, which he has opened (Plate 9, Fig. *b*).

All the Nymphalidae pupate head-downwards in the fashion characteristic of their family. None makes a cocoon, but the pupae of the Dark Green Fritillary, the High Brown Fritillary, and the Painted Lady hang in a tent of leaves bound together with silk. So do those of the Marsh Fritillary, but not of the Glanville and Heath Fritillaries, *Melitaea cinxia* and *Mellicta athalia*, which, it will be noticed, belong to different though closely related genera. The Large Tortoiseshell and the Peacock, both wander far from their food-plant before they pupate. Indeed, the larvae of the latter species often climb trees and attach their pupae at some height from the ground, though they feed on nettle. The Peacock belongs to a genus allied to that of the Large Tortoiseshell and the Camberwell Beauty, *Nymphalis*

a. The Wall Butterfly feeding: the tongue extended (x2)

b. The Swallow-tail: tongue coiled under the head (x4/3)

1. THE TONGUES OF BUTTERFLIES

a. Brimstone: caterpillar ready to pupate

b. Brimstone: chrysalis

c. Large Tortoiseshell: caterpillar ready to pupate

d. Large Tortoiseshell: chrysalids

2. TWO METHODS OF PUPATION IN BUTTERFLIES

a. Girdle in position

b. Larval skin bursts

c. Skin passing under girdle

d. Skin pushed to hind end

e. Cremaster lifted to free skin

f. Skin removed, cremaster attached

3. THE PUPATION OF THE SWALLOW-TAIL

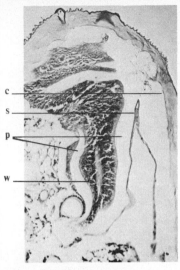

c

s

p

w

a. The wing of an adult
caterpillar (x150)

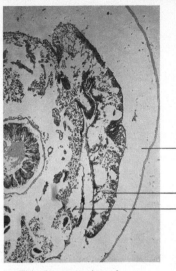

b. The wing at the time of
pupation (x28)

c. The wing removed from a
newly-formed pupa (x27)

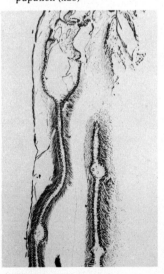

d. The wings during scale-
formation (x34)

In Figs. a and b: w = wing, s = larval skin, p = pocket in skin, c = cuticle

4. THE DEVELOPMENT OF A BUTTERFLY'S WINGS

All figures are sections cut through the wings.

a. Pupa-case bursts

b. Wings start to expand

c. Wings half expanded

d. Wings nearly expanded

e. Wings held apart to dry

f. Ready for flight

5. THE EMERGENCE OF THE RED ADMIRAL (x0.85)

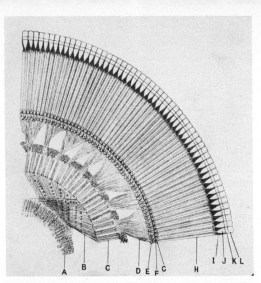

a. Diagram of a section through a compound eye (magnified). Taken from H. Eltringham's *The Senses of Insects,* 1933

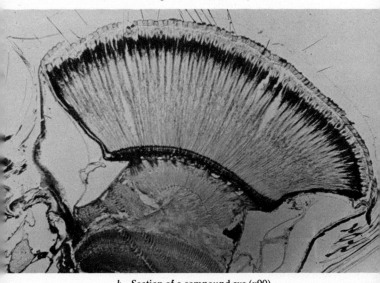

b. Section of a compound eye (x90)

6. THE EYES OF BUTTERFLIES

a. Satyridae (The Grayling)

b. Satyridae (The Small Heath)

c. Nymphalidae (Silver-washed Fritillary)

d. Nymphalidae (Painted Lady)

e. Nymphalidae (White Admiral)

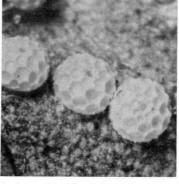

f. Lycaenidae (Small Copper)

7. THE EGGS OF BUTTERFLIES (MAGNIFIED)

Fig. *a:* x 18; Fig. *b:* x25; Fig. *c:* x25; Fig. *d:* x20; Fig. *e:* x30; Fig. *F:* x30

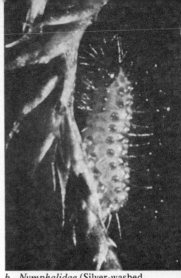

a. Satyridae (Meadow Brown)

b. Nymphalidae (Silver-washed
Fritillary, newly-hatched—
magnified x27)

c. Nymphalidae (Silver-washed
Fritillary, full-grown—x1.5)

d. Nymphalidae (Purple Emperor)

8. CATERPILLARS

antiopa, and, like them, it may once have been a tree-living form. The Purple Emperor, *Apatura iris*, pupates in late June on the underside of a sallow leaf and, though the perfect-insect emerges in about a fortnight, the larva is careful to secure the stalk of the leaf to the stem with strands of silk, lest it fall during this important period.

Typically, the Lycaenidae and the Riodinidae pupate head-upwards supported by a silken girdle; however, various modifications of the method are to be found among them. The pupa of the Brown Hairstreak, *Thecla betulae*, is secured to the underside of a sloe leaf, yet it has neither tail-hooks nor a silken girdle. It is retained in position by the larval skin which it never completely casts, and this is attached to a silken pad by the shrunken remains of the claspers. That of the Green Hairstreak is, I think, unique among our butterflies in any stage of their existence in its ability to make a sound[1]; a slight creaking, which seems to be produced by an imperceptible movement of one segment upon another. It lies loosely among dead leaves at the base of its food-plant with a few threads of silk about it. It is shown on Plate 9, Fig. *e*, and should be compared with the normal Lycaenid type exemplified by the pupa of the Small Copper, *Lycaena phlaeas*, of which there is a photograph on Plate 9, Fig. *d*, and here the silken girth can plainly be seen. The Purple Hairstreak, *Quercusia quercus*, has also lost the tail-hooks and lies loosely covered with a thread or two of silk. The larva feeds on oak, and it has been suggested that it normally pupates under moss on the branches or trunk of the tree. It may be that it often does so, but my father and I were accustomed to find this pupa commonly under moss growing on the ground in the angles between the roots.

The pupation of the Coppers is quite unexceptional, but that of several of the Blues differs from the normal plan of attachment by tail-hooks and a silken girth. In the Silver-studded Blue the hooks remain but are not used, the pupa being hung from the food-plant by several strands of silk. The Long-tailed Blue, *Lampides boeticus*, retains the normal girdle but not the hooks. It protects itself in a cocoon made by spinning together the edges of a withered leaf. The Brown Argus, *Aricia agestis*, may hang supported by a girdle and the larval skin, the remains of the anal claspers being yet entangled in a silken pad. Alternatively, it may be found on the ground attached to the stem of its food-plant by a few threads. Neither the Chalkhill nor the Adonis Blues,

[1] Several moths, however can make a sound.

Lysandra coridon and *L. bellargus*, possess tail-hooks or a girdle. The Chalkhill Blue creeps into any available depression or hole in the ground and pupates without a covering. The Adonis, on the other hand, makes a feeble silken cocoon, and in soft soil it sometimes works its way well below the surface before pupating. The exceptional pupation of the Large Blue, *Maculinea arion*, will be discussed in the next chapter.

All the Papilionidae, including our own Swallow-tail, pupate head-upwards supported by a silken girth, except one foreign sub-family (the Parnassiinae) which form cocoons in or on the ground. Similarly, all the Pieridae pupate head-upwards with a silken girth.

As already explained, the pupation of the Skippers (Hesperiidae) is quite unlike that of the more highly evolved species which comprise the rest of the butterflies. The pupae of our Pyrginae (*Erynnis tages* and *Pyrgus malvae*) are without a girth, and are attached by tail-hooks to loose cocoons of silk and grass. Those of the Hesperiinae are also formed within cocoons of grass, but all except the Silver-spotted Skipper, *Hesperia comma*, and the Large Skipper, *Ochlodes venatus*, are secured by a girth as well as by tail-hooks. These two species are also attached by hooks at the head, as is the pupa of the Essex Skipper, *Thymelicus lineola*, but, strangely, not those of the other species of *Thymelicus* to which it is so closely allied.

THE ADULT INSECTS

Feeding Habits

The individual habits of many of our butterflies in the adult state will be described in the later chapters of this book, which deal with their dispersal and distribution. I propose here to consider only a few general aspects of their behaviour relating to feeding habits and courtship.

Unlike our moths, among which are to be found species with the adult mouth-parts atrophied, all our butterflies are capable of feeding. Many of them use their tongue for sucking the nectar from flowers (Plate 1, Fig. *a*), to which they are attracted by sight (pp. 62–4) as well as by scent. Yet some species show but little interest in such food. Thus the Duke of Burgundy Fritillary, *Hamearis lucina*, will sit on leaves in the sunshine a few inches above the ground or on hot bare patches of earth, but it rarely takes any notice of the blossoms of its larval food, the cowslip and primrose, near which it always flies, or those of any other plant. Furthermore, it has been said that the Grayling never visits flowers. This is an over-statement, but it is certainly true that it seldom does so. It is more inclined to suck the sap exuding from wounded trees, and it will feed at the patches which have been 'sugared' by moth-collectors. Several other species are attracted in a similar way, notably the Peacock and specially the Purple Emperor. Collectors have told me that they have found a dozen or more of the latter butterfly sitting together on a tree from which the sap was running. I have never seen such a sight myself, but it must be a memorable one, for this is among our finest butterflies.

The male, and occasionally the female, Purple Emperor can be taken at carrion, and it may be seen sucking the juices from the rotting corpses in a 'gamekeeper's larder', while a decaying rabbit placed in a suitable woodland ride is a great attraction to it; it may also be found drinking at a foul puddle or at the edge of a stagnant pool. Early in the morning this butterfly will descend and skim swiftly along the paths through the oak or beech woods which it inhabits (p. 133). Long before midday, however, it ascends to the tree-tops, around which it may be seen flying with great power, sometimes leaving them to soar high in the air and at others alighting on the outer branches. Here it presumably sucks the sweet aphis-secretion, called 'honey-dew', which is also a particular delight to several of the Hairstreaks. I once captured numbers of the Black Hairstreak by climbing into a tree and, armed with a net on a long pole, sweeping them off the leaves of a neighbouring oak which was sticky with this substance. I may add that very few of the specimens were worth keeping, so quickly does this insect damage itself on the wing. However, I have usually caught it by disturbing it from the sloe bushes on which it habitually rests, or sitting on privet blossom; and I once saw a specimen of the White-letter *Strymonidia w-album*, and of the Black Hairstreak, together on the same spray, though the latter was much worn as it is the earlier of the two to emerge, the difference being about a week or ten days.

In Britain, with its damp and sunless climate, we do not often see those wonderful associations of butterflies drinking at wet mud, or at the margins of pools and streams, which are such a notable feature of drier parts of the tropics and even of southern Europe. Yet a few species are attracted in this way. The Purple Emperor has already been mentioned as one of these; it mainly visits those which are stagnant and evil-smelling, but the Holly Blue may be found drinking even at running water.

Two of our butterflies whose larvae feed upon low-growing plants (in this instance violets) are yet particularly associated with trees. These are the Silver-washed and the High Brown Fritillaries, *Argynnis paphia* and *Mesoacidalia adippe*, though I do not think they visit them for the sake of honey-dew. Rather, they have the habit of roosting in the higher branches during the night and on dull days. I remember an afternoon in Savernake Forest when, following some hours of cloud, the sun at last broke forth and the High Brown Fritillaries came floating down in numbers from the oak trees around me.

Courtship

No attraction among those so far mentioned is as potent as that which the female butterfly exercises for the male; to the Purple Emperor it even surpasses the appeal of a decomposing rat. It is, of course, one used by moth collectors, who are sometimes able to attract many males to a caged female. This does not seem to have been done in butterflies, but it might well be attempted. It must, however, be remembered that in this group the male often finds the female wholly by sight (pp. 62–4); yet there can be no doubt that scent also plays a part in some species. One may find several male Brimstones, *Gonepteryx rhamni*, attracted to a spot where a female is sitting, sometimes already paired, under leaves in a position quite invisible to them. Scents of this kind are of the group called by Eltringham 'directive'. They are produced by the female apparently from the terminal segments of the abdomen, which are often protruded and withdrawn rhythmically when she is in a condition to attract the male. They must arise from scattered gland-cells, for no special glandular organ which could produce them has ever been identified, and they are perceived by olfactory organs in the antennae of the male. One has the impression that the male can sometimes detect the scent of the female a hundred yards or so away, but no instances are recorded among butterflies of scent perception over great distances such as are known among moths.

The male having found the female by sight or scent proceeds to stimulate her with his own attractive odours. These are disseminated in various ways in the different families. The methods employed by the Danaidae are among the most complex and fully studied. Unfortunately, our only species of this group is the

Monarch, *Danaus plexippus*, which rarely reaches these shores, so that they hardly fall within an account of British Lepidoptera. I shall therefore only refer to them briefly. The males of these insects are provided with extensible brushes at the end of the abdomen and most of the species also possess a patch of secreting cells under a covering of scales on the hind-wings. The butterflies sweep out the scented material from beneath this covering with the brushes and diffuse the odour around the female. Professor G. D. Hale Carpenter has seen the male of the African Danaine, *Amauris psyttalea* Plötz, hover over the female and dust her with the scented powder with which the wing-pocket is filled in this insect, by rapidly protruding and withdrawing its brushes.

In most of our butterflies, the attractive scent of the male is scattered by the androconia, usually situated on the upper side of the fore-wings (pp. 79–87). They are visible as thickenings along the nervures of the Fritillaries, and as small round patches at the apex of the cell in male Hairstreaks. In the Polyommatini (Blues) and the Pieridae they are scattered among the normal scales, and they form a distinct horizontal line on the fore-wings of some male Skippers (Plates 17 and 21). On reaching the female, the male therefore flutters round her and often stands beside her waving his wings, so as to stimulate her with his scent.

As far as is known, none of the directive odours of female Lepidoptera affect the human olfactory sense. It is remarkable therefore that many of the attractive scents of male butterflies are easily perceptible to most people; moreover, they are almost uniformly pleasant to us as well as to the female insect. Some of them are quite strong and easily detected, as is the scent of Lemon Verbena produced by the male Green-veined White. Others appear to us very feeble and can only be noticed by those in whom the sense of smell is well developed. Nor are they produced by every specimen, a circumstance which depends doubtless upon the age of the insect and the state of the secretory cells. In certain species it is possible to detect the odour only from scales which have been scraped from the scent-patch of a fresh male. This applies to the Clouded Yellow, *Colias crocea*, whose male possesses a scent-patch near the base of the costa on the hind-wings, which, by the way, is absent from the closely-related Pale Clouded Yellow, *C. hyale*. The volatile essences produced by the scent-patches of male butterflies can be extracted with alcohol, so that scented solutions of them may be obtained.

My friend, the late Dr F. A. Dixey, made a survey of butterfly scents in collaboration with Dr G. B. Longstaff. He found that the decisions which they reached independently as to the nature of the various odours nearly always corresponded, as far as the difficulties of describing them allowed. Apart from their work, this subject has been very little studied. It is one on which any collector could advance our knowledge, and an account of these scents from the various British butterflies would be well worth preparing. Since the conclusions of Dixey and Longstaff appear to be little known, a summary of them will, I believe, be of considerable interest: see Table 1, in which I have included the continental *Gonepteryx cleopatra* L., which has in fact been recorded several times in England, in order to show the remarkable difference between this and our own very closely related *G. rhamni*.

| | Scent | |
Species	Nature	Strength
L. megera	heavy and sweet, like chocolate cream	slight
M. galathea	distinctly musky	slight
H. semele	sandal-wood, or an old cigar-box	not strong
M. jurtina	old cigar-box	very slight
I. lathonia	heliotrope-flowers	slight
L. boeticus	meadow-sweet	slight
A. agestis	chocolate	rather strong
P. icarus	chocolate	rather strong
P. brassicae	orris root	very slight
P. rapae	sweet-briar	faint
P. napi	lemon verbena	strong
P. daplidice	sweet pea	slight
C. crocea	heliotrope flowers	very slight
G. rhamni	(none)	(none)
(*G. cleopatra*)	rich and powerful, freesia	strong

Table 1 The attractive scent of male butterflies

When the female butterfly has been sufficiently stimulated by the scent of the male, actual pairing takes place. This lasts for a considerable time, in some species for an hour or two. It is shown in progress in the Meadow Brown on Plate 11, Fig. *c*. The process cannot begin until the female has settled. The male grasps the female firmly with his claspers, so that if the pair are disturbed they fly clumsily away together and settle down again elsewhere. In these circumstances, one individual hangs passively and is carried by the other, which may be the male or the female according to the species. The male does not die after fertilizing the female, as in some other orders of insects, and in some instances it is certainly possible for it to pair successfully a second time; and some females may be mated twice.

Hibernation

Having so far considered certain habits of the early stages and of the adults respectively, it will be useful to conclude this chapter with a brief survey of two subjects which require a general study of all periods in the life-history of butterflies. The first of these is hibernation.

One of the most urgent problems which a butterfly has to face in these islands is how to survive the rigours of a British winter. It does so by passing into a period of suspended animation, in which the vital processes are reduced to an exceedingly low level. Many animals hibernate in this way, and the extraordinary effect which the process has upon them is very apparent. Thus bats hang themselves up for their winter sleep, during which their temperature falls to a few degrees only above their surroundings, though these are mammals, whose temperature is, as the elementary textbooks assure us, a constant one. Similarly, the rate of respiration in a hibernating insect is so low that the larvae and pupae of many species can for days be frozen into a block of ice and survive uninjured. The larvae of the Marsh Fritillary live in a web until the autumn, and then spin a somewhat stouter one in which they remain until the spring. During this time they are so dormant that their habitat can be flooded and they may remain for weeks under water without harm, as my father and I often observed in our studies of this insect (pp. 254–5). The hibernating larvae of the Large Copper, *Lycaena dispar*, can also survive for long periods submerged.

It is remarkable that our butterflies, considered as a whole, can hibernate in any of their stages. Nine of them do so as eggs, thirty-five as larvae, eleven as pupae, and seven as adults. Yet, with a single exception, the hibernating phase is always the same in a given species. Only the Speckled Wood can hibernate in either of two stages, the larva or the pupa (pp. 231–2), and that species has consequently been omitted from the list just given. There are four others, the Monarch, the Painted Lady, the Long-tailed Blue and the Clouded Yellow, which must be excluded from it for a different reason. For these are among the

species which reach us only by migration and, being inhabitants
of warmer regions, they have no period of hibernation but
maintain a cycle of broods throughout the year. Consequently,
they cannot perpetuate themselves here. It is remarkable that
others, similarly unable to do so, none the less have a definite
hibernating stage. Very curiously, the two Pale Clouded Yellows
are among these, for they hibernate as young larvae though they
have a still more southern distribution than the Clouded Yellow,
and are even less able to establish themselves in Britain.

It will be seen that by far the largest number of our butterflies
pass the winter in the larval state, but they do so at different
periods within it. Thus the Marbled White and the Small Skipper
hibernate immediately on hatching; they eat their egg-shell but
take no other food until the spring. Many feed for a short time
but hibernate when quite young, for instance the Hedge Brown.
Others hibernate in their later larval stages, the Pearl-bordered
Fritillary, *Clossiana euphrosyne*, does so after its penultimate
moult; while one or two actually pass the winter as fully-fed
larvae. Thus the Dingy Skipper, *Erynnis tages*, completes its
growth in August; it then constructs a tent of grass woven
together with silk. Here it remains until April, when it pupates
where it is, without feeding again. Furthermore, some species
pass the winter in various larval stages, young or old, as does the
Small Copper. Both our species of the genus *Erebia* take two
years to complete their life-cycle, a well-known characteristic of
northern or alpine butterflies. They spend their first winter as a
young larva and their second as a nearly full-grown one. The
statement is frequently made that these insects are in consequence
common only in alternate years. I find this difficult to believe, and
I have myself noticed that it does not apply at all obviously to
the Mountain Ringlet in the English Lake District. It is the type
of assertion often made without proper evidence, and it could in
fact only be established by careful observations over a number
of consecutive years sufficient to eliminate the error introduced
by numerical variations of a less regular kind.

Most larvae make singularly little preparation for their winter
sleep. They generally crawl down to the base of their food-plant
if it is a low-growing one, and there remain in a torpid condition.
This is the habit of all our Satyridae; however, a few species will
awake and eat a little during a spell of mild weather (e.g., the
Meadow Brown). All our Fritillaries marked with silver hibernate
as larvae (except the High Brown Fritillary, which does so as an

egg). They creep into a withered violet leaf and remain curled up in it throughout the winter. However, the Silver-washed Fritillary generally hibernates on the trunk of a tree, to which the young larva makes its way immediately after hatching. Those which normally live in a larval web spin a somewhat tougher one in the autumn, in which they remain until the spring (e.g., the genera *Euphydryas* and *Melitaea*). A very few species make themselves a kind of larval cocoon for hibernation. Thus the Small Blue, *Cupido minimus*, covers itself with a few threads spun on its food plant, but it is in the Skippers that this habit is most marked. As already noticed, several of those which pass the winter as a larva do so in the grass tube or the tent in which they later pupate. The minute newly-hatched larvae of the Small Skipper, however, spin themselves special silken cocoons for the winter, and these are quite unlike those which they make later in life.

None of our small company of butterflies which feed upon trees or bushes passes the winter as a pupa. They almost all do so in the adult state, or else as eggs, which are always attached to the branches. To this there are two exceptions, for the Purple Emperor and the White Admiral, *Limenitis camilla*, hibernate as larvae. They must evidently take special precautions, or they would be left exposed on the food-plant or else fall with the leaves in autumn. The White Admiral solves the difficulty of its winter quarters by constructing a 'hibernaculum' made by spinning the edges of a honeysuckle leaf together and firmly securing its stalk to the branch with silk. The young larva is shown with this structure on Plate 11, Fig. *d*. The Purple Emperor similarly binds the stalk of a sallow leaf to a branch by spinning a quantity of silk round both for a distance on either side of their junction. It then forms a silken pad on the leaf and settles down upon it for the winter. Sometimes, however, it will spin this pad upon a stem and hibernate in that position. The habit which these two insects have evolved of preventing the fall of the leaves upon which they pass the winter, by attaching them to the stem with silk, is a very remarkable instance of adaptation.

The seven butterflies[1] which hibernate as adults do not pair until the spring; they all belong to the Vanessidi except one, the Brimstone. One of them, the Camberwell Beauty, is only a rare migrant with us, but another, the Red Admiral, though a

[1] *V. atalanta, A. urticae, N. polychloros, I. io, N. antiopa, P. c-album, G. rhamni.*

common British species, generally fails to survive the winter successfully here and is maintained by a supply of immigrants from the Continent (p. 152).[1] They all select hollow trees, out-houses, or crannies, in which to pass the winter, except the Comma, which does so exposed on branches or among dead leaves, and the Brimstone, which usually creeps into an evergreen bush.

In more southern latitudes the hot dry summer, not the winter, is the most trying period for insect life, and many butterflies spend it in 'aestivation', settling in a protected spot and remaining there quiescent. That situation is well illustrated by one of our own butterflies, the Meadow Brown (Plate 24), at low elevations in Tuscany. There it emerges from the pupa in early June. After pairing, the males die and the females soon seek shelter in bushes, so that the insect disappears. However, the imagines come forth again in early September to lay their eggs, which are at that time fertilized with sperm received two and a half months previously. Dr Valerio Scali (1971), of Pisa, to whom these observations are due, finds that during aestivation there is a selective elimination of 64% against individuals carrying genes for the higher spot-numbers on the undersides of the hind-wing: those females with two or more spots. Above about 700 metres, however, the Meadow Brown behaves in Tuscany as it does in England. It has been said that the hibernation of certain British butterflies is really derived from such aestivation. For it is not the cold of winter that drives some of them into retreat but such heat as the English summer provides. Since the Small and the Large Tortoiseshells and the Brimstone start to hibernate in early August or even in late July, though the other species remain on the wing until autumn, there may be some truth in this view, but it seems rather speculative. Some larvae also hibernate long before the winter begins (as does the Small Skipper).

PROTECTIVE DEVICES

The Early Stages
Butterflies in all stages of their life-histories employ various devices to protect themselves from their enemies. In general, these fall into two groups, the 'concealing' (or cryptic) and the

[1] This species has a constant succession of broods in more southerly latitudes.

'warning' types. Those which are palatable must escape notice by a close resemblance to their surroundings, and when the adults are upon the wing their safety must depend upon a swift or erratic flight. On the other hand, some species are unpalatable to possible predators owing to a nauseous taste or unpleasant smell, or to the presence of sharp spines. It is to the advantage of these to advertise their distasteful qualities by making themselves conspicuous and easily recognized. Another method is that of deception, in which a palatable species copies a protected one and is therefore credited with disagreeable properties which, in fact, it does not possess; but such 'mimicry' is only found among our Pierinae, copying the aposematic *P. brassicae*; as shown by M. Rothschild.

The eggs of butterflies largely escape attention on account of their small size, their colour, or their position on the under-side of leaves. The newly-hatched caterpillars are too small to be hunted individually by vertebrates, and some of those species which are smooth in their later stages are provided with long hairs or spines when they are young. As they grow larger they become tempting morsels, and they must then employ any devices which enable them to escape insect-hunting birds or other enemies.

Many older caterpillars resemble their surroundings to a remarkable degree. That of the Purple Emperor (Plate 8, Fig. *d*), is most difficult to detect upon sallow leaves, being exactly of their colour, as is the Brimstone upon Buckthorn; and it will be noticed that these are paler beneath and darker above, so as to reduce the effect of shadow. Similarly the green larvae of the Small Copper and of the Green Hairstreak usually escape observation on their respective food-plants, Sorrel (*Rumex*) and Leguminosae. Here the deception is rendered the more complete by their woodlouse-like form, as it is in all the Lycaenidae, owing to which the edges of the body seem to pass insensibly into the surface of the leaf.

In the foregoing instances the larvae evade detection owing to a more or less uniform similarity to the leaves upon which they feed. However, their resemblance to their background may be achieved by means of complex patterns leading to those methods of 'obliterative shading' which render the outline of an object indistinct and so alter its appearance. Thus some of the smooth cylindrical larvae of our Satyridae (that of the Meadow Brown is shown on Plate 8, Fig. *a*) merely match the colour of the grass upon which they feed, being either grass-green, as in the Speckled Wood, or of the brownish tint of a withered blade, as in the Scotch Argus. Several of them, however, are striped longitudinally with green and white (e.g., the Large Heath, *Coenonympha tullia*), so as to give the effect of a number of grass blades, thus disguising the swelling upon the leaf which they would otherwise make. This method of concealment is carried somewhat further by the Silver-washed Fritillary (Plate 8, Fig. *c*), whose large, dark, boldly-marked larva might be thought a conspicuous object upon a violet plant. Yet this is not so; its pattern makes it difficult to detect against the darker ground seen between the leaves. The peculiar colour-pattern of the Purple Hairstreak achieves a similar result on an oak branch. Perhaps the most striking instance of obliterative shading is provided by the Comma, *Polygonia c-album*, in which the nature of the device changes as the larvae grow. In their early stages they are of a brownish shade, crossed with narrow white bars which break up their outline. Yet the pattern of the fully-grown larva is entirely different, being black with an extraordinary saddle-like patch of white along the back, and this conceals their shape effectively.

The very singular habit of the White Admiral must here be mentioned. When young, before hibernation, it often decorates itself with its own frass, producing a strange shapeless object. The older larvae, however, rely upon their green coloration and the spines which they have by this time developed, for protection, and they do not adorn themselves in that way.

The larvae of the Skippers adopt different tactics from those which have just been mentioned, since they do not trust to their own colour for concealment. As already explained, they all hide themselves in tents or foliage, or in a grass tube.

Our conspicuous larvae, possessed of 'warning coloration', are of two types, those armed with spines and those with a nauseous taste or smell. The first group belongs exclusively to the Nymphalidae. Those of the Vanessidi are generally blackish and conspicuous on their food-plants (that of the Small Tortoiseshell is shown when young and gregarious on Plate 11, Fig. *b*). The peculiar behaviour of some of the gregarious forms, increasing their conspicuousness, has already been mentioned (p. 94). It seems that the web spun by the larvae of the Marsh Fritillary, and of the two species of *Melitaea*, has a similar effect, for it is not used for concealment. On the contrary, the larvae sun themselves upon it, making a black spiny mass which is the more evident for its background of whitish silk.

An unpleasant smell and taste is a very frequent form of protection among both the larvae and adults of foreign butter-flies, but it is only found in a few of our own species; notably in the Black-veined White, now probably extinct, and the aposematic Large White. Both of these are gregarious, so increasing their offensive smell (p. 107). The Large White larvae are strongly marked and remain on the outside of the cabbages, sometimes in a conspicuous position. In this they differ from those of their close relative, the Small White, *Pieris rapae*, which are cryptic in colour and burrow into the plant; for these lack the unpleasant smell of the Large White. To me their flavour is bland, wihle that of the Large White is slight but rather unpleasant.

One species has a special cryptic colouring when young which it loses as it becomes adult. This is the Swallow-tail, for the young larvae resemble bird-droppings, but the adults, though green, are conspicuous when feeding in the sunlight, exposed on the Milk Parsley, *Peucedanum palustre*. When alarmed, they erect a contractile process which produces a strong acrid scent somewhat resembling pineapples. This is a pink forked organ ordinarily retracted into a pouch behind the head. It is often shot in and out rapidly like the tongue of a serpent.

The pupae of British butterflies are all protected by a cryptic colour-pattern, by being placed in inconspicuous positions, or by concealment in a cocoon. Many pupae are remarkably well protected by their colour and form, and a notable example is provided by the Orange-tip, whose shape so well resembles a seed-pod. Those of the Vanessidi often resemble a withered leaf both in shape and colour, while the beautiful spots of gold and silver with which most of them are adorned break up their shape. These species, which protect themselves with spines as larvae, therefore acquire a cryptic colouring when they become pupae. The majority of British butterflies place their pupae in incon-spicuous positions on low-growing plants or in cocoons. Some of those which are attached to leaves do not seem to have any obvious protective adaptations, being brown in colour (the Holly Blue and the Brown Hairstreak), but that of the Black Hairstreak resembles a bird dropping to a wonderful degree. Pupae which are placed in exposed positions are subject to considerable colour-variation, sometimes adapting them to the colour of their background, but this subject will be discussed in Chapters 11 and 12.

The Adult Insects

Many of the adaptations used for concealment by adult butterflies will be referred to later in this work. It is only necessary here to point out, with examples, the chief types under which they may be grouped. A number of species, though brilliantly coloured on the upper surface, closely resemble withered leaves when their wings are closed and, in consequence, they are extremely difficult to detect when resting among mixed vegetation. The Large Tortoiseshell provides a good instance of this; also the contrast between the brilliant upperside and the charcoal-like underside of the Peacock is particularly striking. This butterfly often hibernates in hollow trees and dark crevices, and it will be seen that its colour when at rest is admirably suited to protect it in such situations. The Green-veined White possesses a pattern which harmonizes with the blades of grass and rushes among which it sits (Plate 19), while the Orange-tip, *Anthocharis cardamines*, is wonderfully successful in copying the dappled white and green of the heads of several common Umbelliferous flowers. Those Argynnidi which are spotted with silver greatly resemble a broken mass of dead vegetation with light passing between the fragments.

Some butterflies attain a close resemblance to leaves by a combination of shape and colour. Thus the underside of the Brimstone almost perfectly represents a yellowish leaf in shape and outline, and the Comma (Plate 20) a dead brown or blackish one; for that species has a ragged appearance and warm brown (or blackish) colour, while a crack in the leaf is perfectly portrayed by the brilliant white 'C' in the middle of the hind-wings.

The natural outline of several species is hidden by oblique bands or shading (as in the Silver-washed Fritillary and the White Admiral). Many butterflies, however, deflect the attention of enemies from their vital parts by conspicuous eye-like markings at the tips or along the edge of the wings far from the body. A lizard has been observed to pick out the 'eye-spot' of a Small Heath, *Coenonympha pamphilus* (Plate 10, Fig. *a*), which had just settled. The insect escaped, since butterflies can fly with surprisingly large areas of the wings missing. The Grayling combines this type of marking with concealing colours in a very successful way. On settling, it at first displays the eye-spot on the fore-wings, so that any predator which has observed it come to rest may attack it in a non-vital part. Having allowed time for such an event, it assumes, with remarkable accuracy, the appearance of the soil, or of the bark of a tree, by covering the eye-spot with the hind-wings and leaning over at a sharp angle so as to reduce its shadow: it then becomes practically invisible. I have repeatedly marked the place where one of these butterflies has settled, and on creeping up have quite failed to see it until I have disturbed it by my close approach.

There are, however, butterflies with no special concealing colour or pattern on the underside; for example, the Holly Blue (Plate 10, Fig. *b*). These usually hide among a mass of leaves when resting.

The adults of many foreign species have a nauseous odour or a burning taste, and they advertise the fact by means of conspicuous colours and patterns easily remembered. This is called 'warning coloration'. A species known to have such properties which occurs in Britain is the Monarch Butterfly, whose scent, resembling that of a musk-rat, is decidedly disagreeable (p. 158). To a lesser extent the Large White has distasteful properties also. This applies not only to the imago but also to the larva, which, therefore, unlike that of the Small White, is conspicuous and feeds exposed in cabbages.

Quite the most dangerous period which any insect has to face is that during which it emerges from the pupa and dries its wings. It is then unable to escape, while its concealing shape and pattern have not been perfected. It must be saved mainly by the rapidity of the process, yet it may be protected by special devices appropriate to this stage, a novel and illuminating suggestion for which my father (H. D. Ford) was responsible. He observed that the folds and puckers of the unexpanded wings of certain moths (for instance, the Emperor Moth, *Saturnia pavonia*) throw into relief eye-spots or shadings in such a way as to make the insect startling, as in warning coloration. Indeed, the appearance of some species at this time is distinctly disconcerting, and might well discourage a predator from making a closer investigation of them. It would be worth while to examine this possibility in butterflies, in which it has not been studied.

Chapter 6

Relations with Other Insects

Parasites, Association with Ants

PARASITES

The larvae and pupae of butterflies suffer much from the attacks of parasitic insects. These belong to two Orders only, the Hymenoptera (that including bees, wasps, and ants) and the Diptera (the true two-winged flies). In this chapter I do not propose to give lists of the parasitic species and of the butterflies which they infest; for the information on this subject is very imperfect and, even if it were brought up to date by an extensive search of the literature, it would be of interest only to a small circle of specialists. I shall therefore merely give references to such detailed accounts of the species as already exist and confine myself to a short general discussion of the parasitism of butterflies.

The hymenopterous parasites of the British Lepidoptera belong to two main groups, the Ichneumons (super-family Ichneumonoidea) and Chalcids (super-family Chalcidoidea). The first of these is again divided between the true Ichneumons (family Ichneumonidae) and the closely related Braconids (family Braconidae).

According to Morley and Rait-Smith (1933), whose list, however, is incomplete, Ichneumons have been bred from 32 of our British butterflies, and the parasites belong to 64 species, which are included in the 30 genera. A large form, *Apechthis compunctor*, is illustrated on Plate 12, Fig. *d*. It will be seen that it is a wasp-like creature, the hind-wings being considerably smaller than the front pair and closely united with them, a general feature of the Hymenoptera. The body is, however, attenuated, and in this specimen, which is a female, it ends in a long spine-like ovipositor.

Many of the Ichneumonidae are fertilized in the autumn. The males then die and the females deposit their ova in the spring. Most usually they stab a young caterpillar with their ovipositor and inject one or more eggs into the wound. Sometimes, however, the eggs are laid on the skin and the grubs eat into the host when they hatch. Indeed, some species do not ovipost on caterpillars at all but on leaves near them. The larval parasites on hatching then make their way to their victim and burrow into it. In any event they develop internally, but their subsequent habits are very diverse, for they may pupate within the skin of the caterpillar, which then fails to metamorphose, or within the shell of the butterfly's chrysalis. Alternatively, they may make their escape and pupate externally.

The Braconidae are closely related to the true Ichneumons both in structure and habits, but they may be distinguished from them by the neuration of the fore-wings.[1] On the whole they are smaller species and indeed they may be minute, as is *Apanteles glomeratus*, shown on Plate 12, Fig. *d*. This is one of the best known and most thoroughly investigated of the group. It is a parasite of the Pieridae, especially of the Large and Small Whites, *Pieris brassicae* and *P. rapae*, of which it destroys immense numbers, for all the affected individuals die. It is therefore of considerable economic importance since, as is well known, these butterflies do great damage to cabbages and allied crops. Mr J. E. Moss (1933), who made a study of this Braconid in South Buckinghamshire, found that of 3026 caterpillars of the Large White, 2550 or 84·2 per cent harboured it, though only 161 out of 857 Small White caterpillars (18·8 per cent) did so. This difference in infestation is doubtless due to the larval habits of these two butterflies. Large White caterpillars are at first gregarious and remain exposed on the outside of the cabbages, while those of the Small White are much more scattered and bore into the hearts of the plants.

The female *Apanteles glomeratus* lays its eggs in the young larvae, depositing a large number in each; up to a hundred have been recorded. They feed principally on the fat-bodies of their host and remain within it until it has spun the silken pad for the attachment of the chrysalis. The caterpillar then dies without completing its metamorphosis, for at this time the grubs eat their way out from its body. The *Apanteles* now pupate, and the mass of yellow cocoons which they spin surrounding the corpse of their victim is a familiar object on the fences of kitchen gardens (Plate 12, Fig. *c*).

Morley and Rait-Smith (1933) record Braconidae from eighteen species of British butterflies, but their survey of the literature is not an exhaustive one. The parasites belong to seven genera and

[1] The third discoidal and the second apical cells of the fore-wings are confluent in the Braconidae, separate in the Ichneumonidae.

26 species, of which nineteen are included in the genus *Apanteles*. Their habits are in general exemplified by *A. glomeratus*, but they may differ in a number of particulars. Thus *Apanteles rubecula* lays only a single egg in each caterpillar, and the grub, which grows to a larger size, emerges and pupates when its host is only half-grown. It does not parasitize the Large White, but Moss found that of 857 caterpillars of the Small White collected in South Buckinghamshire, 106, or 12·3 per cent, harboured this species.

Chalcids are stouter insects than are Ichneumons, with a shorter and more rounded body, and their neuration is much reduced. They infest numerous moths, attacking their larvae, pupae and, it is said, even their eggs. They are, however, recorded only from four[1] British butterflies by Morley and Rait-Smith, though they must really be far more widespread. These belonged to three species: *Pteromalus puparum* and *P. imbutus* (family Pteromalidae) and *Tetrastichus microgastri* (family Eulophidae), but they are not responsible for a heavy mortality. *P. puparum* is the one which has most frequently been studied. It never makes its attack until the host has reached the pupal stage. Indeed, the female Chalcid has been seen to wait for some hours beside the pupating larva of the Large White until metamorphosis was complete, when it immediately attacked the pupa. It is a gregarious internal parasite which pupates within the butterfly's chrysalis.

The Dipterous parasites of British Lepidoptera all belong to the family Tachinidae or, occasionally, to their close allies. Their occurrence has been analysed by H. Audcent (1942), whose work provides a more complete survey of it than we possess for the Hymenoptera. He records them from 29 species of our butterflies, the infesting Tachinids belonging to 24 genera and 27 species. They are thick-set bristly flies (Plate 12, Fig. *d*, *Phryxe vulgaris*), and the appearance of what seem to be 'house-flies' from a butterfly chrysalis has often occasioned surprise to inexperienced collectors.

The habits of the Tachinids differ rather widely, and they may be either oviparous or viviparous. The eggs, or the already hatched grubs, are most usually deposited on the skin of the host, but in a few instances the female introduces them beneath it by means of a piercing ovipositor. Often, however, they are laid on a suitable plant; the parasites then attach themselves to the skin

[1] *Aglais urticae, Pieris brassicae, P. rapae, P. napi.*

of a passing caterpillar, into which they burrow. A few of the Tachinidae lay very minute eggs upon leaves and these are swallowed by the victim with its food; the grubs on hatching bore through the gut-wall into its body. This is the habit of *Sturmia sericariae*, an important parasite of silk-worms.

They all develop internally, but at some stage they breathe free air either by perforating through to the exterior or by breaking into one of the tracheal tubes of the host. They often feed at first upon the blood and fat-body and later upon the more vital parts, and may leave the caterpillar before its death. Usually they pupate in the soil, but some do so within the chrysalis of the host. This is the habit of *Phryxe vulgaris*, the species illustrated. Its eggs are laid in the young caterpillar, which pupates normally but then dies. The parasite emerges at about the time when the butterfly should appear. This Tachinid has been recorded from seventeen species of British butterflies.

Certain of the Lepidoptera do considerable damage to crops, and some of these have been spread by human agencies to countries previously free from them. Thus the Small White, originally an inhabitant of the temperate regions of the Old World, has become a serious pest in North America and has lately appeared in New Zealand. One means of checking the ravages of this and similar insects is to introduce their parasites also: a step which, however, should be taken only with great caution for fear of the damage that these may do to the indigenous fauna.

In spite of their possible commercial use, the parasites of British Lepidoptera have been very incompletely studied. There are no records of them from some butterflies and but few hosts have been recorded for many of the species: this is almost certainly due to lack of observation. Undoubtedly numbers of species new as parasites of butterflies, if not new to science, await discovery. Here is a valuable field for inquiry. Careful records should be kept of any parasites obtained in breeding Lepidoptera and of the hosts from which they emerge. Those who have not the time or the inclination to identify the parasitic species (which is in any case a matter of considerable difficulty), would still be performing a valuable service by sending any that they may rear, with as much information as possible on their habits, to one of the larger museums, where they would be gratefully received and used to extend our knowledge on a subject which has both theoretical interest and practical applications.

ASSOCIATION WITH ANTS

An association with other insects is not always harmful to butterflies, as it has been in instances so far discussed. It is, of course, favourable to them when it involves a co-operation from which both parties benefit; or when the butterfly larvae become predatory upon other forms. As we shall see, these two situations merge into one another and no sharp distinction can be drawn between them. Such co-operation reaches by far its highest level in the Lycaenidae, whose strange connection with ants deserves rather detailed study.

It has already been mentioned that in this family the larvae often possess a gland on the seventh abdominal segment (the tenth behind the head) which secretes minute drops of a sweet fluid to which ants are greatly attracted. When well developed, this gland is easily visible with a lens as a transverse slit in the middle of the back. The tissue of which it is composed is remarkably sensitive, contracting to the touch or swelling when it is about to secrete. It is surrounded by small bristles, and sometimes by stiff chitinous processes, flattened and star-shaped. These seem to protect the organ while, in addition, the bristles serve to hold the drops of liquid in place. It is found, varying in size, in all the British Polyommatini (Blues); also in two of our Hairstreaks, the White-letter, *Strymonidia w-album*, and the Green, *Callophrys rubi*, in which, however, it is rather small. It generally becomes conspicuous either in the last or in the penultimate larval stage: in the Large Blue, *Maculinea arion*, it is already functional after the second moult.

Most of these larvae constantly associate with ants, a few of which will usually be found in attendance upon them, often caressing and crawling over them; being well armed and pugnacious creatures, they form a powerful deterrent to those insect species which normally parasitize the Lepidoptera. Yet the larvae are never themselves injured by the ants, which treat them with care, as they do the Aphides, which similarly yield them a sweet secretion. At intervals an ant will milk the larval honeygland by touching it with its feet or antennae; a droplet is then exuded from it which the ant licks up. Moreover, ants are known to 'farm' the larvae of the Chalk-hill Blue, *Lysandra coridon*, Silver-studded Blue, *Plebejus argus*, and some other species, for they have actually been observed to carry them in their mouth and place them on the correct food conveniently near their nests.

We have here a true partnership, both ant and larva deriving benefit from the association. In a few instances, however, the gland may have become functionless; perhaps it is so in the Small Blue, *Cupido minimus*, and in the two species of Hairstreaks in which it is known to exist, for there seems to be no record that ants pay any attention to these species.

Though no honey-gland has been identified in any of the Coppers (Lycaenini), the larvae of the Large Copper, *Lycaena dispar*, but not apparently of the Small Copper, *L. phlaeas*, receive similar ant-protection to that accorded to the majority of the Blues. Here, however, a sweet secretion exudes from the skin, seemingly produced by scattered gland-cells.

Doubtless some of the Lycaenidae are more dependent than others upon the security which the presence of ants affords. Indeed, several species, notably the Brown Argus, *Aricia agestis*, do not thrive even in captivity unless ants be present, so that the advantage which these butterflies derive from the partnership is not limited to their relative protection from parasites. That, presumably, was the original benefit which it conferred, but it seems that the physiological activity of the honey-gland, which is stimulated only by ants, has become necessary for the health of some butterfly larvae. In one species, the Large Blue, it is now known that the association has, however, been carried much further, for this butterfly has become absolutely parasitic and dependent upon ants. The credit for this remarkable discovery belongs to Mr F. W. Frohawk, whose work enabled Capt. E. B. Purefoy to undertake the difficult task of making a detailed investigation of its life history, one which he performed with complete success. The description of it which follows is founded upon the accounts given by Mr Frohawk (1924).

The Large Blue (Plate 20) is an exceedingly local butterfly in England (pp. 127-8). The eggs are usually laid in June in the Cotswolds, where alone I have any personal experience of it, but I understand that the species is on the wing slightly later in North Cornwall. They are attached to the buds of the Wild Thyme, and the larvae hatch in about ten days and begin to feed upon the flowers, which they resemble to an extraordinary degree. This food suffices them for their first three stages, which together last for about twenty days. During this time they are great cannibals, the larger individuals devouring the smaller when the opportunity arises, or attacking those which are changing their skin. The honey-gland becomes functional after the second moult, and from that time onwards they are attractive to ants. Having moulted for the third time, a process which occupies three or four days, the larva rests for some hours and then leaves the Thyme and wanders aimlessly about. It never eats vegetable food again. Eventually, perhaps not for some hours, it will meet a foraging ant, which at once takes the greatest interest in it.

As soon as the ant finds the larva it begins to caress and stroke the honey-gland with its antennae and legs, drinking the droplets of secretion which are repeatedly produced. At intervals it walks round the larva two or three times, but soon starts milking it again. Meanwhile other ants may arrive, and though they will remain in the neighbourhood they leave it in the possession of its original discoverer.

After an hour or more the larva assumes an extraordinary attitude, puffing up its thoracic segments whilst its abdomen remains unaltered. At this signal the ant stands astride the larva and, seizing it in its jaws between the third and the fourth segments, carries it off to its nest (Plate 12, Fig. *e*).

The journey is sometimes of considerable length but on arrival the ant, still bearing the larva in its jaws, carries it through one of the entrances and down into the underground chambers. Here it remains in darkness from August until June; and for the first six weeks it grows rapidly, feeding upon the young larvae of the ants. By the end of that time it has greatly changed in appearance, having become fat, white, and grub-like. It now settles down to hibernation in a cavity where the older ant larvae are tended by the workers.

In spring it starts feeding again on ant larvae, remaining in the cavity where it passed the winter, and its growth is completed during the first half of May. It is then of a pinkish-white colour, very shiny and distended in appearance, since from the time that it was carried into the nest it has never moulted, having grown from about 3·2 mm., its size when it ceased to feed on thyme, to about 14·8 mm., entirely by stretching its skin. It now attaches itself by the claspers to a pad of silk, which it spins on the roof of the chamber where it has passed its late larval life, and changes into a white pupa, the process occupying about a week.

The pupa remains hanging for a few days and then drops to the floor. Here it lies among the ants until the perfect insect emerges, about three weeks after pupation. On crawling from the pupa-case the butterfly makes its way up to the outside world. It then climbs a grass-stem or other suitable object and expands its wings, a process which is delayed in order to allow time for its journey through the passages of the nest.

So is completed the life-cycle of the Large Blue, the strangest among our British butterflies. The species which normally act as its hosts are the two common red ants, *Myrmica scabrinoides* and *M. laevonoides*, and they seem to be equally satisfactory. A dull-coloured and dwarf form of the butterfly (of about 28 mm., compared with the normal 40 mm.) is fairly frequent in all the localities, and it is held that this is produced by those larvae which have been adopted by less suitable ants, perhaps the small yellow, *Donisthorpia flava*.

The life-history of a few foreign Lycaenidae is as curious as that of the Large Blue, but none is more so. Among them may be mentioned the Australian *Liphra brassolis* Ww., which preys upon the brood of the ant *Oecophylla smaragdaria*. Yet its adaptations are of a very different kind, for the ants attack it but are unable to injure its hard and slippery cuticle. The insect pupates within its larval skin, so that this continues to protect it. On emerging from the pupa, the brown and orange markings of the butterfly are masked by a mass of loosely attached white scales which stick to the head and jaws of any ants which try to molest it on its way out through the passages of the nest, and divert their attention. The white scales fall off as soon as it begins to fly.

I am inclined to think that the extraordinary habits and larval adaptations of the Large Blue have depended for their evolution upon two characteristics, widespread and specialized among the Lycaenidae but known in other families also. These are, first, the remarkable but quite harmless partnership with ants to which reference has already been made. Here the benefit is mutual, the ant obtaining a sweet secretion and the larva protection from parasitic insects. The second contributing factor is the cannibalism of many Lycaenidae,[1] which are most pugnacious and attack and eat one another fiercely. In some species (e.g., the Short-tailed Blue, *Everes argiades*), this is restricted to the early stages, but in others (e.g., the Green Hairstreak) it persists throughout life. It has been observed in certain of our butterflies besides the

[1] The following species have this habit to a marked degree: *L. boeticus, C. minimus, E. argiades, M. arion,* and *C. rubi.*

Lycaenidae, for example, the Orange-tip, *Anthocharis cardamines*, in its early stages, though it is quite absent from others, including, of course, those which are gregarious when young. It is not uncommon in other groups of the Lepidoptera. Thus the larvae of a common moth, the Dun Bar, *Calymnia trapezina* L., seem to be wholly carnivorous upon those of other species, chiefly Geometridae. A stage in the evolution of such a life-history as that of the Large Blue is represented by the species which ants carry to the neighbourhood of their nests (pp. 116–17). Having brought them so far, it is not unnatural that they should begin to take them farther and bear them down into the cavities of the nest itself. Here larvae already accustomed to attacking and eating others of their own species might well find the ant grubs a congenial food when deprived of their normal diet.

These two tendencies, cannibalism and the association with ants, though originally unconnected are often combined, as they are in the Long-tailed and the Short-tailed Blues. Also the Small Blue and the Green Hairstreak are voracious cannibals, and though they may not now be attended by ants we may be sure that they once were, since they both possess at least the rudiment of the attractive gland. It will therefore be apparent that a general consideration of the structure and habits of the species related to the Large Blue serves to show rather clearly how the strange life-history of that butterfly may have been evolved.

The cannibalism of some foreign Lycaenidae has been developed in other directions, so that they have become completely carnivorous, but not upon ants. Thus the larva of the American *Feniseca tarquinius* F. feeds wholly upon the woolly aphis, *Eriosoma*, while aphides form the sole food of the oriental genus *Gerydus*, which does not seem attractive to ants.

It is apparently not widely known that butterflies other than Lycaenidae enter into an association with ants, indeed the young larvae of many Pieridae obtain protection by this means. These, in the early stages only, possess long glandular setae from which exudes a sweet liquid. This is generally held as a droplet by a fork at the top of the seta and ants seem to be attracted by it. Such secretion has been recorded in all the British Pieridae (including the Bath White, *Pontia daplidice*), except the Black-veined White, *Aporia crataegi*, the Large White, *Pieris brassicae*, and the three Clouded Yellows, so that it occurs in each of the three sub-families.

Attendant ants have been noticed with several of the larvae which produce these droplets of fluid, especially with those of the Orange-tip, but no importance can be attached to the absence of any records of them in others, since the subject has been very little studied. Similarly, I am not prepared to say that the habit of producing a secretion is really absent from the four species just mentioned as lacking it, particularly as the young larvae of the Black-veined White possess forked spines of the droplet-holding type. However, it is at least suggestive that this insect and the Large White are gregarious and seem to derive protection from vertebrate predators by an unpleasant scent. Perhaps this is inconsistent with the attraction of ants, and certainly these two insects are very heavily parasitized.

The association with ants into which the Pieridae enter seems to be very different from that usually found in the Lycaenidae, in which the older larvae only take part and the secretion is produced from a special gland. It may have been acquired independently; possibly, however, the two systems are homologous, having diverged widely from that of the common ancestor. It might even be held that the situation encountered in the Large Copper (p. 117) is to some extent intermediate between the two types.

Finally, attention must be drawn to a peculiar structure characteristic of any British Lycaenidae, the significance of which is yet unknown. A number of the larvae possess a pair of short tubular retractile tentacles behind and below the spiracles on the eighth abdominal segment, that next to the honey-gland.[1] They look very like the defensive organs found in many larvae which are known or presumed to emit a disagreeable odour, and it may be that this is their purpose; a view which receives some support from the fact that they are sometimes thrust out when the larva is suddenly alarmed, as in the Silver-studded Blue. On the other hand, they are repeatedly erected by the Large Blue larva while it is being caressed by an ant. It is, of course, not impossible that a gland normally manufacturing a repulsive scent has in this insect been modified to produce one of an attractive type.

Neither the structure of these retractile tubules nor of the honey-gland seems to have been fully examined, and it would be

[1] They have been described in the following species, and they may well occur in others also: L. boeticus, E. argiades, P. argus, P. icarus, L. coridon, L. bellargus, C. semiargus, M. arion.

of much interest to investigate these organs in detail. Further-more, careful studies of the relationship between ants and butterfly larvae in species other than the Large Blue are greatly needed. Such an association is quite a frequent one, so that there are ample opportunities for this work, and it presents a fascinating and valuable field for amateur research.

Chapter 7

Distribution

Types of Habitat and Geographical Ranges, Changes in the Distribution of Butterflies, Extinction, Species on the Edge of their Range

TYPES OF HABITAT AND GEOGRAPHICAL RANGES

Many of our butterflies are only to be found in a particular type of habitat, and a study of their striking and sometimes mysterious preferences for certain localities is a subject full of interest though beset with unexpected difficulties. As we pass from one part of Britain to another, the change is clearly reflected in these insects; and within any one region the woods, the downs, and the marshes, possess species which are peculiarly their own. Some indeed are catholic in their tastes, and a sunny patch of flowers in late summer is likely to be tenanted by the common Vanessidi wherever it may be. Others, those whose requirements are more strictly defined, are as much a part of the woodland as its trees, or of the wayside as the viatical plants which grow there. They are fitted for life in particular local environments and, though such *ecological preferences* cannot be sharply separated from the broader distinctions of *geographical distribution*, the butterfly fauna appropriate to certain characteristic types of the British countryside is well worth investigation. Yet it must be made clear that all gradations exist between those species which are to be found in many situations and those with the most exacting needs, confining their distribution strictly to a given type of habitat.

We have three butterflies which are limited by geological considerations, being inhabitants only of chalk downs or limestone hills in south or central England, and they may reach the shore where such formations break in cliffs to the sea. These are the Silver-spotted Skipper, *Hesperia comma* (Map 32), the Chalk-hill Blue, *Lysandra coridon* (Plate 18, Map 16), and the Adonis Blue, *L. bellargus* (Map 17). The two latter insects are further restricted by the distribution of their food-plant, the Horse-shoe Vetch, *Hippocrepis comosa*, and possibly by the occurrence of a sufficiency of ants to guard them. Yet any of the three species may be absent from a hillside which seems to possess all the qualification which they need, even though they may occur elsewhere in the immediate neighbourhood. This more subtle type of preference is one which entomologists constantly encounter, and a detailed analysis of it is much needed. A collector who is a careful observer is often able to examine a terrain and to decide, intuitively as it were, whether a given butterfly will be found there, and that rare being the really accomplished naturalist will nearly always be right. Of course, he reaches his conclusion by a synthesis, subconscious as well as conscious, of the varied characteristics of the spot weighed up with great experience; but this is a work of art rather than of science, and we would gladly know the components which make such predictions possible.

The habitats both of the Small Blue, *Cupido minimus* (Plate 20) and of the Brown Argus, *Aricia agestis* (Plate 24, Map 15) are somewhat similar to that just mentioned. Both species occur on downs and rough grassy slopes, but their distribution is far more extensive than that of the insects confined to chalk and limestone; for though these two butterflies strongly favour such formations, they are not restricted to them. The same may be said of Berger's Clouded Yellow (Plate 22), a rare and recently discovered migrant here (p. 88).

The Small Blue is much the more local of the two, since it forms well-defined colonies. It has a wide distribution in southern England, though it is rare in East Anglia and it seems to be unknown in Essex. It is absent from the Isle of Man but occurs in Ireland, where it is widespread though mainly coastal. In the north of England its localities are very few. It exists in Yorkshire and in several places, chiefly railway-cuttings, in Cumberland, and in one of them my father and I caught it. This was on Permian sandstone. It is extremely rare in Scotland, having been reported from a very limited range of localities, though these extend as far north as Muchalls, near Aberdeen, and Aviemore in Inverness.

The Brown Argus is widespread in suitable situations in southrn England and Wales; farther north it is represented by the Northern Brown Argus (Plate 24). This occurs in Furness and spreads through northern Yorkshire to Northumberland, being rare and very local throughout that region. In Scotland it occurs up the east coast at least as far as the Moray Firth. It also passes westwards into Perth and Inverness, perhaps its northern limit.

It is absent from the Western Isles, Ireland, the Isle of Man and the Scillys. This species flies chiefly on chalk-downs and limestone hills, where the Rock-rose, *Helianthemum chamaecistus*, on which it feeds, abounds. But it has an alternative food-plant, the Hemlock Stork's-bill, *Erodium cicutarium*, which grows on sandy soil; and here also the insect is sometimes found, so that it may be taken on sandhills by the sea.

We have several downland butterflies which do not require, though they can well tolerate, chalk or limestone. The Grayling, *Hipparchia semele* (Plate 24) is characteristic of these and it also occurs on dry heaths, but it cannot survive in very damp situations. It is usually stated that the underside of the hind-wings is whiter in specimens from chalk downs than in those which fly among heather or (as they do widely) in coastal localities in Britain. It must be understood, however, that the difference is an average one only, undersides of all degrees of darkness being found in either situation. I have never seen a numerical comparison of them, and this should be made. The butterfly has a wide distribution in Britain, including the Inner and Outer Hebrides, Ireland, and the Isle of Man, but it is mainly coastal.

The Dark Green Fritillary, *Mesoacidalia aglaia* (Plate 16), may be observed flying with great speed and power across the downs. In the south of England, it is not so frequent in woods, where its place is taken by the closely allied High Brown Fritillary, *M. adippe*; though I find it not uncommonly deep in the woodlands of the north, from which the High Brown Fritillary is absent. Yet it also favours the most exposed situations over the whole of its extensive range (pp. 277-8), which embraces the British mainland the and Western Isles, Ireland, and the Isle of Man. It is, however, rare in the eastern counties of England, from Essex northwards, including the whole of Yorkshire, and it is perhaps extinct in East Anglia.

Most downland insects may occur near the sea-shore and, excepting for the three species already mentioned which require chalk, the majority of them are especially fond of sand-hills when covered with Marram Grass and rough vegetation. We have, however, in England three butterflies which are pre-eminently coastal species. The Glanville Fritillary, *Melitaea cinxia* is confined to the southern shore of the Isle of Wight. The Lulworth Skipper, *Thymelicus acteon* (Plate 21, Map 31), is never found more than a few miles inland, and only in Dorset and in one or two places in south Devon. But the peculiar distribution of these two insects in this country will be discussed on pp. 147–8. The third, the Essex Skipper, *T. lineola* (Map 30), is common along the north coast of Kent and the coast of Essex, where it flies in about equal numbers with the Small Skipper, *T. sylvestris*, frequenting particularly sea-walls and dykes. However, it spreads up the Suffolk coast, and inland as far as Cambridgeshire, where it may be taken in Wicken Fen, Huntingdonshire, and Bedfordshire, though it becomes uncommon and very local away from the sea. There are as well a few records from Hampshire; also from central Somerset, where Mr A. T. Pechey has found a specimen (1944) flying with large numbers of the very similar *T. sylvestris*, and there have been previous reports of it from that county. Yet the true home of the Essex Skipper in England is certainly along the southern part of the east coast.

The butterfly fauna of the downland grades rather naturally into that of rough fields, hill-sides, and meadows. Here may especially be found several of our Satyridae. These are: the Marbled White *Melanargia galathea* (Plate 18, Map 4), which is restricted to southern and central England, where it is generally local, though it is a common road-side butterfly in some counties, notably in Oxfordshire and the adjoining part of Berkshire. It is nearly or quite extinct in the eastern counties from Essex northwards, and it has long ceased to occur in Yorkshire where it was once known. The Meadow Brown, *Maniola jurtina* (Plate 24), is distributed throughout Great Britain, the Western Isles (but not the Orkneys or Shetlands), the Isles of Scilly, Ireland, and the Isle of Man. The Ringlet, *Aphantopus hyperanthus* (Plate 22), is chiefly an inhabitant of meadows where the grass is long, and of woodland rides. It is absent from north Scotland and the Isles, but is common over the rest of Britain and Ireland. The Skippers especially associated with these habitats include our two Pyrginae, though in addition they may both be seen in the open parts of woods. The Dingy Skipper, *Erynnis tages* (Map 27), has much the wider distribution, occurring through England and in Scotland, though it becomes rare in the north, while in Ireland it is common but very local, being principally confined to Clare, Galway, and Mayo. The Grizzled Skipper, *Pyrgus malvae* (Plate 21) was formerly found at Arnside and Silverdale on the southern verge of the Lake District; but it now appears to be extinct there, and only inhabits England up to the south of Yorkshire, where it is very local. The Large Skipper, *Ochlodes venatus* (Plate 17), another butterfly of rough fields and meadows, also flies along woodland paths and on coastal cliffs. It has an extensive distribution in Britain, for it is found in the Scottish lowlands and southwards throughout England and Wales, but its reported occurrence in Ireland is probably an error.

Four species combine the two groups of habitats last mentioned: downland and sea-coast, with rough fields, hill-sides and meadows. Two of them, the Common Blue, *Polyommatus icarus* (Plate 19), and the Small Copper, *Lycaena phlaeas* (Plate 22), range over almost the whole of Britain, even to the north coast of Scotland, and Ireland, except that the Small Copper is absent from most of the Scottish Isles, where it is known only in Islay and Colonsay. The Common Blue inhabits nearly all the Hebrides as well as the Orkneys and, as Dr H. B. D. Kettlewell kindly informs me, there is fair evidence that it has occasionally been seen in Shetland. Perhaps it is not fully established there, arriving sporadically as a wanderer (p. 150) and reproducing for a limited period only. Both species occur in the Isle of Man and the Isles of Scilly. The Small Skipper, *Thymelicus sylvestris* (Plate 10), which also flies in forest rides, is almost restricted in England to the region south of the Mersey and Humber, though there are a few localities for it in south Yorkshire, and in Wales, where it is very rare in the north. It is almost certainly absent from Ireland in spite of a few old records. The fourth species, the Large Blue, *Maculinea arion* (Plate 20), is one of the most local of all our indigenous butterflies (Map 18), yet it is found in the most varied habitats; rough low-lying ground, as it was at Barnwell Wold, Northants, where it is now extinct, hill-sides and rough fields on the Cotswolds, and long ago in Somerset, and sea cliffs in north Cornwall and both north and south Devon, though it may be extinct in the last area, as in one or two former localities on Dartmoor. In addition, it has been reported from Wiltshire, while two or three specimens caught in Hertfordshire during the present century suggest that there may once have been a small colony there also. The two latter areas have been omitted from the map; so has the possibility of another, and very different, habitat for this species. Its peculiar life-history, which has already been described in Chapter 6, obviously restricts it to places where the Wild Thyme grows, and where there is an abundance of those ants in whose nest it passes so much of its life. The flight of this butterfly is more powerful than that of most of the Lycaenidae, and its large size and rather iron-blue colour, at least on the Cotswolds (p. 283), make it fairly easy to distinguish on the wing. I have once or twice pursued an especially blue female of *P. icarus* in mistake for *M. arion*, but when I have really seen that species I have seldom been in doubt of its identity. One of its habits, at least on the Cotswolds where alone I have any personal experience of it, does not seem widely known to entomologists: it normally flies only in the mornings and towards evening, and there is little chance of finding any but ovipositing females in the early afternoon.

We have in Britain one species which is especially characteristic of dry open heather moors, though several others, such as the Grayling already mentioned, may also be found there. This is the Silver-studded Blue, *Plebejus argus*. The entomologist who in mid-July steps from his car in one of the great tracts of heather in the New Forest will find himself surrounded by immense numbers of this butterfly. It occurs also on sandy heaths and, in a few localities, by the sea-shore; one of these, where it is common, is south-eastern Dorset. The species has the rather discontinuous distribution indicated in Map 14. It is probably absent from Scotland and Ireland, in spite of a few reports to the contrary. In North Wales, where it is rather widespread, a distinct sub-species, *caernensis* (pp. 279–80), flies at a considerable elevation on limestone cliffs, but this is quite an abnormal habitat for the insect.

We cannot expect that any butterflies will be restricted to such artificial habitats as hedgerows and lanes; and yet a few are so particularly associated with them in the minds of those who love the country that I must especially relate them to such places. In May and again in late July and August the Wall Butterfly, *Lasiommata megera*, will be found sunning itself in warm corners of fields, on shadeless stretches of road, and flitting by the hedges in the full glare of noon. Often a specimen disturbed by the passer-by will fly ahead and settle again, repeating the process time after time, so accompanying him for some distance on his way. The insect is widely distributed through the lowlands of Scotland and southwards in Britain, also in Ireland and the Isle of Man; but it is commoner near the coast than inland, and there are some districts in which it is quite rare. Yet our other member of the genus *Pararge*, the Speckled Wood, *P. aegeria* (Plate 19) is as much an insect of the shade as the Wall Butterfly is of the sunshine. For it generally frequents overshadowed hedgerows and deep lanes bordered by trees, while it also flies along the outskirts of woods. It inhabits the south of England, Wales, and the Midlands, though it is very rare or absent in the eastern counties, from Suffolk northwards. It formerly reached the southern edge of the Lake District, having been taken as a rarity at Witherslack in Westmorland, and perhaps it still exists in south Yorkshire. Its range extends over the whole of Ireland, and it reappears in a few places on the west coast of Scotland: in Islay, Argyll, Inverness, and Skye (Map 1). This remarkable distribution will be discussed on p. 296. The Large Tortoiseshell, *Nymphalis polychloros*, now so rare here (p. 140), is especially to be found along roads bordered with elm trees, upon which it feeds, also in woods where the elm is common. It has always been restricted to the Midlands and southern England, and it was well established until twenty years ago in the eastern part of Suffolk and north Essex.

There are two British butterflies which seem an essential part of the wayside, the one in spring and the other in summer and, probably like most collectors, I cannot think of these seasons without recalling them. The Orange-tip butterfly, *Anthocharis cardamines*, the hedge-garlic, the young green on the hawthorn, and the lady's-smocks in the fields, have always seemed to me an essential part of the English spring; while the Hedge Brown, *Maniola tithonus* (Plate 17), on the bramble blossom, basking on the dusty foliage (for in my childhood tarred roads were unknown), marked the height of summer. This insect, so abundant in the south, becomes very rare in northern England; though in southern Yorkshire it is not uncommon on the east coast. I myself know of but one district within 40 miles of the Scottish border where it can be found. This is on the coast of south Cumberland, but it is absent from the north of that county. In most text-books it is said to occur locally in south Scotland. However, the Baron de Worms, whose knowledge of the distribution of our butterflies is exceptionally thorough, informs me that he has no evidence of its existence north of the border. He most kindly made special inquiries to discover if it is really present in Kirkcudbright, where it has persistently been reported, but he tells me that he can obtain no corroboration of this. In Ireland it inhabits the south only, and is local even there (Map 5). The Orange-tip, however, is common all over Britain, except north Scotland and the Isles, and it is widespread in Ireland, but rather rare in the Isle of Man.

Three of our Theclini are especially frequenters of low scrub

B.   E and hedges. These are the Green Hairstreak, *Callophrys rubi*, which occurs along the borders of woods, but only if such Leguminosae as Gorse, Broom and Dyer's Greenweed be present; also among bushes on the downs and on those moors and mosses of the north which are colonized by these plants. It is found in such situations widely over Great Britain and Ireland. The two others, the Brown and Black Hairstreaks, *Thecla betulae* and *Strymonidia pruni*, feed upon sloe, and accordingly fly only where that plant grows, in hedges and tangled thickets, or along the margins of woods, and beside woodland paths. Yet the distribution of these two species is strictly limited by factors other than their food-plant. In the Brown Hairstreak (Plate 17) these may chiefly be connected with the need for a southern climate for, as indicated in Map 20, it is really quite widespread from the Mersey and the Wash southwards, though apparently now extinct in East Anglia, and in the past it was taken at Silverdale in north Lancashire. Indeed, I expect that it occurs in districts where it is not actually known, since the species is secretive and not often seen upon the wing, even in those places where the larvae are common and may readily be 'beaten' from the bushes. My own impression is that most people look for the butterfly too early in the year. In Oxfordshire I saw ten specimens in an hour and a half one afternoon during the second week in September, though I had often searched in vain for the butterfly during August in the same locality, where the larvae are always common. It is often necessary to beat the sloe bushes in order to disturb the perfect insect. It will be found that an unduly large proportion of the specimens caught in this way are females, as are most of the Purple Hairstreaks which are obtained during sunshine, for the males fly the higher. In dull weather the proportion of the sexes captured becomes more even. The status of the Brown Hairstreak in Ireland is a difficult matter to decide. Most text-books make the ridiculous assertion that it is common in the south and west. The fact is that there are no records since the middle of last century, and Colonel C. Donovan in his refreshingly critical work on Irish Lepidoptera (1936) cannot corroborate them. But Professor Bryan Beirne, of Trinity College, Dublin, points out to me that the Irish records are those of Birchall himself, who was generally reliable when speaking of his own personal experiences apart from his too easy acceptance of the information supplied to him by others. The south and west of Ireland have been very little studied entomologically, and the Brown Hairstreak may yet be found there again.

The Black Hairstreak, *Strymonidia pruni*, is now the most local of all our indigenous British butterflies (Map 23), being confined to a few places in Huntingdonshire, Northamptonshire, and the western edge of Buckinghamshire.[1] There it is to be found, sometimes abundantly but in very circumscribed areas, among sloe along the outskirts of woods and in clearings within them, in overgrown fields, and along hedges. It is remarkable that any butterfly, feeding as does this upon a widely distributed plant, should be restricted to a small area of the Midlands. One would have thought that there would be far more congenial localities for it farther south. This problem arises also in regard to one of the habitats of the Chequered Skipper (p. 135), and it will be discussed on pp. 147–9.

The Brimstone, *Gonepteryx rhamni* is an inhabitant of thickets, hedgerows, and woodland rides where either of the British Buckthorns grow. Yet it is powerful on the wing and wanders over the countryside, particularly after hibernation. Its distribution is really limited by its food plant, for it is absent from Scotland, and occurs southwards from the mountains of Westmorland, where it penetrates as far as Ambleside and even up the valley towards Grasmere, but it does not cross the pass into Cumberland at Dunmail Raise. The butterfly is widespread but rare in southern Yorkshire. It is local in Ireland and found only in the southern half of the country (Map 25).

Woodland is the true home of many butterflies, and the majority of our A gynnidi are to be found there. Among these the distribution of the two Pearl-bordered Fritillaries makes an interesting comparison. Both occur in suitable places throughout most of the mainland of Britain, but the Small Pearl-bordered, *Clossiana selene*, is the rarer in the south and the Large, *C. euphrosyne*, in the north. The latter insect is very scarce in Cumberland, where the Small Pearl-bordered Fritillary is abundant; this situation is maintained up to the north of Scotland, where *C. selene* alone is found. The two species have not quite

---

[1] One extraordinary record exists of the occurrence of *S. pruni* 'within twelve miles of Haselmere', Surrey. Larvae were beaten there from sloe in 1919 by Mr A. A. Tullett, who bred six specimens, which were placed in the Joicey Collection (Talbot, 1920). I have not included this locality in the map, but the species is very easily overlooked and it may really be established as a rarity in Surrey.

the same local requirements. The Small Pearl-bordered affects the damper sites, so that it is absent from woods if these be dry but, unlike the Large species, it flies in marshes in the open country. The Large Pearl-bordered is extremely local and rare in Ireland, though it certainly occurs in a few places, chiefly in Clare and Galway (Map 7), and it has been reported from the Isle of Man. The Small Pearl-bordered seems to be absent there and in Ireland, though one or two records of it in the latter country exist, but it is found in the Western Isles.

The High Brown Fritillary, *Mesoacidalia adippe* appears to be essentially a forest species, inhabiting England south of the Lake District only, where it reaches Witherslack in Westmorland. In Yorkshire it is rare, but becomes commoner in the extreme south of the county. This is the only one of the large Fritillaries which was frequent in East Anglia and Essex, though now it seems to have disappeared there. Its habit of roosting in trees has already been mentioned (p. 100), one which is shared by the other large Fritillary of our woods, the Silver-washed, *Argynnis paphia* (Map 8). This is the more widespread species of the two, but I am not convinced that it occurs farther north than Witherslack and north Yorkshire, where it is rather widely distributed but rare; it occurred in Durham in the middle of last century, but appears to be extinct there. It is rare in Cambridgeshire and perhaps extinct in East Anglia and Essex, though reintroduced into the Ipswich district, but it is common in many parts of the south and west of England. It is less strictly confined to woods in Cornwall than elsewhere, being common also in lanes in that county. Unlike the High Brown, it is an inhabitant of Ireland, where it is well established and sometimes common in most of the suitable woodlands throughout the country.

The Heath Fritillary, *Mellicta athalia*, is really a woodland species, and it only lives where the Cow-wheat (*Melampyrum pratense*) grows, for its alternative food plants, such as Wood-Sage and Plantain, are rarely used. But the extreme localization of this insect must be determined by other factors. It occurs chiefly in north Kent, where it is still abundant. Last century it existed in Essex, and it survived in Sussex until about fifty years ago; however, it became extinct in both these counties and has been reintroduced into them (p. 163). A few little-known colonies also exist in Devon and Cornwall. The species is known to have had a wider distribution at one time, and ancient records from Oxfordshire and Gloucestershire help to bridge the gap between its now isolated western and eastern habitats (Map 10). Indeed, a specimen was taken in a remote part of Gloucestershire thirty odd years ago, while two were caught in the Minehead district of Somerset in 1919. The colonies tend to shift their ground from year to year, and the butterfly favours areas of the woods which have recently been partially cleared. It is one, and I believe they are not many, which has been seriously depleted by over-collecting, but pheasants are even more deadly enemies to it than are unscrupulous collectors. This is another species which, without any real justification, is, in the current text-books, reported from south-west Ireland. Specimens are said to have been caught in Killarney in the 1860s, and its existence there, repeated from book to book, is absurdly maintained today. The region is, in fact, very little known and the insect may really have been found there, for the records are Birchall's own; accordingly it is possible that it may be rediscovered, but this is quite a different matter from the usual uncritical statement of its occurrence.

The Comma, *Polygonia c-album* (Plate 20), really a woodland species, occurs also in lanes and gardens. It has in the last 55 years extended its range, from a centre in Worcester, Hereford, and Monmouth, until it is now found throughout southern England and Wales, and in many midland counties, but this subject will be discussed later (pp. 138–9). The White Admiral, *Limenitis camilla* (Plate 15), which is purely a forest insect, has spread in a similar way to approximately the same extent, but mainly from the New Forest, where a typical locality for it is shown on Plate 13. However, in addition, it was always found in certain other woods, for example, in Suffolk.

The Purple Emperor, *Apatura iris* (Plate 23), whose habits have already been described (p. 99), is also a typical forest species. Though it feeds on sallow, it is confined to extensive woodlands, usually of oak, but it also flies in certain large beech woods. Its distribution is indicated on Map 12, from which it will be seen that it is widespread in southern England, but it is generally rare: at the present time it is perhaps most frequent in west Sussex.

The Duke of Burgundy Fritillary, *Hamearis lucina* (Plate 22), which feeds principally on cowslip but also on primrose, haunts woodland paths and clearings. It is local, but not uncommon where found, in suitable places in the Midlands and the south of England. In the north its habitats are exceedingly restricted, though it is well established and apparently extending its range in the Kendal district of Westmorland. This is probably its northern limit, though there are ancient reports of it from Dumfries. It is absent from Ireland.

The Holly Blue, *Celastrina argiolus* (Map 19), which must have spread from woods into gardens, is common in southern England. Its range in Britain extends to Cumberland, where it is established only in the Keswick district but is rare. It has been taken twice near Carlisle during the present century, and this appears to be its northern limit. It is found throughout Ireland.

The White-letter Hairstreak, *Strymonidia w-album* (Map 22), is restricted to the neighbourhood of elms, in woods and along lanes, also round isolated trees. This butterfly is much attracted to bramble and privet flowers, being in some years common and in others scarce. It is almost exclusively an English species, of the Midlands and the south, but it is rare in west Somerset and Devon, and absent from Cornwall. It occurs just across the border into south-east Wales, and has once been reported from Brecknock. Long ago it was said to be common near Doncaster, but I have no recent information of it from Yorkshire.

The Purple Hairstreak, *Quercusia quercus* (Plate 24, Map 21), is to be found freely in all our larger oak woods in July, and may often be seen in numbers round the higher branches of the trees bordering them. It is fond of sitting on the leaves of the ash, though it never feeds on this plant. It is widespread in Britain northwards to central Scotland, and is local in the southern half of Ireland; the most northerly record being from Inniskillen, County Fermanagh, where it is rare.

The Wood White, *Leptidea sinapis* (Plates 17, 21), is entirely a woodland insect, inhabiting heavily timbered parts of the forest as well as the more open areas and the paths, across which it may be seen to pass uninterruptedly from one thicket to another. Its flight is somewhat weak and flapping but persistent. Though it delights in shade, I have seen it flying in great numbers out of a wood and across a large open area where the trees had been felled. Its curious discontinuous distribution is indicated in the map. It occurred in the south of the Lake District until early in the present century (p. 143), and in north Cumberland up to the 1870s. A few specimens from that county yet survive, and I possess one, discoloured and badly set, which was captured in 1877 in a wood long since cut down which grew two miles west of Carlisle. Formerly it was found in Suffolk and Essex, and it has been extinct in the New Forest for about seventy years. The butterfly appears at the end of May, and a second generation in late July is usual in the south-west of England but not elsewhere. It is local though rather widespread and becoming commoner in southern Ireland. The Chequered Skipper, *Carterocephalus palaemon* (Map 28), is essentially a woodland species also, sunning itself in the grassy rides. It was always thought to be one of our most local butterflies, being confined to a few places in Lincoln, Northants, Rutland and Buckinghamshire, and just over the Lincolnshire border into Nottinghamshire, and in this region it is especially associated with the area of old Rockingham Forest. There are ancient records also from Warwickshire and Oxfordshire. In the last war the astonishing fact was disclosed that this butterfly had been found commonly in western Inverness, where it flies along grass-grown tracks between birch trees.

The most characteristic marsh butterfly which we possess is the Marsh Fritillary, *Euphydryas aurinia* (Map 9). Its food is normally restricted to the Devil's-bit Scabious, *Scabiosa succissa*, but when the supply has failed the larvae have been known to eat Honeysuckle in the hedges. It forms sharply-defined colonies in swamps and damp meadows. Very curiously, it also occasionally inhabits dry chalk hills if its food-plant grows thickly there. This butterfly occurs widely in suitable places in England, though it largely avoids the eastern counties. However, it used to occur near Deal in Kent, and it has recently reappeared in Hertfordshire after a long absence. Formerly it existed in a few places in East Anglia, where it seems to be extinct, and there are one or two localities for it in Yorkshire. The butterfly is widespread in Ireland, but in Scotland it is much rarer and is largely restricted to the west, though it has been taken near Aberdeen.

The Green-veined White, *Pieris napi* (Plate 19), is also essentially a butterfly of damp fields and marshes. It occurs in such places all over Britain, including the Western Isles of Scotland and the Scilly Isles, also throughout Ireland and the Isle of Man. In the Orkneys it is rare, if it occurs, and it is certainly absent from the Shetlands.

The Swallow-tail, *Papilio machaon* (Plate 23, Map 24), is restricted to fens[1] in England, though it flies in varied habitats

[1] Except for the occasional specimens found in Kent, for which see p. 286.

abroad; this fact will be discussed on pp. 147–9. It was until lately an inhabitant of two counties. It became extinct at Wicken Fen, Cambridgeshire, during the last war. It had been abundant in that celebrated locality, a view of which is shown on Plate 13. However, the species is widespread in the Norfolk Broads. According to several text-books it is to be found also just over the border into Suffolk, but this is no longer correct: only occasional stragglers now reach that county. It has been said that the flight of this butterfly is not swift but somewhat feebly flapping, but I must admit that this is not in accord with my own experience.

The interesting distribution of the three sub-species of the Large Heath, *Coenonympha tullia* (Plate 21, Map 6), will be discussed on pp. 276–7. This is one of our northern butterflies. It is locally common throughout Scotland, the Western Isles, and the Orkneys, though its reported existence in Shetland is probably erroneous; also in northern England, as far south only as Shropshire, and to Cardigan. It occurs throughout the greater part of Ireland, even to the extreme south. The species inhabits damp 'mosses' and moors from sea level up to 2000 feet. If these support heather, there must be a plentiful supply of grass mixed with it if this insect is to favour them. In such places there is generally a strong breeze, if not a gale, and on being disturbed the butterflies will rise and allow themselves to be blown far down wind, and a certain number of specimens may usually be observed beating their way back again up wind close to the ground.

The Large Heath is not especially associated with marshes, though it is fond of damp places. Similarly, the Scotch Argus, *Erebia aethiops* (Plate 20), is on the whole found on rather damp soil, with long grass and sparse trees, on hillsides or along the borders of woods: a typical locality for it is seen in Plate 14, near that famous collecting ground Rannoch in Perthshire. The butterfly occurs widely on the mainland of Scotland and on some of the isles, such as Scalpay, the south of Raasay, and the east of Skye. In England there were formerly isolated colonies in Northumberland, Durham, North Yorkshire, Westmorland, and Furness, but today only one of these certainly survives, though one or two others possibly do so (see pp. 273–4).

Our single Alpine butterfly, the Mountain Ringlet, *Erebia epiphron* (Plates 14, 20), flies near the ground and, like that last-mentioned, only in the sunshine: a remarkable circumstance in

insects which inhabit rather sunless regions. In England it is
confined to the Lake District mountains, above 1800 feet, where
it flies abundantly in restricted areas, from which stragglers
range widely over the neighbourhood. Such colonies tend to shift
their quarters every few years. In Scotland the species is more
scattered and widespread over the mountains in Perth and
Inverness, and the Galloway-Kirkcudbright area; and it descends
to a lower level, for it may be taken down to 1500 feet. This is
one of the great prizes awaiting collectors in Ireland, and it seems
to be of a distinct race there (p. 273). The recorded captures
from Mayo and Sligo are certainly correct, but very few specimens
exist, and none has been obtained in recent years. It probably
occurs elsewhere in the country.

We have now briefly surveyed the habitats and distribution of
all the British butterflies excepting three species of more general
occurrence, while such a study is obviously inapplicable to the
migratory Vanessidi and Coliadinae, and to the rare immigrants
(pp. 153–60). Nor is it appropriate to the Large and Small Whites,
themselves greatly reinforced by migration, which are found
mainly in cultivated areas, over the whole of Great Britain,
Ireland, and the Isle of Man, though they are not universally
common in the Western Isles and north Scotland; indeed, the
Small White *Pieris rapae*, is seldom seen in Sutherland and
Caithness. They are absent from the Shetlands, though they are
sometimes fairly common in the Orkneys.

Two of our butterflies, the Small Tortoiseshell, *Aglais urticae*,
and the Peacock, *Inachis io*, are attracted to patches of flowers
anywhere within their range. That of the Small Tortoiseshell
embraces the whole of Great Britain with the isles, and Ireland.
The Peacock used to be restricted in Britain to the centre and
south of England, but it has now spread once more to northern
England and Scotland, which it inhabited long ago (p. 139). It
also occurs in the Isle of Man, where it is uncommon, and
throughout Ireland, but mainly in the south.

Finally, one ubiquitous species must be mentioned. This is the
Small Heath, *Coenonympha pamphilus* (Plate 10), which is
universally distributed over England and Wales, though it
becomes somewhat less common in west Cornwall, and is absent
from the Isles of Scilly. It probably occurs on all the Western
Isles, and on the mainland of Scotland it reaches the extreme
north of the country; I have heard this denied, but I have myself seen specimens flying in Sutherland. However, it has not

colonized the Orkneys and Shetlands. It is to be found over the whole of Ireland and in the Isle of Man. Indeed, it really flies in every conceivable situation; along woodland paths, in marshes, on dry hillsides, by the sea shore, and up to 2000 feet on the mountains, and it is probably the most numerous of all British butterflies.

CHANGES IN THE DISTRIBUTION OF BUTTERFLIES

Since the beginning of the nineteenth century the English countryside has become steadily less favourable for our butterflies. Fens have been drained, waste land reclaimed, and urbanization and industrialism have made vast and hideous advances. Throughout this period there has also been a steady destruction of timber, which, since 1914, has reached alarming proportions. Woodlands were devastated in the first war and never replanted, while the country has been subject to a disastrous forestry policy by which our splendid deciduous trees are being replaced by conifers. Moreover, the great estates, so important to rural communities and to the preservation of wild life, are collapsing under insupportable taxation, and the country will ultimately be infinitely the poorer for their loss. The extent to which our fauna and flora have gained through the establishment of nature reserves and of that admirable institution the National Trust, has been negligible in comparison with such evils.

When we consider these changes, we might reasonably anticipate a corresponding destruction of butterfly life, and expect to find species at the best holding their own but in general becoming rarer and more localized. Superficially, at any rate, such a conclusion has proved false. Up to about 1920 it was apparently being realized; but since that time many British butterflies have undergone a remarkable recrudescence, and numbers of species have for years past been extending their range.

Up to the middle of last century, the Comma was widespread in the south of England and could be taken as far east as Kent and Surrey. But its true home has always been the counties of Gloucester, Hereford, and Monmouth, and to this area it had for many years been virtually confined. However, it began to spread once more during the First World War, and has not only recovered but also far surpassed its former distribution. It is now fairly common throughout southern England from Kent to west

Cornwall (Map 11). I have myself seen it in the latter area in some numbers recently, and it may be taken as far north as Leicestershire, while specimens have even reached the Scottish border.

The White Admiral had for long been restricted to the New Forest and to a few isolated woodlands here and there in the southern counties. It was absent from the south-east but frequented one or two woods in Suffolk. This butterfly also began to extend its range about 1920 and is now a common woodland species in the south, having returned to the south-eastern counties and to Somerset, from both of which it was for many years absent. I have found it commonly in Northamptonshire since 1930, and in an extensive wood in north Berkshire, where, as I well remember, it was seldom seen years ago, it is now one of the most abundant butterflies (Map 13).

The Peacock, always common in the south, for many years reached the Lake District but penetrated no farther. During the last half of the nineteenth century it was almost absent from Scotland and seems to have been taken there less often than the Camberwell Beauty! My father and I collected in north Cumberland for 24 years, and those who had done so in the 1860s told us that they used to catch the Peacock in their youth but that it had for long been absent. Yet we caught a single specimen in each of the last two years that we worked the area, 1935 and 1936. This was the beginning of its return, and it is now actually common in the Border Country and far into Scotland, where it is spreading steadily northwards and has even been taken in Caithness.

The distribution of the Wood White, always a local species, became extremely restricted early in the present century, for it was found in numbers only in South Devon and in the Hereford and Monmouth area. It has certainly been very much more abundant in other districts during the last twenty years, for it is now common in some Northamptonshire woods, extending into Buckinghamshire, and it is reappearing in its old haunts in Surrey.

Several quite common species were for a time absent from localities in which they used to exist, and to many of these they have recently returned: among such insects I may mention the Wall Butterfly and especially the Speckled Wood, which is extending its range in many districts. For example, my friend, Mr R. F. Bretherton, published in 1939 an exceptionally thorough survey of the butterflies of the Oxford district. At that time neither he nor I had seen the Speckled Wood in Bagley during nineteen years collecting in that forest, and Mr Bretherton was able to obtain only one record of its occurrence (in 1922). In the year 1943 I saw six specimens there in a single afternoon, and it is now appearing even in the city of Oxford, so that this butterfly at least has no objection to the horrors of urbanization and industrialism.

The Large Tortoiseshell was not uncommon in southern England up to about 1903, when it suddenly became very rare. Its numbers were therefore reduced at a somewhat later date than in the species so far mentioned. It was not uncommon in some parts of Suffolk and Essex up to the mid 1950s, but now appears to be almost extinct.

The explanation of these facts is decidedly obscure. In a few instances it is possible that local conditions have changed in such a way as to allow a species to establish itself where it could not do so previously. In 1907 or 1908 Canon Godwin liberated large numbers of the White Admiral in Wateringbury Woods, from which the species was then apparently absent, but none survived. Long afterwards, that locality became included within the range of the butterfly, which had extended naturally, and in 1934 Canon Godwin saw at least two hundred specimens in the area where he had unsuccessfully attempted to establish the species in the past. It is doubtful if this really indicates altered conditions in the habitat, for the changes in distribution of the butterflies so far mentioned have been synchronized within each species over the whole country, instead of affecting particular localities only (p. 138). It seems almost certain therefore that they are at least partly dependent upon climatic effects, though none which can be correlated with them has ever been detected by an analysis of meteorological records. But the influence of climate cannot be excluded on that account, for several remarkable instances are known in which unidentified climatic factors apparently exert a notable control upon both the fauna and flora of vast territories. The extraordinary fluctuations in the numbers of fur-bearing animals in Canada provide an example of this kind. These have been studied in great detail by Mr C. Elton, and certain aspects of the subject are summarized by Elton and Nicholson, 1942. Taking as a basis the records of the Hudson's Bay Company, they show that a regular and extreme fluctuation in numbers, having an average period of 9·6 years, has occurred in the population of the lynx and the snowshoe rabbit in Canada for 206 years. So widely synchronized is it that for at least a hundred years the cycle can be shown to have coincided on the two sides of the Rocky Mountains, and its cause is so fundamental that it also affects aquatic species such as the musk-rat and salmon. It seems hardly possible to escape the inference that such fluctuations are at least in part controlled by the climate. Yet no corresponding climatic variation is known, for Elton shows that during the two hundred years covered by the observations the cycle in the abundance of these animals becomes quite out of phase with the curve for sunspot-numbers, which has an average period of 11·2 years. A direct connection between the two phenomena had been suggested, but this is certainly fallacious.

The climatic basis of this Canadian cycle in wild life has escaped detection in spite of extensive research. It would not be very remarkable therefore if some of the changes in distribution to which British butterflies are subject were also dependent upon unidentified climatic variations. Dr J. R. Baker has shown that the stimulus needed to produce striking biological effects is sometimes very small, for he found that bats have a sharply-marked breeding season even in the almost unvarying tropical climate of Hog Harbour, Espiritu Santo, New Hebrides (10° 15′ S. in the Pacific).

It is quite possible that the balanced relationships between some butterflies and their environment may be upset when their numbers increase beyond a certain limit, even though their actual density in the areas concerned is quite small. Such a situation may stimulate limited migrations and extensions of range though the factors leading to the initial effect may be very difficult to detect. They may merely depend upon the occurrence of a few consecutive years of greater sunlight, warmth, or other favourable conditions at some critical stage in the life-cycle of the species.

EXTINCTION

It is certainly gratifying that a number of British butterflies have been extending their range in recent years, even though this may not mean that their status is a satisfactory one (p. 144); but there is, of course, another side to the picture. Several species have become totally extinct, and a few very much rarer, since the beginning of last century. Not only is it interesting to inquire the cause of this, but also such knowledge may help us to save others from a similar fate.

It is my opinion that over-collecting, itself an obvious evil, has not often been responsible for the destruction of butterflies, and that though there are a few species, or rather localized colonies of species, which are actually threatened with extinction by this means, the danger is one which has been unduly stressed. It would not be difficult to exterminate the Heath Fritillary in its localized habitats, and it has certainly been unnecessarily destroyed in some of them. When the Large Blue was discovered in the neighbourhood of Bude, North Cornwall, it was first found abundantly in a restricted area. It was immediately persecuted by collectors, and it would have become extinct in that particular locality had it not been afforded protection.

The cupidity of collectors does, however, appear to have been responsible for the extinction of one of our butterflies, and this the finest of them all, the Large Copper, *Lycaena dispar*. Attempts have been made to disclaim that crime, but they do not bear serious examination. There were certainly additional causes which made over-collecting peculiarly dangerous to this insect, the chief of which was, of course, the drainage of the fens, though this was by no means coincident with the disappearance of the butterfly. The process must indeed have reduced very seriously the habitats available to the Large Copper, but it need not alone have brought about its total destruction. Some of its localities are still in approximately their original condition, and these include Holme Fen, where the last specimens were caught in 1847 or 1848. The truth is that the Large Copper required some degree of protection at a time when the area suitable for it was being rapidly reduced: not only was it given none, but the insect was systematically persecuted to the very end.

In spite of this deplorable event, indirect rather than direct human interference has been the greater danger to British butterflies. No woodland species can survive the destruction of our forests or the awful change from deciduous trees to conifers, while the conversion of moors and wastes into third-rate agricultural land is not always a complete compensation for the loss of natural beauty and of wild-life which is sustained in the process.

Nevertheless, it is true that one of the most potent dangers which our butterflies have to face is, as it were, an intrinsic one. It arises from those, probably recurrent, changes in numbers and areas of distribution to which attention has been drawn in the previous section, and, as already indicated, these seem to be climatic in origin.

Any species can survive such periodic fluctuation provided that its numbers are large enough, and that it is somewhere sufficiently well established, to tide over the dangerous period when it is reduced to its lowest level. Clearly, a 'normal' cycle of this kind may be disastrous to a butterfly which maintains itself precariously, whether in an isolated locality or in the country as a whole. The Wood White survived in Westmorland until about 1905 when it disappeared and has never been seen there again. At that time the species was in general becoming rare (p. 139), and in the south retracting its range to a few favoured places. From these it could, and did, spread once more; but not in the north, where the one isolated colony was wiped out by a process which had no serious consequences elsewhere. Similarly, it disappeared from the New Forest early this century and has not returned. It was said at the time that this was due to over-collecting, and probably that was true. But I suspect that the butterfly was reduced to dangerously small numbers by natural causes, operating there as elsewhere, and for that reason the activities of the collector were fatal.

We have lately had one remarkable instance of the extinction of a butterfly for which no cause is assigned in the text-books. This is the Black-veined White, *Aporia crataegi*, but I do not believe that its disappearance is so very mysterious after all. Consider the history of this insect. It is widespread in Europe and even a destructive pest to fruit-trees, but in England it was on the edge of its range (see the next section). During the last century it was found widely scattered over the southern counties, particularly in the New Forest, and in South Wales; but its true home was always in Kent. By 1900 it had wholly withdrawn there and had become confined to a small area only. Though it was not uncommon in that locality, it was obviously then in great danger. Finally its numbers were reduced in this last refuge also, and it seems to have become completely extinct about fifty years ago. The close parallel between this story, in all but its last phase, and that of such species as the Comma and the White Admiral cannot fail to attract attention. Had the Black-veined White been a little more firmly established here, so as to tide over the period when it was so heavily eliminated, it is quite possible that it would have become commoner and spread once more, as did many other species. The causes which produce fluctuations in numbers and changes in area in some butterflies must inevitably lead to extinction in others.

The fact that a species is extending its range or becoming commoner does not necessarily mean that it benefits from the effects of civilization. If such an apparently favourable situation is less marked than it would have been in normal circumstances, the numbers of the insects may subsequently fall to a dangerously low level. Indeed, the increase in range of many butterflies today does not prove that the present condition of the English countryside is advantageous to them.

Not all butterflies fluctuate synchronously over the whole of their range, but some may do so independently in different isolated localities, as, for example, does the Marsh Fritillary (p. 254). This leads to a great reduction in numbers in any one colony, which may be temporary if there is a sufficient reserve of individuals there; but if not, the species may become extinct in that habitat. Many instances of this might be quoted, but the disappearance of the Large Blue in Barnwell Wold will suffice.

It is possible that the extinction of the Mazarine Blue, *Cyaniris semiargus*, presents a problem of a different nature from those so far discussed. I have therefore reserved it for separate treatment. The impression conveyed in some of the current text-books is that this butterfly was formerly resident in the south of England but became rare in the last century, and finally disappeared between 1870 and 1880. On this view, its history would be somewhat similar to that of the Black-veined White. However, Mr S. G. C. Russell, who discussed the subject in *The Entomologist* for 1943, thinks that it was never really established here but made only sporadic appearances, due to migration, like the Bath White or the Queen of Spain Fritillary (see pp. 154–6). There is at least something to be said for this theory, for the early entomologists, such as Haworth and Lewin, do not give the impression that the Mazarine Blue was frequently caught in their day or that it ever had been: on the contrary, they describe it as very rare. Mr Russell goes on to say 'the only record of a recurrent emergence is that of the late J. C. Dale, who recorded the occurrence of a small colony for several seasons at Glanville Wootton, which eventually died out and never reappeared.' This seems to be a decided understatement of the event. Mr W. C. Dale, quoting from the journal of his father, J. C. Dale, says that the Mazarine Blue 'was common at Glanville Wootton in Dorsetshire, in 1808, once recorded in 1811, once in 1812, common in 1813, 1814, 1815 (one being taken as late as August 1st), and 1816, scarce in 1817 and 1818, common in 1819, 1820, and 1821, scarce in 1822 and 1823, common in 1825, twenty specimens being taken by my father on the 13th June, scarce in 1828, 1830 and 1831, common in 1834 and 1835, only one seen in 1836, a few in 1837, none recorded in 1838, scarce in 1839 and 1840, and in 1841 a pair on the 19th June, being the last ever seen in Dorsetshire.' It is particularly to be noticed that this species was already common when the record starts. We have no evidence therefore that it had not been so for a long while previously, or indeed that it had ever been absent. Some specimens came from this famous colony and were actually captured in Dorset by J. C. Dale. I find that there are only nineteen specimens of the Mazarine Blue in the Dale collection, twelve males and seven females, and that four of the males are labelled 'Cardiff', the remainder being from Glanville Wootton. No conclusions can, however, be drawn from the small size of this set. It fills a line and this, I imagine, was Mr Dale's intention, for the series of the Holly Blue, placed next to it, does so as well and comprises only eighteen insects.

The Mazarine Blue continued to be taken at intervals in the Cardiff district up to the latter part of last century; twelve specimens were caught there in 1876, and there certainly seems to have been a colony there also. On the whole, it is probable that this species maintained itself in a few habitats in the south-west, where perhaps it was indigenous; and little collecting was done in that region in the early days of British entomology. Stragglers may have migrated thence, and these would account for the former persistent occurrence of the species as a rarity in the Midlands and the south-east. In addition, occasional migrants might have reached this country from the continent, as presumably do the few specimens still caught here from time to time. Some of these may, of course, breed and maintain themselves in England for a few generations.

In Chapter 1 it was pointed out that several butterflies not now recognized as British were regarded as indigenous here by the early entomologists. Some of the records of them may be due to error, others to fraud, while it may be that some are genuine and that the species were established here and became extinct at an early date. If any of them fall into the last group, we have no definite knowledge of their fate. The Scarce Copper, *Lycaena virgaureae* (p. 24), may have been present in a few fens only, which were drained; or its disappearance, and that of some others, may be explicable on the same basis as that of the Black-veined White.

The ancient report of the occurrence in Scotland of one continental butterfly merits a brief examination. As already explained (pp. 27–8), when Sir Patrick Walker captured the first British specimens of the Scotch Argus, *Erebia aethiops*, in 1804, it is said that he took in addition to that well-known British butterfly a second species flying with it. This was the Arran Brown, *E. ligea*, an insect which is common in semi-alpine habitats in some parts of the continent. These captures were made on the moors behind Brodick Castle, Isle of Arran, but in spite of repeated investigations no one has ever found the Arran Brown there again. Now it is often held that the reported occurrence of this species must be erroneous. I differ from that view for several reasons. First, two of Sir Patrick Walker's specimens of *E. ligea* are still in existence, preserved in the British Museum, consequently we know that they were at least correctly identified. The possibility remains that they are foreign specimens introduced either by error or fraud. This does not seem likely when we consider the peculiar circumstances. Sir Patrick reported the simultaneous capture of two butterflies new to Britain, and both are species which might reasonably be expected to inhabit the northern part of our islands. His statements in regard to one of them are well known to be perfectly correct, so that it seems improbable that the other was described in error. But we have an additional and more convincing indication of the existence of *Erebia ligea* in Britain. There is now in the Rothschild collection at Tring an Arran Brown labelled 'Galashiels', which was found in the collection of the late A. E. Gibbs, where it was included in a series of the Scotch Argus for which it had evidently been mistaken owing to the close resemblance between the two species. It is possible therefore that specimens of *E. ligea* occur as rarities among the population of the Scotch Argus in some parts of Scotland. Much of that country is quite unexplored entomologically, and a remote district may yet be found where *E. ligea* is not uncommon. It is, of course, possible that the species was on the verge of extinction and has now disappeared, but we have only to consider that the Chequered Skipper could exist unknown in Inverness until 1941 to realize that remarkable discoveries may still be made among Scottish butterflies.

There are several very different forms of *E. ligea*. However, the presence of one or more small white marks on the underside of the hind-wings, absent from *E. aethiops*, is a safe guide in distinguishing it from *E. aethiops*, in which these are absent.

SPECIES ON THE EDGE OF THEIR RANGE

The habitats chosen by some of our most local butterflies can seldom be related in any obvious way to their needs, for they may be absent from districts which appear to be as well, or better, suited to them than those which they select. Attention has already been directed to this circumstance in discussing the distribution of those species which are restricted to a few inland localities in the south-eastern Midlands (pp. 131 and 135). Moreover, there are others whose range in these islands is yet more remarkable, since they are limited to a particular type of environment here, though it is not one to which they are confined on the Continent. Thus in England the Lulworth Skipper (Plate 21) only flies within a mile or two of the sea. It is most abundant in the 'Isle' of Purbeck, from Swanage to Weymouth, where, near Lulworth Cove (Plate 14), it was originally discovered (p. 29). The butterfly does not necessarily require a calcareous soil, as, for example, does the Chalkhill Blue, for though it occurs on the chalk for a few miles west of Lulworth, it does not do so to the east of that locality, and colonies of it also exist upon the Old Red Sandstone of south Devon.

Similarly, the Glanville Fritillary is now restricted to the southern coasts of the Isle of Wight, where it is to be found here and there in great numbers. As we pass along the south coast from the Needles, the chalk of which that headland is composed is replaced first by Wealden Clay and then by the Lower Greensand. The clay often breaks down to the sea in a series of small cliffs which in some places may merely be steep banks fifteen to twenty feet in height, separated by rough grassy slopes and ledges; while farther east where the cliffs are higher there may be a considerable area covered with rank vegetation between them and the shore. These 'undercliffs' are the chosen haunts of this butterfly, its larvae feeding upon the Narrow-leaved and Sea Plantains (*Plantago lanceolatus* and *P. maritima*) which grow there. The Glanville Fritillary was first found in the Isle of Wight by Edward Newman in 1824. At some places along the coast it has become extinct since his day, but at others it has greatly multiplied and has even spread for a short distance inland in recent years. Previous to this discovery it was an insect of great rarity here, but it seems to have occurred in one or two small areas on the coasts of Kent and Sussex. The ancient records, mostly of the eighteenth century, from inland localities in the south-eastern counties are probably erroneous; perhaps the butterfly was then confused with the Heath Fritillary.

Neither the Lulworth Skipper nor the Glanville Fritillary is a particularly maritime species abroad. It is probable that they both require a greater amount of sunlight than our climate normally affords, but this does not account for their strict limitation to the coast and their extreme localization there. The truth is that species on the edge of their range, such as these, can only survive by adapting themselves closely to the environment which they find in certain places which chance to suit them particularly well. Thus they form local races whose probable physiological modifications may or may not be reflected in their colour-patterns. British specimens of the Lulworth Skipper and of the Glanville Fritillary are not distinguishable from those caught on the Continent, but the Swallow-tail, which has also survived here by adapting itself to peculiar conditions, has come to differ visibly from any other race in the process (pp. 285–6). This butterfly is purely a fen insect in England,[1] though that is not its normal habitat abroad. It is worth noticing that other organisms, for example plants and birds, may be found in abnormal localities near the edge of their range.

The restriction in unfavourable circumstances of the White Admiral to the New Forest and some other woods, and the Comma to Hereford and the neighbouring counties, must be regarded as further instances of species limiting their distributions to regions which are for some reason especially suitable for them. Yet these two butterflies do not seem to be deeply committed to life in their chosen habitats for, as already mentioned, they are able to spread outwards from them when the conditions are satisfactory.

The peculiar limitation of the Black-veined White to a region in Kent, so unlike its toleration of diversified habitats abroad, should now be less mysterious; for in England it was at the

[1] Except for specimens of the Northern French race which are occasionally found in Kent (pp. 285–6).

extreme limit of its distribution, and to that circumstance, combined with a severe decrease in numbers, it probably owed its extinction. It is fortunate for the survival here of the Lulworth Skipper and the Glanville Fritillary that they do not appear to be species whose numbers undergo violent fluctuations, for those which do so run grave risks of extinction in areas near the edge of their range.

Chapter 8

Dispersal

Migration, Artificial Introduction

MIGRATION

Some butterflies are great migrants and, having remarkable powers of flight, they may reach countries far distant from their original home. A number of them form vast migrating swarms at long intervals, probably as a result of over-population; for they occasionally undergo notable fluctuations in numbers (pp. 138–41), giving rise to excessive abundance. Others seem to overflow their territory frequently, while there are foreign species which maintain themselves in favourable conditions throughout the year by migration, as do many birds. Thus the Monarch, *Danaus plexippus*, which sometimes finds its way to Britain, is a permanent resident only in the south of the United States, Central, and tropical South America. However, it annually migrates northwards in the spring, travelling far into Canada, and there is a return migration in the autumn, a succession of broods being maintained at all seasons.

The phenomenon may best be studied by dividing our butterflies into groups according to their habits of migration. Specimens of all the species now and then wander far from their normal haunts, and, if they be fertile females, they may produce a brood in distant localities where they could not perpetuate themselves. There is indeed abundant evidence of such exceptional behaviour in those which are not normally regarded as migratory. Thus the Wall Butterfly, *Lasiommata megera* has been captured at least twice at the Outer Dowsing Light Vessel thirty miles east of the Norfolk coast. The Small Copper, *Lycaena phlaeas* (Plate 22), and the Meadow Brown, *Maniola jurtina* (Plate 24), have been caught at the Royal Sovereign Light Vessel seven miles south-east of Eastbourne, and the Common Blue, *Polyommatus icarus* (Plate 19), at the Corton Light Vessel four miles north-east of Lowestoft, while the Small Heath, *Coenonympha pamphilus* (Plate 10), has several times been observed coming in from the sea. These are isolated instances, but mass movements of the so-called non-migratory forms are sometimes detected inland in our own country. A number of specimens of the Brimstone, *Gonepteryx rhamni* have been seen migrating near Tavistock, and a considerable migrating swarm of the Peacock, *Inachis io*, has been reported from Surrey. Clearly a small party of species with such habits, whether indigenous here or not, might sometimes reach these shores.

The wandering of the Meadow Brown *Manida justina*, seven miles across the sea near Eastbourne, just mentioned, must be an occurrence of extreme rarity. In our ecological genetic work we have captured this species on a scale never before approached, and we have studied its habits in great detail for a quarter of a century. Even on the Isles of Scilly we must, over the years, have caught, and often released after marking, many thousands of this butterfly. Yet we have never seen it migrate across the sea. The specimens flying out over the water turn back after a distance of, perhaps, up to a hundred yards, as they do over unsuitable country. Thus a hundred yards of grass kept short like a lawn by the grazing of cattle proved a complete barrier to the insect on the Island of Tean (Ford, 1971).

Two of our resident butterflies, the Green-veined White, *Pieris napi* (Plate 19), and the Small Tortoiseshell, *Aglais urticae*, though not normally migrant, are none the less augmented by small streams of immigrants from the Continent which occasionally reach considerable proportions. But these do not depend upon such additions for their survival here. The Green-veined White is not infrequently reported as migrating in considerable numbers within this country; it has been observed to do so in Leicestershire, in Northumberland, and at a high elevation on the moors around Alston in Cumberland, while specimens have sometimes been caught at light vessels at sea. The Small Tortoiseshell is not often observed to migrate, though hundreds were found on Flamborough Head on 22 March 1935 before our own hibernated individuals had become common. It has also alighted on boats in the middle of the English Channel and has repeatedly been captured at the East Dudgeon Light Vessel thirty miles from the Norfolk shore.

The next stage is in general similar to the last, but it is one in which migration has become of much greater importance to the species. Two more of our butterflies, though indigenous and well able to maintain themselves here, are at frequent intervals reinforced by vast swarms which reach us from the Continent. These are the Small White, *Pieris rapae*, and the Large White,

Pieris brassicae, the latter being the greater migrant of the two. Immense flights of both these species have been encountered in mid-Channel making towards England, and they have been observed from the shore coming in across the sea in myriads. I have not myself seen them in such numbers as to darken the sun, as is reported of them, but I have witnessed such a cloud of them that it looked like an oncoming snowstorm. After such an immigration on the south coast every field seemed alive with the insects, and their astonishing numbers may be judged by the fact that they were freely remarked upon even by those who had no interest in butterflies. These are the only two species we have which are any serious danger to crops, and their periodic excessive abundance is certainly due to immigration from the Continent.

We next come to those curious insects, the Red Admiral, *Vanessa atalanta*, and the Painted Lady, *V. cardui*, which, though common British butterflies, are quite unable to maintain themselves here. They hibernate as adults and though a few, at least of the Red Admirals, survive our winter, the majority perish, so that without migration they would rapidly become extinct in these islands. In spring, numbers of these butterflies arrive from the Continent and lay eggs which produce a large autumn generation of British-born specimens, which is often reinforced by further immigration on an extensive scale. The immigration of the Painted Lady is the more irregular, so that it is rare in some years and abundant in others, but the Red Admiral population also fluctuates, though to a lesser degree, for the same cause.

These two butterflies arrive in considerable numbers almost every year. Three others, similarly unable to maintain themselves as an indigenous stock, only appear at considerable intervals, for the area in which they are truly endemic is farther to the south. These are the Clouded Yellow, *Colias crocea* (Plate 21), and the Pale Clouded Yellows, *Colias hyale* and *C. australis* (Plate 22), which are much the rarer.

A few specimens of the Clouded Yellow reach us nearly every spring and lay eggs which produce a thin sprinkling of butterflies in the autumn. Sometimes, however, we receive a considerable party of immigrants whose offspring may make the butterfly abundant during the late summer in the south of England; while in seasons in which they are exceptionally plentiful they may spread sparsely into Scotland, the Isle of Man, and Ireland.

Though there have been a number of years during the present century in which the Clouded Yellow was common, none has equalled 1941, when the species attained the extreme degree of abundance reported of it in the 'great edusa year' of 1877.[1] I was in Cornwall in August of that year and in some places on the Lizard peninsula the fields were yellow with these butterflies as if scattered with flowers, and a distant 'white' was almost as likely to be a specimen of the pale female form *helice*[2] as a member of the Pierinae. Practically every one of these butterflies would be killed off during the ensuing winter, and the species was, in fact, scarce during the following summer, for this insect has no hibernating stage but maintains a constant succession of broods throughout the year. It is therefore wholly unsuited to be a permanent resident of Britain.

The migratory habits of the Pale Clouded Yellow are quite similar, yet it reaches our shores far more rarely than the Clouded Yellow, so that it becomes really common with us only at very long intervals; 1900 was the last year in which it did so, though fair numbers have been taken in some seasons since then. It never spreads as far north as does the Clouded Yellow, and it is practically unknown in Scotland. One might have expected this butterfly to be the more suited to our climate, for it at least possesses a definite hibernating phase in the larval stage. The insect cannot establish itself here, apparently because continuous damp is fatal to it. So, it is said, is a temperature below 40° F., but this is an error. Mr J. Shepherd informs me that he has twice brought the larvae successfully through an English winter without artificial heat, and that on one occasion they survived a temperature as low as 19° F.

A number of species unable to survive our winter reach us only as stray immigrants, and the recently recognized *Colias australis* (pp. 86–8) is to be placed among them. Now and then they may arrive in the spring and produce a small autumn brood, but they nearly always remain rarities.

The Camberwell Beauty, *Nymphalis antiopa*, long regarded as

[1] At that time this butterfly, now called *Colias crocea*, was known as *C. edusa*.
[2] The pale female form *helice* (p. 250) of the Clouded Yellow, *C. crocea*, is not always easy to distinguish from the female Pale Clouded Yellow, *C. hyale*. It is, however, much more heavily marked with black, particularly on the hind-wings. Also the black border on the fore-wings of *C. crocea* not only reaches the tornus but *turns slightly down the inner margin*, which it never does in *C. hyale* (see Plates 21 and 22).

the great prize of British butterfly collecting, is remarkable among these vagrants in several ways. Unlike the others, it comes to us from Scandinavia rather than from France and Belgium, so that it is more often found along the east than the south coast. Also a considerable swarm has occasionally arrived here, when the butterfly has appeared in numbers, so that it was called 'The Grand Surprise' by the early Aurelians. It was not uncommon in the years 1789, 1846, 1872, and 1880, while in 1819 many dead specimens were seen floating in the sea off the Durham coast.

This species is a late summer, not a spring migrant, consequently it seems never to have bred here. The few adults which survive the damp of our winter are so widely scattered that they fail to find a mate, for pairing takes place in the spring. The borders of the wings are a rich yellow when the insect first emerges, but they gradually fade and become white. In many specimens, however, the scales along the edges of the wings are imperfectly formed, being curled and devoid of pigment. The border is then white even at emergence, and the condition sometimes extends inwards making the blue spots rather dull in colour. It was formerly supposed that a white, instead of a yellow, border distinguished a genuine British example. Indeed, an old specimen in the British Museum had had its borders painted white by a dishonest dealer, who knew that he could not sell it as a native when they were yellow. The fraud was not discovered until the series was examined under ultra-violet light, when the border of one insect was seen to fluoresce brilliantly while that of all the others remained dark. There is some truth in the old belief, for Dr E. A. Cockayne has found that this scale abnormality is present in the great majority of the specimens caught in this country. He is inclined to think that it is particularly common in Scandinavia, which would account for its frequency here and for the tradition that a genuine British Camberwell Beauty may be recognized by the white borders of its wings.

Most of our rare migrants, however, never appear in numbers. These include the Queen of Spain Fritillary, *Issoria lathonia*, which was known as British in the eighteenth century. It has bred in this country once or twice, a spring migrant having produced an autumn brood; but it has been even rarer during the present century than in the past, for only one or two specimens have been recorded in a year and sometimes none for several years together.

These statements are true also of the Bath White, *Pontia daplidice*, with one shining exception. This was in 1945, when Dr H. B. D. Kettlewell at Falmouth, west Cornwall, and Mr C. S. H. Blathwayt at Looe, east Cornwall, each saw many dozens in a day or two, and there were numerous records of smaller numbers along the south coast of England and in North Cornwall that year. Vast numbers of eggs must have been laid, principally on Weld, *Resida luteola*, but the species was rare or absent in England in 1946. Dr Kettlewell found that the young larvae were destroyed by mites, a virus, and by the Braconid, *Apanteles glomeratus*, as well as by the climate. This insect is subject to occasional great numerical increases. Apart from assemblages at damp mud in the tropics, I have never seen any butterfly so common as was the Bath White one year in Rome: the ground was shimmering white with this insect on the Palatine Hill, and it was pouring over the precipice into the Forum like a cascade.

The Long-tailed Blue, *Lampides boeticus*, has been recorded less than thirty times since its first capture was announced in 1859, but it might easily be passed over on the wing as the Common Blue. It is rather a difficult insect to catch, for its flight is swift and powerful and longer sustained than is usual in the Lycaenidae. In 1926 Mr W. T. Kerr saw a number of specimens in his garden in Torquay and captured three of them. One of these was found sitting with its wings yet limp from emergence, an undoubted instance in which this species has bred in England. It could never maintain itself here, however, as it is a southern form which does not hibernate but depends for its existence upon a succession of broods throughout the year.

The Short-tailed Blue, *Everes argiades*, is among the rarest of all our casual immigrants, less than a dozen specimens having been recorded here in all, though at Falmouth in 1945 my friend, Dr H. B. D. Kettlewell, had a Bath White and a Short-tailed Blue in his net together. However, it could very easily be mistaken for the Silver-studded Blue, *Plebejus argus*, and I think it probable that this has happened. But that error should not arise if it is possible to see the underside, for this much resembles that of the Holly Blue except for a small orange spot within the outer margin of the hind wings, close to the anal angle, which is diagnostic. Indeed, it is not clear why the species is not indigenous here, since it hibernates and maintains itself successfully as near us as

Brittany. It is not impossible that small colonies of it in reality exist in this country.

Occasional specimens of the extinct Mazarine Blue, *Cyaniris semiargus*, are still reported in England: a female is said to have been caught in 1938, no locality being given, and a male was taken in south Cornwall in 1934. These probably reach us as immigrants, but the extinction of this butterfly has already been discussed on pp. 144–5.

Specimens of the Swallow-tail, *Papilio machaon* (Plate 23), are sometimes reported from places widely scattered over the southern, and even the midland, counties of England. They are, however, much more frequent in Kent than elsewhere: a subject which will be discussed on pp. 285–6. Those which have been critically examined do not belong to our British fen race, which is a recognizably distinct one, but are Continental specimens, either immigrants or their descendants, or they are imported insects which have been released.

As already mentioned, the American Painted Lady, *Vanessa huntera*, has been caught in England about a dozen times, and twice in Ireland. Possibly it has been imported in its early stages or has flown into a ship and been brought here as an adult butterfly.

I have reserved the Monarch Butterfly for treatment as the last of our rare visitors since it presents rather exceptional problems. It was first captured in Britain in 1876 and by 1944 157 specimens had been reported as seen here, 62 of which have been captured. Most of the records of those which were not caught are probably correct, since this is such a large and unmistakable insect. It is, as already mentioned, an inhabitant of America, and the Milkweeds (*Asclepias*) upon which it feeds are not indigenous in this country, so that it could not possibly maintain itself in Britain.

As the species is a noted migrant, it has often been maintained that the specimens which are caught here have flown the Atlantic. It seems to me that this view involves great difficulties. To perform such a feat the butterfly must obviously fly all night as well as all day, or be capable of resting on the sea in mid-ocean. Even so, it may well be asked why it should reach Britain at all. It only penetrates as far as the northern United States and Canada by migration each summer (p. 150), so that it should be immensely commoner in the Iberian Peninsula and along the west coast of France than here. Now the Monarch has only been recorded six times from continental Europe (twice from France and four times from Spain and Portugal), for we may neglect the specimen found in a greenhouse in The Hague. Considering the conspicuousness of the butterfly, these records seem too few from countries where, if it really migrates, it should be far commoner than in Britain; I think this is true even allowing for the scarcity of observers abroad. Similarly, in that event, it should mainly be found on the west coast of Ireland when it does reach these islands, but only three of the records are from that region. Is it not remarkable, moreover, that such a striking insect was never reported until 1876 if it has really always been making its way here? And we must bear in mind the extensive knowledge of British butterflies already possessed by the end of the eighteenth century (p. 33).

We may, in fact, be confident that the Monarch Butterfly usually crosses the Atlantic on ships. The purser of one vessel, himself a collector, has stated that on the American side numbers were generally to be seen flying round the potato-locker on his boat. Some of these would survive the voyage, and he had seen them fly away when the locker was opened on reaching England. Few if any specimens would reach us until the Atlantic service became frequent in the latter part of last century, and before fruit-boats, with which the species is particularly associated, were introduced.

Yet there seems some slight indication that this notable migrant may occasionally travel from America by its own powers of flight. Perhaps a great migratory swarm left that country in 1933, a minute proportion of which survived to swell the exceptional total of thirty-eight seen in Britain that year. Two pieces of evidence tend to support such a view. It is said that several specimens were captured on a steamer outward bound from Glasgow about 1880 when two or three hundred miles from British shores, though none of these appear to have been preserved. Also one settled on the rail of H.M.S. *Abelia* in mid-June 1941, when the ship was 800 miles due west of Queenstown. Unfortunately, it was not captured.

The North, Central, and South American sub-species of this butterfly are recognizably distinct. The racial characteristics of only 22 of those taken in Britain seem to have been examined, and all but one of these was of the North American type. The exception, a specimen caught in Cornwall in 1885, is said to be of Central American origin.

This is the largest butterfly seen in Britain, though but few collectors have the pleasure of encountering it. Yet it was my good fortune to do so on the evening of 30 August 1941 at Kynance Cove, Cornwall, within two miles of the most southerly point in Great Britain. Those who know that exquisite spot, now largely spoiled through having been popularized for tourists, will remember that the steep path up the cliff reaches a short piece of level ground just before the summit. Climbing from the cove, I arrived, net in hand, at this place at 6.20 p.m., double summer time, and glancing to the left saw a Monarch Butterfly about twenty feet away flying inland perhaps fifteen feet from the ground. It was slowly flapping and gliding and looked immense, and the honey-coloured underside of the hind-wings showed clearly. It quickly reached a small rocky hill and disappeared over the top. Now every collector knows that if one loses sight of a butterfly one rarely sees it again. It was with a sinking heart therefore that I gained the top of the hill, and, turning to the left in the direction which the insect had taken when last seen, found my way barred by a steep rocky slope. I threw myself over, landing in a heap at the bottom and, on picking myself up, beheld with joy the Monarch about fifty yards away. It was hovering over a path, no more than a foot above the ground, and then slowly rose. By the time I arrived it must have been about two feet above the heather, and I caught it with a single stroke of the net. It proved to be a female in good condition.

On this occasion I was much impressed by the resistance of this species to pressure and by its leathery consistency; a well-known characteristic of these protected insects, which indeed allows a bird to peck them sufficiently to realize their disagreeable qualities without killing them. As this specimen was too large to go into my killing bottle or boxes, I kept it in the net and repeatedly pinched it. This would have cracked the thorax of a large Nymphalid and caused its immediate death, but after each pinch this insect would lie still for a few minutes and then revive apparently none the worse. A faint musky odour hung about it, and I was greatly tempted to bite into it to determine if it were unpalatable but, having regard to the interest of the specimen in other ways, I thought it well to restrain my curiosity in this respect. I have now eaten it in the USA.

Very exceptional acts of migration undoubtedly bring to this country butterflies ordinarily unknown here. Among them *Gonepteryx cleopatra,* a close relative of our Brimstone, has

already been mentioned (p. 102). Other foreign species have
occasionally been found in Britain. Thus there is an authentic
instance of the capture by N. S. Brodie, of *Clossiana dia* L. near
Christchurch in 1887, and the specimen is now in the Hope
Department of Entomology at Oxford. Another is said to have
been taken at Cookham Dean in 1837. This insect was regarded
as British by the early entomologists, and known as Weaver's
Fritillary. It is, of course, possible that such specimens have been
purposely released, though some of the species are very unlikely
to have been bred or imported alive by collectors. Thus several
examples of the European Skipper, *Pyrgus alveus* Hb. were
caught on the Norfolk coast in 1860.[1]

Few British entomologists have experience in separating the
Fritillary *Mesoacidalia niobe* L. from the High Brown, *M. adippe*,
a small specimen of which it much resembles (Higgins and Riley,
1970, give an excellent account of the distinctions between
them, with illustrations in colour). *M. niobe* occurs, though not
commonly, along the north coast of France, including the Calais
district, and Belgium, while in Scandinavia its distribution extends
at least as far north as the Shetlands. Furthermore, several
specimens of it have in fact been caught in England, mainly in the
south-east but once in Suffolk (in 1879). Thus there is just a
possibility that this butterfly exists here unrecognized.

One instance of this type of discovery presents certain remarkable features and merits rather fuller discussion. Between 3 and
11 August 1911 Mr A. W. Bennett chanced to walk up a narrow
wooded valley near Tintagel in north Cornwall and noticed
several very large Fritillaries soaring about and settling on
Purple Loosestrife (*Lythrum salicaria*). Having collected in his
youth, though he had long ceased to do so, he realized that these
insects differed somewhat from Silver-washed Fritillaries,
Argynnis paphia, which he had at first thought them to be.
Accordingly, with great difficulty he managed to catch one in his
cap and pinch it. He brought it back to his hotel and set it with
an ordinary large-headed pin on a flat piece of wood. On
examining his capture later, he realized that the underside did
not resemble that of any Fritillary he had seen, the fore-wings
being salmon pink and the hind-wings green with silver bars. He
showed the specimen to me, but I did not then know the European
butterflies and could make nothing of it. Accordingly, I advised

[1] I am, of course, aware of the recorded capture in Surrey of a pair of
Charcharodus alceae Esp. in June 1923.

him to send it for an opinion to a celebrated entomologist who a few years previously had published one of the best-known works on British butterflies and moths. However, this expert did not see fit to reply to Mr Bennett, merely knocking off one of the antennae of the specimen and pencilling the words '*Argynnis paphia*' on the wrapper when he returned it. Had he given it more than a casual glance he would have realized his mistake.

In later years it became apparent to me that Mr Bennett had secured the only known British specimen of the largest and most magnificent of all European Fritillaries, *Argynnis major* Cr. (=*pandora* Schiff). Long afterwards, I exhibited it to the Royal Entomological Society, giving a full account of what had taken place, and the specimen, a female originally in perfect condition though a little damaged in the setting, is now in my own collection. Had it not occupied excessive space for a species caught but once in Britain, I would have figured it in this book.

It is very remarkable that Mr Bennett saw several specimens of the butterfly. I have been told that it occurs in Brittany, though it is usually stated that it does not exist in northern France. It seems an improbable species for any one to breed and liberate in this country, and it is possible that its occurrence here represents an extraordinary act of migration. If so, being single-brooded, it must have succeeded in surviving at least one winter, for a few migrating specimens would hardly all have reached the same spot. Another specimen has subsequently been caught in England.

Two general characteristics of migratory butterflies are noteworthy. First, Lepidoptera are much more quickly damaged by contact with grass and bushes than they are by sustained flight. Migrating specimens do not encounter such obstacles, and therefore they often arrive after immense journeys almost as if newly emerged. The statement is constantly made that a rare species must have bred in England because an example of it has been obtained here in perfect condition. This is quite worthless evidence. For instance, a female Pale Clouded Yellow which I caught at the foot of White Horse Hill, Berkshire, on 12 June 1934 was perfectly fresh, yet it must certainly have been an immigrant. Secondly, the urge to migrate is something quite distinct from the ordinary habits even of the most notable migrants. Thus, on arrival, they will often settle down in a restricted area for the rest of their lives and their progeny may remain there also, so that one may discover little colonies of such species. For instance, my father and I found the Clouded Yellow not uncommonly on the Solway coast of Cumberland in 1922, yet the butterflies were restricted to a stretch of about half a mile, and were to be seen nowhere else in the immediate neighbourhood.

The cause of large-scale migrations is quite unknown, but it is probable that they may be produced in several distinct ways. Some species may be stimulated to migrate in vast swarms by over-population, when the food-plants have been so depleted by the larvae that little remains on which the females can lay their eggs. However, so simple an explanation certainly does not cover all the facts. The food-plants are not always exhausted when species begin to migrate, and the Vanessidi, which have been known to reach this country in large numbers in the autumn (*A. urticae, N. antiopa*), do not pair until the spring, when the damage done by their larvae should largely have been made good. It seems likely that the conditions responsible for an extension of the range of some butterflies may stimulate extensive migration in others. Their nature is not understood, but they have been briefly discussed on pp. 138–41, where it was pointed out that hitherto unrecognized climatic changes may cause an increase in numbers up to a point at which the ecological balance of the species is upset. There are indeed strong indications that migration may occasionally be controlled by some general and widely-acting phenomenon. For example, the record captures in England of 50 Queen of Spain Fritillaries and 35 Bath Whites, both migrants from central and southern Europe, coincided in the year 1872. Much more striking, however, is the fact that this was also one of the very exceptional seasons in which the Camberwell Beauty has indeed been taken in numbers here, though that butterfly comes to us mainly from Scandinavia. Such an observation suggests the operation of some widespread climatic factor either in that year or acting cumulatively for some years previously.

Our knowledge of migration has been greatly extended by the labours of Dr C. B. Williams, who has collected an immense amount of information on this subject from all parts of the world (Williams, 1930). Also by Captain T. Dannreuther, R.N., who for long analysed the records of observers in different parts of the British Isles. His surveys of them have appeared in *The Entomologist* for many years. This organized scheme of recording migrants is no longer maintained, but it is still true that collectors would be doing good work by publishing such information.

ARTIFICIAL INTRODUCTION

Attempts to introduce butterflies artificially into new localities are to be recommended only in exceptional circumstances, for they may do considerable harm in vitiating studies of the habitats of the species concerned and of their natural means of dispersal. When it has been decided to undertake such work, the project should be advertised as widely as possible, so as to reduce to a minimum the possibility of falsifying genuine records of distribution. The risk that such publicity will lead to over-collecting, or to the extermination of the new colony by some fanatic (p. 166), must, I think, be taken, as it is the lesser evil; and this danger is not very great, especially when the site chosen is on private property, as it probably would be.

By no means all attempts to establish a butterfly artificially are likely to be successful. We have only to consider how often a species is absent from one of two adjacent and apparently similar habitats to realize how imperfect is our information on the requirements of the Lepidoptera. The greatest chance of success will probably be obtained by releasing fertile females, since these will be able to choose the best places in which to lay their eggs. This will generally be preferable to stocking a locality with one of the earlier stages and forming our own opinion as to the appropriate plants on which to establish them, or to liberating unpaired insects, for with the small numbers which can be used, some of the females might never become fertilized.

I have already given an instance in which a large number of White Admirals, *Limenitis camilla*, were indeed liberated quite unsuccessfully in a wood which subsequently proved entirely suitable for the species, though it is just possible that this was due to a change which had taken place in the interval. It will be worth while to describe briefly four successful instances of the artificial introduction of butterflies, which appear to be justified by the exceptional nature of the circumstances. These illustrate the chief aspects of such work, since they provide examples of the establishment of an existing British butterfly in two different habitats, one being colonized from the other; of the re-establishment in the British Isles of a species which had become extinct here; and of the successful introduction of a foreign butterfly.

The Heath Fritillary, *Mellicta athalia*, has been re-introduced into a wood near Hadleigh, Essex, where it seems to have existed up to the latter part of last century. Specimens were brought from North Kent and liberated there about fifteen years ago, and the butterfly has maintained itself successfully in its new home ever since. It is said that this Essex race has now become recognizably distinct from the Kentish form from which it was derived, being smaller and darker; but I have seen no exact quantitative comparison of the two, without which such a statement cannot safely be made.

Five years ago this Essex stock was used to re-establish the species in Abbot's Wood, Sussex, where it had formerly occurred but had become extinct. So far, the colony has done well and in 1943 it was estimated to comprise about five hundred specimens. The original form from Abbot's Wood was, on the average, paler than that from Kent or Essex, and it will be interesting to see if in time the new population comes to resemble it or changes its appearance in any other way.

The Heath Fritillary requires a plentiful supply of Cow-Wheat (*Melampyrum pratense*), and thrives best in woods which undergo a certain amount of systematic clearing. It is one of our most local species and has disappeared from districts where it was formerly established. In fact, in North Kent, its chief stronghold at the present day, it is still to be found in numbers; but it is in some danger from over-collecting and even more from pheasants which are very destructive to its larvae. Attempts to secure the wider distribution and greater safety of this butterfly in England thus appear to be justified.

By far the most notable attempt to establish a butterfly artificially has been the re-introduction of the Large Copper, *Lycaena dispar*, into the British Islands (Committee, 1929). As already explained (p. 24), the occurrence of this insect in England was first reported in 1795; for a time it was found commonly in some parts of fenland, but by 1840 it had become rare, and the last specimens seem to have been caught in 1847 or 1848. It is widely distributed on the Continent, but the old English race, sub-sp. *dispar*, differed from all others and was the finest of them.

In 1909, G. H. Verrall announced that he had liberated larvae of the Continental sub-species *rutilus* Wern in Wicken Fen, Cambridgeshire. This attempt at naturalization was a failure, for the locality was not suitable, as the food-plant, the Great Water-dock, *Rumex hydrolapathum*, was uncommon there. However, the same sub-species, *rutilus*, has been successfully established in southern Ireland on a site selected and prepared for it by Captain E. B. Purefoy. This is a snipe-bog at Greenfields, Tipperary, which was partially cleared and stocked with Great Water-dock. The experiment began in 1913, when only four fertile females were available, but in 1914 about four hundred imagines were released there. The colony was a great success and was still flourishing when last examined. This was in 1928, and apparently it has not been visited by an entomologist since that date! The original butterflies were obtained as larvae in the neighbourhood of Berlin and were bred in captivity. The sub-species *rutilus* is a less magnificent insect than the original English *dispar*. It is smaller, and differs from *dispar*, especially on the under side of the hind-wings, for the marginal red band is narrower and becomes indistinct towards the apex, while the ground colour is but little suffused with pale blue; moreover, the white-ringed black spots on the under surface of both fore and hind-wings are not as large as in *dispar*.

An attempt was made in 1926 to introduce the sub-species *rutilus* from Ireland into a marsh in Norfolk. Over five hundred butterflies were liberated, but the stock survived only for a couple of years. Since this site had proved unsuitable, much more extensive preparations were made to establish the Large Copper at Wood Walton Fen, Huntingdonshire, which is in the custody of the Society for the Promotion of Nature Reserves. The ground had become excessively overgrown, so that extensive clearing was necessary and the Great Water-dock had to be planted on a large scale before the insect could be introduced.

A new race of the Large Copper, the sub-species *batavus* Oberth., had been discovered in 1915 in the Province of Friesland, Holland. This resembles the old English *dispar* far more closely than does any other, and indeed the two can only be distinguished with difficulty. They are of approximately the same size and colouring, but on the under side *batavus* is the less heavily spotted, while the red sub-marginal band on the hind-wings is slightly narrower than in *dispar*, and a few other minute differences can be detected.[1] The sub-species *rutilus* is widespread on the

[1] On the upper-side, the hind-wings of the female may be predominantly black or predominantly copper within the submarginal band in either face.

Continent, but *batavus* occurs only in a few fens in Friesland, and even there it is a rarity. Drainage schemes threaten its habitats, and as soon as its existence was made known it became a prey to collectors, so that in a few years it was on the verge of extinction. It was therefore decided to make a great effort to stock Wood Walton Fen with this form, so like the one which flew there in years gone by. It proved extremely difficult to obtain specimens, but all obstacles were eventually overcome and the first butterflies were liberated in 1927. During the following winter occurred one of the worst floods on record, which for sixty days turned the site of the experiment into a vast lake many feet deep; yet the submerged larvae survived, producing a large number of butterflies in 1928, and the species has thrived in the fen ever since.

In view of this success, it was decided to establish *batavus* also at Wicken in Cambridgeshire. Several acres of that part of the fen which is the property of the National Trust were accordingly planted with the Great Water-dock during the winter of 1929–30, the work being admirably done by Mr G. H. Barnes, the well-known keeper. Half-grown larvae were liberated in the following May and nearly all of them produced imagines. This colony has become extinct but on Plate 10 is a photograph of a living specimen of the Large Copper, sub-species *batavus*, in its natural surroundings at Wicken; and part of the fen itself is shown on Plate 13.

The Great Water-dock grows easily on the banks of streams, yet it is not favoured by the Large Copper in such positions, but rather on level ground when surrounded by natural cover, and here it is not easy to establish it. The butterfly is very fond of flowers and a sufficiency of these seems to be essential for its welfare, particularly such species as *Lythrum salicaria* and *Thalictrum flavum*. Given the right conditions, it is an adaptable species, prepared even to lay its eggs on a dull day. Its most vulnerable period is not during winter floods but the last three weeks of its larval life, when it is much parasitized, and the three weeks spent as a pupa. At that time it is extensively preyed upon by birds, particularly on the day before emergence when it turns black and becomes very conspicuous, this being enhanced by the fact that with infinite folly, the pupae are frequently placed in full view on the upper-side of a leaf.

The work of establishing the Large Copper in England has been conducted by the committee appointed by the Royal

Entomological Society for the Protection of British Lepidoptera. Captain E. B. Purefoy has freely given his valuable help, and entomologists will be grateful to the members of this committee, by whose care and energy the most magnificent of our butterflies has been restored to us again almost in its original form. Yet the fens in which it has been naturalized cannot be left unattended, otherwise they would revert to a jungle into which the naturalist could not penetrate and in which the butterfly would not survive. Considerable expense is incurred in cutting the reeds and keeping the growth of undesirable plants in check, and in providing a watcher. Entomologists who care to contribute to this worthy object should send their subscriptions to The Royal Entomological Society, 41 Queen's Gate, London, S.W.7.

Finally, the successful introduction into England of a foreign butterfly must briefly be noticed. This was the charming little Vanessid *Araschnia levana*, an insect of great interest, since it provides one of the most remarkable known instances of seasonal variation. There are two broods in the year, and the chief difference between them is on the upper-side: that appearing in May resembles a Fritillary, being fulvous-brown with black pencillings, while specimens of the second generation, which fly in July, look like small White Admirals, for the wings are blackish and are crossed with an oblique white bar. The pattern of the under-side is similar in the two broods, but the colour is much richer in the second generation than in the first, though the difference is small compared with that of the upper-side.

The species feeds on nettle and occurs widely in Europe, even in the north-eastern Departments of France, but it is absent from the north-west of that country. It was introduced into the Forest of Dean, Monmouthshire, about 1912, and a second small colony was also established near Symond's Yat, Herefordshire. It not only survived but also increased in numbers for several years, when it was ruthlessly exterminated by a collector (whose identity was widely known), who thought that no foreign butterfly ought to be introduced into Britain. His arbitrary action was an improper one; for he should at least have consulted a considerable body of entomologists, for example the Entomological Society, before taking a step which was by no means his personal business alone and on which many other people had as much right to an opinion as he. For myself I am inclined to think that the introduction of this insect was less exceptionable than the establishment of a British species in a new area. It could not be confused with our native fauna, to which, however, it added an element of decided interest, its remarkable seasonal variation being unlike anything that can be seen here. The butterfly seems able to maintain itself at least in the south-west of England, and I should not object to a further attempt being made to naturalize it in this country.

In general, it is certainly true that the distribution of our butterflies should be interfered with as little as possible. Attempts to introduce species into new areas, or to re-introduce them into old ones, are sometimes valuable, but they should only be made in special instances in which the possibility of confusion with natural changes in distribution is reduced to a minimum, and only under the auspices of some representative body.

Chapter 9

Theoretical Genetics

Simple Inheritance (Segregation), Linkage, Multiple Allelomorphs, Sex, Conclusions

SIMPLE INHERITANCE (SEGREGATION)

Genetics is the study of heredity and variation: it is therefore a subject of special value to the collector of butterflies. Not only does it enable him to appreciate the significance of the otherwise chaotic mass of individual aberration which he meets, but it also invests it with that interest which knowledge alone can supply. Further, it provides opportunities for amateur scientific research of real value which, in my experience, a large number of collectors would be eager to undertake within the ordinary limits of their hobby if they could see more clearly how to conduct it. If one must find a reason for such work beyond the delight of satisfying one's curiosity on natural phenomena, that is easily done. For the principles of genetics are of universal application to living organisms, plant and animal. The breeder of butterflies who studies variation is obtaining evidence which may throw light upon problems arising in the culture of plants or the successful rearing of other animals. Moreover, certain aspects of such work have an especial bearing upon heredity in Man, whose blood-groups are examples of polymorphism (p. 247). Those who have no aspirations beyond forming a collection will yet be wise to call genetics to their aid. Putting it at its lowest, it will be of value in obtaining desirable varieties by breeding.

The complaint is often made that genetics is a subject for specialists: not indeed too difficult for any ordinarily intelligent person, but requiring more intensive study than the amateur entomologist is prepared to accord it. There is no reason for this view. It is quite easy to master the essentials of genetics sufficiently to open up new and exciting possibilities to the collector of butterflies, and I hope that the following account will provide the means for doing so. It will be necessary in the course of it to introduce a few technical terms; for to avoid them would cause much circumlocution, and a knowledge of them is presumed in the genetic literature which the reader may later wish to consult. However, they will here be reduced to a minimum.

Every character which we can study is the combined product of heredity and environment, to both of which organisms must always be exposed. On the other hand, variation in a character may be the result of hereditary, or of environmental, influences alone, or of the two acting together. It will be convenient to consider these agencies separately, taking first the part played by heredity.

It has already been pointed out that the living material in the bodies of animals and plants is sub-divided into microscopic units known as cells. Now the first cell of a new organism results from the union of two reproductive cells produced respectively by the male and the female. These, the sperm and the egg, may in a sense be regarded as half a cell each, since from their fusion arises the first cell of the offspring.

Now it seems clear that some sort of 'hereditary factors', responsible for the production of particular characters, must be transmitted from generation to generation if heredity has any physical basis at all. These unit-factors are called *genes*, and the hereditary constitution of any individual consists of a great many of them. Each may, in reality, influence a number of characters, and one character is undoubtedly affected by many genes (p. 211). However, the simplest situation is one in which any given character is controlled by *two* genes, one received in the sperm from the father and the other in the egg from the mother. The pairs of genes derived in this way, controlling particular characters, are called *allelomorphs*. They are carried in every cell of the body and the members of any given pair of them may either be similar or dissimilar, according to the constitution of the two parents from which they were respectively obtained. When similar, the pairs forming the allelomorphs are said to be *homozygous*, and when dissimilar, *heterozygous*; the animals carrying them being called *homozygotes* or *heterozygotes* in respect of the allelomorphs concerned. Any individual may be homozygous for some pairs of allelomorphs and heterozygous for others. That is why the terms 'pure-breed' and 'hybrid', which refer to the organism as a whole, are not appropriate alternatives for homozygote and heterozygote.

It will be realized that we have assumed the two parents to be equally important in heredity, as indeed they are. At this point an important question is bound to occur to the logically minded.

Consider any two different genes constituting, for instance, a heterozygous pair of allelomorphs. Do these contaminate one another when brought from distinct parents into the very same cell of the offspring? The answer is that they do not; on the contrary, they remain permanently distinct. Thus when the offspring in its turn forms reproductive cells, the members of each allelomorphic pair are able to separate cleanly from one another again and pass into different reproductive cells, sperms or eggs, according to the sex of the individual. These once more are worth but half a cell each: they possess one member only of each pair of allelomorphs. This separation from one another of the members of every allelomorphic pair of genes, and their passage into different reproductive cells, is called *segregation*.

All organic inheritance depends upon this clear-cut segregation. No blending or contamination of the hereditary material takes place. This essential principle was enunciated in 1865 (and first published the following year) by the renowned Father Gregor Mendel, Abbot of the Augustinian monastery of St Thomas at Brünn (now Brno) in Moravia. His work passed almost unnoticed at the time and only received recognition in 1900, sixteen years after his death.

We may now apply this 'Mendelian' mechanism of heredity to the needs of entomologists, illustrating it by means of examples. The first of these will be taken from the common Currant Moth, *Abraxas grossulariata* L., for that species provides a special simplification not yet detected in British butterflies, from which, however, all other instances will be drawn.

The Currant Moth is white, sprinkled with black dots and marked with orange. In a rare variety, *lutea* Cockerell, the white pigment is replaced by one of a deep yellow, almost of a sulphur shade. This difference in ground-colour, white or yellow, is controlled by a single pair of allelomorphs, the members of which have been derived respectively from the two parents. The pair in question may be denoted C^wC^w in the normal white insects and C^yC^y in var. *lutea*.[1] These are homozygous pairs, composed of members which are similar in the white and in the yellow moths respectively.

---

[1] I suggested this nomenclature, to be used in the absence of 'dominance', in my work, *Genetics for Medical Students*, where its advantages are explained. In the present instance, C =colour production, its type being indicated by the index *w* (white) or *y* (yellow).

When these insects produce their reproductive cells, segregation will take place, so that the sperms or eggs to which they give rise will receive one member only of the allelomorphic pair concerned. It is immaterial which is the male and which the female; but assuming the male to be white, all the sperms would contain C^w, and all the eggs C^y, only.

Consider a cross between the white and the *lutea* forms of the Currant Moth. The cells of the progeny will once more possess a *pair* of allelomorphs determining colour. This will now be a heterozygous pair C^wC^y, the members of which have been derived respectively from the two parents, C^w from the one and C^y from the other. Such individuals, having one dose of the white determinant and one of the yellow, are intermediate in appearance between the two parents, being of a pale yellowish tint, a form called *semi-lutea* Raynor. These specimens constitute what is known as the *first filial generation* (denoted F_1) of the cross, while the parents are said to belong to the *first parental generation* (P_1). This nomenclature can be extended in either direction. Thus the grandparents may be called P_2, while the F_2 generation is that which results from inter-breeding the F_1 individuals.

It is instructive to perform the latter operation. Half the reproductive cells manufactured by var. *semi-lutea* will receive one type of allelomorph (C^w) and half will receive the other (C^y), as a result of the segregation of the heterozygous pair C^wC^y. Thus, when these F_1 insects are inter-bred, the chances are equal that a sperm carrying C^w will meet an egg carrying C^w or C^y, resulting in the combinations C^wC^w and C^wC^y in equality. So, too, for the equally numerous sperms bearing C^y which, uniting with the two types of eggs, will give rise to C^wC^y and C^yC^y, also in equality. That is to say, the next, or F_2 generation, will consist of three forms: the ordinary white one (C^wC^w), *semi-lutea* (C^wC^y), and *lutea* (C^yC^y) in a ratio of approximately 1 : 2 : 1 (see Text-fig. 3).

This result is always to be expected from a mating between two individuals heterozygous for a given pair of allelomorphs. Indeed, such a ratio must inevitably arise when two objects having corresponding and alternative forms are combined at random: it is not a special property of genetics. If we toss two pennies together a hundred times, they will fall both obverse approximately twenty-five times, one obverse and one reverse approximately fifty times, and both reverse approximately twenty-five times: forming three classes in a ratio of 1 : 2 : 1, as in the F_2 generation of the Currant Moth, and they appear in the same proportion for the same reason.

It will, of course, be appreciated that the genetic results, like those obtained by tossing coins, are average values only, subject to the laws of chance, and that in general the larger the numbers used the closer is their approach to the theoretical expectation.

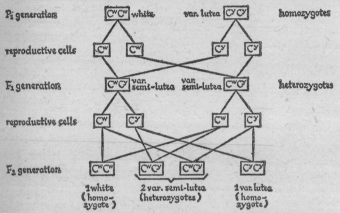

Fig. 3   Segregation in the second hybrid generation (F_2) of a cross between the normal white Currant Moth and its variety *lutea*.

It is therefore important to determine whether a given departure from an expected ratio (say, one of 1 : 2 : 1) is or is not within the ordinary limits of probability. Those limits are by convention reached when an event can take place fortuitously only once in twenty trials, or less.[1] For pure chance becomes so important when it may be expected to occur more frequently than this, that we have then no right to ascribe an occurrence to any other cause. Methods for calculating this probability are given by Mather (1943).

It is well to reflect briefly upon the mating which has just been outlined. On crossing the white with the deep yellow form *lutea*, the result in the F_1 generation was a blend so far as the *character*

[1] This level is adopted because the chances that an event shall be due to luck decline so rapidly beyond it. Thus we estimate the significance of, e.g., an average by calculating its standard error. The chances are 1 in 3 that the true value lies outside the standard error ×1, there are 1 in 22 (approximately our 20 : 1 level) that they lie outside the standard error ×2, but only 1 in 370 that they lie outside the standard error ×3. The probability of a merely fortuitous result is therefore much reduced when the value giving a 1 in 20 chance is only slightly exceeded.

(wing colour) was concerned; for the offspring were of an intermediate shade (var. *semi-lutea*). But the hereditary factors concerned must have preserved their identity without contamination. For, on inter-breeding the *semi-lutea* of the F_1 generation, the original types crystallize out, as it were, among the F_2 progeny. Moreover, they prove to be as pure as they were in original P_1 generation. It would be possible by breeding together two of the 'extracted' whites, or two of the 'extracted' *lutea*, to found true-breeding white or deep yellow strains, and these would not be diluted or be in any way less 'pure' because the determinants which control them had been passed through a 'hybrid' mixture.

Blending leads to uniformity, and that is the very antithesis of these results. Had the hereditary units contaminated one another, the F_2 generation would have been less variable than the F_1. This was not so. The F_1 generation consisted of a single form only, *semi-lutea*, while the F_2 comprised three forms, white, *semi-lutea*, and full *lutea*. Though the *character*, wing-colour, had indeed blended in the F_1 generation, the *genes* controlling it preserved their identity unimpaired.

We have just studied a mating between two heterozygotes, from which we have inferred certain features of heredity. Now the deductions of science should enable one to make predictions. Indeed, it should at this stage be possible without additional information for any one to discover what will be the result of mating a heterozygote with a homozygote. In the instance which we have chosen, this would be a cross between *semi-lutea* and either of the other two forms. As we have seen, *semi-lutea* possesses the allelomorphic pair C^wC^y, producing in equality reproductive cells bearing C^w or C^y. Suppose we cross it with the normal (white) form, C^wC^w, which manufactures but a single type of reproductive cell, carrying C^w only. The combinations C^wC^w and C^wC^y must thus arise and with equal frequency, so that two classes (normal and *semi-lutea*) are produced in a 1 : 1 ratio (see Text-fig. 5, p. 176).

Such a mating, between a heterozygote and a homozygote, is called a *back-cross*, and it leads to segregation in equality. It will be obvious that a corresponding result would have been obtained had we crossed *semi-lutea* with the other homozygote, the full *lutea*. The offspring would then have comprised *semi-lutea* and *lutea* in equal numbers.

By taking a small additional step it will now be possible to relate all that has so far been said in this chapter to the special needs of butterfly collectors. The preceding instance is one in which the heterozygote is intermediate in appearance between the two homozygous types. That condition is uncommon. Indeed, it has not yet been reported in British butterflies; though there is no reason why it should not be found among them, and it may well be the good fortune of someone who reads this chapter to make the discovery. More frequently, the heterozygote is indistinguishable from one of the two homozygous classes. In these circumstances, two of the terms in the 1 : 2 : 1 ratio cannot be separated by inspection, so producing a ratio of 3 : 1. The character which is as fully developed in the heterozygote as in the homozygote is called a 'dominant', that which is obscured in the heterozygote, appearing only in the homozygote, is called a 'recessive'. The slight modifications introduced by this phenomenon of *dominance* may best be explained with the help of an example.

The Small Copper Butterfly, *Lycaena phlaeas* (Plate 22), is a species whose affinities, habits, and distribution have already been described. In a rare variety, *obsoleta* Tutt, the copper band is absent from the hind-wings. It may disappear almost completely; alternatively, a trace of it may remain in the form of short copper lines along the nervures, and specimens in which these are present are sometimes called var. *radiata* Tutt. However, the distinction is of doubtful value, since the two conditions grade into one another, and a few copper scales are present on the nervures in nearly all specimens in which the band is lost. Mr J. W. O. Holmes has demonstrated that the development of this band is controlled by a single pair of allelomorphs, which may be represented as *oo* in *obsoleta* and *OO* in the normal form (the nomenclature adopted here is explained on pp. 176–7). If these two forms are crossed, whether *obsoleta* be the male or the female is immaterial, the resulting F_1 generation will consist of heterozygotes of the constitution *Oo*, produced precisely as were the *semi-lutea* individuals of the corresponding generation in the Currant Moth example. They differ, however, from that example since, instead of being intermediates between the two homozygotes, they exactly resemble one of them, the typical banded parent. An intact copper band on the hind-wings is thus dominant to a fragmented one, which is recessive. Thus the F_1 individuals are normal in appearance but heterozygous in constitution, and they produce reproductive cells in which the members of the allelomorphic pairs have segregated, so that half carry *O* and

half *o*. The sperms bearing *O* combine with the eggs bearing *O*
or *o* to give the combinations *OO* and *Oo* in equality; while the
equally numerous sperms bearing *o* combine with the two types
of eggs to produce *Oo* and *oo*, also in equality. Three classes of
offspring, *OO*, *Oo*, *oo*, thus arise, and they are distributed in a
ratio of 1 : 2 : 1, as they were in the F₂ generation of the Currant
Moth. But since in the Small Copper the heterozygotes (*Oo*)
cannot be distinguished from one of the homozygous classes, the
normal one (*OO*), only two visibly separable forms appear in the
F₂ generation: normals and var. *obsoleta*, in a ratio of 3 : 1 (see
Text-fig. 4).

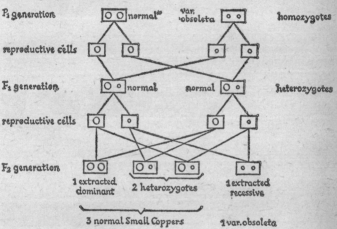

Fig. 4   Segregation in the second hybrid generation (F₂) of a cross
between a normal Small Copper (dominant) and its variety *obsoleta*
(recessive).

It can be demonstrated by breeding that three classes, distributed as 1 : 2 : 1, are concealed within this 3 : 1 ratio. If we
cross with var. *obsoleta* the normal individuals that appear in the
F₂ generation, it will be found that one-third of them produce
normal progeny only while two-thirds produce normals and
var. *obsoleta* in equality: clearly two distinct types, homozygotes
and heterozygotes distributed as 1 : 2, are included among the
apparent normals. For when var. *obsoleta* (*oo*) is mated with the
homozygous normals (*OO*), all the offspring will have the constitution *Oo* and will manifest the dominant normal character.

But when we mate var. *obsoleta* with the heterozygous normals (*Oo*), we perform a back-cross, as in the Currant Moth (p. 173), resulting in segregation in equal numbers (Text-fig. 5). This is the back-cross between the heterozygote and the recessive. Evidently the other one, that between the heterozygote and the dominant homozygote, must produce a brood of normals only, since all of them will receive at least one *O*, supplied by their homozygous parent. But it could again be shown by breeding that such uniformity is deceptive; that homozygotes and heterozygotes are once more present in approximate equality. The appropriate method of doing so would be similar to that used in analysing the 3 : 1 ratio into its components of 1 : 2 : 1; that is to say, the individuals to be tested should be mated with recessives. In this way, the factor having the dominant effect can be brought in by one parent only; thus that producing the recessive character will be unmasked.

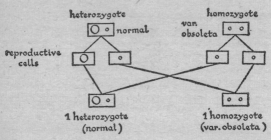

Fig. 5 A back-cross (heterozygote × homozygote) between a normal, but heterozygous, Small Copper (as produced in Fig. 4) and its recessive variety *obsoleta*. The progeny segregate in a 1 : 1 ratio.

The type of nomenclature adopted in the last example should always be employed when dominance is complete or nearly so, and this is by far the more usual situation. A small letter is taken to represent the gene producing the recessive condition, while the capital of the same letter indicates that having the dominant effect. This system is convenient since it at once makes the dominance effect of a particular gene clear, while the use of the same letter, whether large or small, denotes that the genes are both members of the same allelomorphic pair; a matter of importance when several pairs are studied simultaneously. The letter employed should, where possible, be the initial of the varietal rather than of the normal form. It is thus easier to obtain a suitable selection of letters for use in the same species.

We have so far followed the distribution of a single pair of allelomorphs controlling a given pair of contrasted characters. It will now be necessary briefly to consider the segregation of two or more pairs of allelomorphs when these are studied together. This situation was examined by Mendel himself, who provided an interpretation of it which we now know to be generally, though not always, correct. He stated that the distribution of any one pair of allelomorphs is not affected by the distribution of any other pair, a rule usually called the Law of Independent Assortment. Consider two pairs of allelomorphs each controlling a pair of contrasted characters in which dominance is complete. Each of them, treated separately, will segregate in the F_2 generation so as to produce two classes in a ratio of 3 : 1, as already explained (p. 174). The law of independent assortment tells us that, taken together, they will give the result obtained by combining two 3 : 1 ratios at random; that is to say, four classes, distributed in a ratio of 9 : 3 : 3 : 1.

I do not think that this type of mating has yet been studied experimentally in a British butterfly. To illustrate it we must therefore take an example which is in some degree fictitious, though I should be greatly surprised if it proved to be incorrect. Albino forms are extremely widespread among animals, and the vast majority of them appear to be inherited as simple recessives. One of them is well known, as a rare variety called *alba* Tutt (Plate 22), in the Small Copper Butterfly. Here the copper is replaced by pure white, while the black markings are unaffected. It is reasonable to assume, though it has not been proved, that the normal Small Copper is a simple dominant to the albino. The F_1 generation of a cross between these two forms would thus be of the ordinary copper colour while, when such F_1 specimens are inter-bred to produce the F_2 generation, normals and albinos would appear in a 3 : 1 ratio. The genes responsible for var. *alba* may be represented as *aa*, and their normal allelomorphs as *AA*.

We can now examine the combination of two pairs of allelomorphs. If we were fortunate enough to secure a cross between the vars. *alba* and *obsoleta* in the Small Copper, *L. phlaeas*, the two dominant conditions would manifest themselves in the F_1 generation, for each parent would contribute the normal allelomorph of the other type. Thus we may represent *alba* as *aaOO* and *obsoleta* as *AAoo*. The members of each allelomorphic pair will segregate, one passing into each of the reproductive cells. Those produced by var. *alba* will therefore carry *aO*, and those produced by *obsoleta* will carry *Ao*. The F_1 generation will consequently be of the constitution *AaOo* (Text-fig. 6). Such specimens must be copper in colour and possess an intact band. The recovery of the normal form upon crossing two varieties used to be regarded as somewhat mysterious. Its explanation should now be clear.

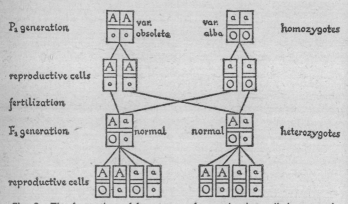

Fig. 6   The formation of four types of reproductive cells by normal Small Coppers of the F_1 generation of a cross between the recessive varieties *obsoleta* and *alba*. Members of the same pair of allelomorphs are separated by a single line, different allelomorphs by a double line.

The normal but doubly heterozygous specimens of the F_1 generation will all produce four types of reproductive cells: *AO*, *Ao*, *aO*, *ao*. For *A* has an equal opportunity of segregating with *O* or with *o*, like its equally numerous allelomorph *a* (Text-fig. 6). On inter-breeding two of these F_1 specimens, the four types of reproductive cells to which each gives rise can be combined with one another in sixteen ways, which produce nine distinct genetic types,[1] and these give rise to four visibly distinct forms. In all, twelve will be normally coloured and four will be albinos (a 3 : 1 ratio), while twelve will possess an intact and four a

[1] These are *AAOO, AAoo, AaOO, AAOo, AaOo, aoOO, Aaoo, aaOO, aaoo*, in a ratio of 1 : 1 : 2 : 2 : 4 : 2 : 2 : 1 : 1. Without dominance, each of them would be visibly separable.

	AO	Ao	aO	ao
AO	AAOO normal	AAOo normal	AaOO normal	AaOo normal
Ao	AAOo normal	AAoo var. obsoleta	AaOo normal	Aaoo var. obsoleta
aO	AaOO normal	AaOo normal	aaOO var. alba	aaOo var. alba
ao	AaOo normal	Aaoo var. obsoleta	aaOo var. alba	aaoo var. obsoleta + alba

F_2 generation: 9 normal Small Coppers, 3 var. obsoleta, 3 var. alba, 1 var. obsoleta + alba.

Fig. 7   The recombination at fertilization of the F_1 reproductive cells whose formation is illustrated in Fig. 6. They produce an F_2 generation of four types in a ratio of 9 : 3 : 3 : 1.

fragmented band on the hind-wings (also a 3 : 1 ratio). Taken together, nine will be normal Small Coppers, three will be var. *alba*, three will be var. *obsoleta*, while one will be a new form combining *alba* and *obsoleta* (see Text-fig. 7).

This double recessive may be used to demonstrate the result of a back-cross involving two pairs of allelomorphs. Having the constitution *aaoo*, it can produce a single type of reproductive cell only, carrying *ao*. We have already seen that the normal but doubly heterozygous Small Copper (*AaOo*) forms four kinds of reproductive cells in equality. Thus four combinations must arise on mating these two forms: *AaOo* (normals), *aaOo* (*alba*), *Aaoo* (*obsoleta*), and *aaoo* (*alba-obsoleta*). Evidently they will appear in equal numbers, as is always to be anticipated in a back-cross. This result, the union of the single type of reproductive cell carrying *ao* with the four types produced by the double heterozygote, is illustrated in the lowest horizontal line of Text-fig. 7.

LINKAGE

It will be apparent that the property of independent assortment allows us to bring together distinct varieties and to combine them in the same specimen, yet such opportunities are not unlimited. To understand the check imposed upon them it will be necessary very briefly to discuss the manner in which the genes are transmitted.

Every cell in the body contains in its nucleus microscopic structures, the *chromosomes*, which can be demonstrated by staining with certain dyes. This can only be done when the cell divides, yet we know from indirect evidence that they persist, in some form, from one cell-division to the next. The number of chromosomes in each cell is normally constant in all the individuals of a species, though it may not be the same in different species: the total may be less than ten and rarely exceeds a few dozen. Chromosomes are present in pairs, each of which is, in certain respects, different from any other: the two members of each pair are said to be *homologous*. This distinction between the different sets of chromosomes is particularly obvious when, as often, the individual members differ from one another in size, for two of every size are included within each cell. The members of a homologous pair are derived respectively from the two parents. When an individual produces its reproductive cells, the two chromosomes of each homologous pair separate, *one* passing into every sperm or egg. Thus the reproductive cells are, from this point of view also, worth but half a cell each, since they contain only half the number of chromosomes found in the body cells. That number is, however, restored at fertilization, when a sperm and an egg fuse.

The remarkable parallel between the distribution and behaviour of the chromosomes and of the allelomorphs cannot fail to attract attention, and it is now known that the chromosomes are the actual bearers of the genes. But since their number is small, and that of the genes must be great, amounting to thousands in any species, it is clear that each chromosome must carry many of them. This must limit the application of the law of Independent Assortment as enunciated by Mendel, who worked before chromosomes had been discovered. The genes do indeed assort independently of one another so long as they are carried in different pairs of chromosomes. When, however, they are situated in the same pair, the segregation of the allelomorphs is not independent, since they are travelling in the same vehicles and therefore they usually reach a common destination. The tendency for different pairs of allelomorphs to assort together because they are carried in the same pair of chromosomes, is called *Linkage*.

No instance of linkage has yet been reported in butterflies, though the condition has been encountered in moths. The chief reason for this is that breeders of butterflies have so seldom studied the inheritance of two varieties of a species simultaneously. It must be added that the chromosome numbers are rather large in the Lepidoptera, generally ranging between one dozen and three dozen pairs; so that linkage is bound to be much less frequent than in groups with a lower chromosome number. Man has 23 pairs of chromosomes and the fruit-fly, *Drosophila melanogaster*, on which so much genetic work has been done, has only four pairs.

The study of linkage is of great importance, for it throws much light upon the mechanism of heredity, demonstrating as it does the relation between the behaviour of the chromosomes and of the genes which they bear. One example only of this need be mentioned. All the genes carried in the same chromosome will evidently be linked with one another. Consequently, they are said to belong to a single 'linkage group'. If the account of heredity given in this chapter is a valid one, there must be as many such linkage groups as there are pairs of chromosomes, and there can be no more. The number of the one is estimated by the result of breeding, that of the other by a microscopic examination of cells. The agreement of the two findings, obtained in numerous plants and animals by means so distinct, provides convincing testimony of the truth of genetic theory.

It is not my intention to discuss in any detail a phenomenon such as linkage, which is as yet unknown in butterflies. But it would be unfair to withhold a few directions which may lead to its discovery: a prize which awaits any one who breeds these insects.

If we look once more at the example used to illustrate independent assortment, that of the Small Copper Butterfly, *L. phlaeas*, it will be noticed that four classes appear both in the F_2 generation and in the back-cross. Two of them resemble the original parents, while the other two are the 'recombination classes' in which a pair of characters has been interchanged. That is to say, we started with one var. *obsoleta*, having the normal copper colour, and one var. *alba* having the normal intact band on the hind-wings. These two forms reappeared in the F_2 generation and in the back-cross. But with them were the two recombination classes, one composed of insects that were normal, and the other of insects that were abnormal, in both respects. If the hereditary factors controlling these two characters were carried in the same pair of chromosomes, the two recombination classes would be unduly rare or absent; for, in such circumstances, the genes cannot readily be interchanged.[1]

The example of the Small Copper was so arranged that the original parents each possessed *one* of the two recessive characters; so that the two recombination classes, subsequently obtained, are those with neither and those with both recessive characters. Had we, on the other hand, started with these latter types, an ordinary Small Copper and the double variety *alba-obsoleta*, the recombination classes would, of course, have been different: comprising those specimens which are *alba* alone and those which are *obsoleta* alone.

The deficiency of the recombination classes is more easily detected in the back-cross, in which all four classes should appear in equality, than in an F_2 generation. In the latter, linkage will lead to an excess of the two middle terms of the 9 : 3 : 3 : 1 ratio if the recombination classes are the double dominants and the double recessives; if they are those with one recessive character each, the first and last terms will be in undue excess.

Any one who breeds butterflies should, where possible, study the inheritance of two pairs of allelomorphs, each controlling a pair of characters in which dominance is complete. If he finds that his recombination classes fall below expectation, he should suspect that he has discovered an instance of linkage. In these circumstances, if unacquainted with the subject, he would be well advised to read the sections on linkage and crossing-over in any up-to-date text-book of Genetics. He should also consult a work on statistical methods in order to discover if the numbers which he has bred are large enough for the necessary conclusions to be drawn from them (e.g., Mather, 1943).

[1] That they can be interchanged at all will, without additional information, seem curious. But, when the reproductive cells are formed, a reciprocal transference of material between homologous chromosomes can be demonstrated. This allows some degree of recombination between the genes which they carry (an occurrence called 'crossing-over').

MULTIPLE ALLELOMORPHS

It would not be right to leave this subject without giving some information which may help entomologists to make original genetic discoveries of another kind. For there exists an important phenomenon known as *multiple allelomorphism*, which must certainly occur throughout the Lepidoptera, though, as with linkage, it has been recognized among the British species only in moths. It has, however, been studied extensively in other groups of insects; for example, the Diptera.

As already explained, allelomorphs can exist in alternative states, thus producing contrasted characters. Yet they are not necessarily restricted to two phases. Three, four, or more forms of the same gene have on occasion been encountered, so giving rise to 'multiple allelomorphs'. Since in nearly all animals (though not necessarily in plants) the homologous chromosomes which carry the allelomorphs exist in pairs only, not higher values, no more than two members of any multiple allelomorph series can be employed by the same individual insect.

The changes which any gene can undergo appear to be strictly limited to produce modifications of a single character or set of characters. We do not find, for instance, that a gene can exist in two phases, one of which controls colour but not wing-shape and the other wing-shape but not colour. On the contrary, multiple allelomorphs can be arranged in a series affecting progressively the development of the characters for which they are responsible. Moreover, the dominance relationships of multiple allelomorphs are characteristic of them. The normal wild-type condition, produced by one member of the series, is usually dominant to the varieties determined by each of the other members. But when two of these recessive forms are combined, the effect is an intermediate one: dominance is here absent. Thus it is frequently found that the gene responsible for albinism may be replaced by other allelomorphs which do not completely prevent colour-production, as well as by that responsible for the normal full coloration. To take an instance from mammals, rabbits possess a series of this kind comprising six known terms: the normal brown, dark chinchilla, light chinchilla, pale chinchilla, Himalayan (white with black extremities), and the true albino (white with pink eyes). Any two, but no more than two, of these can be brought together in the same individual. Brown is fully dominant to each of the others, while the five recessives give intermediate results when combined. The genes responsible for such a series should be indicated by the same letter, the capital being used for the dominant and the lower-case, distinguished by an index, for each recessive. The index is, however, omitted for the most extreme of the recessive forms. Thus A, a^h, and a represent the genes for brown, Himalayan, and albino coloration in rabbits.

There can be no doubt that many such series await discovery in butterflies, and I think it highly probable that one of them is associated with albinism in the Small Copper. A deep cream-coloured form, *schmidtii* Gerh, is known in addition to the pure white *alba*. I suspect that when either *schmidtii* or *alba* is crossed with the normal form, the F_1 generation will be normal and that a ratio of 3 normals to 1 *alba* (or *schmidtii*) would be obtained in F_2. This would show that these forms behave as simple recessives. Assuming such knowledge, we may consider a cross between *schmidtii* and *alba*. Two possibilities confront us. First, it may be that the genes controlling them are not allelomorphic. In that event, each form would carry the normal allelomorph of the other, and the F_1 generation would all be of the full copper colour (a situation similar to that obtained in the cross *obsoleta* × *alba*, p. 178). In these circumstances, the *schmidtii* gene should be called s and the *alba* gene a. *Schmidtii* would have the constitution $ssAA$, and *alba* $SSaa$, so that the F_1 generation would be double heterozygotes $SsAa$. I do not anticipate such a result. Rather, I would here suspect multiple allelomorphism. On that assumption, a cross between *schmidtii* and *alba* should produce an F_1 generation in which all the specimens were of a creamy-white shade, intermediate between the two parents. For, in these circumstances, only a single pair of allelomorphs would be concerned in the production of the two varieties. The *schmidtii* gene would then be represented by a^s, and the *alba* factor by a; *schmidtii* would have the constitution $a^s a^s$ and *alba*, aa. One would not possess the normal allelomorph of the other, so that specimens of the F_1 generation would have the constitution $a^s a$, and the normal allelomorph would be absent from them.

These two F_1 results sufficiently distinguish the behaviour of characters when controlled respectively by genes which are not allelomorphs and those which are. Of course, the F_2 generations arising in each of these situations would also be distinct. If two pairs of allelomorphs were concerned, the F_2 insects would comprise normals and pale forms in a ratio of 9 : 7. This would really be a ratio of 9 : 3 : 3 : 1 in which the last three terms are not separable owing to the close similarity of vars. *schmidtii* and *alba* and the absence of dominance between them. With multiple allelomorphs on the other hand, no normals at all would appear in F_2. That generation would segregate in a ratio of 1 : 2 : 1, in which the two end terms would be *schmidtii* and *alba*, while the middle one would comprise intermediates. These three classes would almost certainly grade into one another owing to the similarity of the two pure types, so giving an F_2 generation composed wholly of pale forms which would merely appear rather variable. The fact that pure-breeding lines can at once be established by mating together two *alba* or two *schmidtii* respectively, distinguishes multiple-allelomorphism from the condition in which a gene has a somewhat variable expression (p. 218).

The collector should now have no difficulty in detecting multiple allelomorphism should he be fortunate enough to encounter it among the butterflies which he breeds. The phenomenon is of much interest from evolutionary and other points of view and is known in foreign butterflies.

SEX

Sex is a character which is inherited, and in definite proportions generally approaching equality. It therefore segregates and, moreover, nearly always in a clear-cut fashion, for though intermediates between the two sexes are known, they are very uncommon. These facts remind one of the mechanism which has so far been discussed in this chapter. It is right that they should do so, for sex is indeed controlled by genes carried in the chromosomes. Their method of transmission must now briefly be studied.

It has already been mentioned that the chromosomes are present in corresponding pairs (homologous chromosomes), the members of which are derived respectively from the two parents. In the male, in Lepidoptera, the genes responsible for sex-determination are carried by one of these pairs, whose members are called *X-chromosomes*. The female, however, possesses but a single X-chromosome, for its partner bears very few genes of any kind and none controlling sex; this is called the *Y-chromosome*.[1] The X- and Y-chromosomes are together known as *sex-chromosomes*. All the other chromosomes (the so-called 'autosomes') are present in homologous pairs in both sexes, and they are not directly concerned with the differential control of sex.

It is now known that the actual agents which determine sex are the X-chromosomes. If an extra Y-chromosome be added, owing to an abnormal cell-division, it is without effect; but an additional X-chromosome profoundly influences the sex of its possessor. In butterflies, every sperm receives one X-chromosome, owing to the segregation of the XX pair in the male. Half the eggs receive X and half receive Y, owing to the segregation of the XY pair in the female. The chances are then equal that a sperm, necessarily carrying X, fertilizes an egg with X or with Y, so producing males (XX) and females (XY) in equality. This simple distribution is illustrated in Text-fig. 8.

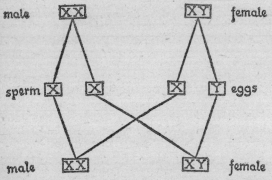

Fig. 8   The sex of a butterfly is determined by the number of X-chromosomes in its cells. Note that the sex-control is quantitative since the X-chromosomes are interchanged between the sexes at successive generations.

In Mammals, and therefore in Man, the chromosome outfit controls only the reproductive glands, deciding whether they shall be male or female (testes or ovaries). These glands then

[1] In the majority of animals, including Mammals and Man, this arrangement is reversed, the male possessing the XY pair and the female the two X-chromosomes. However, the female is of the XY type in birds and some fish, as it is in the Trichoptera (Caddis-Flies), from which the Lepidoptera are derived.

produce a special type of secretion, a 'hormone', which, when passing into the blood-stream, circulates through the body and determines the sex of all other parts. In these circumstances, early castration will obviously have a profound effect upon the body. Not so in insects, for here the sex of every part is controlled directly by the chromosome-constitution of the cells composing it. Hence the sexual characters are unaffected by the removal of the ovary or the testis, or even by their transplantation; operations which have successfully been carried out on the Lepidoptera.

Yet such a situation is extremely sensitive to abnormalities which may affect the distribution of the sex-chromosomes. One of the two X-chromosomes in a male is occasionally lost during a cell division, so leaving one of the daughter-cells with but a single X. But this converts the cell to the female type, so that all parts of the body to which it gives rise will be female; for the absence of the Y-Chromosome is irrelevant, since it is nearly functionless and quite so in regard to sex. The resulting individual, of mixed sex, will be one in which male and female parts develop simultaneously side by side, and a sexual mosaic of this kind is called a *gynandromorph*. It is one form of *hermaphrodite*, a term applied to any animal in which the two sexes are combined, by whatever means this may be done.

In insects, the first cell of the new individual, arising from the fusion of the sperm with the egg, divides into two cells which will form the right and left halves of the adult body. Therefore if one of the two X-chromosomes of a male is lost at the first cell division, giving rise to one cell with the original two X-chromosomes and the other with one, one half the adult body will be male and the other half female. The line of division in such a 'bilateral gynandromorph' is remarkably sharp, passing down the length of the body, the two halves being of opposite sex not only in colour and pattern but also in structure: consequently they are generally of different sizes. Should the abnormality in cell-division occur at a later stage in development, a small patch only of the inappropriate sex will be produced.

Evidently the loss of one X-chromosome will lead to the production of an individual which is half, or more than half, male, but not to one which is more than half female. Yet that condition can also arise, but in a slightly different way. The chromosomes grow, and each splits into two before the cell divides, so that the two daughter cells each receive the same number of them that was possessed by the single cell from which they were derived. But the products of the division of the X-chromosomes may occasionally fail to separate. If this happens in a male, with two X-chromosomes, one of the resulting cells will have three X-chromosomes, and will die, and the other will have one. This would, as before, produce a patch of female cells if it occurs at a later stage, but it could not give rise to a bilateral gynandromorph (owing to the death of the other cell). If the same thing happens in a female, with one X-chromosome, one of the two resulting cells would be left with no X-chromosome. This would die, and the other would be left with two, as in the male. In this way, a patch of the male sex may appear in a female. For example, in the Silver-studded Blue, *Plebejus argus*, the right fore-wing may be scattered with the blue scales of the male. It is not as blue as that of a normal male, probably because it chances that in this species the products of cell-division are no longer dispersed with perfect regularity at this late stage in development.

Gynandromorphism has been extensively studied in other insects (Diptera) and it has been found that the tendency to produce it is often inherited. Indeed, it may be due to a single pair of allelomorphs. Thus, though gynandromorphs have been recorded in almost every species of British butterfly, they seem to be especially frequent in some of them and commoner in some districts than others. For instance, it has been said, I am sure correctly, that the phenomenon is much more often encountered in the Irish than in the British race of the Common Blue, but it is exceedingly rare in all races. Similarly, later stages in female gynandromorphism sometimes occur in the Chalk-hill Blue, *Lysandra coridon*, in which a small patch of the male colour will be found on one or more wings, usually affecting their size also. Specimens of this kind have certainly been found more frequently at Royston in Cambridgeshire than elsewhere, and are named *roystonensis* Pickett. It is noteworthy that corresponding stages in male gynandromorphism are much rarer in this insect. This entirely agrees with what we know of the genetics of gynandromorphism. Hereditary factors determine not only its occurrence but also its type; whether taking place in the male or the female, or at a late or an early stage in development.

The loss of an autosome may give rise to a mosaic condition, but one not associated with a sexual abnormality. Though not unknown, this is very rare, for such failures in cell-division are nearly always fatal except when they affect the X-chromosomes, which are adjusted to vary normally from one to two.

Two phenomena, linkage and multiple allelomorphism, have so far been discussed in this chapter, which, though well known in moths, still await discovery in British butterflies, and the study of sex supplies two more. These are intersexuality and sex linkage. The four of them are likely to provide notable rewards for the investigator who is prepared to use simple methods carefully.

Intersexuality is a form of hermaphroditism quite different in origin from gynandromorphism. We may look once more at Text-fig. 8, for certain considerations not yet mentioned follow from a consideration of it. It will be observed that the sex of the female offspring is due to the presence of a single X-chromosome. Yet this was derived from their father, and was partly responsible for making him a male. The sex of the male offspring is due to the presence of two X-chromosomes, one of which comes from their mother, where it was the very agent which determined her sex as female. That is to say, the X-chromosomes are constantly shuffled across from one sex to the other. They cannot therefore carry genes for the respective sexes; on the contrary, their action must be quantitative, one dose evoking one sex and two doses the other. Indeed, it is known that in Lepidoptera the autosomes carry genes determining femaleness and the X-chromosomes genes determining maleness. The genes for maleness are in effective excess when present in the double dose, supplied by the two X-chromosomes, and those for femaleness are in effective excess when balanced against a single X-chromosome only.

So long as this quantitative relationship is observed, sex determination will work correctly, whatever the absolute values of the male and female determinants may be. The male type might, for example, amount to twenty arbitrary units and the female to thirty. But in another race of the species evolving in isolation, the absolute values may have changed, becoming, for instance, 30 for the male type and 45 for the female. This system would work correctly in each race, the varying dosage of male units (in the X-chromosome) being in effective excess or deficiency compared with the fixed dosage of the female ones (in the autosomes). But difficulties may arise if such races are crossed. A male determinant of value 30 from one race might then be balanced against a female determinant, also of value 30, from the other. Such a situation leads to the production of an individual in which the effective separation of the sexes is not achieved. In these circumstances it will develop for a time as its correct sex and then switch over and continue its development as the opposite one. Individuals of this kind are called *intersexes*. Not only do they differ from gynandromorphs in their origin, but they also do so in two other ways. First, the male and female parts do not develop simultaneously but one after the other, so that all the earlier formed structures are of a different sex from those formed later. Secondly, the two sexes do not necessarily occupy distinct areas of the body or wings: some regions may have characteristics of an intermediate type.

Intersexuality has been studied in detail by Goldschmidt (1933) on the Gipsy Moth, *Lymantria dispar* L., a species formerly found in the English fens but now extinct. He obtained different degrees of inter-sexuality by crossing different European and Asiatic races of it. Should the collector cross two geographically isolated races of butterflies (say from England and Ireland) and obtain sexual abnormalities among the F_1 or F_2 offspring, he will probably have encountered intersexuality. This could be verified by an examination of the sex characters of the specimens, which, as explained, would differ from those of gynandromorphs. Such a discovery would be an important one, since the appearance of sexual abnormalities on crossing geographical races marks one of the principal steps towards their conversion into distinct species.

It has been pointed out that when two or more pairs of allelomorphs are carried in the same pair of chromosomes they fail to assort independently, that is to say, they are 'linked'. Now the X-chromosomes usually bear some genes other than those for sex, and so control characters entirely distinct from it. Such genes must be linked with those responsible for sex-determination and therefore distributed relative to sex, instead of being independent of it as are those carried in the autosomes, which comprise all those so far known in British butterflies.

A detailed analysis of sex-linkage would require somewhat extensive treatment, which would not be justified in discussing butterflies, in which the phenomenon has not yet been found. Yet it is bound to occur in the group, so that the following guide to its detection may be welcome. A recessive sex-linked character would only rarely appear in a male butterfly, since the genes controlling it (carried in the X-chromosome) would have to be homozygous. It would be much commoner in females, because in that sex a single gene suffices for its production[1]: for the Y-chromosome being practically functionless, the operation of genes carried in X cannot be masked by normal allelomorphs in Y.

It may at any time be found that when a female variety is crossed with a normal male all its offspring are normal, but that in the F_2 generation half the females are varieties, while all the males and half the females are normal. This is a 3 : 1 ratio but distributed relative to sex, and it indicates the existence of sex-linkage. This should, if possible, be verified by breeding the male form, which could be done by mating a female of the variety to a heterozygous male. All four types (male and female varieties, and normal males and females) should then appear in equal numbers.

Sex-linkage was originally detected in a moth, and it provided the first known association between a gene and sex. This was in 1906, and the form used was the pale variety *dohrnii* Koenig (then called *lacticolor* Raynor) of the Currant Moth, *Abraxas grossulariata*. It has never yet been found in a butterfly: I hope that this discovery may not be long delayed.[2]

CONCLUSIONS

The principles of genetics which have been examined in this chapter depend fundamentally upon the circumstance that the genes are extremely permanent, for they do not contaminate one another when brought together into the same cell, but retain their identity intact. This has the highly important consequence that genes which have arisen far apart in time or in space can be brought together in the same individual, so allowing a wide combination of distinct characters. Yet such permanence can only be achieved if the further condition is fulfilled that, apart from contamination by others, the genes themselves seldom

[1] Its difference in frequency between the two sexes can be exactly defined. If p be the fraction of females in a wild population which show a recessive sex-linked character, the fraction of males which do so is p^2. Consequently the ratio of such females to males is 1 : p. Thus if a sex-linked recessive variety is found in one female butterfly in a thousand under natural conditions, it will occur in one male in a million.

[2] The existence of 'partial sex-linkage' has been detected in some animals including Man. It has not been discovered, but may well occur in the Lepidoptera. A discussion of the subject is outside the scope of this book; for an account of it, see Ford, 1973, *Genetics for Medical Students* (7th Edition) London: Chapman & Hall Ltd.

change. Obviously, they must sometimes do so, otherwise they could not exist in different states (allelomorphs), but the occurrence is a very rare one. It is called *mutation*, and on the average it takes place in a given gene in perhaps one individual in a million, though a gene will occasionally be found which mutates in one individual in fifty thousand. This, which represents about its upper limit of frequency, is still a very rare event, and butterfly collectors are unlikely to encounter it; though both the existence and the rarity of mutation are matters of fundamental importance in evolution. When a gene mutates, it does so suddenly. Moreover, it can change not only from the normal to an 'abnormal' state, producing a variety which is thereafter inherited in the ordinary Mendelian way, but back from the 'abnormal' to the normal; evidently, therefore, the act of mutation does not involve irreparable loss or damage to the gene concerned.

We have so far regarded the genes as units having characteristic effects. Neither their possible interactions with one another nor with the environment have been considered. Before discussing this subject, however, it will be helpful to apply the theories which have just been outlined to the practical needs of butterfly collectors.

a. Satyridae (Meadow Brown)

b. Satyridae: the underground chrysalis of the Grayling (x1.5)

c. Nymphalidae (Purple Emperor)

d. Lycaenidae (Small Copper—x3)

e. Lycaenidae (Green Hairstreak— x 2.8)

f. Hesperiidae (Grizzled Skipper, cocoon opened—x2.5)

9. THE CHRYSALIDS OF BUTTERFLIES

a. Small Heath (x1.5)

b. Holly Blue (x1.5)

c. The imported Large Copper alive at Wicken (natural size)

d. The Dingy Skipper sitting 'like a moth' (natural size)

e. Small Skipper at rest in sunshine (x1.5)

f. Meadow Brown after an attack by a bird (natural size)

10. BUTTERFLIES AT REST: AND ATTACKED BY A BIRD

a. Butterfly laying a cluster of eggs: Small Tortoiseshell (x4/3)

b. Gregarious caterpillars: Small Tortoiseshell

c. Butterflies mating: Meadow Brown

d. White Admiral: Caterpillars and hibernaculum (x4)

11. LARVAL AND ADULT HABITS

a. Normal scales in position (x35)

b. Normal scales and scent-scales removed (x42)

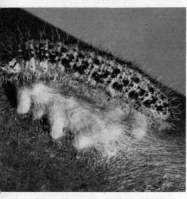

c. Large White caterpillar, with cocoons of *Apanteles glomeratus* (x2.5)

d. *Apanteles glomeratus, Apechthis compunctor, Phryxe vulgaris* (x1.75)

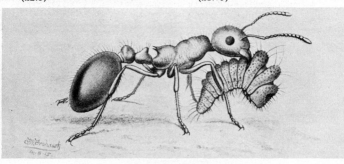

e. Ant carrying caterpillar of the Large Blue (x11)

12.

a. Wicken Fen, where the Swallow-tail, and the recently imported Large Copper, fly

b. A ride in the New Forest; the haunt of the White Admiral, Silver-washed Fritillary, and other woodland species

13.

a. Near Rannoch, Perthshire, where the Scotch Argus flies

b. Lulworth Cove, Dorset: the country of the Lulworth Skipper

14.

15. THE WHITE ADMIRAL (x1.25)

16. THE DARK GREEN FRITILLARY (x1.17)

Chapter 10

Practical Genetics and Breeding

The Application of Genetics to Butterfly Breeding, Single-Factor Differences — Known Instances — Probable Instances, The Distribution of Genetic Types in Wild Populations

THE APPLICATION OF GENETICS TO BUTTERFLY BREEDING

I have been astonished to find how much time and material is wasted in breeding butterflies when the work has not been properly planned. The analysis of Genetics undertaken in the last chapter, elementary as it was, should at least make it clear that the first essential in producing, as in studying, varieties is to keep each brood separate; yet I could give instances of the use of haphazard matings to maintain a valuable form. It seems almost incredible that any one should multiply labour and reduce results by such a practice, which is as opposed to common-sense as it is to genetic requirements. The progeny of matings between pairs of homozygotes, pairs of heterozygotes, and between heterozygotes and homozygotes, are thus brought up together indiscriminately: a procedure which baffles analysis and impedes the segregation of recessives. The facts already discussed should warn the student to avoid such a gross error of technique. More than that, they make it possible to frame a few simple rules for the guidance of any one who obtains a variety and wishes to secure further specimens of it by breeding.

If the variety is a female which has been caught in the open, it will almost certainly have been impregnated already by a male of the normal form. The method to be adopted should depend upon the type of brood raised from its eggs. This will constitute the F_1 generation, the P_1 individuals being the original variety and its, generally unknown, mate. Consider first the situation in which the offspring are all normal. We must then act on the assumption that the variety is a simple recessive. In these circumstances, it is essential to interbreed the F_1 brothers and sisters; on no account must they be crossed with individuals outside their own brood, if this can possibly be avoided. The resulting F_2 generation will be the inbred grandchildren of the original

H

variety, and one-quarter of them are expected to be of the desired form. Such 'extracted recessives' must be homozygotes (as all recessives are), so that it is only necessary to mate them together to found a pure strain of the variety. If it be desired to maintain such a stock, it would no longer be necessary to interbreed; so long as two similar recessives are used, all the progeny will be of the recessive type, whatever their source. Unfortunately, some lepidoptera suffer severely from the effects of inbreeding. The reason for this will be explained later (p. 210), but the danger may to some extent be avoided by founding two distinct recessive lines at the earliest possible stage. These may subsequently be crossed with impunity should either or both of them show signs of becoming weak or sterile. The resulting offspring will probably be more vigorous.

Thus, as soon as we can mate two individuals of the same recessive form, a pure-breeding strain will be produced. But unexpected difficulties may be encountered on the way. First, we may not succeed in pairing a brother and sister of the F_1 generation, so that it may be necessary to fall back upon crossing an F_1 specimen with an unrelated individual. As already mentioned, every effort should be made to avoid this, Not only does it necessitate breeding at least one additional generation, but it also involves rearing far more individuals per generation as well. The F_1 specimens are all heterozygotes. If we cross them with un-related males or females we perform a back-cross, so that the resulting progeny will be heterozygotes and homozygous dominants in equality, and these types, being normal in appear-ance, are indistinguishable. All that can be done is to inter-breed them, and only one mating in four will produce varieties in the next generation, the third from the original capture. A number of separate broods must therefore be raised in order to include the required cross, and sixteen of them are needed to make reasonably sure of doing so.

It will therefore be seen that it will not be worth while attempt-ing to breed a variety if we cannot mate brother and sister among its offspring, should these all be normal in appearance, unless it is a very valuable one, financially or scientifically. The black variety of the Swallow-tail Butterfly, *Papilio machaon*, is a simple recessive. The first known specimen was seen flying near Ranworth in Norfolk. After many attempts, it was caught by a fisherman in his landing net.

When initial success is obtained and we are able to interbreed the offspring of a variety (supposing, as we are, that these are all normal), disappointment may yet attend our efforts; for the desired form may not reappear in the resulting F_2 generation. But the breeder should take heart: failure is less probable than success, and if encountered, may be due to one of several causes. First, the variety may be environmental (pp. 230–5), due perhaps to extremes of temperature or humidity, and not inherited at all. Secondly, the genetic situation itself may be more complex than the single-factor difference which we are considering; this is rather an unlikely alternative, but it is known in the Green-veined White. Thirdly, the variety, though a simple recessive, may be less hardy than the normal form. The mortality of the early stages will then be a differential one, so that the extracted recessives in the F_2 generation will fall below numerical expectation. This will reduce the chances of obtaining the variety. But even if quite vigorous, a recessive may fail to appear in a small brood when expected only in one quarter of the individuals. Thus we require to know the minimum number of specimens which should be reared in order to include at least one specimen of such a form with fair probability, and the answer is, again, sixteen.

We may now turn our attention to the situation in which the offspring of a variety caught in nature are not all normal but include the desired parental form. It is, of course, just possible that a recessive has mated with a heterozygote, a member, probably, of its own brood.[1] This is less unlikely in those species which remain gregarious as larvae for a considerable time, as in the Marsh, Glanville and Heath Fritillaries. But otherwise such an occurrence is an improbable one, and we may reasonably assume that a variety is not recessive if it appears among the progeny of a captured female.[2] This does not mean that it is a dominant, and it should never be reported as such until the heterozygote and the homozygote have been compared and found to be similar. It may merely be an example of the condition, illustrated on p. 172 by the *semi-lutea* form of the Currant Moth, where the heterozygote is intermediate in appearance. But

[1] The possibility that two recessives have mated in nature also exists, but it is extremely remote.

[2] The two situations can, of course, be distinguished by the ratios involved, if the numbers bred are large enough to allow of such discrimination. For a recessive would segregate in one quarter, and a heterozygote in one half, of the offspring. It may be noted that the smallest number of individuals capable of discriminating between these alternatives is 56.

the mistake is repeatedly made of calling a form a dominant when the homozygote has never even been seen!

A heterozygote in natural conditions will nearly always mate with a typical insect; thus varieties and normal specimens will appear in equality among the insects reared from it, for this is a back-cross. In these circumstances, two of the varieties should be interbred so as to produce the F_2 generation. The advantages of doing so are twofold compared with mating the variety with the normal form (whether a member of the same brood or not). First, a higher proportion of varieties, three-quarters instead of one-half, will appear in the next generation. Secondly, one-third of them (one-quarter of the whole brood) will be the rare homozygotes. Now it is particularly valuable to obtain these. For if a heterozygous form is rare, we can be fairly confident that the homozygous one is entirely unknown. It may merely be rather more extreme in appearance, or it may be very different from the heterozygote. Further, though the complete dominance of the wild type over a variety is very usual, the complete dominance of a variety (unless polymorphic, pp. 247–52) is very rare indeed. Thus if the heterozygote is distinguishable at all, it is very probable that the homozygote will differ from it. Consequently if a collector catches a variety, breeds from it and obtains it again among the progeny, he usually has within his grasp the opportunity of securing a rare or unknown form merely by raising the F_2 generation. It is extraordinary how seldom such homozygotes have been examined, even when the heterozygotes are clearly polymorphic and therefore relatively common, as they are in the Clouded Yellow, *Colias croceus*, var. *helice*, and the Silver-washed Fritillary, *Argynnis paphia*, var. *valezina* Esp.; yet very few homozygous specimens of these varieties exist and they have never been properly studied. It is, however, probable that they are complete dominants.

It will be realized that it is quite easy to maintain a stock of a heterozygous variety even without inbreeding; for, when such a form is crossed with unrelated normal individuals, it will constantly be recovered in half the resulting generation. Nevertheless, an opportunity should always be taken of mating two of the varieties together, so as to obtain the homozygotes.

It has so far been assumed that the initial variety is a captured female. Should it be a captured male, it will be very difficult to breed from it, simply because a suitable female with which to mate it is not usually available. If the variety is a particularly interesting one, it is just worth while attempting to pair it with a freshly captured female, on the chance that this may be a virgin specimen. But it is not likely to be so; for as the males appear first (p. 243), the females are usually mated as soon as they begin to fly, or even sooner. I have several times found female Marsh Fritillaries already paired before their wings were expanded. This was in a restricted colony in which the species was extremely abundant, so that the opportunities for early pairing were great. If a butterfly is very rare, captured females are all too frequently virgin, as was a female Pale Clouded Yellow, *Colias hyale*, which I found in May flying at the foot of White Horse Hill, Berkshire.

Females have undoubtedly been known to mate twice, producing broods of mixed paternity. This has very rarely been observed, but I have obtained genetic evidence of it in the large African Swallow-tail Butterfly, *Papilio dardanus* Brown. I do not think, however, that it is worth while to provide a male with a fertile female in the hope of such an event. The possibility of it should, however, be borne in mind as a conceivable source of error in experimental breeding.

Varieties sometimes appear unexpectedly in the breeding cage. They can then usually be mated as desired, whether they be males or females. When a large brood is emerging, they may be in *copula* when first seen. If their chosen mate be normal, this will retard the work by one generation when the variety is the female. If it is not, such delay may be avoided in some species at any rate, for a single male can successfully impregnate several females. This has been denied, but it has been established in more than one African butterfly, and Mr R. F. Bretherton has proved it in our own Scarlet Tiger Moth. The fact is an important one, since it can be used to simplify genetic analysis. Not only can a number of broods sometimes be raised from a single male variety, but also these may so be arranged as to include different types of crosses.

Though many moths pair readily in captivity, butterflies do not, and this is partly responsible for our extreme ignorance of their genetics. Yet the great deficiency of our knowledge in that respect should be a splendid encouragement to butterfly collectors to undertake simple breeding experiments, now that the difficulties of pairing these insects have, to some extent, been overcome; for almost all the genetic data which they may obtain will be new and useful.

In the past, it was not realized that fresh air and sunshine are the chief requirements for the successful pairing of butterflies. Most moths will pair in confined quarters, but butterflies need more favourable conditions. Pairing-cages may be constructed in various ways: some are elaborate and the size of a small greenhouse. However, one of the most satisfactory and inexpensive is that designed and used with great success, by Mr J. Shepherd, and I am much indebted to him for allowing me to describe it here.

This cage consists of a cubical wooden frame, each side of which is fifteen inches in length externally. The floor is a platform, to which an upright is attached at each corner. These uprights are joined at the top by side-pieces. The top and three of the sides are covered with tiffany, usually sold by drapers as butter muslin. A piece of glass is fixed in the fourth side, to act as a door.

The floor may be made of a single piece of wood, fifteen inches square, into which is cut a round hole just large enough to fit under the eyelets at the top of an ordinary galvanized iron pail. From this the handle is removed, and the eyelets which held it are bent outwards at right-angles. The eyelets rest on top of the platform and are fixed to it by nails. Two holes are made in the pail, one on each side half-way between the eyelets, and a nail is driven through each into the edge of the platform. Any chink between the top of the pail and the platform can be stuffed with cotton-wool. Mr Shepherd himself constructs the platform a little more elaborately, and his plan, though slightly more trouble, has certain advantages. He makes it of a square wooden frame, each corner strengthened with a piece of wood attached cross-wise below. The inside width of the frame should equal the diameter of the top of the pail. The four triangular spaces between the pail and the corners of the frame are then filled with Portland cement. A larger cage should be used for butterflies the size of the Red Admiral and upwards: one of three feet high by fifteen inches square is suitable for them.

The pail should have a few holes punched in the bottom for drainage. It is filled with earth and holds the growing food-plant. This will usually suffice the young larvae until they can be handled without much difficulty, but a jar of the fresh food can be placed inside if needed.

When used for pairing, this cage should be stood in the open, where it will receive fresh air and sunshine. However, some butterflies will pair indoors if there is sunshine, or even in dull weather should the temperature be fairly high.

It is usual to feed captive butterflies on sugar and water, soaked up on cotton-wool. Both Mr Shepherd and I have found this unnecessary, provided that a bunch of fresh flowers (for example, Valerian) be placed in the cage, and to this he attached considerable importance. The females of many species certainly pair before their first flight, but it must be remembered that those which hibernate as butterflies (the Vanessidi and the Brimstone) do not do so until the spring.

A cage of the kind described here can be used not only for pairing butterflies but also for rearing the larvae and hibernating them. Should it be employed for this purpose, the pupae (or, preferably, the nearly fully-fed larvae) should be taken out of it, as it is difficult to remove the butterflies when they have dried their wings and are ready for flight.

By the use of such pairing cages, it has been possible to keep butterflies in captivity for a number of generations. Species belonging to nearly all the families found in Britain have been mated in this way. In the event of failure, artificial pairing might be tried, a device used with success by collectors in Africa. The wings of the female should be held with a clip; the type used on retort-stands is convenient, but a cleft cane will serve. The male and female genitalia are then brought into the correct juxta-position. Very slight pressure on the sides of the two abdomina will usually induce the male to clasp the female, after which he is allowed to hang freely. The insects should then be placed in a box; if they appear restless, this should be dark. Some males refuse to pair in this way, but the method is often highly satis-factory, and abroad extensive breeding work has been done by this means.

Many butterflies are easily reared in captivity, and the possi-bility of pairing them allows us not only to make genetic in-vestigations but also to maintain stocks of some of the varieties. These may then be used in studies such as those on linkage and multiple allelomorphism. In discussing these subjects, it was assumed that two rare forms were available for mating. The chances of obtaining them would be exceedingly remote were we to depend upon the fortuitous capture of such insects when required. But work of this kind would be by no means so difficult if collectors would endeavour to breed from and main-tain stocks of any rare variety which they may encounter. Those

engaged in genetic work might then advertise for the forms
which they need in one of the entomological journals, such as
The Entomologist, The Entomologist's Monthly Magazine, or *The
Entomological Record.* In these periodicals, space is already
devoted to advertisements from those who wish to exchange
specimens, and even now they occasionally contain inquiries for
experimental material. The facilities therefore already exist for
effective collaboration between those engaged in genetic investigations in the Lepidoptera.

SINGLE-FACTOR DIFFERENCES (KNOWN INSTANCES)

We may now review the very small amount of information
which is available in British butterflies on the effects of single
pairs of allelomorphs. Having done so, it may be useful to go
further and to indicate which of the better known varieties not
so far examined genetically are most likely to be controlled in
this way: for it should be easy to determine the true status of
most of them experimentally. The various examples will be used,
where appropriate, to illustrate points of technique or of genetic
interest. All instances of the interaction of genes with one
another, with sex, or with the environment, are reserved for
study in the next chapter.

Astonishing as it may seem, only four forms inherited as
simple recessives had been analysed in British butterflies up to 15
years ago, so that there is a great field for investigation here. Those
proved to be inherited as heterozygotes (or dominants) are subject
to a slight additional complexity which makes it desirable to examine them later (pp. 223–30). The recessives are the following:

(1) The Ringlet, *Aphantopus hyperanthus* var. *lanceolata*
Shipp. In this variety, the rings surrounding the spots are
enlarged and distorted into ovals, generally contracted to a point
on the outer side. Mr J. Shepherd bred from a captured female
lanceolata and obtained an F_1 generation of 32 insects, all
normal. He inbred these and produced a total F_2 of 30, of which
23 were typical *hyperanthus* and seven *lanceolata*: a result entirely
in accord with the view that *lanceolata* is inherited as a simple
recessive.

(2) The Small Copper, *Lyaaena phlaeas* var. *obsoleta.* This has
already been discussed (pp. 174–5).

(3) The Green-veined White, *Pieris napi.* There exists a variety
hibernica Schmidt (often wrongly called *citronea* Frohawk) of

this species in which the white ground-colour is replaced by bright yellow both above and below. It is of excessive rarity, having been seen in wild specimens on three or four occasions only. However, a stock derived from a yellow female of Donegal origin has been maintained in captivity for many years. It has now been widely distributed, and all the larger collections contain examples. Their monetary value has thus declined from several pounds, which single specimens would fetch fifteen years ago, to about ten pence each. The genetics of this variety have been studied by Mr J. Shepherd (1942). He showed that when inter-bred with the ordinary white *napi* of its own Irish form, *hibernica* behaves as a simple recessive. Consequently a mating between two specimens of this variety produces offspring all of which are yellow, and these must necessarily be homozygotes. A cross between *hibernica* and ordinary British *napi*, however, gives a more complex result which has not yet been fully analysed. It will be discussed in Chapter 13, where the significance of this strange diversity in genetic behaviour will be considered further.

(4) Varieties of the Swallow-tail Butterfly are very rare. The most striking of them is var. *nigra* Reutti, in which the yellow areas are suffused with a blackish-brown shade so that the black markings become indistinct, though they are unaltered in form. The blue scales are developed in the normal way, but these are the only component of the pattern that stands out clearly.

This wonderful black variety has been captured on the wing (p. 194), and specimens of it have several times been bred. On one occasion a stock originating from Ranworth larvae produced large numbers of typical specimens for two generations. However, among many normal butterflies comprising the third generation, at least seven were var. *nigra*. One of these, a female, was paired with a typical male from the same stock. It produced thirteen normal offspring and six var. *nigra* (three males and three females).

The genetics of this situation should be obvious, but the inter-pretation put upon it when published constitutes a valuable warning to those who breed butterflies. Since the parents of the seven black specimens which first appeared were normal, the variety cannot be a heterozygote or a dominant. The breeder assumed, correctly, that it was a simple recessive, and mated a black female with a normal male which, being taken from the same brood might well be a heterozygote. There was a reasonable probability of this, and the hope was, in fact, fulfilled. The authors who conducted and reported on the work fully realized that such a procedure should lead to segregation in a 1 : 1 ratio, for it involves a back-cross. Yet they bred thirteen normals and six *nigra*. Struck by the inequality of this result, they attempted to explain it by an additional and complex hypothesis. They suggested that the black form may be controlled by the interaction of two pairs of genes, each without effect by itself, and showed that segregation in a ratio of 10 : 6, a nearer approach to that encountered, could be obtained on this basis. Now it is especially to be noticed that this system of genic-interaction was invoked to surmount a difficulty which does not exist. Had the authors calculated the probabilities involved, they would have found that a distribution of 13 : 6 does not constitute a mathematically significant departure from equality, for it would be obtained entirely fortuitously slightly more often than once in ten trials. Such an occurrence is certainly not rare enough to require an additional hypothesis for its interpretation. That made on this occasion might well have been shaved away with William of Occam's razor, *essentia non sunt multiplicanda praeter necessitatem*; for there is here nothing to suggest that var. *nigra* is other than a simple recessive. Let the breeder of butterflies who finds that his ratios depart somewhat from expectation determine whether or not they do so significantly before advancing special theories to account for them. Appropriate methods for making such calculations are given by Mather (1943).

It has often been postulated that the interaction of two pairs of genes is necessary for the production of a single character. This has usually been done to overcome some apparent difficulty, but further analysis has nearly always shown that such an assumption is invalid. It is therefore one which should be made only when the facts absolutely demand it, and it should then be checked by further experimental breeding.

The breeding technique employed on this occasion provides still further material for fruitful study. When the black form of *P. machaon* first appeared, a specimen of it was crossed with a normal male. This was wisely chosen from the same brood, so that there was a fair chance that it might be a heterozygote. Had the normal male been an unrelated specimen, the variety would not have reappeared among the offspring. It may be that the obviously desirable pairing between two black specimens could not be obtained, for such extreme forms are sometimes difficult to mate among themselves. Even so, the method adopted could have been improved upon, for it would have been better to breed from one of the black males rather than from a black female. An attempt could then have been made to pair it with more than one normal female, which would much have increased the chance of securing a back-cross; for obviously there was some danger of introducing a dominant homozygote at this stage which would prevent the segregation of var. *nigra* among the progeny.

It will be noticed furthermore that two generations comprising only normal specimens preceded that in which var. *nigra* appeared. Therefore all the heterozygotes must have been mated with dominant homozygotes in the first generation raised in captivity. Were these the progeny of wild larvae, as appears likely, matings between heterozygotes could certainly not have been ensured because brother and sister pairings could not have been made. If, on the other hand, they were derived from eggs laid by one or more captured females, the segregation of var. *nigra*, though not anticipated, would with greater probability have occurred a generation earlier had the technique recommended on pp. 194–5 been adopted.

SINGLE-FACTOR DIFFERENCES (PROBABLE INSTANCES)

Certain varieties not yet studied genetically may with some confidence be ascribed to the action of a single pair of allelomorphs. It may indeed prove that a few of them are not inherited in this way. Nevertheless they should provide suitable material for simple genetic studies, for though some are very rare others are not difficult to obtain.

Single pairs of allelomorphs must also be responsible for the production of many known forms not included in this list. There must also exist an almost unlimited store of genetic variability capable of producing varieties not yet encountered by entomologists. Means for tapping this great reserve will be discussed at the end of this chapter (pp. 209–10).

It is thus probable, but not yet proved, that the following varieties are inherited as simple recessives or, in a few instances, as heterozygous forms:

The Pearl-bordered and the Small Pearl-bordered Fritillaries, *Clossiana euphrosyne* and *C. selene*. Rare varieties of both these butterflies occur in which the sub-marginal row of silver spots on the underside of the hind-wings run inwards as rays. They are probably simple recessives. The black markings on the fore-wings of *C. euphrosyne* may become enlarged to varying degrees and coalesce. These are probably multi-factorial conditions (pp. 209–19). However, a form is occasionally found in which a broad black band crosses the wings on the upper-side. This may merely be an extension of the tendency just mentioned, or it may be a distinct condition. If the latter view is correct, it is likely to be inherited as a simple recessive. Similar variations occur in *C. selene*, but they are still rarer.

The Dark Green Fritillary, *Mesoacidalia aglaia*. In the variety *charlotta* Haw., silver blotches are formed at the base of the hind-wings, owing to the confluence of some of the spots. It is not a great rarity in some districts, almost unknown in others, and it is probably inherited as a simple recessive.

The High Brown Fritillary, *M. adippe*, var. *cleodoxa* O. The silver spots are largely, or wholly, absent from the under-side in this variety; they are replaced by pale yellow non-metallic marks. Possibly it is a simple recessive, but I think this unlikely for, though exceedingly rare in England, it is quite common in southern Europe. Perhaps it is produced environmentally; alternatively, it may be an instance of polymorphism affecting part only of the insect's range, as is true in the *valezina* form of *Aglaia paphia*. If so, the variety *cleodoxa* would be hetero-zygous, not recessive. In view of these varied possibilites, *cleodoxa* would be a most interesting form to breed.

Some of the varieties encountered in the Marsh Fritillary, *Euphydryas aurinia*, are doubtless simple recessives. Others are probably multi-factorial. This is an exceptionally variable species.

In the Peacock, *Inachis io*, the normal maroon ground-colour is sometimes replaced by one of a dull, slightly olive-brown, shade, having rather a greasy appearance. This effect can be produced artificially, by exposing a Peacock Butterfly to the vapour of strong hydrochloric acid and subsequently neutralizing with ammonia. The resulting change is a permanent one. Such facts may ultimately throw some light on the action of the genes concerned. The natural form of the variety is not very rare, and families containing several such specimens have sometimes been reared without precise details being recorded. Mr Richard South, the well-known author of *Butterflies of the British Isles*, reports that he selected larvae from a single large brood and at all of them produced butterflies of this coloration. Unfortunately, he does not state the number, even approximately, so that it is difficult to interpret this result. The variety is almost certainly a simple recessive. So is the Blind Peacock, var. *belisaria* Ob., in which the beautiful eyelike spots on the fore- and hind-wings are represented only by a whitish cloud.

The White Admiral, *Limenitis camilla*, Plate 15. The white band on the upper-side of this species may be reduced to a few more or less indistinct marks, var. *semi-nigrina*, or lost altogether, var. *nigrina* Weym., while the under-side becomes highly abnormal. These *nigrina* forms have long been prized by collectors. Though rare, they occur with greater frequency in some woods than others, and they are certainly reported much more often now than formerly. Whether they are becoming relatively commoner, as some consider, or whether they are merely more often observed owing to the extraordinary increase and spread of the White Admiral during recent years (p. 139), does not seem clear. It might well be suggested that *semi-nigrina* is the heterozygote of which *nigrina* is the homozygote. Yet I think this unlikely. True *nigrina* seems to occur much too frequently compared with *semi-nigrina* to be maintained in that way.[1] Moreover, if favoured by a polymorphism, for which they are far too rare (p. 247), the variety would probably have become dominant (p. 246). I think that *nigrina* in both its forms is most likely to be a simple recessive with variable expression of the character.

A corresponding form, *iole* Schiff, is known in the Purple Emperor, *Apatura iris*, Plate 23. Considering the much greater scarcity of that species, *iole* is perhaps not proportionately rarer than the *nigrina* forms of the White Admiral and, like them, is presumably recessive.

Most varieties of the Blues are instances either of 'continuous variation' or of 'sex-controlled' inheritance, and both these subjects are considered in Chapter 11. However, var. *fowleri* South of *Lysandra coridon* is probably a simple recessive. Though always very rare, it has been found in some districts and not in others. It is a form in which the black border on the upper-side of the wings is replaced by white. Though occurring in both sexes, it appears to be commoner in males than in females. If this is substantiated, it will probably prove to be an instance of the well-known phenomenon of partial sex-control, in which a gene

[1] They are certainly much commoner proportionately than the *lutea* forms of the moth *Abraxas grossulariata*, in which the heterozygote is distinct from the homozygotes.

is not always able to exercise its effect in the environment provided by one of the sexes.

There exists also a variety known as *arcuata* in which the most posterior of the basal spots on the under-side of the fore-wings is joined in a curved line to the last of the outer row. It occurs in at least three of the British Blues (the Chalkhill, *arcuata* Courv.; the Adonis, *arcuata*, Courv.; and the Common Blue, *arcuata* Weym.), being found throughout their range; nor is it very uncommon, though intermediates are seldom seen. The two sexes are equally affected. Possibly these *arcuata* forms are simple recessives in all three species.

It is probable that the form of the Small Copper with blue spots inside the copper band on the hind-wings, var. *caeruleopunctata* Stgr., is inherited as a simple recessive with rather variable expression.

The Hairstreaks are notably invariable, except for the development of the series of white dots on the under-side of the Green Hairstreak, *Callophrys rubi*, and this will be discussed on p. 213. A few very rare varieties have been found in all the species. One of these is the var. *bellus* Gerh. of the Purple Hairstreak, *Quercusia quercus*, Plate 26, in which an orange patch appears at the end of the cell on the fore-wings. My father (H. D. Ford) and I captured in Cumberland on 21 August 1919 one of the very few recorded British examples. This is a very late date for the species even in the north of England, so that, though a female, it is in poor condition. Unfortunately, it laid no eggs. Sandars (1939) incorrectly states that this variety is restricted to the male. It would almost certainly prove to be a simple recessive.

Both in the Large White, *P. brassicae*, and the Small White, *P. rapae*, a parallel variety to var. *hibernica* of the Green-veined White, is known, in which the white ground-colour is suffused with a bright yellow shade. This also occurs in the Orange-tip, *Anthocharis cardamines*, and gives it some resemblance to several allied species (e.g., *A. gruneri* H. Sch., *A. eupheno* L., and others). This, however, is superficial, for in these the yellow ground-colour is developed in the male only. Such varieties are of the greatest rarity. It is probable that they would prove to be recessives.

The Wood White, *Leptidea sinapis*, Plate 21. A rare form of this butterfly, with buff, instead of the usual black, markings is probably recessive.

Distinct varieties are hardly ever obtained in the British Skippers (Hesperiidae) save in two species. In the Grizzled Skipper, *Pyrgus malvae*, occurs the well-known var. *taras* Bergstr., in which the white spots on the fore-wings run together to a varying degree, forming patches. Though never common, it seems to be found in the south-west of England more frequently than elsewhere. On the other hand, in the Chequered Skipper, *Carterocephalus palaemon*, the yellow markings may completely disappear, leaving the upper side of an almost unicolorous dark brown. This form has very seldom been reported, for the species itself is extremely local, but it has already been found in the newly-discovered Inverness race (p. 284): perhaps it is more frequent in these Scottish insects. These two varieties are probably both simple recessives.

This list may be concluded with a few generalizations. Albinos are found in so many butterflies that I did not include them in it. They will usually be inherited as simple recessives. They must be distinguished from those 'pathological' conditions in which no pigment is present in certain areas, large or small, owing to the imperfect development of the scales. The whitish spots and blotches sometimes found in the Meadow Brown, in the fulvous areas of the Fritillaries, and in many other species, are usually of this nature. Such defects are easily identified by the use of a dissecting microscope, or even of a good hand-lens, when it will be seen that the scales are curled or otherwise deformed. This abnormality may be due to disease; but it must not be forgotten that it may itself be inherited, even on the simplest basis. The primary effect of the hereditary factors would then be exercised upon scale-development, which would secondarily be responsible for the imperfect coloration.

It may be said that rare varieties are more likely to be inherited as simple recessives than produced in any other way, especially when the following conditions are satisfied: (1) When the variety is found more often in some localities than in others, or has recurred in the same place after some years. (2) When the variety is itself fairly constant in form. This is rather a poor criterion since, as will be explained in Chapter 11, variations may occur in the *effect* of a given hereditary factor. (3) When the variety is not connected with the typical form by a series of intermediates. Should such exist, and the more normal members are found to be commoner than the less normal (suggesting that the fluctuation is not occurring round a separate mean), it is unlikely that the variety is controlled by a single pair of allelomorphs.

THE DISTRIBUTION OF GENETIC TYPES IN WILD POPULATIONS

The existence of a recessive variety necessitates that some of the normal specimens are heterozygous for the gene concerned. It may well be asked what is the relation between the proportion of recessives and that of their corresponding heterozygotes in natural conditions. This is easily determined. If we have a population breeding at random, and the three genetic types, the dominant homozygotes, the heterozygotes, and the recessives, are equally hardy, then the number of individuals in the heterozygous class is twice the product of the square roots of that in the two homozygous classes. Thus if the number of insects in the homozygous dominant class is p^2, and if the number in the recessive class is q^2, the three classes are distributed in the ratio:

$$p^2 : 2pq : q^2$$

Consequently, if we know the proportion of individuals in any one class, that in the two others can readily be calculated. As will shortly be explained, this fact is of great importance from a theoretical point of view, but it may also have practical bearings. For instance, it becomes possible to answer such questions as the following, which I have repeatedly been asked. If a recessive variety is unusually frequent in a particular locality, what are the chances that a captured female may have mated with a heterozygote (or that a normal specimen obtained for mating purposes will be heterozygous)?

It will, of course, be obvious that the distribution of genetic types which has just been indicated is not restricted to the situation in which dominance is complete. It is directly applicable to that in which a variety is a heterozygote, so allowing us to determine how rare the homozygotes may be. Further, the suggestion may be made that two known varieties represent corresponding heterozygotes and homozygotes. For instance, this has been done, wrongly, I believe, in the *semi-nigrina* and the *nigrina* forms of the White Admiral (p. 205). Should these be common enough to obtain the necessary data, it can be asserted, even without breeding, that such a suggestion is incorrect if the proportions prove to depart significantly from those expected on such an hypothesis. On the other hand, if the proportions agree with the distribution of the three genetic types in a random mating population, the view at least receives sufficiently strong support to warrant detailed investigation.

Percentage of recessives	Percentage of heterozygotes
25	50·0
20	49·4
15	47·4
10	43·2
5	34·7
1	18·0
0.1	6·2
0.01	2·0
0.001	0·6

Table 2. The percentages of heterozygotes corresponding to various percentages of recessives in wild populations breeding at random

In Table 2 I have listed the corresponding percentages of heterozygotes and recessives expected in a wild population. Naturally this may equally well be used to obtain the proportions of heterozygotes and the rarer homozygotes when the latter are dominants or when all the genetic types are distinguishable. It will be obvious that at the lower frequencies the proportion of heterozygotes declines very slowly compared with that of the homozygotes, so that when a recessive variety occurs in only one individual in 10,000, the heterozygotes actually occupy about 2 per cent of the population. This is a fact of the utmost importance and of the widest application: it is as true of Man as of butterflies. Its significance will briefly be discussed in Chapter 12, and only one of its consequences need be dealt with here.

It will now be evident that even when recessive varieties are very rare, their heterozygotes must be quite widespread in the population. For, owing to the fact that the hereditary units do not contaminate one another (p. 170), such variability is almost indefinitely preserved. Further, the number of allelomorphs in any insect must be large, amounting at least to some thousands. Consequently, every butterfly must be heterozygous for a large number of pairs, and some of them will be responsible for the production of recognizable varieties. Indeed, as already indicated, living organisms contain a vast store of heritable variation, and it is to some extent possible to avail ourselves of it. In order to do so, we may take advantage of the fact that inbreeding leads to homozygosity. Were self-fertilization possible in butterflies, as it is in many plants, the amount of heterozygosity would actually be halved at each generation, so that the variability normally cloaked by recessiveness would rapidly be unmasked. This process is considerably slower when the closest inbreeding that we can perform is a mating between brother and sister, but it is still very effective, and the butterfly collector should not fail to make use of it. His technique should be to breed from captured females of species in which he is interested and, by crossing brothers and sisters among the offspring, to obtain the F_2 generation in each line. It is quite probable that recessive varieties will appear at this stage, owing to the tendency of inbreeding to increase the proportion of homozygotes at the expense of the heterozygotes. A further reduction in heterozygosity would naturally be obtained by raising the F_3 and later generations. But the largest effect occurs in F_2, so that it is a better policy to use time and material in producing more broods of that generation than to raise subsequent ones. Recessives tend to be disadvantageous (p. 246), and their appearance during inbreeding is responsible for the deleterious effects of that process in some species which chance to possess a particularly harmful set of them, but it is not likely to hamper the production of F_2. The device of securing new recessive forms by inbreeding from wild individuals has been employed with the greatest success in many animals, yet it seems never to have been applied to butterflies and moths. Those collectors and experimenters who adopt it will open up new and exciting possibilities from which they may reap a rich harvest.

Chapter 11

Genetic Interactions

Factor Interaction, Sex-Controlled Inheritance,
Environmental Variation

FACTOR INTERACTION

An important addition must be made to the account of Genetics given in the two previous chapters: that characters may be variable even when inherited as simple recessives. For hereditary factors (see note, p. 213) interact with one another, as well as with the environment, to produce the results for which they are responsible. Yet the factors themselves remain unaltered in the process, for such interactions only modify their working. In discussing this subject it will be convenient at first to omit the influence of the environment, which will be considered separately on pp. 230–5.

A number of different genes may have similar effects and, should they act cumulatively, they may give rise to a graded series of varieties in which distinct segregation cannot be recognized, as in the inheritance of human height.[1] It has already been shown (p. 178) that two pairs only of heterozygous allelomorphs produce nine genetic types in the next generation, which all differ in expression when dominance is absent. If such allelomorphs control the same character quantitatively, even these few classes would merge almost imperceptibly into one another. Should three pairs of allelomorphs be concerned, the number of genetically distinct classes would be raised to 27, of which eight would have distinct effects even if dominance were complete. It will be evident therefore how easily variation may become 'continuous' if a number of hereditary factors approximately equal in their contributions are responsible for it.

This condition is a very usual one. In the absence of dominance, it leads to a series of varieties in which the intermediates are commoner than the extremes.[2] Such variation must be due to

---

[1] This character is partly inherited and partly environmental.

[2] Their proportions are such that when the numbers are plotted, as ordinates, against the class-values, the result is a bell-shaped curve, known as the curve of 'normal distribution'.

heredity, rather than to other causes, if the amount of heterozygosity becomes greater as we approach the middle of such a
series, while the two end terms are homozygous for all the
allelomorphs concerned. In such circumstances, an approximately
pure-breeding line may be obtained when both the parents belong
to one, or to the other, extreme form. On the other hand, a cross
between two of the intermediates should lead to the production
of intermediate offspring, subject only to a moderate degree of
variability; but the whole series, or an approach to it should be
recovered when the succeeding inbred generation is reared. Such
variation is inherited, since relatively pure stocks of the extreme
types can be obtained; moreover, it is Mendelian (p. 170), for the
F_2 generation is more variable than the F_1, as opposed to a system
of blending inheritance in which the reverse would be true.

Many quantitative characters in butterflies must be inherited in
this way, and size, as measured by wing-lengths, is doubtless one
of them. In addition, certain dwarf forms are sometimes found
which appear to be of a distinct kind since intermediate specimens
connecting them with the normal are rarely or never taken.
Some of them must indeed be environmentally produced, as are
the dwarf specimens of the Large Blue, *Maculinea arion*, encountered from time to time, which may have lived with the
wrong species of ant (p. 119). Others are certainly inherited,
and on a basis which produces sharp segregation: probably they
are simple recessives. Thus the average wing-expanse of the
Orange-tip, *Anthocharis cardamines*, is about 42 mm., but I
possess four specimens of which the average is 34 mm. They
were all captured, with others like them, at the same place in
Cumberland but in different years, and no intermediates were
discovered. These dwarf specimens have been reported from
many localities, and it is said that they appear in advance of the
typical insects.

Two remarkable dwarf races of butterflies occur on Great
Orme's Head, North Wales, and I am much indebted to Mr J.
Anthony Thompson for the information on them which he has
given me. One of them, the race *thyone* Thompson of the Grayling, *Hipparchia semele*, is not known elsewhere (p. 274). Its
average wing-expanse is about 41 mm. in the male and 43 mm.
in the female (in normal specimens it is about 48 mm. and 52 mm.
respectively). The other, the race *caernensis* Thompson of the
Silver-studded Blue, *Plebejus argus*, is found also on a few other
cliffs in Caernarvon (pp. 279–80). The males average about 25·5

mm. and the females about 21·5 mm.: each about 4 mm. less
than usual. Both sexes also differ consistently in colour from
the normal form.

The dwarf forms of these two very dissimilar butterflies both
emerge some weeks earlier than do the normal ones in the same
district. It seems probable that they, and the dwarf specimens of
the Orange-tip to which reference has just been made, are
produced by a gene which speeds up development; thus they
emerge at an early date and the larvae do not have time to attain
their full growth, so that they give rise to small imagines. Genetic
studies on the sizes of butterflies would be well worth undertaking.
They should include both an examination of 'continuous variation' and of the inheritance of distinct dwarf forms.

Characters such as colour and markings must often be controlled by means similar to that responsible for ordinary size-
variations: by a number of genes having approximately equal
effects and acting without dominance. For example, the development of the spots on the wings of the Large Heath, *Coenonympha
tullia*, fluctuates round an average value and may do so rather
widely, particularly in some Cumberland colonies. A further
instance is provided by the line of white dots on the under-side
of the Green Hairstreak, *Callophrys rubi*. This varies from a
single spot on the costa of the hind-wings (which may perhaps
disappear too, though I have never seen a specimen in which it
did so), to a complete row across the fore-wings as well as the
hind, the most usual condition being an intermediate one.
Numerous other examples might be cited.

Many of the varieties prized by collectors must be controlled
by the system which has just been discussed, but complicated by
the phenomena of dominance. If a character is due to a number
of genes, all of approximately equal importance, dominance will
prevent it from varying to a corresponding extent on either side
of a mean, as it did in the previous instances. On the contrary,
the normal form will then be the common one, since this is
generally dominant (except in polymorphic species, pp. 247–52);
the others will constitute varieties departing from it in one direction only and becoming progressively rarer the more marked
they may be.[1]

[1] Thus a cross between two individuals differing in three pairs of allelomorphs, each controlling a dominant character, together give an F_2 ratio
of 27 : 9 : 9 : 9 : 3 : 3 : 3 : 1. Here all the factors are segregating, but, in
nature, when some or all of the allelomorphs producing the recessive

Numerous examples suggesting such 'multi-factorial'[1] inheritance involving dominance will occur to the mind of every
collector. I shall mention a few only of the more obvious or
interesting of them.

The Hedge Brown, *Maniola tithonus*. A varying number of
extra 'eye-spots' may be developed in a row posterior to the
single one normally present on the fore-wings (Plate 17). These
extra-spotted specimens are not uncommon, and they certainly
occur more often in some localities than in others. In my experience, they are particularly frequent in Cornwall.

The Ringlet, *Aphantopus hyperanthus*. A series illustrating the
reduction of the spots on the under-side of this butterfly is shown
on Plate 22, giving normal specimens from above and below. It
will be seen that these 'eye-spots' consist of a dot surrounded by
a circle. It is this circle which is gradually reduced in diameter
and finally lost, leaving only the dot. The number of eye-spots is
also variable, being rather less in those specimens in which they
are smaller in size. These varieties may thus be divided into two
main classes: those in which some or all of the rings persist,
though in a reduced state, and those in which they are altogether
lost, so that the dots alone remain, both shown on Plate 22.
Specimens possessing the reduced rings are often referred to as
var. *arete* Müll., and those with the dots only as var. *caeca*
Fuchs. However, this does not appear to be the correct use of
these names, a view endorsed by Seitz (1906–10), who holds that
arete applies to the specimens in which the ring is lost, and that
var. *caeca* must be reserved for those instances in which both
rings and dots have vanished, the insect being immaculate. Such
a form has been illustrated in drawings (see Newman, 1869), and
it may even exist. Yet I have never seen it, although I have had
an unusually large experience of the varieties of this butterfly,
extending over many years, for I must have caught and examined
(but not necessarily killed!) over a thousand of them. Moreover,
when a very few small points alone remain on the wings, these
are not easily seen in faded specimens, and the few that I have
found treated as immaculate in collections have really been of

characters are rare, the proportions at the normal, or left-hand, end of the
series may be increased to any degree.
  [1] This term, rather than 'multi-' or 'poly-genic', should be used when a
character is controlled by a number of different pairs of allelomorphs; for
the term 'gene' should be employed only for the members of a given
allelomorphic pair.

this kind. Mr J. Shepherd, whose knowledge of this species is very extensive, tells me that his experience coincides with my own.

These varieties are much commoner in some districts than in others. They are exceptionally frequent in the neighbourhood of Carlisle, Cumberland (Ford, H. D., 1920). I myself obtained but scanty results in studying them experimentally, since I had a heavy mortality in breeding them. However, Mr J. Shepherd has been much more successful and has several times reared considerable broods from *arete* females which had been paired in nature. They always produced typical insects, *arete*, intermediates, and various mixtures between the two forms: specimens in which the fore-wings were normal and the hind *arete*, those in which the fore-wings were *arete* and the hind intermediate, and other combinations. Though more detailed experiments are desirable, in which the male as well as the female parent is known, these results are quite in accord with the supposition that the reduction of spots in *A. hyperanthus* is controlled on a multi-factorial basis; the contrast with the genetics of var. *lanceolata* (p. 200) is particularly striking.

Much of the variation in the Marsh Fritillary, *Euphydryas aurinia*, must also be due to 'factor interaction'. This species forms more or less isolated colonies dependent, among other things, upon the presence of its food-plant, the Devil's-bit Scabious; and at intervals, often of many years, such colonies become highly variable (pp. 254–6). A few of the varieties are clear-cut and distinct, and these may well be controlled by single genes. However, the majority of them can be arranged in a series grading into the normal colour-pattern. The work of Mr J. Shepherd on this butterfly provides an excellent example of the effect of selection upon multi-factorial variation. He bred it for fourteen generations, selecting consistently the darkest individuals obtainable, and finally produced a brood of completely black specimens.

The situation in the Glanville Fritillary, *Melitaea cinxia*, and in the Heath Fritillary, *Mellicta athalia*, is much like that in the Marsh Fritillary; but both species are far less variable, probably because they are not subject to such extreme cyclical fluctuations in numbers. Varieties of a less striking kind, passing insensibly into the normal condition, are found in both of them, as are some very rare and remarkable forms that are sharply distinct, such as the var. *pyronia* Hb. (=*eos* Haw.) of *M. athalia*.

The amount of black on the fore-wings of the Duke of Burgundy, *Hamearis lucina* (Plate 22), is always less in the females than in the males. It is subject to a certain amount of graded variation.

A set of parallel variations is to be found throughout the Polyommatini. In all the species the spots on the under-side may be reduced in number and may finally disappear, leaving the specimen immaculate. The discal spots, in the centre of both the fore- and hind-wings, must be controlled by a different gene or genes, for they often remain fully developed when all the others have vanished. On the other hand, any of the spots may elongate into lines and rays. This can affect all of them, but it is frequently limited to those on the fore-wings. All stages are to be seen from the normal to the extreme types in the reduction and elongation of the spots, and such variations affect both sexes. Many striking examples of them are found in the Chalk-hill Blue, *Lysandra coridon* (Plate 18). The diversity of these variations is extraordinary: some spots may be fully developed while others are absent, or all may be correspondingly reduced. Further, combinations between the two types are known, in which a few spots only remain, but these produced into streaks. Specimens with additional spots also occur. Such varieties are often unsymmetrical. Moreover, they are not infrequently associated with alternations in the ground-colour. In the unsymmetrical specimens, the spots and ground-colour generally vary together, the wings that are more normal in marking being also more normal in colour. This asymmetry is probably due to the fact that the normal complement of genes is adjusted to give the most favourable set of characters within the range of environmental changes to which the species is ordinarily exposed: that is to say, it produces a very constant effect. But a rare variety cannot have been adjusted in this way, so that it tends to respond unequally to the unequal stimuli which it must often receive. To use a term which will be familiar to physiologists, but not to the general reader, the normal form must be more closely 'buffered' than the abnormal.

These varieties are hunted assiduously not only by those collectors with a genuine interest in natural history but also by others who, like magpies, are concerned only to amass curiosities: the different forms are sub-divided, minutely described, and named, with all the seriousness normally accorded to a game. This proceeding seems effectively to have cloaked their real interest, so that our information on their distribution and relative frequencies is very small, though they are well known to be much more plentiful in some localities than in others. We are largely ignorant of their genetics, and we know nothing of the extent to which they may be differentially eliminated in nature. These subjects would be well worth investigating.

It is interesting to notice that though such varieties occur in all the British Blues, they are far commoner in some of them than in others. They are found most often in the Chalkhill Blue, and after that in the Adonis Blue, *L. bellargus*. In the Common Blue, *Polyommatus icarus*, they are less frequent, and they are very rare in the other species, though known in all of them. In the north of England they are fairly common in the Brown Argus, *Aricia agestis*, but not in the remainder of its range. I once captured a strikingly rayed specimen of the Silver-studded Blue on the Lizard Peninsula, but I believe the form to be extremely scarce. The spots on the upper-side of the Large Blue and on the lower surface in the two species of Coppers, are subject to a similar series of variations.

The development of the black markings on the Green-veined White, *Pieris napi*, is doubtless controlled by a number of factors, and it may be that the effects of some only of them are dominant. This is probably true of the other, and less variable, species of the Pieridae.

The breeding results to be obtained when multi-factorial inheritance is associated with dominance are of a characteristic kind. A mating between two of the less extreme varieties should lead to a partial return to normality. Its extent cannot be predicted, for it depends, among other things, on the proportion of allelomorphs in the rarer homozygous phase possessed in common by the parents. An increase in variation may be expected in the F_2, compared with the F_1 generation. The more extreme varieties should, however, breed fairly true when paired among themselves. Much more often a variety would have to be mated with a normal specimen, and it will usually have done so if it be a captured female. In that event, departure from the typical form will be small in the F_1 generation, but greater in the F_2. The fact that such forms are inherited, which can thus be proved when they are bred, will be strongly indicated in natural conditions if they are commoner in some localities than in others.

The genetic interactions so far discussed have been such that all the genes concerned produce approximately equal effects.

Very often, however, one of them exercises a major control while the others play the subsidiary part of modifying its operation, having little or no influence save in its presence. These are sometimes called 'specific modifiers'. Every gradation is found between specific modifiers in the strict sense, which can be detected only in the presence of a particular gene which 'sensitizes' them, and those types of interaction in which a number of genes are in varying, or equal, degrees capable of producing a given character.

Evidently we must be prepared to encounter variation even in those characters which are *controlled* by single pairs of allelomorphs, whether or not they be simple recessives. Attention has already been drawn to the existence of this phenomenon, and it clearly opens up exciting possibilities to those who are prepared to undertake simple breeding experiments. For it must especially be noticed that minor variation of this kind is *inherited*, being due to the segregation of genes additional to that responsible for the production of the variety which is being studied. Thus by breeding from the more extreme forms even of simple recessives, the varietal characters could be intensified, just as they could be diminished by selection in the opposite direction. Some remarkable consequences and extensions of this process must be reserved for later discussion (pp. 244–7).

Experience both with moths (p. 247) and with mammals (mice) demonstrates that quite striking results may be attained even in two or three generations. It is only necessary to choose both parents from among the most extreme individuals, to pair brothers and sisters, and to repeat the process in succeeding generations. Thus even if, as I suspect, the *nigrina* forms of the White Admiral, *Limenitis camilla*, should prove to be simple recessives, it should be possible to produce the true *nigrina* from the *semi-nigrina*, and, on the other hand, to obtain intermediates more nearly approaching the normal than those usually found. Similar results could doubtless be obtained, though less easily, with the variations of the whitish form of the Clouded Yellow, which is a heterozygote (see pp. 227–8). In general terms, the use of selective breeding should enable us to modify, in the direction either of more or of less extreme variation, any of the forms which have so far been mentioned, and many others that may be encountered, whether they are under the major control of a single pair of allelomorphs or not.

The various parts of the body provide different internal

environments for the genes. Consequently, though they are present and identical in every cell, they have not the same effects in one tissue as in another. Thus not only do the wings bear diversified patterns but the fore and hind pair are of different shapes and, usually, they are differently marked. But variations sometimes occur in the internal environment provided by the body, leading to the formation in one region of characters appropriate to another. For example, part of the fore-wing pattern or structure may appear in one of the hind-wings. Variations of this kind constitute the phenomenon of *homeosis*. We have no definite evidence of its nature in butterflies, though it has been studied in other insects (*Drosophila*) and shown to be genetic; it is very rare.

An important consideration bearing directly upon the subject of this chapter is the fact that the genes have multiple effects. This is difficult to illustrate from British butterflies since their genetics have been so little studied. However, if, as seems possible, the race *caernensis* of the Silver-studded Blue is controlled by a single gene, this alters both the size and colour of the insect. Yet in foreign butterflies genes are known which produce several distinct characters (Ford, 1937). Thus in the African Nymphalid, *Hypolimnas dubius* Beauv., a single gene changes the dominant form *dubius* into the recessive *anthedon* Doubl.; these have different colour-patterns and different habits. The frequency with which a single gene influences the length of life and fertility of the form which it produces shows us that such multiple effects, modifying also the working of the body, are exceedingly common, perhaps universal, attributes of genic action.

The genes, then, have multiple effects and interact with one another to produce the characters for which they are responsible. Thus they form a combined system or *gene-complex* (Ford, 1971), which may influence the expression of any one gene within it. The existence of such genic-interactions is often particularly clear in the offspring of a cross between distinct species.

It has already been explained that individuals may be regarded as belonging to the same species if they can inter-breed and produce fully fertile progeny (p. 72). This definition is not adequate for plants, but it is quite satisfactory for the higher animals including the Lepidoptera. Distinct species are usually wholly sterile with one another even if they can be induced to pair, but they sometimes produce sterile offspring (like the mule) or offspring which, though capable of reproduction, have poor fertility. In many instances these hybrids are of one sex only; or if both sexes are present, one of them may be rare, or sterile when the other is fertile. Professor J. B. S. Haldane long ago showed that if one sex is sterile, rare, or absent, among the progeny of a mating between different species, it is always that with the unlike (XY) chromosome-pair. This is the female in the Lepidoptera but the male in Mammals.

Species-crosses have been studied rather extensively in moths, in which a deficiency of females among the hybrids is often apparent; but unfortunately exceedingly little is known about them in butterflies. Dr H. B. Williams has pointed out to me that Klemann (1933) seems to have obtained a successful pairing in artificial conditions between a male Green-veined White, *Pieris napi*, and a female Small White, *P. rapae*. Both sexes were represented among the few offspring produced, which were intermediate in appearance between the parents. Among the Polyommatini, a variety, *polonus* Zell., is thought to be a natural hybrid between the Adonis and Chalkhill Blues, but the evidence for its origin in this way is purely circumstantial. Individuals belonging respectively to these species are occasionally found *in copula*; but this has little significance in itself, since pairings between most dissimilar butterflies, belonging even to different families, are sometimes encountered, and there is no suggestion, nor indeed possibility, that offspring result from them. However, *polonus* seems only to be found where the Adonis and Chalkhill Blues both fly, and it appears rather earlier than the latter species (usually near the beginning of July), so that its time of emergence is often between that of the presumed parents. Two forms of the male[1] are known. One is approximately intermediate in appearance, the fore-wings being more like *L. bellargus* in colour (and with the very narrow dark edging of that species) and the hind-wings more like *L. coridon*. The other is unlike the colour of either parent, or indeed of any other British 'Blue', being dull with a strong sheen of violet; the markings, however, are somewhat intermediate, though more like those of *bellargus*. The existence in a species-hybrid of characters unlike those of either parent is a well-known and singular occurrence. It indicates that the hereditary factors produce abnormal results when they work in an exceptional gene-complex, derived half from one species

[1] A few *polonus* females have been recorded, flying with the males. They are apparently intermediate, in so far as it is possible to state this of species whose females are so much alike.

and half from another. The gene-complex will be discussed further in Chapter 12, but one additional aspect of it may conveniently be considered now.

SEX-CONTROLLED INHERITANCE

The interactions which have so far been described take place during the rather complex developmental processes which link the hereditary factors with the characters they produce. Clearly, therefore, a given gene may have somewhat different effects in different individuals, depending upon the genetic setting in which it finds itself. Now one of the striking distinctions between different members of a species is that of sex, so that we may expect, and in fact we find, that the action of the genes is not always the same in males as in females. Moreover, many of them only become operative in the environment provided by one of the two sexes, to which therefore the characters they produce are restricted. This is called *sex-controlled inheritance*. It should clearly be recognized that the *genes* concerned in it exist in, and are transmitted equally by, both sexes; it is their effects which are confined to one of them. Sex-controlled inheritance is thus fundamentally distinct from the sex-linked type (pp. 190–1), in which the characters appear more often in one sex than the other for purely mechanical reasons; the genes responsible for them being carried in the sex-determining chromosomes. Consequently they are not transmitted equally by the male and female, nor in their operation wholly confined to one sex.

Evidently the features which normally distinguish the two sexes are sex-controlled; not only those associated with the actual sexual mechanism, but also such subsidiary qualities as wing-shape, colour, and marking. Since these remain true to their specific type, they must be inherited, but the set of factors responsible for the equipment of one sex must be inoperative or produce different effects in the other. However, sex-controlled inheritance is not confined to the maintenance of the ordinary sexual distinctions, for the appearance of certain forms and varieties is restricted to one sex only. Logically these fall into two quite different groups. First, variations in those characters possessed only by one sex must of necessity be sex-controlled. Thus any genes which may influence the shade of the orange patch in the Orange-tip butterfly could only be detected in the male, because orange coloration is absent from the female.

Secondly, characters possessed by both sexes may vary in a particular way in only one of them, because some genes cannot operate in males while others cannot do so in females. An orange ground-colour is possessed by the two sexes of the Clouded Yellow, *Colias crocea*. There is no *apparent* barrier to prevent the gene which converts it to a cream colour from acting in the male just as it does in the female, yet such a barrier exists, for cream-colour in males is unknown.[1] It is due to the type of environment required by the developmental processes which lead to the production of the pale pigment, and that is provided only by the female sex.

In the following brief summary of some of the more outstanding instances of sex-controlled inheritance in British butterflies (from which the ordinary sexual differences will, of course, be excluded), I shall not formally introduce the distinction which has just been drawn. It should none the less be clear to which type each of the examples belongs.

The Meadow Brown, *Maniola jurtina*, Plate 24. Some males possess no orange on the upper-side except the narrow ring surrounding the 'eye spot' on the fore-wings. In the majority of specimens, however, slight orange patches are present posteriorly to this and these occasionally become of considerable size, even as large as that found in the less marked of the females. It is indeed possible that while the amount of variation may be approximately similar in the two sexes, it is more obvious in the male, in which there may be an almost total suppression of orange, than in the female, in which the amount of that pigment is so much greater that it is never entirely lost. Well-marked forms in which the males were more like the females, or poorly-marked ones in which they were more distinct from them because destitute of orange, could almost certainly be produced by selective breeding.

The Silver-washed Fritillary, *Argynnis paphia*, provides a famous instance of sex-controlled inheritance, for the males are all alike in that their ground colour is of a rich brown, while two forms of the female exist. These are the normal one, much resembling the male in colour, and var. *valezina*, which is of a dark olive-green shade. This variety is inherited as a sex-con-

---

[1] They have once or twice been reported. I possess one of the supposed examples, but it is of a shade never found in the female form and it is, in fact, a different variety. The pale form of the male has, however, been reported as a great rarity in other species of *Colias*.

trolled 'dominant'. It is excessively rare throughout the whole British range of the species except in the New Forest, and a typical locality for it there is shown on Plate 13. Unfortunately, no trustworthy estimate of its frequency in that locality seems to have been made, though it is much needed. Any collector who obtained one would perform a valuable service (see pp. 256–60 for the necessary methods). However, general indications suggest that probably 5 to 15 per cent of the New Forest females are *valezina*. The great majority of these must be heterozygotes, for, at this frequency, no more than 0·07 to 0·66 per cent of the whole population would be homozygous *valezina*; a fact easily established if we calculate the distribution of the three genetic types by the means supplied on pp. 208–10. We are here assuming that the rare homozygotes are as hardy as the heterozygotes, which I do not believe; for this is an instance of 'polymorphism', in which the heterozygotes are likely to be at an advantage over both the homozygous classes. I fancy therefore that homozygous *valezina* must be much rarer than the calculated values, though it is known that they can be produced and that they do not differ in appearance from the heterozygotes.

The three genetic types are, of course, distributed in the same proportions among the males as among the females, so that 5 to 15 per cent of normal females caught in the New Forest should produce *valezina* offspring, which will have inherited the condition from their male parent, though this must have been an apparently normal specimen. Indeed, it is worth noting that half the *valezina* genes possessed by the population are carried, and therefore concealed, by the males. This suggests that the variety is not likely to be seriously reduced by over-collecting.

Eighty-five to ninety-five per cent of the *valezina* females in the New Forest, themselves heterozygotes, will have mated with normal homozygous males. They will therefore produce equal numbers of typical and of *valezina* females. It is especially to be noticed that those who breed from this variety will, on the average, obtain it in not less than half of the female offspring. But 5 to 15 per cent of *valezina* should have paired with heterozygous males and should, in theory, produce normals, heterozygotes, and homozygous *valezina* in a ratio of 1 : 2 : 1. If the latter class is less hardy than the others, this ratio should approach that of 1 : 2 instead of 1 : 3, which would be expected if dominance is complete.

The *valezina* form has been studied experimentally on the

Continent, and it was reported that such a 1 : 2 ratio was actually obtained. The explanation put forward to account for this was somewhat technical and need not be considered here, for that adopted on pp. 250–1, in discussing polymorphism is both easier to follow and more probable. It has been found that the optical stimulus which a female of this species must provide in order to be recognized by a distant male consists of the normal brown yellowish colouring when kept in rapid motion by the fluttering of the wings, and that the greenish colour of *valezina* is useless for this purpose, so that females of that form must be at a reproductive handicap. However, the butterfly is often common in its special haunts, so that when feeding on flowers *valezina* females are likely to meet males ready for copulation. At any rate, when caught in the wild it has generally been found that *valezina* females have in fact been fertilized, though they will probably have had to wait longer than the normal form before pairing is accomplished.

The ordinary brown females of the Chalkhill Blue Butterfly are occasionally marked with the male colour, but of a slightly deeper shade. Only a few blue scales may be present, but every gradation is found between that stage and one in which they spread over the greater part of the wings. At the same time the under-sides become progressively paler, so approaching the male. Such forms are called *semi-syngrapha* Tutt. Specimens are also known in which the whole upper-side of the female is blue. These are named var. *tithonus* Meigen (=*syngrapha* Kef.). Superficially they are very like the male, from which they can be distinguished at a glance by the presence of orange lunules on the border of the hind-wings, a character of the female not found in the male.

These blue females are especially prized by collectors, some of whom spend a great deal of time in hunting for varieties of this butterfly. They are well known to be far more frequent in some colonies and in some years than in others. Thus at Royston in Cambridgeshire, var. *semi-syngrapha* was for a number of seasons quite common, and fairly extreme forms of this and other varieties were not difficult to find there. In many places, however, hundreds of females may be examined without discovering more than one or two very slightly marked with blue.

It might reasonably be supposed that the completely blue females, var. *tithonus*, represent the last term of the *semi-syngrapha* series which appears to lead to them. Yet I am sure that this is incorrect, for their geographical distribution is quite different. I do not think that var. *tithonus* has been found at Royston, where *semi-syngrapha* was relatively common. On the other hand, var. *tithonus* formerly occurred not very uncommonly in a restricted locality on the Chilterns, but *semi-syngrapha* was very rare there and seemed to be no more frequent than elsewhere on the hills.

We have no exact information on the genetics of these varieties, but it may safely be asserted that both are inherited. *Semi-syngrapha* is probably multi-factorial. Var. *tithonus*, on the other hand, may well be controlled by a single pair of allelomorphs; it may be heterozygous or, more likely, a simple recessive. On the single occasion that, to my knowledge, eggs obtained from an example of it have successfully been reared, one female only was bred, and that normal. Such a result throws no light on its genetics, except to exclude the possibility that var. *tithonus* is controlled by a number of factors without dominance.

Females lightly scaled with blue are very much commoner in the Adonis than in the Chalkhill Blue. Though uniformly chocolate-brown specimens are the more usual, even those with a considerable amount of blue are not really infrequent, and they seem to occur in most of the localities. However, the more extreme forms are very seldom found. A completely blue female, much resembling the male, also exists but is of great rarity. It is known as var. *ceronus* Esp. and it is comparable with the var. *tithonus* of the Chalkhill Blue. The genetics of the corresponding forms in the two species are probably similar.

The situation just described in the Adonis Blue is in a sense intermediate between that in the Chalkhill and the Common Blue (Plate 19). For in the latter insect a scattering of blue scales is actually normal in the females. Those destitute of them are really quite uncommon. The specimens can be arranged in a continuous series up to the wholly blue var. *caerulea* Fuchs., which resembles the male, though it is of a more violet tone. There is no evidence to suggest that this is genetically distinct from the intermediates, as there is in var. *tithonus* of the Chalkhill Blue. All these forms of the Common Blue are probably due to multiple factors, which must be widespread in the species.

Females possessing a small but varying amount of blue scaling are found occasionally throughout the range of the Silver-studded Blue, *Piargus*, and, as will be explained, they are characteristic of the local races *masseyi* and *caernensis*. It will readily be appreciated how easily such a situation as that in the Chalkhill

Blue, in which blue females are much commoner in some localities than others, could give rise to a distinct geographical race: the parallel with the Silver-studded Blue requires no further emphasis.

The genus *Colias*, comprising the Clouded Yellow Butterflies, has an extremely wide distribution and includes a large number of species. These may be placed for convenience in one or other of two main groups. First, that in which the males are pale yellow and the females whitish. Secondly, that in which the males are of a deep orange shade and the females are of two forms; one of them, the commoner, resembling the male in colour, the other and rarer varying from primrose to white. Our own species, the Pale Clouded Yellow (Plate 22) and the Clouded Yellow (Plate 21) provide an example of each kind.

The pale female variety of the ordinary Clouded Yellow, the form *helice*, is inherited as a sex-controlled dominant. Several estimates of its frequency in nature have been made, but I can find no more than three of them carried out in Britain which involve counts of more than twenty specimens (Ford, 1942*b*); these are given in Table 3.

Two obvious sources of error may affect such sampling. First, since *helice* is a rarity prized by collectors, there is a tendency to make a special effort to catch it when the normal form might have escaped, so that the variety will appear to be commoner than it is. Both the 1865 and the 1928 estimates are possibly subject to this defect. Secondly, specimens may be counted twice

Locality and date	Normal females	helice	Total
Cornwall, 1865	182	8 (4·2%)	190
Suffolk, 1928	133	17 (11·3%)	150
Cornwall, 1941	55	9 (15·8%)	64

Table 3. The proportions in natural conditions of the two female forms of the Clouded Yellow Butterfly.

unless some means for avoiding that danger be taken. In the 1865 count, it is asserted that every specimen was killed; such unnecessary carnage at least increases its accuracy. The succeeding one, however, may to a small extent be vitiated by recaptures. The third in the list, that of 1941, I made myself and I know that it is subject to neither of these criticisms. All specimens seen were caught as far as this was possible, regardless of form.

Before being released, they were marked with a dot of cellulose paint (p. 257) so that they should not be counted twice.[1] Since it was clear to any practised observer that *helice* was not only absolutely but also relatively common in Cornwall in 1941, we may perhaps regard the estimate for that year as approaching the upper limit of its frequency: 5 to 10 per cent of all females is probably a much more usual figure. In these samples the proportion of *helice* chances to be higher in the more recent years, but this is purely a coincidence.

The situations provided by the *valezina* variety of the Silver-washed Fritillary and the *helice* variety of the Clouded Yellow are remarkably similar. Both species have a single form of male and two forms of female, of which the rarer is inherited as a sex-controlled 'dominant'. The chief point of difference between them is due to their habits; for the Clouded Yellow is a great migrant, owing its occurrence in these islands entirely to that fact. It would obviously be impossible therefore for *helice* to be restricted to a particular locality, like *valezina*.

All that has been said of the genetics of the *valezina* form may be taken to apply to *helice*. If we breed from a specimen of it, half the offspring will usually be of the normal deep yellow shade and half will be *helice*, and we cannot obtain less. It has, however, already been pointed out that we anticipate our expectation to be realized only within the ordinary limits of chance. An example drawn from the species now under discussion should help to clarify this generalization, which is one of the widest description. Two entomologists, particularly careful and accurate workers, recently reported the following result. On breeding from a female of the *helice* form they obtained twelve males and sixteen females, of which four were *helice*. Not only did they fail to breed equal numbers of the two female forms, though they had a right to anticipate doing so, but they obtained a different and well-known Mendelian ratio, that of 3 : 1. They correctly attribute what they describe as their 'abnormal figures' to the operation of chance; but it is particularly important to notice that these figures are not 'abnormal', since they do not depart *significantly* from equality, the chances against obtaining such a result merely fortuitously being well under 20 to 1 (p. 172). A distribution of 12 to 4 is simply incompetent to distinguish

---

[1] They could also be marked for this purpose, though less satisfactorily, by taking a small nick out of the edge of a wing at a fixed place with a pair of forceps.

between ratios of 1 : 1 and 3 : 1 therefore. Let the breeder remember that he is expecting certain results within certain limits, and that he would be wise to determine what those limits are for each result which he obtains. Appropriate methods for doing so are given by Mather (1943).

Just as a normal female Silver-washed Fritillary may produce *valezina*, since the gene determining it can be carried by either sex, so also may a normal female Clouded Yellow produce var. *helice*. The proportions of the genes carried by the two sexes are the same and, if we may assume 10 per cent to be a fair average figure for the frequency of *helice* females, it is also the frequency of heterozygous males, so that 10 per cent of the *normal* females will produce *helice*. Further, 10 per cent of all *helice* would have mated with a male carrying the *helice* gene. They should give a ratio of 3 *helice* to 1 normal female if the variety be fully domin-ant, as it probably is, and if the rare homozygotes are as hardy as the heterozygotes, which is decidedly unlikely. Indeed, as in *valezina*, a ratio of 2 : 1, or an approach thereto, is probably to be anticipated in these circumstances (pp. 249–50). The only known instance of a pairing between *helice* and a heterozygous male seems to be that recorded by Chapman, in which 79 males, 52 *helice* and 19 normal females were produced. Unfortunately, these numbers are not sufficient to distinguish between a 3 : 1 and a 2 : 1 ratio. Those who obtain F_2 generations from *helice* (by inter-breeding the *helice* offspring with their brothers) would perform a valuable service in helping to provide the additional data which are required for this purpose.

A further interesting feature of *helice* is its variability. Though due to a single gene, it is itself variable, ranging in colour from a primrose shade to white. Various names have been given to these forms, such as *helecina* Ob., *pallida* Tutt, and others. The only conceivable justification for naming arbitrary stages in a series such as this is the pleasure of doing so. But we must really curb our passions, and remember that such names are much worse than useless, especially when, as in this instance, they obscure a single-factor difference. Indeed, they seem effectively to have prevented its recognition in this species by some writers.

It is theoretically possible that these variations of *helice* are environmental in origin, but it is far more likely that they are wholly or partly due to the segregation of additional allelomorphs acting as 'specific modifiers'. That is to say, they represent instances of the phenomenon discussed on pages 218–19. Unfortunately, var. *helice* would not be a very satisfactory form on which to conduct selection experiments. This would almost certainly modify it in the direction either of greater yellowness or whiteness but, as the male situation would always be unknown, selection would be confined to one sex in each generation and its effect therefore retarded.

Specimens of the Orange-tip are occasionally found in which the orange on the fore-wings is replaced by a pale lemon yellow. The genetics of this variety are quite unknown; but it may well be inherited since, though it is very rare, two or more examples have sometimes been reported from the same district and in different years. It has, for instance, been encountered in the Isle of Man on several occasions.

Very rarely specimens of the Brimstone, *Gonepteryx rhamni*, have a large orange blotch covering most of the fore-wings. It would be particularly interesting to study this variety, the genetics of which are not known, since such specimens closely resemble the related continental species. *G. cleopatra*. This only differs in appearance from *G. rhamni* in the possession of such a blotch in the male, and in its less shapely angled wings by which the females alone can be distinguished.[1] It is quite likely that the development of the orange patch is homologous in the two species, having become rare in the one and a specific character in the other. It would be easy to mistake this variety of our Brimstone for *G. cleopatra*, a few specimens of which have indeed been recorded as taken in England. Some of these records may therefore be erroneous, but I believe that at least one or two of the specimens have been correctly identified as the foreign species.

When one sex undergoes gynandromorphism, any sex-controlled character which would have manifested itself in the other will actually do so in the sex-converted area. Thus specimens of the Silver-washed Fritillary are known which are half male and half *valezina* female, or one type may be limited to a small region only. Corresponding sexual and varietal mixtures of the Clouded Yellow also occur, being partly male and partly *helice* female.

The different aspects of factor-interaction discussed in this chapter all lead to variation. The part which they play in evolution will be considered briefly in Chapter 12, yet it will already

[1] See p. 102 for the difference in scent between the males of *G. rhamni* and *G. cleopatra*.

have been realized that they raise numerous and interesting problems which could be investigated by simple means. Collectors who devote their time to such work will find it well spent.

ENVIRONMENTAL VARIATION

The hereditary factors interact not only with one another to produce the characters for which they are responsible, but also with the environment in which they find themselves, as in sex-controlled inheritance. Thus we may reasonably expect that external conditions modify their effects and so influence the colour and pattern of butterflies; a conclusion which is fulfilled.

Temperature is among the most easily studied of such environmental agencies, and its influence on the production of melanin is particularly striking. It will be recalled that this substance is responsible for the black and brownish colours of butterflies, and that in these insects it is formed by the interaction of an enzyme, tyrosinase, in the blood, with a colourless substance, tyrosin, localized in those areas of the wings and body where the pigment will later be laid down.

A high temperature tends to restrict melanin production and a low one to promote it, at least within the range to which organisms are normally exposed. Thus heat restricts the deposition of tyrosin in the Vanessidi, and cold tends to extend it. A writer in *The Entomologist*, who had bred large numbers of the Small Tortoiseshell, expressed surprise that the specimens of the second brood, which had been reared in a cool sunless period, were darker than those of the first brood in warmer conditions; but this is just what one would expect in that species; a fact fully demonstrated in temperature experiments. These produce the contrary effect with increasing heat, which produced imagines with a bright reddish ground-colour and reduced dark markings, so making an approach to the local race *ichneusa* from Corsica.

On very rare occasions a most remarkable variation of the Small Tortoiseshell has been taken, in which the black markings are greatly extended in such a way that the normal pattern is quite altered; thus the result is very different from that produced by low temperatures. On the other hand, I have heard it said that it has appeared in temperature experiments. Perhaps it is due to an extreme (presumably low) temperature acting upon a particular genetic constitution. For not only may the action of the hereditary factors be altered by external agencies, as the very existence of environmental variation clearly shows, but also certain genes produce their known effects only at a given temperature: a phenomenon which has already been investigated in moths (Kettlewell, 1944), but not in butterflies.

The simple effect of temperature upon melanin formation may be modified by the hereditary constitution of the species. Thus dark individuals of the Pierinae are produced by warmth and pale ones by cool conditions: a reversal of the situation found in the Vanessidi, which is that due to a direct environmental control of the melanin reaction.

Clearly temperature alone could produce seasonal variation in butterflies, and it is indeed partly responsible for that well-known phenomenon. Those larvae which pupate in the cool of the autumn or the spring will have been subjected to lower temperatures than those which do so in high summer. For example, the first brood of the Small White, *Pieris rapae*, is made up of more lightly marked insects than the second brood, and this is true of the Large and the Green-veined Whites, *Pieris brassicae* and *P. napi*, also. A low temperature seems to favour melanin production in the Wood White, *Leptidea sinapis*, as it does in the Vanessidi, for specimens of the first generation possess more black pigment than those of the second. This need cause us no surprise, since this species is very distinct from our ordinary 'Whites' and belongs to a different sub-family, the Dismorphiinae.

Yet temperature is only one of the agents which may make the environment of an early brood unlike that of a later one, and any or all of them may play a part in the production of seasonal variation. Alterations in the rate of growth must sometimes affect the appearance of butterflies, for it is known that changes in it do not influence all the developmental processes to an exactly equal degree: a circumstance which may modify the colour-pattern of these insects since, as we have seen (pp. 51–2), this is due to the accurate timing of different processes in the body.

Only one British butterfly can pass the winter in either of two stages. This is the Speckled Wood, *Pararge aegeria*. Those individuals which hibernate as pupae come out in April or even late March, and their white markings are then unusually large. They are followed in late April and May by those which pupated in the early spring. Their pale areas are smaller, and

such specimens are indistinguishable from the second generation, which is on the wing from July to September. Our race of
this insect is the sub-species *aegerides* Stgr. The typical sub-
species, *aegeria*, occurs here only as a very rare variety, but it is
the normal one in southern Europe and North Africa. Its dark
markings are reduced in size, and the pale areas, instead of
being whitish, are of a rich brown shade, so that the insect bears
a superficial resemblance to the Wall Butterfly. It is unknown
whether the difference between *aegeria* and *aegerides* is produced
by environmental conditions, presumably temperature, or if it is
genetically controlled. Temperature experiments on the two sub-
species followed if necessary by crosses, would be most instructive and not difficult to perform.

A type of seasonal variation similar to that of the Speckled
Wood is found in the Comma, *Polygonia c-album*. The first
generation of this butterfly is divisible into two parts. The earlier
section, which appears in late June and early July, is the product
of larvae which fed up quickly, and is composed of specimens
which are immediately distinguishable from those produced at
any other time of year. They have a yellowish-brown underside,
the ground colour of the upper-side is bright and rather fulvous,
and their shape is quite characteristic, for the wings are decidedly
less scalloped and angled than in the typical form. Such specimens
are known as var. *hutchinsoni* Robson (Plate 20). They pair at
once and produce the second generation in September.

The later section of the first brood arises from larvae which
have fed up slowly, and it appears in late July and in August.
These specimens precisely resemble those of the second brood
(Plate 20), having a blackish underside, a rich reddish ground
colour above, and deeply scalloped and angled wings. All insects
of this type hibernate as adults and do not pair until the spring,
when individuals of the second part of the first generation and
those of the second generation mate indiscriminately. It is
unknown what determines whether their individual offspring
shall feed up quickly to produce *hutchinsoni*, or slowly to produce the normal form differing from that variety so markedly in
colour, shape, length of life, and mating habits.

Such a system is not likely to be wholly independent of
temperature. Indeed, very rarely specimens of *hutchinsoni* appear
in the autumn. It is said that this happens more often in hot than
in cold summers. If this is so, and the subject has not been
extensively studied, the temperature reaction cannot be of a simple

kind, since *hutchinsoni* is normally produced by larvae pupating earlier in the year, and on the average in cooler conditions than those which give rise to the normal form.

The most famous instance in which temperature reacts with rates of development to produce seasonal variation is supplied by *Araschnia levana*, and this is one which has been investigated in detail (Süffert, 1924). Reference has already been made to the extraordinary difference between the spring and summer broods of this butterfly, which was once so successfully established in England (pp. 166–7). The offspring of the Fritillary-like first generation, *levana* L. normally produce the White Admiral-like second generation, *prorsa* L.; but if subjected to cold as larvae or pupae, the summer insects are of the spring instead of the summer form, or else they are intermediates, called *porima* O. When caterpillars are cooled, the whole course of the insect's development is retarded, so that temperature then produces a general effect upon metabolism in addition to influencing the colour-pattern; if the pupae are so treated, they develop at the normal speed on being returned to the ordinary temperature (which the larvae do not). The response is then more localized, and the pupae are only susceptible for a limited period, the first 24 hours after they are formed, the hind-wings being affected slightly earlier than the fore-wings.

Yet in this butterfly temperature acts indirectly through its influence on the rate of development, rather than directly upon pigment formation. For if the larvae are cooled to a moderate degree, so that the emergence of the summer brood is spread over a long period, all the earlier insects to appear are of the *prorsa* form, as they should be, but those which come out towards the end are intermediates (*porima*), and the latest of all may even be *levana*. Furthermore, the hibernating pupae cannot be made to produce *prorsa*, or *porima*, by the application of heat during the susceptible pupal period or at any other time: on the contrary, they invariably emerge as the ordinary spring form *levana*. Presumably it is impossible to speed up sufficiently the development of individuals which are adjusted to survive the winter.

It may seem rather surprising that the susceptible period during which the pupa can be affected by temperature is not shortly before emergence when the pigments are appearing in the wings, but much earlier. In fact, however, the chemical processes which precede the manufacture of these substances, as well as those which control the development of the scales, must involve a lengthy series of reactions which may be influenced at given times during their early stages.

In southern England, but not indeed in Ireland, the Holly Blue, *Celastrina argiolus*, appears twice in the year. Specimens of the first generation, which flies in April and May, have fed on ivy, and they are of a brighter blue and are less heavily marked with black than those appearing in July and early August. This second brood is the product of larvae which have fed principally on holly; but it is only partial, for some of the offspring of the first generation do not emerge in the summer but remain as pupae until the following spring. Since the characteristics of the spring and summer specimens are preserved, this seasonal variation must be controlled by temperature, not by larval food or length of development.

The colours of some butterfly pupae are either thought or known to be affected by their environment, but the subject is not well understood. It is said that those of the Small White are more often green than dark-coloured on green surroundings, and this is reversed when they pupate on a brown or blackish background. Similarly, the pupae of the Small Tortoiseshell, the Peacock, the Red Admiral, and some other Vanessidi are yellow or golden when attached to their food-plant, but blackish when they have pupated on fences or tree-trunks.

Many years ago Professor E. B. Poulton (1892) studied this subject extensively on the Small Tortoiseshell, and showed that those larvae exposed to a yellow light produce pale pupae, while members of the same brood form blackish pupae in a blue light. He found that the larva was susceptible to this colour-stimulus for a short period only. This is after it has ceased to feed and during the time when, having selected its site for pupation, it remains quiescent before spinning the silken pad by which the pupa will be attached.

Poulton believed that the effect of light is a more or less direct one acting upon the surface of the body and not controlled secondarily through the eyes, for he found the response unaltered after the ocelli had been covered with black varnish. Yet Brecher (1921), who repeated his work on an extensive scale, reached the opposite conclusion. For she reports that if the ocelli are varnished blue, the dark type of pupa is produced irrespective of the background; similarly, a yellow varnish on the ocelli always gives light pupae. The whole subject is in need of further investigation, and it does not seem possible to form an opinion on it in the present state of our knowledge.

It will now be evident that variation may be due to either of two causes: to changes (mutations or recombinations) in the genes, or to changes in the environment affecting the *action* of the genes. Normally, these two agencies both contribute to produce the diversity of living organisms which we find in nature.

Chapter 12

Evolution

*Natural Selection – The Nature of Selection – Dominance –
Polymorphism, Evolution and Fluctuation in Numbers, Methods
of Studying the Numbers of a Population, The Rate of
Evolutionary Changes*

THE NATURE OF SELECTION

The theory of Natural Selection was given to the world on 1 July 1858, in the famous Darwin-Wallace lecture. In over eighty years it has been disputed, discussed, and amended and, since the First World War, it has come to be accepted more nearly in its original form, and with its original implications, than for more than a generation previously. Any theory which can stand searching examination for so long and remain so essentially unshaken must possess remarkable qualities: these reside in its apparent simplicity, its fundamental nature, and its universal application to living organisms. It will be necessary briefly to explain the modern version of the Darwinian theory of selection and then to consider some of the ways in which it throws light upon the natural history of butterflies.

On the farm or in the laboratory we can choose those individuals which are to be the parents of the next generation and, in so far as their characteristics are inherited, the choice will influence the type of offspring to which they give rise. But in natural conditions, those animals or plants which possess the most advantageous qualities and are the best fitted to their environment will most often succeed in reproducing their kind; consequently, they will contribute more to posterity than those which are less well endowed. Moreover, the characters which have ensured their success will thus tend to be disseminated through the population, causing it to change or 'evolve'. This simple statement requires a closer examination.

In the first place, selection implies the possibility of choice: there must be a superabundance of individuals above what is needed to perpetuate the race, and usually the excess is great. A pair of butterflies may produce several hundred fertile eggs, but from them, on the long average, a pair only will survive to reproduce if the species is to maintain itself at a constant level.

Secondly, selection could have no meaning in the absence of variation, for choice is merely fortuitous when exercised on a group whose members are identical. Thirdly, though it may be perfectly true that some individuals are better fitted for life than others, and more often survive to reproduce their kind, the natural selection which has favoured them can contribute nothing to evolution unless the chosen qualities are inherited. The reality of *selection* would remain, but it could produce no permanent effect. That is to say, the process cannot bring about an evolutionary change in the population if the variations upon which it works are purely environmental; a fact which is indeed self-evident, though it has now been subjected to rigorous proof.

We have seen that the characteristics of butterflies, as of other organisms, are due to genes working in a given environment, and that variations may be genetic, and therefore inherited, or else environmental, or both. These insects indeed, like other sexually reproducing organisms, possess a vast reserve of inherited variation maintained indefinitely by the Mendelian system of heredity. Further, the elimination which occurs during their life-history is enormous, but it is not always clear that it is due to anything but chance. The opportunities for natural selection to bring about evolution certainly exist, but it may legitimately be questioned if use is made of them.

It is essential to realize that the effects of selection are not necessarily large and spectacular. Even a very minute advantage will have an important effect over the long periods of time available for evolution if it causes one form to contribute slightly more than another to future generations. Yet it is not easy to demonstrate this in simple terms. A more detailed study of genetics makes it possible to show that genes having small, as well as great, advantageous effects are in fact being spread through wild populations by selection (Ford, 1971, pp. 88–90). Here we can only mention a few instances of selection operating on butterflies, and remark that some of the agents responsible for eliminating these insects in nature are capable of distinguishing between their varying colour-patterns, both in their early and adult stages. However, the reality of selection will become apparent also from the discussions to be found in the later sections of this chapter.

The variations of caterpillars, though often remarkable, have been studied far less thoroughly than have those of adult butterflies, and here is a valuable field for research. J. H. Gerould (1921) investigated a variety of the American Clouded Yellow, *Colias philodice*, a species much resembling our own *C. croceus*. It was one in which the normal grass-green colour of the larva is replaced by a blue-green shade. He showed that the condition is inherited as a simple recessive, and that the gene probably acts by modifying certain digestive processes. The green pigments of these larvae are apparently derived from those of their food-plants, which are due to the presence of a number of substances: blue-green chlorophyll-A, yellow-green chlorophyll-B, yellow xanthophyll, and orange-red carotin. It seems that the blue-green caterpillars can use only the chlorophyll-A. Consequently, they no longer match the leaves of the clovers upon which they feed. Gerould brought up a mixed batch of larvae in the open and found that all the blue-green specimens were eliminated by sparrows, while the normal yellow-green ones, protected by their concealing coloration, escaped.

In this country, Carrick (1936) conducted a series of valuable experiments on the effect of protective adaptations in insects. Most of the Lepidoptera which he used were moths, but he also worked with the larvae of three species of butterflies. Two of these, the Brimstone, *Gonepteryx rhamni*, and the Small White, *Pieris rapae*, are cryptically coloured, for both of them are green and match the leaves upon which they feed. The third, the Small Tortoiseshell, *Aglais urticae*, is in its later stages conspicuous, being black with a variable amount of yellow markings, and it possesses powerful spines which are no doubt protective; however, when young it is brown and clothed with very short hairs.

Carrick conducted his work in the field, exposing the larvae near the nests of small insectivorous birds which were feeding their young. Some specimens whose colours were of the concealing (cryptic) type were placed upon backgrounds which they matched, others on inappropriate ones. The cryptic butterfly larvae all fall within the latter group, and it will be seen from Table 4, in which I have summarized a part of Carrick's data, how heavily they were eliminated. This is in striking contrast to the adult larvae of the Small Tortoiseshell, which proved to be nearly immune to attack, even though highly conspicuous. On the other hand, when young, before the spines are developed, they are apparently very vulnerable.

In addition, I have added to Table 5 the data obtained with

Species	Protec-tion	Back-ground	Number offered	Number eaten	Predator
A. urticae (adult)	warning	right	30	1	Sedge Warbler
A. urticae (young)	?	wrong	6	6	Willow Warbler
G. rhamni	cryptic	wrong	7	6	Willow Warbler
G. rhamni	cryptic	wrong	6	6	Whitethroat
P. rapae	cryptic	wrong	6	6	Sedge Warbler
L. hirtaria	cryptic	right	22	4	Sedge Warbler
L. hirtaria	cryptic	wrong	12	7	Sedge Warbler

Table 4. Experiments performed by Carrick (1936) to demonstrate selection in nature.

one of the cryptic moth larvae, the twig-like Brindled Beauty, *Lycia hirtaria* Clerck, in order to show that such forms receive relative protection on the right background compared with the wrong one. The difference between the proportion of specimens taken in these two situations is, however, not fully significant.[1]

Moss (1933) showed that birds eat large numbers of butterfly pupae. He placed 148 pupae of the Large White, *Pieris brassicae*, in positions differing in their degree of exposure. Group 1 were in full view on the surfaces of walls, tree, and fences. Group 2

Group	Number of pupae	Number left in spring
1	37	2 (5·2%)
2	97	11 (11·3%)
3	14	12 (85·7%)
	148	25 (16·9%)

Table 5. The elimination of pupae of the Large White placed in various positions.

were partly concealed under window-sills and eaves, and Group 3 were placed inside outhouses. I give his results (with percentages added) in Table 5, which is based upon his own tabulation.

A heavy elimination during the pupal stage is clearly indicated by these results, and the nature of the damage showed that the destroyed pupae had been pecked by birds. Moss further observes that they demonstrate 'that situations that appear to the

[1] This is measured by $\chi^2 = 2·737$, which, with one Degree of Freedom, gives a value of P, which just exceeds 0·10.

human observer to afford concealment really do provide it'. Probably he is right, but I am doubtful if he has actually proved his point. On calculating the error involved, which he unfortunately omitted to do, I find that the difference between Groups 1 and 2 is not significant.[1] That between Groups 1 and 3 is clearly so; but it would be possible to infer that pupae receive a greater degree of protection from birds inside open buildings than outside, even though all situations out of doors were equally dangerous. I do not, of course, imagine that this is so. Indeed the difference which Moss observed between Groups 1 and 2 is in the right direction, and it would probably become significant with larger numbers.

Poulton and Saunders (1898), however, obtained more definite results, though they worked with the Small Tortoiseshell, which only remains in the pupal stage between ten days and three weeks. They exposed the pupae in various situations: on a bank, on fences, on walls, and attached to the food-plant (nettles). I have summarized their results in Table 6. The numbers on walls and

Site	Number of pupae	Number which survived
Banks	219	84 (38·3%)
Fences	98	8 (8·2%)
Walls	26	12 (46·2%)
Nettles	35	15 (42·9%)
	378	119 (31·4%)

Table 6. The elimination of pupae of the Small Tortoiseshell placed in various positions.

attached to nettles are small, but this work demonstrates a considerable difference in elimination between pupae placed respectively on banks and fences.[2] Unfortunately they obtained their results by using pupae of varying colours, a distinction which they do not seem fully to have analysed. They say, however, that part of the pupae were placed on a background which accorded to some degree with their own shade, and that part were reversed in this respect. We must presume therefore that the influence of colour may be excluded in so far as the site chosen for the pupae is concerned, a statement which can be

[1] The difference is 6·1 ±4·9%, so that it is only 1·25 times its Standard Error.
[2] The difference, being 30·1 ±4·3%, is heavily significant.

made with some confidence because the effect of position is such a large one.

The importance of colour in protecting pupae on different backgrounds is a matter of much interest. It is one on which information is greatly needed and it would provide an ideal subject for amateur research. It is not difficult to obtain light or dark, brown or green, pupae of some of our butterflies (p. 234). These should be divided into four groups: for instance, green pupae on green and dark backgrounds, dark pupae on green and dark backgrounds, and the amount of elimination recorded.

Work demonstrating the operation of Natural Selection in respect of the colour-patterns of the perfect insect would be particularly valuable and, though perhaps less easy, it is also well within the scope of any collector. It would be necessary to breed one or more large families segregating for the normal form and a variety. The specimens should then be marked (p. 257) and released in a suitable place, and the elimination determined by subsequent captures. Alternatively, if those who catch quantities of Lycaenidae, for instance the Chalkhill Blue, *Lysandra coridon*, merely to fill their cabinets with curios, would undertake work on the effect of selection they would probably derive more pleasure and interest from their studies and, incidentally, obtain information of much value. It would be necessary to choose a variable population, as was that of the Chalkhill Blue at Royston for many years, and to mark, release, and recapture at intervals, normal specimens and varieties. Differences in the marking can easily be made to indicate whether the individuals were fresh or worn when first caught, and the date of release. Naturally the work need not be restricted to the Lycaenidae: it could be done on any species in which variable colonies may be found, for instance the Marsh Fritillary, *Euphydryas aurinia*. Those who undertake such studies would be well advised to submit their results to a statistician, or to read a simple book on statistical methods (e.g., Mather, 1943), before publishing their results, if they chance to be unacquainted with the necessary mathematical technique.

So little attention has been given to investigations of this kind that we have very few direct observations on the effect of selection on adult butterflies (but see pp. 261–5). However, I have by other means demonstrated its operation in an African Swallow-tail, *Papilio dardanus*. The females, but not the males, of this insect are polymorphic and most of the forms are mimetic (p. 107).

B.   K

That is to say, though they are themselves palatable, they copy species which are protected by a nauseous taste and so escape their enemies by deception. A very large and random collection of butterflies had been made at Entebbe in Uganda, and I found that this included 111 female specimens of *P. dardanus* in several of its forms, together with 1949 examples of the various species which they copy. A similar random collection was also formed near Nairobi in the mountains east of Lake Victoria. Here *P. dardanus* is not uncommon and 133 females were included in the captures. However, the models are very rare in this mountainous region, which provides an exceptional habitat in which the Swallow-tail can live without their protection, and only 32 of them were obtained. In the Entebbe sample, four specimens (3·6 per cent) of the mimic belonged to forms in which the resemblance to the model is imperfect, but at Nairobi 42 (32 per cent) were of this kind. These figures show that at Entebbe the models are 73 times commoner relative to their mimics, and the forms of *P. dardanus* which copy them but imperfectly are nine times rarer, than at Nairobi.

The importance of selection in maintaining the correct pattern of the mimetic forms is here well illustrated, since it fails to do so when the models are rare. This example also demonstrates an important consideration which will be developed further on pp. 255–6: namely, that selection tends to produce uniformity, so that the inherited variation of any species is in equilibrium between Mendelian recombinations (and mutation), tending to increase it, and selection tending to diminish it.

It may be well to draw attention to an obvious fallacy in considering the effects of variation in adult butterflies. This is the conclusion that, since by far the greatest amount of elimination takes place in the early stages, the colour-pattern of the adults must be relatively unimportant. Such a point of view is ridiculous, though it has often been maintained: yet it should be evident that as the individuals become fewer during the life-history of an insect, so the survivors become progressively more valuable. I do not know what the average numbers at different stages would be, and they would, of course, vary according to the species. But let us suppose that a female lays 300 eggs, that 100 become half-grown larvae, 30 become pupae, and that 5 become imagines. The elimination of a single butterfly before reproduction would then be six times as important as that of a newly-formed pupa, twenty times as important as that of a half-grown larva, and 60 times as important as that of an egg.

The habits of the two sexes are so different in butterflies that their elimination must be dissimilar. Very little is known of this subject, and there is here a considerable field for inquiry. There is a general tendency for the males to emerge before the females, and this is carried to an extreme in some species, of which the Hedge Brown, *Maniola tithonus*, and the Meadow Brown, *M. jurtina*, are examples: more than a fortnight may elapse between the emergence of the earliest males and the earliest females of these butterflies. As Mr R. F. Bretherton has pointed out to me, a balance must have been reached here. The prior appearance of the males ensures that a maximum number of females are fertilized before their adult elimination takes place. On the other hand, the death-rate of the early males must be compensated in one of two ways: either the sex-ratio must depart from equality, males being much the commoner, or polygamy must be the rule. It should be quite possible to decide between these alternatives, or to dis over if they are to some extent combined.

The agents which are responsible for the great destruction which occurs during the lives of butterflies are, of course, exceedingly varied: inclement weather, parasites, and disease (especially fungus diseases) take a heavy toll of them in the early stages, and, to a small extent, predaceous insects, especially dragonflies and Hymenoptera, are a danger in the adult state also. But it must principally be vertebrate predators which are responsible for the type of selective elimination against which the colour-pattern provides the chief defence. In this country, birds are by far the most important of these: lizards play a very small part here, though they become more serious enemies in warmer climates.

Detailed observations on the extent to which birds eat butterflies are sadly lacking, and collectors are earnestly requested to obtain data on the subject. However, Professor G. D. Hale Carpenter (1937) has brought together an imposing array of evidence to show that they do so extensively.

The frequency with which birds attack butterflies, particularly in the adult state, seems to be much underestimated by naturalists. The act is rapid and easily overlooked, and its interest has not been sufficiently evident to warrant recording it when seen. Moreover, butterflies are so quickly reduced to unrecognizable fragments after being swallowed that they are likely to pass unnoticed in an analysis of the stomach-contents of birds.

However, difficult as they are to see, most entomologists will have witnessed such attacks on many occasions. For instance, I have repeatedly watched small birds of various species perching in the neighbourhood of flowering Buddleias in order to catch the butterflies which were attracted to the blossoms; in these circumstances I have never observed one molested when it was at rest, but only when flying round the bush. It is remarkable how often on these and other occasions the birds miss the insects, or seize them only by the wings instead of by the body. They will then usually carry them off and peck them to pieces on the ground, but often they attempt to alter their grip at once, while still in the air, when the butterfly not infrequently escapes. Its wings then bear the imprint of the bird's beak, and on Plate 10 I illustrate a specimen which shows this clearly.

The leathery consistency of the distasteful groups of butterflies (e.g., the Danaidae), common in the tropics, allows them to be caught and pecked by a bird sufficiently to determine their nauseous qualities, when they are released often but little the worse for the experience (p. 158). Consequently, such beak-marks are found far more frequently on 'protected' species than on those which appear to be palatable, a fact successfully established by Professor Carpenter (1941). The accurate vision of birds probably makes them rigorous agents in eliminating those varieties whose colour-pattern provides the less satisfactory protection. It would be well worth while to survey the relative frequency of such beak-marks on normal specimens and varieties, for it is possible that their differential elimination may sometimes be large enough to be detected by such means.

Butterflies themselves seem to appreciate extreme departures from the typical form, for varieties of a marked kind, irrespective of sex, are sometimes mobbed by the normal insects. In colonies in which a species is very abundant, for instance in the Chalkhill Blue, many specimens are occasionally seen flying together and apparently jostling one another in the air. Such an association frequently contains an extreme variation, a fact well known to collectors.

It has already been pointed out that, in some species at least, the male butterfly finds the female by sight, and that variations in colour greatly affect his power to do so. This must certainly constitute a powerful selective agent in maintaining the normal coloration of such insects. Thus, as explained on pp. 63–4, when Dr H. Eltringham and I bleached Pearl-bordered Fritillaries,

Clossiana euphrosyne, and dyed them different colours, those of approximately the correct shade were visited by the male thirteen times in half an hour and the other colours not at all. Also when Dr Eltringham dyed paper models green, blue, red, tawny-yellow (the natural shade), brown and a clear pale yellow, those of the natural colour attracted twenty-seven individuals, the red ones eighteen, the pale yellow two, and the other colours none.

On a subsequent occasion, I bleached six dried specimens of the Small Pearl-bordered Fritillary, *C. selene*, and pinned them, with six normally-coloured dried examples, to the ground where the butterflies were flying. The untreated specimens received eleven visits in an hour while the bleached ones, in which the ground-colour was nearly white, did not receive any. Now a white variety of this species actually exists as a great rarity in nature, but it is commoner in some localities than others. When it occurs in the female sex it seems unlikely that it would ever be fertilized. Here we have a striking instance of the action of sexual selection: a process which must ensure that, in species such as this, certain varieties shall contribute less to posterity than the normal form, so that they will tend to be eliminated. It is clear that variations in the strength or quality of the attractive scents emitted by butterflies would also be particularly subject to selection of this kind.

DOMINANCE

Natural selection was to Darwin a process which rejected the worse and preserved the better elements in the population, but to us it is something more; for we know that it is capable of modifying the *effects* of a gene, so as to diminish its influence if they are harmful or to enhance it if they are beneficial. That is to say, selection has not merely to play the part of accepting or rejecting the variations presented to it, but it has some power of adjusting them to the needs of the organism. It does so by the selection of other genes which modify the influence or expression of the particular one in question. This possibility is one which follows naturally from the facts discussed in the last chapter. It was there pointed out that the genes have multiple effects and that they interact with one another to produce the characters for which they are responsible. Consequently, variation may occur in a structure controlled by a single pair of allelomorphs and, though part of it may be environmental, some of it will be inherited. Thus it can be modified by selection; whether this be exercised consciously by the breeder or whether it be the 'natural selection' to which butterflies, like other organisms, are exposed throughout their lives.

A study of Table 2 (p. 209) shows that when a gene is rare it occurs much more frequently in the heterozygous than in the homozygous state. Evidently, therefore, the influence of selection in modifying the effects of rare genes will be almost entirely confined to heterozygotes; and among them, those individuals will be favoured whose disadvantageous characters are the least accentuated. Clearly, therefore, selection will tend to spread through the population a genetic constitution which minimizes the action of harmful genes when they are heterozygous. On the other hand, the species will not be able to adjust itself to the homozygotes, since these will be so very rare that it will have had scarcely any experience of them. Nor should we necessarily expect that a condition which cloaks the action of a gene in a single dose will be able to do so when the dose is a double one.

Now to suppress the action of a gene when heterozygous but not when homozygous is to make it *recessive*, hence there is a general tendency to press the effects of deleterious genes into the recessive state, and they will, on the whole, be eliminated during the process. On the other hand, they will constantly be maintained in small numbers by recurrent mutation, so giving an opportunity for the population to be adjusted to them by selection acting on other genetic factors which modify their expression.

The converse process will, of course, operate in favour of any genes which confer a benefit upon the organism. Those individuals in which their effect is most pronounced when they are heterozygous will leave the most descendants, and selection will thus spread through the species genetic constitutions which tend to enhance the valuable qualities for which such genes are responsible, and so make them dominant. This effect will be rather a rapid one, because the advantageous genes will spread through the population, giving increased opportunities for selection to modify their action.

During the course of the last three chapters it will have been realized that the dominance or recessiveness of an inherited character is one of its most important attributes and it will now be clear that this is determined by selection, a conclusion for which Professor R. A. Fisher was originally responsible (1928).

It was a most welcome one, for the apparently haphazard way in which dominance is associated with some genes, and recessiveness with others, had seemed to introduce an arbitrary feature into the otherwise logical system of genetics.

A great bulk of circumstantial evidence has accumulated which demonstrates the evolution of dominance by selection, but the theory has very seldom been put to actual experimental proof. This was done first by Professor Fisher himself (1935), who worked upon certain characteristics in poultry which had become dominant owing to unconscious artificial selection. The second experimental test of dominance-modification was carried out on the yellow variety *semi-lutea* of the Currant Moth, *Abraxas grossulariata* (Ford, 1940b). This is the only occasion on which such work has so far been conducted on wild material; and the selection to which domesticated stocks are exposed is, of course, of rather a special kind. We thus return to the original example used to introduce the subject of genetics in Chapter 9. By dividing a stock into two lines in one of which the darkest, and in the other the lightest, heterozygotes were selected for four generations, I was able to make the yellow variety nearly a dominant on the one hand and nearly a recessive on the other. At the end of the work I was able to show that the gene itself had been unaffected by the process. This was done by crossing modified heterozygotes to wild unselected normal specimens, a process which went far towards restoring the original condition after only two generations: thus it was the response of the moth to the gene, not the gene itself, which had been changed.

Work demonstrating the influence of selection on the effect of the genes could be conducted rather easily on British butterflies, and it would be of much interest and importance. Evidently it would also be possible to demonstrate in them the evolution of dominance and recessiveness by selection, in the same way that it has actually been done in the Currant Moth.

POLYMORPHISM

Polymorphism is a term that is often loosely used. The definition of it now accepted is, the occurrence together in the same habitat of two or more distinct forms of a species in such proportions that the rarest of them cannot be maintained by recurrent mutation (Ford, 1940a). It is necessary to explain this definition, for the situation with which it deals is of special interest to butterfly collectors. In the first place, it excludes seasonal variations and geographical races, for it relates to forms which occur together in the same population. Secondly, it deals not with graded character-differences, as in the reduction of spots in the Ringlet, *Aphantopus hyperanthus* (p. 214), but with those which are sharply contrasted. Further, polymorphism will very seldom be due to environmental variation, for individuals flying together in the same locality will be subject to very similar conditions, and such diversity as they encounter will not be of a kind likely to produce alternative forms whose respective characters are clearly defined.

We must therefore consider heritable variation. From the point of view of selection, the genes all fall under one of three headings: those which are advantageous to the species, those which are disadvantageous to it, and those which are neutral as far as their survival value is concerned. But this last group is very rare, for R. A. Fisher (1930) has shown that the balance of advantage between the members of a pair of allelomorphs must be extraordinarily exact if their selective value is a negligible one. Moreover, unless a gene is favoured by selection, it will take an immense time to spread through a species until it occupies even 2 or 3 per cent of the individuals. If actually disadvantageous, it would never, in normal circumstances, progress so far, for it would tend to be eliminated and would disappear altogether were it not maintained at a low level by rare recurrent mutation. As we have seen in the last section, the effects of such genes will generally become recessive and though, as a whole, they are responsible for a vast amount of heritable variation, each one of them must be very uncommon.

It will thus be clear that if a form occupies even a small percentage of a population, it must normally have reached that frequency because it is beneficial. Here we are confronted with two possibilities: either the form is a favourable one which is in process of spreading, or it must be maintained at a constant level by a balance of selective advantages. These two alternatives merit rather careful examination.

Since mutation is recurrent, advantageous genes will very seldom be found in the process of establishing themselves, for they will generally have been able to do this long ago. On the other hand, we must remember that all environments are liable to change, and a gene which was unsatisfactory in one may be useful in another: evidently this may well be true of the effects of civilization. While a gene is actually spreading in a new environment, the character to which it gives rise will fall within our definition of polymorphism; but it will sweep through the population, which will become effectively uniform again when the process is complete. I have therefore described this situation as 'Transient Polymorphism'. I know of no instance of it in our British butterflies, but it has been observed in a number of British moths, in which the most striking examples are provided by the phenomenon of 'industrial melanism'.

It is a most extraordinary fact that, within the last eighty years or so, almost the whole population of a number of species, belonging to different groups of our moths, have lost their normal concealing coloration and become black in manufacturing areas and their neighbourhood. This represents one of the most considerable evolutionary changes which have ever been witnessed in any living creature in the wild state. It therefore has an interest and importance which stretch far beyond the confines of entomology. Various theories have in the past been put forward to account for it, but none of them has appeared to me to be satisfactory. I therefore advanced a new interpretation of it which I have been able to verify experimentally (Ford, 1940*b*). However, industrial melanism can only be touched upon here in so far as it provides an example of transient polymorphism. To take an instance, the black variety *carbonaria* Jordan (=*doubledayaria* Mill.) of the Peppered Moth, *Biston betularia* L., was first caught in 1848 near Manchester, where previously only the normal form was known. This latter is speckled black and white, so that the moth resembles a patch of lichen when at rest upon a tree. However, the black variety has spread through the population until the typical insect has now become a rarity in the Manchester district. While the process was taking place, the species provided an example of transient polymorphism.

Polymorphism may also arise in a very different way from that just described. A form may confer some benefit on the species, but it may be of such a nature that its advantage wanes as it becomes commoner, and is finally converted into a disadvantage. Consequently, such a form can never establish itself throughout the whole population, but reaches a frequency at which it is in equilibrium: it does so when its value is balanced by the harm which would result if it were to become more abundant. I have described this situation as 'Balanced Polymorphism', and it is a lasting one.

Now the selective opposition to the spread of an advantageous gene may be either environmental, arising from the very nature of the advantage itself, or it may be genetic. The distribution of the two sexes provides an example of the first of these two types of balanced polymorphism. It will evidently be important for one sex to occur in a given fraction of the population but no more, and the proportions of the sexes will be balanced against one another in equilibrium which in most, but by no means in all, animals will be in the neighbourhood of equality. If one sex were for some reason to become too rare, selection would favour its spread again up to a given percentage, but no further.

Sex provides rather a special case with, usually, a special genetic control. Normally a balanced polymorphism will be established genetically when a heterozygote is at a greater advantage than either of its corresponding homozygotes, for evidently the whole population cannot be maintained in a heterozygous state. Moreover, as Table 2 (p. 209) shows, the proportion of individuals belonging to the rarer homozygous class increases rapidly as the heterozygotes become commoner. Consequently, the spread of a gene which is advantageous when heterozygous may be brought to a standstill at a fairly early stage if it i very harmful when homozygous. Indeed, many instances ar known in which such homozygotes are markedly unhealthy o actually unable to survive.

We have two famous examples of polymorphism (in addition to sex) among our British butterflies; these are, the *valezina* form of the Silver-washed Fritillary, *Argynnis paphia*, in which the ground-colour is blackish-green instead of the normal orange-brown, and the whitish *helice* form of the Clouded Yellow, *Colias crocea* (Plate 21). Magnus (1958) has discovered a situation which opposed the spread of *valezina*. He finds that the optical stimulus provided by a female *paphia* to stimulate a distant male consists of the normal orange-brown colouring of this butterfly kept in motion by the fluttering of the wings. The greenish shade of *valezina* is useless for this purpose and must be a real handicap. However, as he points out, this species is often common in its localities so that *valezina* females feeding on flowers are likely to meet males ready for copulation. Indeed, when caught wild, *valezina* females generally have been fertilized, though they will at any rate have had to await copulation longer than the normal form and so lay fewer eggs.

In both *A. paphia* and *C. crocea* two female forms exist flying together in the same habitats; the commoner one occupying from 85 to 95 per cent of the female population, and the rarer which is inherited as a simple complete 'dominant'. These rarer forms could not have reached so high a frequency as 5 to 15 per cent unless they had some advantage, and they would have continued to exploit their superiority until they had supplanted the normal ones had they not carried with them some counterbalancing drawback. This will almost certainly be found in an inferiority of their corresponding homozygotes, which are probably delicate, sterile, or altogether inviable. It would be possible to test the accuracy of this conclusion by making up matings which would normally lead to segregation in a 3 : 1 ratio; it may then be found that a ratio of 2 : 1, or an approach to it, is actually obtained, indicating a deficiency of the class representing the homozygous variety. The type of cross which is required to produce such families has already been described (p. 223), and any collector who is able to provide these data will be performing a valuable service.

It chances that in both these examples the variety is sex-controlled and limited to the female, but this is not a necessary feature of such polymorphism, as a study of foreign butterflies, or of British moths, would show. Thus the variety *hospita* Schiff. of the Wood Tiger Moth, *Parasemia plantaginis* L. supplies an instance of sex-controlled polymorphism limited to the male. The form is one in which the ground-colour is white instead of yellow, and it is found only on mountains: in the Lake District and in the Scottish Highlands. On the other hand, the Riband Wave Moth, *Ptychopoda aversata* L., exists in two polymorphic forms, *remutata* L. (the commoner) and *aversata*, and these occur equally in the two sexes.

It is especially to be noticed that a species may be polymorphic in a part only of its range. This is indeed to be expected, since the advantages involved are very closely adjusted to the needs of the insect, and a form may be an asset in one type of habitat but not in another. Thus in Britain the polymorphism of the Silver-washed Fritillary is restricted to the New Forest (Plate 13). Only there does *valezina* occupy approximately 10 per cent of the female population; throughout the remainder of the insect's range it occurs merely as a rare variety, probably less than one female in 500 being of that form. Similarly, the *hospita* form of the Wood Tiger has evidently some advantage on mountains, but otherwise it must be stringently eliminated, for it is quite unknown elsewhere. On the other hand, the Riband Wave is polymorphic throughout its range: so also is the Clouded Yellow Butterfly, but since this is a notable migrant, one which cannot survive the winter in this country, it would not be possible for *helice* to be restricted to particular localities.

It will be apparent that the existence of a polymorphism always indicates a situation of special interest, one which invariably repays study (Ford, 1965, 1971). It either shows that a variety is in the actual process of spreading in nature, so that we have the opportunity of examining an evolutionary change in progress, or that an advantageous form is balanced by some disadvantage; a situation capable of throwing considerable light on the working of natural selection.

EVOLUTION AND FLUCTUATION IN NUMBERS

Selection operating on inherited variation is capable of bringing about evolutionary changes. As Huxley (1942) has pointed out, evolution includes a variety of processes of which one, the origin of species, has received perhaps undue attention. Among the remainder may especially be mentioned the evolution of adaptations, the establishment of non-adaptive characters, the evolution of genera and of larger groups, and the processes which lead to extinction, and there are others. I do not propose to survey these in any detail, but attention must be drawn to a few of the evolutionary trends which they involve.

The evolution of adaptations is one of the most obvious effects of selection. Those individuals which are the best fitted to their environment will contribute most to posterity, so that the characters to which they owe their success will be disseminated through the population. Now a few points in this apparently simple situation require a brief study.

All the animals, and obviously all the insects, which we know today are really rather highly organized creatures, and it is difficult to make changes in a highly organized system which will promote its harmonious working: variations in it are very much more likely to be harmful than beneficial. Now the genes have multiple effects, and evidently we can be sure that when one of them is advantageous the others will very rarely be so too. Thus when a favourable character is spread through the population by selection, it will in addition carry with it certain disadvantages. However, these can often be minimized by selection modifying the effects of the genes in the manner already outlined (pp. 244-7).

Some organisms succeed by being 'euryplastic' (Huxley, 1942, pp. 444 and 519); that is to say, they have a general high viability and can adapt themselves to a wide range of conditions. Those, on the other hand, which are 'stenoplastic' (ibid.) are narrowly adapted to a particular environment. These tend to become more and more closely fitted for life in their own special type of surroundings and less able to live in any other. But environments are not permanent things: sooner or later they will change, and those forms which are deeply committed to them will be unable to readjust themselves and will become extinct. Close adaptation is indeed a very usual evolutionary process, and yet it carries with it a high probability of extinction: the vast majority of evolving lines are heading for ultimate destruction, and evolution is far more often in the long run a failure than a success. As the more highly specialized groups or species are eliminated, so the less highly specialized ones have an opportunity of evolving, and of occupying their places. There is indeed to be discerned in evolution a general 'upward' tendency or 'advancement', independent of human values for, as J. S. Huxley has pointed out, the more highly evolved organisms have on the whole become less dependent upon their environment. But the process is accompanied by an extreme wastage and repetition of failure.

The evolutionary origin of species has attracted the greatest amount of attention, partly, no doubt, owing to the title of Darwin's most famous book. It requires, in addition to selection operating on inherited variation, the existence of some degree of isolation, using that word in the widest sense. Something, that is, which can check the free flow of genes throughout a population: whether it be geographical isolation, seasonal isolation, or isolation due to adaptations to different types of habitat within the same area. Only in isolation can a form evolve independently until it becomes specifically distinct. But the evolution of subspecies leading, in certain circumstances, on to that of species, will be discussed in the next chapter. It is here necessary to point out that the course of evolution in isolated colonies may be very remarkable. It is one which the collector of butterflies often encounters, and he is in a particularly good position to study it. I propose therefore to draw attention to a few of its special characteristics.

Colonies of a species may be localized by a variety of conditions. They may be cut off on islands, or they may be restricted to a particular type of habitat, such as mountains, marshes, moors, or woods, and any of these may be completely isolated from places of a similar character. It is probable that in Great Britain the course of civilization is increasing the isolation of colonies, and thus actually facilitating the evolution of local forms.

Now it has already been explained in Chapter 7 that fluctuations in numbers and in areas of distribution take place throughout the whole population of certain butterflies, but isolated colonies of a species are particularly susceptible to such fluctuations, whether as part of the more general trend or in response to local conditions. In an isolated habitat the food-supply may partly fail, circumstances may for a season or more favour the parasites or the diseases of an insect, or bad weather may occur at some critical stage in the life-cycle. Any of these events may greatly reduce an isolated population and cause it to fall far below the numbers which the area could support in favourable conditions. When these return, a recrudescence of the colony may be expected, so that the population will fluctuate over a long or a short period according to circumstances.

Such fluctuations allow special opportunities for minor evolutionary changes to take place, and these constitute a fascinating study. It will be convenient first to illustrate them by means of an example and then to discuss them.

My father, H. D. Ford, and I kept a colony of the Marsh Fritillary, *Euphydryas aurinia*, under observation for nineteen years (Ford & Ford, 1930). It was situated in Cumberland, where it was isolated by several miles from any other in the district; indeed it was confined to a few swampy fields, from which the butterflies rarely strayed, even for a short distance, into the adjoining woods and meadows. Records of its conditions had been kept by collectors for a period of 36 years before we began our work, and preserved specimens obtained at intervals during that time were available for us to examine. Thus a fairly thorough study of this population could be made over a period of 55 years, and during that time an extreme fluctuation in its numbers took place.

The species was quite common in 1881, and gradually increased until by 1894 it had become exceedingly abundant. After 1897 the numbers began to decline, and from 1906 to 1912 it was quite scarce. From 1913 to 1919 it was very rare, so that a few specimens only could be caught each year as a result of long-continued search, where once they were to be seen in thousands. From 1920 to 1926, a very rapid increase took place, so that by 1925 the butterfly had become excessively common, and so it remained until we ceased our observations in 1935.

The amount of variation was small during the first period of abundance and while the species was becoming scarce, and it may be said that a constant form existed at this time, from which departures were infrequent. When the numbers rapidly increased, an extraordinary outburst of variation took place so that hardly two specimens were alike, while extreme departures from the normal form alike in colour, pattern, and shape, were common. A high proportion of these were deformed in various ways, and some could hardly fly. When the rapid increase had ceased, such abnormalities practically disappeared and the colony settled down once more to a comparatively uniform type. This, however, was recognizably different from the one to be found during the first period of abundance.

Various interpretations have been placed on this remarkable occurrence and on the association between fluctuations in the numbers and the variability of a colony of which it is an example. It will be noticed that it was not due to the segregation of recessives consequent upon inbreeding (pp. 209–10) when the community had become very small, since the variation did not occur until the numbers were rapidly increasing. In order to make this phenomenon clear,[1] we must return to the point developed on p. 242 that genetic variability is in a state of equilibrium between recombination (and mutation) tending to increase it, and selection tending to diminish it.

If the numbers of a population are being reduced, some aspect of the environment, in the widest sense, must have become particularly severe, and selection will be exceptionally rigorous in eliminating all but those forms which are best able to survive. Consequently much variation will be unlikely at such times and the population will be reduced to smaller numbers than the locality could normally accommodate. Accordingly, when the conditions become more favourable again, the numbers will rapidly rise until they attain the level at which reproduction is balanced by elimination; meanwhile selection will be less stringent than usual, so that the population will become variable.

[1] I am, of course, aware of the ill-informed explanation of Sewall Wright; see the criticisms of Fisher, 1941a.

Once the numbers have reached the normal limit, stricter selection will be restored and marked variations will no longer be possible.

The period of rapid increase in numbers thus provides a special opportunity for genetic recombinations to take place, many of which would very seldom be realized in a stable population. The great majority of these will be unfavourable and would never survive in normal conditions, but among them one or two may be found more satisfactory than those of which the colony has had previous experience. These will be favoured when the selection becomes stricter again, so that a stable form will be produced differing from that which existed before the fluctuation in numbers.

In support of this view it is especially to be noticed that many of the more extreme varieties which occurred from 1920 to 1926 were deformed, some of them grossly, and we may reasonably suppose that they would have a lower survival value than the typical specimens. This is corroborated by the fact that they became very rare after the period of rapid increase.

Though the causes of the relation between fluctuation in numbers and the variability of a colony may be somewhat obscure, there is less doubt about its effects. Clearly it allows the species to adjust itself to its environment more rapidly than it would otherwise do, and it enables us to examine actual instances in which an evolutionary change takes place in nature.

METHODS OF STUDYING THE NUMBERS OF A POPULATION

Isolated populations of many species of butterflies occasionally undergo extreme fluctuations in numbers, and the Marsh Fritillary provides an example of this not only in the colony which we studied but also throughout its entire range. Moreover, an outburst of variation has more than once been casually noticed in several localities at the time when the population was increasing. Thus good opportunities exist for collectors to make observations on this remarkable occurrence. When doing so, it would be very desirable to obtain information on the actual numbers at different times, and it will be valuable to describe a method by which this can be done. It may be added that there are many other circumstances in which it would be extremely interesting to estimate the absolute numbers of a wild population of butterflies or moths.

As long ago as 1930, I suggested that this could be calculated by marking, releasing, and recapturing specimens. Fundamentally, the method depends upon the following proposition. Suppose that we mark 100 butterflies in any colony, release them and allow them to become thoroughly dispersed; then, if we catch another 100 and find that 10 of them are marked, we can estimate the population as:

$$100 \times 100/10 = 1000.$$

The practical details and the theoretical possibilities of this method have been fully explained by Dowdeswell, Fisher, and Ford (1940), and I shall here briefly summarize a part of our results.

It seemed to me important to discover if it were possible to mark butterflies satisfactorily for work of this kind, and to show not only that it enables the numbers of a population to be estimated at any given time, but also that it allows the changes which they undergo, owing to emergence and to deaths, to be analysed. For this purpose Professor W. H. Dowdeswell and I camped on an uninhabited island (Tean, Isles of Scilly), where we studied the population of the Common Blue, *Polyommatus icarus*, from 26 August to 8 September 1938, and a previous period of investigation was also necessary. We felt that if marking could be successfully carried out on so small a species, it could be used widely.

In such work it is essential to know not merely whether any specimen which may be taken had been caught before, but also the date of its first capture and of any subsequent recaptures. For this purpose we marked each insect with a dot of cellulose paint. This seals the scales on to the wing and is then permanent and waterproof. It dries very rapidly, so that it becomes sufficiently hard in about ten seconds after application. The butterflies were placed in separate boxes as they were caught and, when the desired sample had been obtained, they were taken back to one of our tents for marking. They had then been for some time in the dark, so that with care the wings could be held with a pair of forceps while the paint was applied. This is better done with a pointed stick then with a brush. It was given time to dry before the specimen was returned to its box. At the end of the work the boxes were carried to a central point on the island, at the foot of the highest hill, and there the butterflies were released. They were then allowed some hours of sunshine during which to

distribute themselves throughout the colony before another
sample was taken on the following day.

Tean is approximately half a mile long and a quarter of a mile
broad at its widest part. We caught marked specimens freely at
the farthest points from the central releasing station, and we
were careful to collect as far as possible at random over the whole
area in which this could be done (some parts of the island were
covered by an impenetrable jungle of brambles).

On the first occasion that a specimen was caught, it was
marked on the underside of the hind-wings, the position (left or
right) and the colour of the paint indicating the date. Subsequent
recaptures were similarly marked, but on the fore-wings: we
found no difficulty in making as many as three marks on the
same fore-wing of even so small an insect as the Common Blue.
The fore-wings are less easily examined than the hind, so that
when a specimen was captured it was unnecessary to look at
them unless the hind pair bore a mark, and that could be seen at
a glance.

The Common Blue is not a migratory butterfly; moreover, by
making extensive captures at the nearest point on the neighbouring island of St Martin's, we were able to show that no significant
amount of migration took place. Thus additions to our population were due, at least principally, to emergence, and losses
from it were due to death. We were anxious to analyse these
changes, and the ingenious form of tabulation shown in Text-fig.
9, which was devised by Professor R. A. Fisher, has made this
possible.[1]

This table contains a complete record of the numbers caught
on one day and recaptured on another. These data are arranged
diagonally. The top line comprises the dates, from each of which
lines descend forwards and backwards at 45° so as to intersect.
Thus about the middle will be seen (in heavy type) the number
11, meaning that 11 butterflies marked and released on 30 August
were re-caught on 3 September. The totals captured and released
on these two dates are given at the ends of the diagonals: whence
it will be seen that 52 specimens had been caught and 50 released
on the 30th and that 50 had been caught and 50 released on
the 3rd.

Since the totals captured and released differed on different
days, a calculation was made to show the number of recaptures

[1] It is reproduced by kind permission of the Editor of *The Annuals of
Eugenics.*

on the basis of those actually obtained, supposing that 100 had been taken and 100 released on each occasion. Thus, dividing 11 by the total number released on the 30th, namely 50, and the total number captured on the 3rd, also 50, and multiplying by 10,000 (to give convenient whole numbers), the lower number 44 (in small type) is obtained; so that these lower numbers represent frequencies of recapture allowing for the numbers released and caught on the two relevant dates.

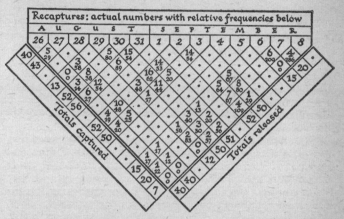

Fig. 9   Actual number of captures, releases and recaptures of *Polyommatus icarus*, with relative recapture frequencies.

This type of trellis diagram provides a means not only of calculating the numbers in a population at a given time but also of distinguishing changes in it due to the addition of new individuals by emergence (or immigration) or to loss through death (or emigration). If no new individuals were added, the proportion of the population which had been marked on any previous day would remain approximately the same for all subsequent samples: the adjusted frequencies (in small type) would then be constant, apart from sampling errors, on lines running diagonally up the table from right to left. If, on the contrary, there were no losses, though the population might be increasing by new emergences, the proportion of recaptures on any fixed subsequent day must be approximately the same for the samples released on different prior occasions: the adjusted frequencies would then be constant, apart from sampling errors, along the lines running diagonally upwards from left to right.

It will in fact be observed that in Text-fig. 9 there is a general tendency for the calculated frequencies (in small type) to increase largely as we pass up from left to right, but that the changes encountered as we pass up from right to left are small and fluctuating. It is clear therefore that the emergences are small compared with the number of deaths.

An estimate of the population on the first day (26th) may be obtained by the direct calculation:

$$43 \times 40/5 = 344.$$

But, of course, the value to be attached to this evidence depends on the consistency of the observed changes. The detailed analysis of this table is a little too complex to be undertaken here, but it may be obtained in full from our paper already cited. It leads to the conclusion that a considerable emergence (approximately of 50 per cent) took place between 2 and 3 September, that throughout the fortnight of observations about 450 to 500 insects died in all, including about 100 which had emerged during that period, and that the population decreased progressively from about 350 to almost nothing. Thus it was possible to distinguish both emergences and deaths, and to estimate them, as well as the total numbers, throughout the whole time that we were at work. It will be seen that no data are available for 28 August, and 1, 4, and 5 September. This was due to bad weather.

A direct estimate of the numbers in a butterfly population can be made by marking and releasing specimens on one or, preferably, on several occasions. The result may then be obtained by the simple direct calculation given above. However, it is to be hoped that many collectors will study the nature of the changes which take place in a butterfly community, since this is a matter of exceptional interest. For this purpose it is essential that they should arrange their data, as they obtain it, in the manner shown in Text-fig. 9, otherwise confusion is certain to arise and valuable work may be wasted. They should then consult the detailed analysis to which a reference has just been given, or, if they are not inclined to examine their results themselves, they should obtain the help of a statistician; but the practical side of such work could be conducted by any one interested in insect populations. Indeed, it is a study admirably suited to the collector or naturalist who wishes to increase the value of his hobby. It will be realized that the methods suggested here are capable of revealing to an unexpected degree the numerical status of a population and the changes which occur in it.

ECOLOGICAL GENETICS

Charles Darwin had realized the importance of actually detecting and studying evolution in progress in wild populations but, wrongly as we now know, he reached the view that the process, even when most rapid, must be too slow for that work to be possible. Subsequently, he did indeed suggest that an evolutionary change in a species reproducing annually might perhaps be observed in about fifty years in natural conditions.

The results of a numerical fluctuation in the Marsh Fritillary butterfly (pp. 254–6) suggested, however, that Darwin might well have been too pessimistic, for the reason that he much underestimated the force of selection for advantageous qualities in nature. That mistake was still, in general, being made up to thirty years ago or less. Somewhat earlier still, in 1930, Sir Ronald Fisher, a great authority on evolution and on quantitative methods in biology, concluded that a 1 per cent selective advantage must represent something like an upper limit in the wild, and he was criticized for putting it so high. Today we know that values of 20, 40 or 60 per cent and more are common and usual in nature. It should be noticed that in 1924 Haldane had calculated that, when heterozygous, the black form of the Peppered Moth, *Biston betularia*, had a selective advantage of 50 per cent over the normal pale one. But this was regarded as an entirely exceptional response to an abnormal situation, that in an industrial area (see the volume on Moths in the New Naturalist Series).

Two types of study made possible the discovery of the high selection-pressures operating in nature. In the first place, though later found not to be always necessary, it seemed essential to pick upon situations in which natural selection was likely to be exceptionally powerful; their identification being an important aspect of the matter. Secondly, the chosen examples were analysed by observations in the field together with genetic experimentation in the laboratory: a combined technique constituting what is known as *ecological genetics*.

The field-work involves methods for making numerical estimates of wild populations and of assessing the selective forces acting upon different genotypes or upon races occupying diverse habitats; also the founding of artificial colonies and other relevant techniques. The laboratory work necessitates not only the genetic analysis of the forms that are studied in the field but also an assessment of their relative survival in different environments and the impact and effect of artificial selection on them. Such work is today being extended to include the study of protein variation by means of electrophoresis.

In general, Darwin was right in regarding isolation, in some form, as important for the evolution of adaptations in nature. However, we now know that selection can be so powerful as to produce clines, and even sharply-contrasted groups, in continuous populations.

Work on ecological genetics has now been carried out on the most diverse organisms, both in plants and animals. Though the Lepidoptera provide particularly useful material for it, especially in polymorphic mimicry, which is so striking a phenomenon in the tropics, these investigations have included one well-known British butterfly, the Meadow Brown (Plate 24).

In that species the underside of the hind-wings may bear small black spots placed sub-marginally in a curving row. They may be absent, or present in any number up to five. Their variation has proved to be a useful character for quantitative study in order to compare populations and to detect changes in them.

The genetic aspect of the work conducted by McWhirter (1969) shows that the variability of these spots is partly environmental and partly multifactorial. At about 15°C. the latter component is negligible in the males but responsible for 63 ± 14 per cent of the female variation in spot numbers. McWhirter later found that the relative effects of the genes become greater as the temperature rises, being responsible for about 47 ± 20 per cent of the variation in the males and 78 ± 16 in the females at 22°C. There is thus adequate opportunity for the selective adjustment of spotting in this species. For though it is indeed possible that these small spots are of no importance to the individual, there is clear evidence that this is not true of the genes controlling them, which can be powerfully influenced by selection.

The male situation chiefly shows modifications of a plan that is 'unimodal' (having a single maximum) at two spots, the analysis of which can throw valuable light on the adaptations of this insect. It will, however, be best largely to confine the present brief account to the females, since in them its features are more strikingly displayed. Throughout much of England and Scotland, as well as the greater part of Europe from the west coast of France at least to Rumania, spotting is unimodal at 0 spots in that sex (the 'Southern English' form). This is the condition in the south of England from the North Sea to about central Dorset, where a region of genetic instability starts. It continues across Devon and for a few miles into Cornwall; whence, westwards, throughout the eastern and central part of the county the female spotting is bimodal, with a greater maximum at 0 spots and a lesser at 2 (the 'East Cornish' form). The change between this and the Southern English type is restricted to the region of instability just mentioned. There it occurs along a more or less north to south line or band, the position of which can move twenty miles or so between generations, of which there is one a year. In some seasons the boundary between the two types is more or less gradual, covering a distance of many miles; in others it takes place abruptly in a few yards even where no effective physical barrier exists, as at a field hedge or even in the middle of a field.

The insect becomes rarer towards the Cornish isthmus between Hayle and Marazion, but is common on the Land's End peninsula both north and south of the granite intrusion occupying the centre of that region. Here in the extreme west of the county the butterfly takes on a new form, the female being unimodal at two spots like the males, though much more variable than they.

A striking and important situation occurs on the Isles of Scilly. Those on which it has been studied may be classified as 'large', 282 acres or more and 'small', 40 acres or less: a difference of at least seventeen times. The female spot-distribution is approximately similar on each of three large islands, St Mary's, St Martin's and Tresco, with more or less equal values at 0, 1 and 2 spots, but it differs greatly from one small island to another; the characteristic frequencies being maintained season after season. This distribution is due to the local ecology. The small islands differ markedly from one another, each having its own characteristics, while the large ones are of sufficient extent to include widely differing habitats. The butterfly can, therefore, adapt itself to the individual local situations found on each small island, but only to the average of those found on the large ones, and averages tend to approximate to one another.

It has also been possible to study the Meadow Brown on two

small islands on which a sudden and profound ecological change occurred: on Tean, due to the removal of a herd of cattle long maintained there, an event which transformed the vegetation; also on White Island, which is somewhat hour-glass shaped, at a time when it was temporarily subdivided following a great storm which washed sand and shingle across its central isthmus. Both events produced a significant change in the spotting of the butterfly; the new spot distribution being as constant after the environmental change as the old had been before it.

It is clear, therefore, that the spot distributions are selectively maintained and are not due to the migration of the butterflies, an almost unknown event in Scilly, or to random genetic drift: that is to say, the slow chance spread of genes effectively neutral in survival value. Indeed, it was possible to calculate the selection pressures involved: on Tean, for instance, this proved to be 64 per cent against non-spotted individuals in a single generation.

Returning to the mainland, when the boundary between the two spotting types has remained for several years at the same place, a 'reverse cline' in spotting can develop there; that is to say, the difference between the two becomes greater as we approach the position where they meet. Evidently, the less well adjusted specimens which arise by crossing between the two forms tend to be eliminated. Yet both types can tolerate extremely varied conditions within their own range without responding to them, at least visibly: acid or alkaline soils, open grassland, marsh or woodland, the semi-Continental climate of east Suffolk and the Atlantic one of the Dumnonian peninsula. Each type is therefore buffered against ecological diversity.

As Handford (1973a and b) points out, all the aspects of the environment can no doubt change in more or less continuous and to a considerable extent independent ways as one passes across the country. Yet it is most unlikely that the response of the animals to such changes can be similarly independent, for the reason that genes interact to produce their effects. There will thus be a limited number of gene-complexes available to the organism and these must therefore change sharply from one to another. That situation will tend to build up a region where such genetic substitutions can effectively take place, ideally in a manner complete and abrupt. Consequently, even if such changes are at first gradual for a considerable distance, the butterflies will be forced towards sharp discontinuities of spotting within a limited area: that is to say, in the Meadow Brown, the region of genetic instability that has just been mentioned. As already explained, this was originally detected by a study of spot *numbers*. Its existence has now been confirmed from three additional and independent lines of evidence.

McWhirter and Creed (1971) have examined the *positions* of the spots upon the hind-wings, which may be more costal or more anal (nearer the anal angle). They find that there is an east to west anal to costal cline in female spot-placing which extends across England from the North Sea to the Isles of Scilly, but this is reversed over the 'boundary area', and yet it has been demonstrated that spot numbers and spot-placing are independent characters.

So also Handford (1973*a* and *b*), studying protein variation in this species, has detected polymorphisms which are independent of one another and of either aspect of spotting. Their frequency indicates that in both of them the 'boundary area' from mid Dorset to the Devon/Cornwall border is a region of genetic disturbance in the Meadow Brown. It is indeed striking that the four criteria by which the boundary effect has been assessed should independently confirm each other.

Thus, as exemplified by the Meadow Brown, it is possible to analyse variation and to study evolution in progress by means of ecological genetics. This butterfly illustrates indeed one aspect of such work, that dependent upon multifactorial variation. Furthermore, it has already been pointed out that powerful advantages and disadvantages must be contending to maintain a polymorphism. Evidently that situation must also provide great opportunities for ecological genetic studies to reveal the effects of selection. This has already been done in the work of Kettlewell and others investigating melanism in moths, as well as in the beetle *Adalia lipunctata* by E. R. Creed, though the polymorphism of British butterflies has not yet been utilized in the analysis of evolution by observation and experiment.

to one of them are no longer fertile with those of another, or else when crossed they produce sterile offspring only. They have then reached the status of full species.

Yet, contrary to the view often expressed in the past, sub-species are not always 'species in the making', as Huxley (1942) has shown. The Independent type do, indeed, represent potential stages in the evolution of specific differences, though, of course, the process may never be fully completed. Dependent sub-species, or Independent ones which have extended their range until they meet and exchange genes, are much less likely to evolve into distinct species. It is, however, possible for them to do so, particularly when the environmental differences between the ends of a cline become more pronounced and at the same time pass more abruptly from one type to the other. The necessary adjustments to them will then tend to become sharply defined, and the flow of genes between the two relatively constant populations will be progressively attenuated, until the sub-species become Independent.

Every gradation may be found leading up to the formation of clearly distinct sub-species. Any geographical distinction between groups of animals or plants, recognizable by whatever means, may be said to constitute a *geographical race*, but at what stage it is desirable to regard two such races as definite sub-species and to assign names to them is, to some extent, a matter of convenience. In general, it may be said that geographical races should not be treated as sub-species if they differ from one another in a single character only, unless this be a distinctive one and universal in the population. The wider the basis of the distinction between them becomes, the less likely is it that we are merely dealing with the effects of a single gene or with purely environmental influences. Further, if an adjustment to different habitats does not affect the colour-pattern of a butterfly, it is seldom practicable to separate the two forms as sub-species even though the difference between them may be a very real one; for it is then difficult, or impossible, to discriminate between specimens when preserved in collections.

This point may usefully be illustrated by examples. For this purpose I will select three virtually non-migratory species having comparable geographical ranges: for each is found both in England and Ireland but not in Scotland, so that the two areas which they inhabit are completely cut off from each other by a wide stretch of sea. First, though the spring and summer generations of the Holly Blue, *Celastrina argiolus*, are distinguishable from one another in appearance, either brood is quite similar throughout the entire range of the butterfly in these islands. In England both occur,[1] but in Ireland only one, for there the summer generation is absent, even in the extreme south of the country. Thus there is a real distinction between the races, but it would not be practicable to treat them as sub-species because they are not visibly separable. Secondly, the Silver-washed Fritillary, *Argynnis paphia*, has the same colour-pattern everywhere in the British Isles,[2] but the Irish specimens are slightly larger than the English. It seems that the species has diverged to some extent in the two countries, but the contrast between the geographical races which it has formed in them, depending only upon an average difference in size, is not one which could conveniently be regarded as sub-specific, especially as it may only be environmental. Thirdly, the English and Irish races of the Wood White, *Leptidea sinapis*, differ both in colour and markings, and though the species is partially double-brooded in south-western England, it is single-brooded in Ireland, as it is in central England. These two races are therefore sufficiently distinct to be treated as sub-specific.

We sometimes find that a single independent sub-species may have a discontinuous distribution, having become broken up into separate populations since it was evolved. One or more of these may sometimes be distinguished from the others by constant features which are but slight and involve a single character only. These are conveniently termed *forms*: clearly they are potential sub-species in the same sense that such sub-species are potential species. They may be distinguished by a name with the abbreviation *f.* (= form), added after that of the sub-species. Thus, a distinct sub-species of the Mountain Ringlet, *Erebia epiphron* (Plate 20), is restricted to Britain. This is called *mnemon* Haw., and it is divided into two dissimilar populations, inhabiting the Lake District and part of the Scottish Highlands and Lowlands. Specimens from these two regions are similar except that those from Scotland are consistently a little the larger and brighter, and they have been called the form *scotica* Cooke. We

---

[1] The second generation is, however, not quite a complete one, for some of the pupae produced by the first generation fail to emerge in the summer but give rise to butterflies in the following spring.

[2] The variety *valezina* has, I believe, never been reported from Ireland.

can therefore sub-divide our British Mountain Ringlet as *Erebia epiphron mnemon* f. *scotica* from Scotland and *E. epiphron mnemon* f. *mnemon* from the Lake District. The name of the sub-species is to be repeated for the typical form in the same way that the specific name is repeated for the typical sub-species.

THE GEOGRAPHICAL RACES OF BRITISH BUTTERFLIES

I shall now illustrate the principles discussed in the previous section with a brief account of the sub-species and clines of British butterflies, together with a number of the more important forms, and of other types of geographical races, the status of which is not always clear. I propose to give brief descriptions of them since, perhaps in the majority of instances, they are omitted from the current text-books. It is indeed remarkable that most of the information on the geographical races of British butterflies remains scattered in periodicals and is not easy to obtain. It will be convenient to discuss these races in the classificatory order of the species (pp. 79–87), and to point out the nature of each when possible, rather than to attempt to group them under such headings as Independent and Dependent sub-species, clines, and forms. For the status of a number of them is uncertain, while different species would be scattered by such treatment and valuable comparisons between them obscured.

A number of distinct races occur in the Western Isles of Scotland. Our knowledge of the insect fauna of this highly interesting region was for long most inadequate, but it has of late been greatly extended by the labours of Professor J. W. Heslop Harrison and his colleagues. His results have been published at frequent intervals in *The Entomologist* for a number of years past. Most of the information on the butterflies of these islands that is contained in the present section is derived from this source.

The genus *Erebia* comprises arctic or alpine butterflies which have reached this country during a glacial period (p. 294). They have accordingly survived here only in the north, and there in mountainous or hilly districts. The Mountain Ringlet, *Erebia epiphron* (Plate 20), cannot live in England at an altitude of less than 1800 feet, but in Scotland it is able to descend to about 1500 feet, and I have met with it at this elevation in Perthshire. It is found in four isolated areas: the English Lake District, the

a. The Brown Hairstreak (x1.25), underside

b. The Wood White (x1.5), underside

c. The Large Skipper (x1.25), male

d. The Large Skipper (x1.17), female

e. The Hedge Brown (x1.3), male upperside

f. The Hedge Brown (natural size), male underside

a. The Chalkhill Blue, male (x1.7)

b. The Chalkhill Blue, female (x1.7)

c. The Marbled White (natural size)

d. The Marbled White (x1.4)

18.

a. The Common Blue, male (x1.25), upperside

b. The Common Blue, female (x2.0), underside

c. The Green-veined White (x2.0), underside

d. The Speckled Wood (x1.25), female, Generation 1, part 1

20 a. Scotch Argus, *Erebia aethiops*, male upperside (Perthshire); b. Scotch Argus, female underside (Perthshire); c. Mountain Ringlet, *Erebia epiphron*, male upperside (Cumberland); d. Comma, *Polygonia c-album*, female underside (Oxfordshire), Gen. 1, Part 1; e. Comma, female underside (Oxfordshire), Gen. 2; f. Comma, female upperside (Oxfordshire), Gen. 2; g. Small Blue, *Cupido minimus*, male upperside (Berkshire); h. Small Blue, female upperside (Berkshire); i. Large Blue, *Maculinea arion*, male upperside (Cornwall) (x0.8)

21 *a.* Clouded Yellow, *Colias crocea,* male upperside (Cornwall), typical;
b. Clouded Yellow, female upperside (Cornwall), typical; *c.* Clouded Yellow,
female upperside (Cornwall), *helice; d.* Wood White, *Leptidea sinapsis*, male
upperside (Northamptonshire); *e.* Wood White, female upperside
(Northamptonshire); *f.* Large Heath, *Coenonympha tullia*, male upperside
(Perthshire); *g.* Large Heath, male underside (Perthshire); *h.* Large Heath,
male upperside (Shropshire); *i.* Large Heath, male underside (Shropshire);
j. Grizzled Skipper, *Pyrgus malvae,* male upperside (Berkshire); *k.* Lulworth
Skipper, *Thymelicus acteon,* male upperside (Dorset); *l.* Lulworth Skipper,
female upperside (Dorset) (x0.8)

22 *a.* Pale Clouded Yellow, *Colias hyale*, male upperside (Kent); *b.* Berger's Clouded Yellow, *Colias australis*, male upperside (Berkshire); *c.* Duke of Burgundy, *Hamearis lucina*, male upperside (Berkshire); *d.* Duke of Burgundy, female underside (Berkshire); *e.* Small Copper, *Lycaena phlaeas*, male upperside (Caernarvon); *f.* Small Copper, female upperside (Staffordshire); *g.* Small Copper, female underside (Oxfordshire); *h.* Ringlet, *Aphantopus hyperanthus*, male upperside (Worcester); *i.* Ringlet, male underside (Hampshire); *j.* Ringlet, male underside (Cumberland), var. *arete*; *k.* Ringlet, male underside (Cumberland), var. *caeca* (x0.9)

23 *a*. Purple Emperor, *Apatura iris*, male upperside (Sussex); *b*. Purple Emperor, male underside (Sussex); *c*. Swallow-tail, *Papilio machaon*, female upperside (Norfolk) (x0.8)

24 a. Meadow Brown, *Maniola jurtina*, male upperside (Oxfordshire);
b. Meadow Brown, female upperside (Oxfordshire); c. Meadow Brown, female
underside (Berkshire); d. Meadow Brown, female underside (Oxfordshire);
e. Grayling, *Hipparchia semele*, female upperside (Berkshire); f. Grayling, male
underside (Berkshire); g. Brown Argus, *Aricia agestis*, male upperside
(Berkshire); h. Purple Hairstreak, *Quercusia quercus*, male upperside
(Oxfordshire); i. Purple Hairstreak, female upperside (Oxfordshire); j. Purple
Hairstreak, female underside (Oxfordshire); k. Brown Argus, male underside
(Berkshire); l. Northern Brown Argus, *Aricia artaxerxes*, male underside
(Aberdeen); m. Northern Brown Argus, female upperside (Aberdeen) (x0.9)

Scottish Highlands, and on a few mountains in Ireland (Map 2). Since this book was first published, it has been discovered on the Galloway-Kirkcudbright mountains. These populations are cut off from one another, and they have evolved independently. As already mentioned, the Scottish form, *scotica* Cooke, is larger and brighter than the English, but otherwise the two are much alike and they both belong to the sub-species *mnemon* Haw. This is chocolate-coloured and is marked with a dull orange band on the fore- and the hind-wings which is interrupted by the nervures and bears black dots. In the female these are often pupilled with white below and, rarely, on the upper side also. It is undoubtedly true that the Mountain Ringlet exists in Ireland, but the where-abouts of only three Irish specimens seems to be known. These are preserved in the Dublin Museum and I have seen photo-graphs of one of them but not the specimens themselves. These Irish specimens appear to belong to an entirely different race from the British (Warren, 1936) one, which is much less strongly marked. For they seem to be examples of the sub-species *aetheria* Esp., form *nelamus* Bdv. (p. 294) and, strange to say, this is found elsewhere only at a high altitude in the Alps. In it the orange band is faint and unspotted though continuous on the fore-wings but absent from the hind pair. Though it would be premature to determine the nature of the Irish race on the evidence of three specimens, their characteristics do at least suggest that it may be very distinct from the English one. Thus it would be a most interesting piece of work to obtain and study this species in Ireland, where it has so far been reported on two or three occasions only from mountains in Sligo and Mayo, but the extent of its distribution is, in reality, quite unknown. The possible significance of the marked difference between the British and Irish races of the Mountain Ringlet is discussed on p. 289.

Our other member of the genus *Erebia*, the Scotch Argus, *E. aethiops* (Plate 20, Map 3), is a northern but not a mountain species, though it often flies in hilly country, and tends to replace the Meadow Brown at higher altitudes in the Scottish Highlands. With the exception of the Yorkshire race shortly to be mentioned, it is not possible to distinguish English and Scottish specimens, though they have certainly lived in isolation, for the species is not at all migratory. It is not uncommon in the Lowlands and it used to occur in Northumberland and Durham; poss-ibly it still does so in some remote places. Formerly it was also found in several localities in an area comprising a small part of Westmorland and North Lancashire at the south of the Lake District, and here one colony yet survives. This latter population has on the west been quite cut off from Scotland, where the butterfly is established in one or two places even in south Dumfries; for, contrary to the assertions repeated, I think, in all the current text-books, it is absent from Cumberland. Indeed, I believe I possess the only extant specimen which has certainly been taken there: this was caught near Keswick in 1899. Nor has it become extinct in recent times, as it apparently has in Durham, for J. B. Hodgkinson, who collected extensively in Cumberland during the first two-thirds of last century, knew of but one specimen from the county.[1] In general, it seems that the Scotch Argus has not responded to isolation by evolving a series of geographical races here. Our specimens belong to the typical sub-species, but they are divisible into two forms: the normal one, f. *aethiops*, and f. *caledonia* Vty. The first of these is the smaller (ranging from 35 to 42 mm., compared with 40 to 45 mm.), with narrower fore-wings and relatively narrow bands. *Caledonia* occurs wherever the typical sub-species is found, but both in Scotland and England it is much commoner than the normal form.

A single very distinct race of the Scotch Argus has, however, arisen in Britain: this is the one which used to be found in north-west Yorkshire. It is said to be extinct, but Mr W. G. Clutten obtained it not uncommonly as recently as 1923, and perhaps it yet survives. Specimens from that district cannot be confused with any others occurring in these islands, for the orange markings on the upper-sides of the males are nearly obsolete, and in the females they are scarcely more developed than in an ordinary male. It seems to have arisen in isolation as an inde-pendent sub-species.

A remarkable dwarf race, *thyone* Thompson, of the Grayling, *Hipparchia semele*, occurs on Great Orme's Head, North Wales (p. 212), where it comprises the whole population. Its average wing-expanse is about 41 mm. in the male and 43 mm. in the female (normally it is about 48 mm. and 52 mm. respectively); moreover, it emerges several weeks before the ordinary form, from which is is isolated by a gap of about 2500 yards. I am indebted to Mr J. Anthony Thompson for my information on this race.

[1] *Entomologist's Weekly Intelligencer*, 7.

The Meadow Brown, *Maniola jurtina*, has produced three distinct sub-species in Britain, in addition to the widespread one which is represented on Plate 24. Two of these have evolved in isolation, in Ireland and in the Isles of Scilly respectively, but the third, *splendida* B. White, has a distribution which is rather difficult to interpret. It is found only in Scotland, from Dumbarton to western Sutherland, and in some of the Scottish islands: in Baleshare, South Uist, and Vatersay, also in Barra; though the species is frequent throughout the rest of the Inner and Outer Hebrides, it is fairly typical in appearance. Professor W. H. Dowdeswell and I found an intermediate form on the little-known island of Cara off the coast of Kintyre. It is just possible that *splendida* originated on an island and then extended its range but, more probably, it represents the response produced by some genetic constitutions to the environment of the north-west, and that it is a Dependent sub-species separated by a sharp cline from *M. j. jurtina*.

The sub-species *splendida* is a more magnificent insect than the ordinary Meadow Brown, being larger and brighter. The male is a rich dark brown with an extensive orange patch on the under-side of the fore-wings. In the female the orange band invades the central area of the wings on the upper-side, forming a large blotch. The under-side is rather mottled, and there is a greyish band on the hind-wings in both sexes. The Irish race, sub-species *iernes* Graves, has in the female a bright orange band and a separate orange patch in the centre of the fore-wings. The under-side is more uniform in colour than in *splendida* and the band on the hind-wings is greyish. This seems to be the normal form in Ireland. A distinct sub-species, *cassiteridum* Graves, inhabits the Isles of Scilly. The upper-side resembles that of *iernes* but the under-side has a mottled appearance, and the hind-wings are marked with a pale band. It is generally said that this is of a creamy-buff shade and that it bears black spots, often with white pupils. I have an extensive experience of *cassiteridum* and have caught and examined a large number of specimens. I find that there is considerable variation in the colour of the band and that the black spots are often absent. The whole population of the Meadow Brown on the Scillys appears to belong to this sub-species, and I have compared sets from several of the islands and can detect no constant differences between them, a situation to be contrasted with that found in the Common Blue (p. 282). It is said that specimens approaching *cassiteridum* exist as rarities in west Cornwall and it may be so, but I have not myself encountered them. This race and *iernes* may both safely be considered independent sub-species.

Attention has already been drawn to the cline shown by the Large Heath, *Coenonympha tullia* (Map 6). This provides a valuable example of certain aspects of geographical variation and deserves discussion. The species occurs in most suitable localities (p. 136) in the Orkneys, the Outer and Inner Hebrides, and the Highlands of Scotland. In this region it is of a rather pale light-brown colour above and greyish on the hind-wings beneath, while it is almost devoid of 'eye-spots' on either surface (Plate 21). This is the sub-species *scotica* Stgr. In the Lowlands the specimens gradually approach the Cumberland race, sub-species *tullia*. Here the males vary from a slightly deeper brown to a chocolate tint. The females also are darker and in both sexes eye-spots are developed above and below. Still farther south, the characteristics of the sub-species *philoxenus* Esq. are gradually assumed, in which both sexes are very dark and the eye-spots large and distinct. This is found in Lancashire, Yorkshire and Cheshire (Plate 21), the most southerly point reached by the butterfly in England.

Here we have a typical cline. Moreover, this insect illustrates that clines are not unique, but may be repeated in different directions (p. 268). Thus going west from the *philoxenus* of Cheshire into Wales the characteristics of *tullia* once more appear and may even be surpassed, producing what are practically the Lowland forms again on reaching the region approaching and around Lake Bala.

The sub-species within the British cline are found elsewhere intermingled. It appears that in the island of Islay *scotica* predominates, but that the intermediate sub-species *tullia* is not uncommon and that even specimens closely approaching *philoxenus* occur. Here the population must have evolved upon somewhat independent lines. The situation in Ireland is almost as curious. The Large Heath is found in suitable places throughout the greater part of that country, even in the extreme south. The specimens are larger than those from Britain, but otherwise they are not distinguishable from them. The sub-species *philoxenus* does not occur, but *scotica* and *tullia*, with their intermediates, fly together in the same localities. This is actually true in Cork, where, at the most southerly point reached by the species in the British Isles, the northern race *scotica* is still present. The failure of the races to assort themselves into distinct habitats in Ireland may in part be related to the fact that the climate and country-side are far more uniform there than they are throughout the British range of the species. It may be added that *tullia* and *philoxenus* are both found on the Continent, but that *scotica* appears to be unknown there.

It should be noticed that even closely allied species may respond to geographical changes in very different ways, for some vary markedly in relation to them while others remain wonderfully constant over great distances. Thus though specimens of the Large Heath from Perthshire, Cumberland, and Shropshire are extremely dissimilar, the nearly related Small Heath, *Coenonympha pamphilus* (Plate 10), which occurs throughout the whole mainland of Britain and Ireland, is everywhere almost identical, though it is slightly paler in Scotland than in the south.

The Ringlet, *Aphantopus hyperanthus* (Plate 22), is in Britain subject to a slight cline in the colour of the under-side. This is of rather an ashen tint in Scotland and the north of England, but becomes of a rich chocolate shade in the south.

Only three[1] Fritillaries are established in the Western Isles, and all of them have evolved local races there. The sub-species *insularum* Harrison of the Small Pearl-bordered Fritillary, *Clossiana selene*, differs from the ordinary form of that insect only in being brighter above and below, and it is perhaps doubtful if it merits a distinct name. It occurs in Rhum, Soay, Skye, and Scalpay, and the entire population of the butterfly on these islands seems to belong to this form.

A magnificent sub-species of the Dark Green Fritillary, *Mesoacidalia aglaia*, has developed on a number of the Western Isles. This is called *scotica* Watkins; it is large and very dark, indeed the females are sometimes so thickly sprinkled with black and greenish scales that only a trace of the normal tawny ground-colour appears, in the centre of the fore-wings. *M. aglaia* is found on nearly all the islands of the Inner and Outer Hebrides, and on many of them it is of the *scotica* form. This occurs on the Outer Isles all the way from Berneray at the south of the Barra Group,[2] northwards to Benbecula; and on the Inner Isles it is to be found on South Rona, where it is of a very extreme type, and on the south-east of Rhum. However, the normal form inhabits

[1] Professor Heslop Harrison has reported a single specimen of *Argynnis euphrosyne* from Rhum, but it is not otherwise known in the Isles.
[2] Not to be confused with Berneray between North Uist and Harris.

the remainder of that island, where apparently the two sub-species (*scotica* and *aglaia*) meet but on the whole preserve their identity in the manner outlined on p. 269, though some intermediates occur.

It may at first sight seem strange that the largest race of one of our butterflies should be found on islands, a habitat often associated with particularly small specimens, and one in which wingless forms have repeatedly evolved in certain groups. It will, however, be realized that such evolutionary trends are generally encountered on wind-swept islets where insects with large wings are in danger of being blown out to sea, and this does not apply to the localities frequented by the *scotica* race of *M. aglaia*. However, the principle that a large wing-span is dangerous on exposed places is demonstrated by the very small pale form of this butterfly discovered by Professor Heslop Harrison on the wind-swept and wave-swept little island of Flodday, situated to the south-west of Vatersay at the southern extremity of the Outer Hebrides. It is low, devoid of shelter, and exposed to the full force of the Atlantic, and here large specimens might well be at a disadvantage compared with small ones.

The Dark Green Fritillary is fairly constant in appearance throughout the rest of Britain, but in west Cornwall the females are larger and much suffused with dark scales; indeed they suggest an approach towards *scotica* once more. The Irish race is not remarkable, except that the males are of rather a rich reddish-brown tone.

The Marsh Fritillary, *Euphydryas aurinia* (Map 9), is the third member of the *Argynnidi* inhabiting the Western Isles, and it has been found by Harrison on Gunna, Tiree, and Rhum in a form closely approaching the Irish sub-species *praeclara* Kayne. This is a brightly coloured race in which the lighter markings are a clear pale yellow or even whitish. The majority of the specimens from the Oban district also resemble it. In addition, this butterfly occurs in Islay, where it is also very like *praeclara*, as Mr R. L. Wilkes, who has taken it there, kindly informs me, and this race is also found in Jura. The species is not known from any other of the Western Isles, except that in the Hope Department at Oxford are two specimens caught in the Isle of Mull in 1900 by E. F. Tylecote. They are of an ordinary English form. The bearing of these facts upon the distribution of the species is discussed on p. 300. The sub-species *praeclara* itself is found throughout Ireland, where it is widespread in suitable localities. It is decidedly more constant than the British race *aurinia*. This is a duller insect, whose pale spots are buff-coloured or light brownish, and it is often exceedingly variable. Alternatively, it may be very uniform for many years in a given locality and then undergo a great outburst of variation for a few seasons, after which it will resume a constant form again which may differ from the previous one. This phenomenon has been discussed on pp. 254–6, and its existence makes it almost impossible to trace geographical trends in the colour-pattern of this butterfly throughout England and Wales. Occasionally an English colony may rather closely approach *praeclara*, but it is rare to find specimens which could really be mistaken for it.

The little-known south-western race of the Heath Fritillary, *Mellicta athalia* (Map 10), which exists in a few localities in Devon and east Cornwall, differs slightly from that found in Kent. It seems to be a little smaller with more pointed wings, and the ground-colour is rather duller and less reddish in tone.

The Silver-studded Blue, *Plebejus argus* (Map 14), is among the less variable of our Polyommatini, but the males from localities on the chalk are of a paler blue with narrower borders than are those taken where the soil is dark and peaty. The females normally have blackish-brown wings edged with orange crescents, which, however, are not infrequently absent. The ground-colour is sometimes powdered with blue scales, and these bluish females supplant the normal form in a few localities, where they characterize distinct geographical races. One of these, *masseyi*, occurs in the damper parts of the 'mosses' on the borders of Lancashire and Westmorland. It was formerly abundant at Witherslack in the latter county, but it has been almost exterminated there by over-collecting. I understand, however, that it is increasing again owing to the protection which it is now given. This race is of the average size and it emerges at the usual time, flying in July. The females are invariably marked with blue, except for a patch on the discal area of the fore-wings, while the under-side of both sexes is unusually pale. The way in which such a race might arise is discussed on pp. 225–6.

The sub-species *caernensis* Thompson is also one in which the females are bluish. This is much smaller than the typical form; the males vary between 22 and 27 mm. in expanse, and the female between 19 and 24 mm. (compared with the ordinary British form, which ranges from 24 to 32 mm. and 23 to 28 mm.

for the males and females respectively). Furthermore, it emerges earlier in the year, often appearing even in the second week of June. As already mentioned (pp. 212–13), the precocious emergence and small size of *caernensis* are probably both due to a tendency for the larvae to feed up rapidly. The males are of an unusually pale shade of blue and their black border is much reduced. The females are always marked with blue; the amount is much more variable than in *masseyi*, and it may suffuse the whole upper surface. The orange lunules are inconspicuous or absent, never well developed. This sub-species feeds on Rock Rose (*Helianthemum*), an unusual food for *P. argus*, and it is to be found at a considerable elevation on limestone cliffs at several places on the north coast of Caernarvon. It never flies with the normal one, which is not uncommon in that county, occupying a very different type of habitat: sandy heaths and low-lying waste land. It appears therefore that *caernensis* is a rather distinct sub-species.

Since this book was first published, some evidence has suggested that the Brown Argus, *Aricia agestis* Schiff. (1775) is divided into two species (Plate 24): *A. agestis* itself, the true Brown Argus, and *A. artaxerxes* F., which may reasonably be called the Northern Brown Argus.[1]

The northern limit of *A. agestis* is reached in southern England and northern Denmark, while *A. artaxerxes* inhabits parts of northern Britain, Norway, Sweden and Finland. Several characteristics help to separate these two butterflies. One is provided by the larger orange lunules on the upper-side of the wings of *A. agestis* (these are reduced and often absent on the fore-wings in *artaxerxes*); another by its more heavily marked larvae. Yet these features are variable and can overlap. The real criterion between the two species is the fact that *A. agestis* is double brooded and *A. artaxerxes* is single brooded. This condition is genetic not environmental, by means of temperature or length of daylight: *artaxerxes* remains single brooded when reared in southern England.

In *A. agestis* there is a black spot in the centre of the fore-wings, though it is inconspicuous owing to the dark brown

[1] Higgins and Riley (1970), in their authoritative work, use the name 'Scotch Argus' for *A. artaxerxes*. But since this is generally applied, and indeed by them, to *Erebia aethiops*, that designation is not acceptable (while, of course, we are free to recast the English nomenclature since the International Rules do not apply to it). Furthermore, now that the distinction between these two *Aricia* species seems established with fair probability, *artaxerxes* (Fabricius, 1793) takes precedence of *allous* (Geyer, 1837).

ground-colour. In nearly all the specimens from Scotland this central spot is white, while the under-side spots lack their black centres. Thus the Scottish form, which is, in fact, restricted to the east of that country, is immediately distinguishable from the Brown Argus of southern England. It is now known that the Northern Brown Argus occurs also in Northumberland, Durham and Lancashire, where it is local and rare, and there about 10 per cent of the butterflies have white spots on the fore-wings, while the black centres of their under-side spots are sometimes reduced.

This north English race was known as *salmacis*, while it was to the Scottish one that the name *artaxerxes* was originally applied. The white spot on the upper-side of the fore-wing occurs also, as a great rarity, in *A. agestis*, while occasional specimens in which it is replaced by black have been found in Scotland. This distinction in spotting, affecting both the upper- and under-side, is a single-factor difference, the Scottish form being a simple recessive (Høegh-Guldberg, 1968). Consequently, the two phenotypes cannot be judged as indicating a subspecific difference.

In experimental crosses, there was no differential mortality between the sexes when *artaxerxes* was the female parent, but all the male offspring died when the female parent was *agestis*. This indicates a degree of interspecific sterility, and there are other instances in which its effects are known to be influenced by the direction of the cross. For example, it is easy to mate male *Smerinthus ocellata*, the Eyed Hawk Moth, and female *Lathoe populi*, the Poplar Hawk and produce an F_1 brood, but the reverse cross has hardly ever succeeded. As Haldane pointed out in 1922, when one sex is sterile, rare or absent among the progeny of an interspecific cross, it is the heterogametic sex that is so affected. This is generally regarded, though on very scanty evidence, as the female in the Lepidoptera (but the male in Mammals). The situation in *Aricia* is the reverse of what is to be expected on that view. The necessary cytological evidence is lacking, but Remington (1954) has already seen grounds to question if the females are heterogametic in the Lycaenidae.

Høegh-Guldberg has suggested that a long warm period may have favoured the evolution of a double brooded from a single brooded species in *Aricia*, and that both *agestis* and *artaxerxes* have spread northwards following the last glaciation. *A. artaxerxes* would then be the better adjusted to higher latitudes, where a longer growth period is needed; and there it would subsequently undergo further divergent evolution.

The Common Blue, *Polyommatus icarus* (Plate 19), inhabits the whole of the British Isles with the doubtful exception of the Shetlands (p. 299). Scottish females are often more brightly coloured than are those taken farther south but, though numerous aberrations are known, the butterfly is not subject to distinct geographical variation on the British mainland. In Ireland, however, occurs a characteristic and brilliant sub-species, which has arisen in isolation there. The specimens are large and tend to have rather pointed wings, while the females are heavily marked with blue, and the orange crescents along the outer margins of their wings are exceptionally well developed. It would indeed be possible for an experienced collector to determine, with but a small margin of error, whether or not any unlabelled female specimen came from Ireland. It has already been pointed out that though the sub-species of butterflies must necessarily be *identified* mainly by their colour-patterns, they may often differ from one another also in other ways which are less easily detected. The Common Blue provides an example of this, for gynandromorphs are very much more frequent in the Irish than the British race.

Throughout the greater part of its range, *P. icarus* is double-brooded, and specimens of the second generation tend to be a little smaller than those of the first. In the north of Scotland, and it is said in Northern Ireland, the summer brood is omitted and the butterflies do not emerge until June, instead of appearing in May as they do farther south. A remarkable race inhabits the tiny island of Tean in the Scillys. I have not collected on, or seen specimens from, all the islands of that group which it could inhabit, but the normal form is found on St Mary's, Tresco, and even St Martins, which is only 300 yards from Tean at one point, though elsewhere the shores fall away from one another rapidly. This isolation is not very surprising, for the species is not at all migratory, and Professor W. H. Dowdeswell and I obtained considerable evidence, from marking and releasing specimens, that the populations on these two neighbouring islands are effectively distinct. In this race the majority of the females obtained in the summer (I have no knowledge of the spring form) have an extensive scattering of pale silvery-blue scales, so that they are most unlike those found elsewhere, which are either blackish or else marked with a violet shade. Moreover, the form from Tean is associated with a characteristic variation on the under-side of the hind-wings, which affects both sexes; for in a large proportion of the specimens the two spots placed along the coastal margin are united, forming a short curved line, and other varieties in spotting are frequent. We seem to have here a stage in the evolution of an independent sub-species. The Common Blue is at least partly triple-brooded on the Isles of Scilly.

It is generally supposed that the Large Blue, *Maculinea arion* (Plate 20), is today restricted to two small areas: the Cotswolds and the north coast of Cornwall (Map 18). In the latter region it is found near Bude, and then eastwards in small isolated colonies until it crosses the Devon border. On the Cotswolds it appears in June or even in late May, and it is of a rather dark iron-blue shade. The species emerges a little later in Cornwall, where the specimens are of a clearer blue, while the spots on the upper-side are larger, though they may be less numerous than in the Gloucestershire examples which resembled the extinct race from Barnwell Wold, Northamptonshire. Ancient specimens from the Langport district of Somerset, where the species is also presumably extinct, are similarly of the darker blue shade, but they are remarkable for the large size of their spots, either on the upper- or the under-side of their wings, or both. Those from the Salcombe district of south Devon on the whole resemble the Cornish form, though some of the specimens are of rather a duller tint. The butterfly does not appear to have been caught in this area for a long time, though it was formerly thought to be its chief stronghold, but I have seen specimens that were taken there in 1892.

It is clear that in England there is a tendency for the Large Blue to be of a brighter colour in the peninsula of Devon and Cornwall than elsewhere, though the discontinuity is not a large one. Somerset specimens tend to bridge the gap between the south-western habitats of this butterfly and those of the Cotswolds.

Reference has already been made to the extraordinary distribution of the Wood White (Plates 17, 21), which is found in England, now only in the south, and in Southern Ireland, where it has a fairly wide range, but is very little known (Map 26). This Irish race, which clearly represents an independent sub-species is now being described by Dr H. B. Williams. On the upper-side of the fore-wings the faint black lines posterior to the apical spot are more strongly developed in the Irish insects; but the chief distinction is on the under-side, where the markings are exceptionally well developed and of a dark olive-green shade, instead of pale greyish as in the English insect. Indeed, on the lower surface the Irish sub-species has a decided resemblance to the Continental species, *L. duponcheli* Stgr.

The Green-veined White, *Pieris napi* (Plate 19), often has a very distinct appearance in its two broods and in different, even though neighbouring, localities so that it is hardly possible to sub-divide it into geographical races in Britain, though the markings of the Scottish specimens are usually especially clear. However, they are far more strongly developed in the Irish insects, in which the black scaling is particularly pronounced and the spots on the fore-wings of the females not infrequently tend to coalesce into a band. Moreover, the white areas are generally rather cream-coloured and the yellow pigment on the under-side is especially bright. The Irish and British races have diverged sufficiently far from one another to give different breeding results when crossed with the bright yellow variety, *hibernica*, so that one can have no hesitation in regarding them as markedly distinct sub-species.

The hind-wings of the Orange-tip, *Anthocharis cardamines*, are in the female, but not in the male, stained with yellow in the majority of Irish specimens. This condition is rare but not unknown in Britain. Irish examples are also the more subject to variation, and this butterfly seems to be forming an incipient sub-species in that country.

One of the most extraordinary events in British entomology in recent years has been the discovery of the Chequered Skipper, *Carterocephalus palaemon*, in western Inverness by Lt.-Colonel Mackworth-Praed (p. 135, and Map 28). The race occurring there is darker and decidedly more greenish in tone, especially on the under-side, than the English one; also it must have a different food-plant, though certainly a grass, for *Brachypodium* and *Bromus*, upon which the larva lives in England, are absent from the newly-discovered Scottish haunts of this insect.

It will have been noticed that the more extreme local races of the British butterflies are those which have arisen in the greatest isolation: in Ireland, and in other islands. Yet it is especially to be observed how diverse is the response of different species to isolation of a similar degree. Some have formed sub-species, though others have not, in circumstances which are apparently identical. We can be certain that this is not due to any difference in their potential variability, for all our butterflies must possess vast and largely unexplored reserves of genetic recombinations (pp. 209–10), but rather to a greater tolerance of environmental change by some constitutions than by others; and no doubt also to the circumstance that by no means all adaptations are reflected in the colour-patterns of the adult insects.

THE INDEPENDENT EVOLUTION OF BUTTERFLIES IN BRITAIN

It is a remarkable fact that very few butterflies have evolved independently in Britain and on the Continent in such a way that specimens from these islands are, in general, distinguishable from those taken elsewhere: a situation which is decidedly less uncommon in birds. A number of butterflies have indeed given rise to unique forms in some part of their range here; for instance, the Scottish sub-species of the Brown Argus, and the Irish sub-species of the Wood White, and various others, are unknown abroad. But such races are not characteristic of the entire British population, and only three species have evolved as a whole here in a distinct way. One of them, the Large Copper, *Lycaena dispar*, is extinct in England and its special features have already been described (pp. 164–5).

The Mountain Ringlet, *Erebia epiphron*, has in Britain evolved into the sub-species *mnemon*, which is divisible into two forms (pp. 271–2). This is found nowhere on the Continent, and it differs from the typical sub-species, which is restricted to the Hartz Mountains, in its smaller size and much less well developed band and spotting, a feature which is particularly clear on the underside of the hind-wings. It has already been pointed out that the strange Irish race of this butterfly may be one which is known in the Alps (*aetheria*), though this statement requires confirmation from additional specimens.

The third butterfly which has evolved into an independent sub-species here is the Swallow-tail, *Papilio machaon*. With us it is well-established only in the Norfolk Broads; but it is by no means limited to such country on the Continent. Furthermore, our race constitutes a distinct sub-species, *britannicus* Seitz, which cannot be confused with any other, of which there are several in Continental Europe. It will be seen that the English insect has a distinct appearance, being considerably the darker. Its ground-colour is of a deeper yellow. On the fore-wings the dark lines along the nervures are much heavier and the dark sub-marginal band is not only wider but also more triangular, becoming relatively broader as it approaches the inner margin, while in the French specimen it is of nearly the same width throughout. On the hind-wings, the broad submarginal band, marked with blue, extends nearer to the dark mark at the end of the cell in the English than in the continental sub-species.

As already explained (p. 148), the Swallow-tail butterfly seems to have survived here, at the edge of its range, by adapting itself closely to a specialized type of habitat in the fens. However, Dr H. B. Williams has pointed out to me that its occurrence in Kent merits more consideration than it has received. It is well known that specimens of the French sub-species are sometimes taken in south-eastern England. Now these are not freely scattered along the coast of Kent and east Sussex, as would be anticipated if they were purely immigrants, but are largely confined to Kent itself.[1] Moreover, they are less infrequent than is generally supposed, and for at least a century they have been captured every few years. Sometimes a number of specimens are seen in several consecutive seasons, and the caterpillars have repeatedly been found feeding on wild or cultivated carrots: for the food-plant of the continental races of the Swallow-tail is not confined to the Milk Parsley, *Peucedanum palustre*, as is that of the sub-species *britannicus*.

The Hythe district was known to the early entomologists as a locality for the Swallow-tail at a time when that butterfly seems to have been more widespread here than it is today. But it is unlikely that the specimens now found in Kent are the descendants of that ancient stock. Probably they are the progeny of occasional immigrants which can perhaps maintain themselves at least for a number of generations if the conditions are favourable for some years, though they may need to be recruited now and then by foreign specimens. It does appear, however, that Kent more nearly provides the required conditions for the continental race of the Swallow-tail than do the adjoining counties, and we may regard it as maintaining a precarious footing there. This observation shows rather clearly how a species may find in an otherwise inhospitable country some restricted habitat to which it might ultimately adjust itself.

It is not at all clear, however, why so few butterflies have evolved independently here and on the Continent, when unique sub-species of some of them have originated in a part of their

[1] Occasional scattered records from other counties may reasonably refer to stray immigrants or to specimens which have been released.

range in our islands. Furthermore, many are quite isolated in this country, since they migrate to a negligible degree. It may be, however, in some instances at least, that the special adaptations of our butterflies do not chance to evoke modifications of their colour-pattern; and the fact that several of them are limited to habitats in Britain to which they are not restricted abroad suggests that they may well have acquired distinct physiological adaptations in our islands. Some indication of this might be obtained by inter-breeding British and continental specimens. An unexpected distinction might then be found in their genetic behaviour, at least if varieties are introduced into the cross, as in the British and Irish races of the Green-veined White.

Chapter 14

The Origin of the British Butterfly Fauna

All our butterflies have a fairly wide distribution on the Continent, so that none of the species can have evolved here. They must have reached us since the maximum of the third Pleistocene glaciation, when the whole of these islands, except England south of the Severn and Thames and the extreme south-west of Ireland, were covered with ice. The sequence in which the various species made their way to England is very difficult, sometimes impossible, to determine, nor has the subject received much attention from entomologists. Professor Bryan Beirne (1943) has, however, begun the analysis of it and, though I depart rather widely from his views, it is a pleasure to draw attention to his pioneer work.

It seems to me that we have rather definite indications that our butterfly fauna is the result of two waves of colonization during warm periods, separated by glacial or semi-glacial conditions when our three northern or alpine butterflies may have arrived; but it is much more probable that two of them did so in the latter part of the previous glaciation. In order to reach any conclusion on the relative dating of these events, it will be necessary very briefly to survey the glacial history of these islands since the end of the Pliocene Period. This subject has been much affected by the results of recent research, and I am most grateful to my friend, Mr Charles Elton, for the valuable help which he has given me in analysing it. Though it is one on which diverse opinions are held, the following scheme seems to be in accord with the views of the most recent authorities.

Four Glacial and three Interglacial Periods occurred during Pleistocene times in the British Isles, but it is unnecessary to consider any earlier than the second of the Interglacials. This was of very long duration, with a warm or temperate climate much like that of today and vegetation very similar to our own; the implements associated with it are of the Acheulean type, fashioned by men who were very different from ourselves and perhaps belonged to a different genus. It was followed by the severe third glaciation already mentioned, which was contemporary with Mousterian implements; these were made by Neanderthal Man, a species distinct from our own. The third Interglacial Period which succeeded it was shorter and less pronounced than the second, being dry and rather cool, and it was followed by the fourth and last Pleistocene glaciation, which was much less severe than the third. At this time there were at any rate glaciers on some of our mountains, with tundra in their neighbourhood, and the ice had blocked the entrances to certain caves in Derbyshire which contain evidence of a previous Aurignacian culture, the work of our own species, *Homo sapiens*. It is at present impossible to form an opinion on the length of these various Pleistocene ages, except to say that some of them must have occupied immense periods of time: to be measured in tens of thousands of years. However, it can be asserted that the last ice-cap in Sweden began to recede about 11,000 BC, and it may well have done so in Britain about the same time, but this is not certainly known.

When the ice of the last glaciation retreated, a Magdalenian culture appeared, and we pass from Pleistocene into Holocene times; an approximate dating of subsequent events now becomes possible. The new phase opens about 8300 BC with a 'Pre-boreal or sub-arctic' climate lasting for about 1500 years. Pine, birch, and willow grew over a large part of Britain, and during this time the Dogger Bank sank beneath the North Sea. About 6800 BC a Boreal Age supervened. The climate was then of the 'continental' type, with warm summers and cold winters. Oak and mixed deciduous woods were spreading, but pine was yet largely predominant. These conditions continued until about 5000 BC. Meanwhile the land was still sinking, and it is probably during this phase, approximately contemporary with Noah's flood in the plains of Mesopotamia, that the land-connection between England and the Continent was finally severed, in part by subsidence and in part by erosion through the chalk. The succeeding 'Atlantic Age' was wet and warmer than today, the climate being 'oceanic'. It was marked by an increase of oak, alder, and other deciduous trees, and a decrease of pine and birch, and near the end of it the Neolithic culture appeared. The main sinking of the land was now ended. Somewhere about 2500 BC we passed into a 'Sub-boreal phase', with a continental climate. This was not long before that great event, conveniently dated a little earlier than the year 2000 BC, the beginning of the Bronze Age in England, when we reach familiar pre-history.

The sub-atlantic conditions, with an oceanic climate characteristic of the present day, began about 1000 BC.

It is especially to be noticed that the climate in south-west England, on the west coast of Scotland, and in south-west Ireland would be much milder during the last ice-age and in the early Holocene than that described in the foregoing account. Some members of the pre-glacial fauna and flora therefore survived in those regions.

Now it is not possible to suppose that Britain and Ireland have been united at any time in the Holocene, for it seems generally agreed that the alterations in land-level which have taken place since the last retreat of the ice have been insufficient to close the gap between them, nor does the vertebrate fauna of Ireland accord with such a view. The most recent warm period during which the two countries can have formed a single land-mass is the third and last Interglacial Age of Pleistocene times, that between the intense third and milder fourth ice-ages. It is generally admitted that the land-bridge linking them must have been between Ulster and south-west Scotland a little to the north-west of the North Channel. The most obvious site for it is from the Inishowen Peninsula, Co. Donegal, to Argyll through the islands of Islay and Mull, for here the sea is much shallower than at any other point between the two countries and an elevation of 30 fathoms would unite them. However, its exact position must remain in doubt, since it is not safe to deduce the land connections of past times from present-day map contours. First, because of the possible existence of former glacial deposits now washed away and, secondly, because changes in land-level are not all 'eustatic'; that is to say, they are not always uniform risings or sinkings but may in part be due to a tilting of the whole country.

The Shetlands also were probably still united with the British mainland in the last Pleistocene Interglacial Period, for the Wood Mouse, *Apodemus sylvaticus,* inhabits them; and it would certainly have been destroyed had it been isolated there during the severe third glaciation. However, these islands must have been cut off soon afterwards, for the sea between them and Caithness is over fifty fathoms deep, nor does their fauna contain post-glacial elements.

The sea between Scilly and Land's End reaches but does not exceed 40 fathoms in depth, slightly shallower than that between Orkney and Shetland. Consequently we may suppose that the

Scillies were connected with Cornwall during the last Interglacial Period, but not in the Holocene.

The faunistic relations of the Isle of Man are decidedly Irish, though deeper water separates it from Ireland than from England, but the changes in level involved may not be eutaxitic. The matter requires further study.

It is unbelievable that any of the butterflies which must surely have existed here during the long warm second Interglacial Period could have survived the severities of the intense third Pleistocene glaciation. Accordingly, we may suppose that the earlier colonists among those found today arrived in England during the third and last Pleistocene Interglacial Period (or a few of them towards the end of the third glaciation), and that many made their way across the land-bridge to Ireland. They would be driven south in both countries by the fourth glaciation, but a proportion of them would maintain themselves in the south-west of England and Ireland, as well as on the west coast of Scotland and its isles, during that not very rigorous time. Some of these have since remained in the south of the two countries, but others recolonized the north of one or both of them when the increasingly milder conditions of the Holocene supervened. That period would also allow new species to make their way into England from the Continent, and these formed a second wave of invasion before the English Channel broke through to the North Sea during the Pre-atlantic Age, probably near the end of it, between seven and eight thousand years ago.

Professor Beirne divides the butterflies of our islands into two main groups (with sub-divisions), excepting of course those normally maintained here by migration from the Continent, which must be omitted from any such discussion as this. His Section A comprises species confined to certain limited areas or having a discontinuous distribution, and many of these form sub-species. His Section B includes those occurring in south-east England and possessing a wide and continuous distribution, and a smaller number of them form sub-species. He considers that Section A arrived here in 'late glacial' times and that the remainder are post-glacial. However, it has been pointed out in Chapter 7 that some of our butterflies are subject to great cyclical changes in their distribution-areas, which may be widely extended at one time and contracted at another (pp. 138–41), while there is good reason to think that the distribution of a few of them has been converted from the continuous to the discontinuous type quite recently, owing partly to such changes in area and partly to the effects of civilization. Taking these and other considerations into account, I reach certain tentative conclusions on the past history of our species. These results are, however, very different from those of Professor Beirne, as is the geological setting in which I place the various waves of immigration.

Certain of the species which do not depend upon supplies from the Continent for their existence here are none the less well known to be immigrants or occasional wanderers, and this fact must be taken into account in considering their history. Others have rarely or never been known to stray from their main habitats, in spite of the extensive observations which have been conducted on this subject, nor do most of the common British species absent as residents from Ireland seem to appear as vagrants there. We may therefore exclude migration as an important factor in the distribution of such insects, and certainly from those found only in the south.

In the first edition of this book, published in 1945, the fact that a butterfly had evolved a local race in isolation was taken into account when suggesting its long residence in these islands. For at that time the great power of selection for advantageous qualities in wild populations, and therefore the possibility of rapid race-formation, had not been appreciated as it has now. We may take an example from birds. Moreau, a well-known authority on the subject, had in 1930 estimated 5000 years as the minimum time required for the formation of distinct local races in that group. We now know that a definitive local form of the Sparrow has evolved round Mexico City in 30 years. So, too, the rate at which a butterfly can in favourable conditions extend its range had been much under-estimated. For instance, the Essex Skipper was introduced into North America at London, Ontario, about 1910. It has now spread thence into New Jersey and New Brunswick, distances of approximately 400 and 700 miles.

We may certainly feel, however, that if a butterfly is not known in Scotland but exists in England and the southern part of Ireland, the two populations have been long isolated, having origins in the Holocene and the last Interglacial periods respectively. This will also be true of such a species as the Silver-washed Fritillary, found throughout Ireland but, except formerly as a great rarity in south Yorkshire, not in Britain north of the line from the Mersey to the Wash. A similar deduction may with some safety be made in regard to the Chequered Skipper, which exists here only in two restricted areas: in the Northamptonshire–Lincolnshire district and in western Inverness. A somewhat comparable situation characterizes the Speckled Wood, which in Britain occurs only south of the Mersey–Wash line, except for occasional instances in Yorkshire and Furness, and in the coastal region of Argyll and Inverness; that is to say, at the end of the last land-bridge to Ireland, where indeed the species is widespread.

With one exception, no butterfly not known as at least an occasional wanderer inhabits the Isles of Scilly: thus the Large, Small and Green-veined Whites are established there, but not the Orange-tip. It is the Meadow Brown whose position, widespread in that archipelago, is particularly doubtful. Except for a strange record from the *Royal Sovereign* Light Vessel seven miles south-east of Eastbourne, we have exceptionally clear evidence that this is neither a migratory nor wandering insect. A unique and highly characteristic form of the butterfly exists throughout Scilly. Though as just indicated, the speed of race-formation is a hazardous criterion by which to judge distribution, I am inclined to regard the Meadow Brown as an Interglacial relic in those islands.

In spite of the uncertainties that have just been indicated, it seems worth endeavouring to divide the butterflies of the British Isles into groups reflecting their geological history, omitting, of course, the well known migrants. This is attempted in Table 7, in which those species whose distribution is uncertain are placed in brackets.

GROUP I. *Erebia epiphron, Coenonympha tullia.*
We have in these islands three[1] alpine or northern butterflies. These have probably reached us during glacial times and spread north in the wake of the ice, where they are now cut off. It might be suggested that they all did so during the interval which separated the first and second waves of colonization, that is to say in the last Pleistocene glacial period; but I believe that only one of them, the Scotch Argus, *Erebia aethiops*, arrived at that time (p. 297). The other two, the Large Heath, *Coenonympha tullia*, and the Mountain Ringlet, *Erebia epiphron*, must have been established here much earlier, for they have both crossed to Ireland; assuming, as I think we may, the Irish occurrence of the

[1] Four if, as I believe, *Erebia ligea* really occurred here.

latter species. These two insects must therefore be the most ancient of our butterflies, and their arrival here must be dated to the latter part of the third Pleistocene glaciation.

Group	Probable period of arrival	Species
I	3rd Pleistocene glaciation, towards end	*E. epiphron, C. tullia*
II	3rd Pleistocene Interglacial Period	
a (1)		*M. tithonus, (M. athalia), (T. betulae), L. sinapis, G. rhamni*
(2)		*C. euphrosyne, Q. quercus, E. tages*
b		*A. paphia, C. argiolus*
c		*P. aegeria, C. palaemon* Scotch
d		*M. jurtina, L. megera, M. aglaia, E. aurinia, H. semele, C. pamphilus, A. hyperanthus, C. minimus, C. rubi, P. napi, A. cardamines*
III	4th Pleistocene glaciation, near end	*E. aethiops*
IV	Holocene	
a		*M. galathea, C. selene, M. adippe, N. polychloros, A. iris, H. lucina, P. aegon, A. agestis-artaxerxes, L. coridon, L. bellargus, S. w-album, A. crataegi, P. malvae, C. palaemon* English, *T. sylvestris, T. lineola, H. comma, O. venatus*
b		*M. cinxia, P. c-album, L. camilla, M. arion, L. dispar, S. pruni, P. machaon, T. acteon*
V	(Doubtful)	*A. urticae, I. io, P. icarus, L. phlaeas*

Table 7. The Origin of the British Butterfly Fauna. Doubtful species are in brackets. (For sub-groups, see text.)

The status of the Mountain Ringlet would have to be reconsidered if the Irish race really proves to be the high Alpine sub-species *aetheria* f. *nelamus* (p. 273).[1] In that event, it might

[1] This possibility lacks confirmation, since only three Irish specimens seem to be known.

at least be suggested that the Irish insect descends from a high Alpine race which reached us during the rigorous third Pleistocene glaciation and that the British one, *mnemon*, arrived at a later date, during the last glacial period when the connection with Ireland seems to have been severed.

GROUP II This consists of the succeeding colonists, those which presumably reached us during the third Interglacial Period of the Pleistocene. The evidences of their antiquity are of various kinds, and some produce a more convincing picture than others, so that this group may be subdivided as follows:

GROUP II (*a*) Species occurring in Ireland but absent from the north of that country.

(1) *Maniola tithonus*, (*Mellicta athalia*), (*Thecla betulae*), *Leptidea sinapis, Gonepteryx rhamni*.

These butterflies are not now found in Scotland or the extreme north of England. Thus they are today cut off on both sides from the land-bridge to Ireland. The Heath Fritillary, *Mellicta athalia*, and the Brown Hairstreak, *Thecla betulae*, can only be included here if the old records of them from Ireland are substantiated. Otherwise, they belong to Group IV.

(2) *Clossinia euphrosyne, Quercusia quercus, Erynnis tages*.

These have extended their range farther north in Britain so as to include at least part of Scotland, where the Purple Hairstreak, *Q. quercus*, is now limited to the south, while the Dingy Skipper, *E. tages*, is very local.

It is reasonable to suppose that the butterflies placed in Group II (*a*) spread northwards in a warm period sufficiently far into Scotland to reach the north-eastern end of the land-bridge to Ireland, which they crossed. The advancing cold of the last glaciation no doubt drove them south. There they have remained in Ireland, but those placed in the second division of the group have reached Scotland again in the Holocene.

GROUP II (*b*) *Argynnis paphia, Celastrina argiolus*.

These are species which have spread throughout Ireland but in Britain have not penetrated again into Scotland. Indeed, the Silver-washed Fritillary, *A. paphia*, is hardly to be found north of the Mersey–Wash line, while the Holly Blue, *C. argiolus*, though reaching the south of the Lake District, is almost unknown in north Cumberland and is absent from north-eastern England.

GROUP II (c) *Pararge aegeria, Carterocephalus palaemon* in Scotland.

These two species exist in isolation in southern England and north-west Scotland. They probably represent a double colonization of the British islands, the Scottish group in each being Interglacial in origin, a fact particularly clear in *P. aegeria*, which has reached Ireland, where it is widespread. The Chequered Skipper has not colonized that country, while in Scotland it is limited to a small area north of Fort William, whence, south-wards, it is not found again until Lincolnshire. It appears likely that the southern populations of these two butterflies, extremely restricted in the Chequered Skipper but widespread in the Speckled Wood though absent from the north of England, are Holocene in origin.

GROUP II (d) *Maniola jurtina, Lasiommata megera, Meso-acidalia aglaia, Euphydryas aurinia, Hipparchia semele, Coeno-nympha pamphilus, Aphantopus hyperanthus, Cupido minimus, Callophrys rubi, Pieris napi, Anthocharis cardamines.*

We have here eleven species that occur in England, and at least as far north as southern Scotland, and are widespread in Ireland. They are not on the whole likely to have established themselves in the latter country as wanderers. Three of them require special mention.

The Wall Butterfly, so common in Ireland, might have arrived there by means of stragglers during Holocene times, since it has been reported as a stray out at sea (p. 150). It is, however, absent from Scilly though found in west Cornwall and, at least normally, it is by no means an insect of sustained flight.

Much the same may be said of the Small Heath, which has been observed coming in from the sea (p. 150). It is widespread both in Ireland and the Isle of Man; yet it has not reached Orkney or Scilly, though found at the extreme north of Scotland and at Land's End.

The Green-veined White is the most migratory of the species placed here as Interglacial in origin: obviously this is much less probable in this instance than in the others so treated. It has been pointed out (p. 151) that race formation can no longer be regarded as contributing a criterion in favour of long residence in these islands. Yet this is the butterfly in which, if at all, such evidence is to be admitted, since the Irish race of *P. napi* is one of the most distinct to which any British butterfly has given rise. Indeed it has diverged so far that exceptional breeding results are obtained when it is crossed with the English form.

GROUP III *Erebia aethiops.*

When we consider our three northern or mountain butterflies, we see that the situation in regard to the Scotch Argus is different from that of the other two: the Mountain Ringlet or the Large Heath. The latter species is a northern insect, down to sea level, for its range extends beyond the Arctic Circle in Scandinavia. The Mountain Ringlet actually reaches its northern limit in Britain, but it is a true inhabitant of the mountains. Many cold-adapted Lepidoptera will have had a wide distribution during the fourth Pleistocene glaciation and will have been cut off in Scandinavia and in the Alps, and other southern European mountains, in the Holocene. This seems true of the Mountain Ringlet, although it did not reach, or has not survived in, Scandinavia.

On the other hand, the Scotch Argus is not a northern butterfly, nor essentially a mountain one. It, too, attains its northern limit in Britain. Yet it occurs down to sea level on the coast of Belgium and north-eastern Germany. It is also found across the great plain of Europe though, in addition, it inhabits the Alps and other mountainous regions. In Britain it seems to be a species that has survived at the edge of its range by means of adjustment to a special type of habitat, in this instance adaptation to cold, so that it flies in northern districts while it is sometimes restricted to higher altitudes there. It may even have arrived here later than the last glaciation, a possibility which its absence from Ireland tends to support.

GROUP IV Here are included those species that are absent from Ireland and occur in the south of England, some with extensions into Scotland. They may most reasonably be regarded as Holocene colonists which arrived across the land-bridge from the Continent after that to Ireland was broken, for they are not noted as migrants or wanderers.

GROUP IV (*a*) *Melanargia galathea, Clossiana selene, Meso-acidalia adippe, Nymphalis polychloros, Apatura iris, Hamearis lucina, Plebejus aegon,* the *Aricia agestis-artaxerxes* super-species, *Lysandra coridon, L. bellargus, Strymonidia w-album, Aporia crataegi, Pyrgus malvae, Carterocephalus palaemon* in England, *Thymelicus sylvestris, T. lineola, Hesperia comma, Ochlodes venatus.*

These eighteen species occur in the south-east of England, whence some have spread. Two require special comment.

Possibly the Small Pearl-bordered Fritillary is an Interglacial survival, for it is much commoner in the north than in southern England. In this it contrasts with the Pearl-border; indeed the distribution here of these two species may be thought consistent with their occurrence in Europe. Though both are found to the extreme north of Scandinavia, the Pearl-border flies in Italy and Sicily while the Small Pearl-border goes no farther south than the Alps. However, though the latter butterfly is the more northern of the two in Britain, it has not crossed to Ireland (unless it has become extinct there). Moreover, it may easily have gained its present distribution even if arriving in the Holocene.

Secondly, the Northern Brown Argus is restricted to Scotland, mainly the east, and the north of England. This might suggest a butterfly which had entered Britain during the last glacial period, its extremely close ally being Holocene. But it seems more probable that both reached this country after the last retreat of the ice, and it will be noted that the northern insect is absent from Ireland; though in this respect, negative evidence carries far less weight than positive. As Høegh-Guldberg (1968) suggests, a warm period in Europe may well have favoured the evolution of a double-brooded from a single-brooded *Aricia.* The double brooded species would have an obvious advantage in the south and the single brooded in the north, where the growth period is longer. The two could colonize this country in the Holocene, the one being favoured in the south and the other in the north. In Europe, the Brown Argus has not advanced farther north than Denmark, while the Northern species is established in Norway, Sweden and Finland.

GROUP IV (*b*) Eight species occurring in southern England but not in the south-east corner of the country are placed here.

Melitaea cinxia, Polygonia c-album, Limenitis camilla, Maculinia arion, Lycaena dispar, Strymonidia pruni, Papilio machaon, Thymelicus acteon.

GROUP V There seems no point in attempting to relate four of our resident butterflies to their period of origin in this country. These are: *Aglais urticae*, *Inachis io*, *Polyommatus icarus*, *Lycaena phlaeas*.

All seem well established in Ireland. However, a trickle of immigrant Small Tortoiseshells yearly reaches England from the Continent, and several migratory swarms of the Peacock have been observed. Both species could evidently have crossed to Ireland at any time. The Small Copper is almost universal in Europe except for northern Scotland. In some seasons it is common in Scilly and it has been caught at lightships. So also has the Common Blue, which is abundant in Scilly. If the (already fairly circumstantial) reports of it as occasionally sighted in Shetland are confirmed, its power to wander over considerable distances of sea would be well attested.

The facts which have just been discussed suggest that it is possible to draw conclusions as to the relative times at which many of our non-migratory butterflies arrived in Great Britain. Those placed in Group II, which arrived here in the last Pleistocene Interglacial Period, have in Ireland presumably been augmented by no further arrivals since that time, after which the land-bridge to Scotland was severed. In Britain they would, of course, be in direct connection with the Continent until the English Channel was formed. Some species might accordingly have been driven south even beyond the limits of the British Peninsula during the last glaciation and returned later. The statement that certain butterflies are interglacial in origin of course means that such species have maintained themselves in some part of Britain or Ireland continuously since that epoch; it is not suggested that they were never recruited from the Continent during the earlier part of the Holocene Period.

I may add that Heslop Harrison (1943) has discussed the origin of the fauna of certain of the Scottish islands. He points out that the Marsh Fritillary, *Melitaea aurinia*, approaches the Irish sub-species *praeclara* very closely on Gunna. This is a small island a few hundred yards from Coll, where are to be found several Irish plants absent from the Scottish mainland (*Spiranthes gemmipara*, *Sisyrinchium angustifolium*, *Eriocaulon septangulare*). Further, the humble bee, *Bombus smithianus*, and the moth *Nyssia zonaria* Schiff., are both found in Coll, Tiree, and Gunna, as well as in the Outer Hebrides and in the west of

Ireland; while the Transparent Burnet Moth, *Zygaena purpuralis* Brunnich, occurs in Gunna and west Ireland (but I have also received specimens from Skye). It further survives in North Wales, as does *Nyssia zonaria*. From these facts Harrison concludes 'that not only has the Tiree-Coll group been severed from Scotland prior to parting company with Ireland, but also has received some of its plants and animals from the latter country'. Further, that Ireland, the Coll-Tiree group, and the Outer Hebrides 'must have been linked together, and not with Scotland, at some fairly recent time, possibly in early post-glacial times or in some inter-glacial period'.

The Irish element in these islands is undoubtedly strong (as it is in Islay, where *M. aurinia* also approaches *praeclara*), but I think we may dismiss the possibility of their connection with Ireland in post-glacial times (p. 290). It is to my mind more likely that certain interglacial colonists survived at some places in the relatively warm Western Isles and in western Ireland, just as it seems that others did on the west coast of the Scottish mainland. Indeed, *M. aurinia praeclara* does not provide very strong evidence for the relatively recent connection of some of the Western Isles with Ireland but not with Scotland, since that sub-species (or a very close approach to it) occurs also in the neighbourhood of Oban and indeed it is fairly widespread in that district. It is indeed possible that *praeclara* represents the race present in interglacial times, and that *M. aurinia aurinia* is a Holocene arrival.

It will, of course, be realized that extensive sources of error exist in any such analysis as that attempted in this chapter. Species may have occurred widely in Britain and Ireland and have retracted their ranges of distribution southwards in both countries in recent times. Some of those found only in south-east England may have been early colonists driven there by the advancing cold of the last glaciation, but it is much more likely that they would have survived in the south-west than the south-east. Various other possibilities exist, but it seems probable that the majority of the species placed in the first four main groups of Table 7 do in fact represent distinct waves of colonization.

It is noteworthy that the feature which has attracted generations of naturalists to collect butterflies and moths is the one which fits these insects so well to act as tools in the study of evolution: that is to say, their beautiful colour-patterns, which make it possible to analyse their variation with exceptional facility. Moreover, it has already been pointed out that the power of selection for advantageous qualities in nature is much greater than was appreciated twenty or twenty-five years ago. Consequently the speed of race formation and other types of evolution can be correspondingly greater, too. For that reason, the fact that a butterfly has produced local forms in particular areas cannot itself be taken into account as an indication of antiquity. It will none the less be true that those insects which have been long established in Britain have had more extended opportunities for adjusting themselves to the conditions of their different habitats. Partly for this reason, those whose arrival here goes back to the last interglacial period are on the whole more characterized by special local forms than are the invaders of Holocene date. But there is a more telling basis for that conclusion. The species established here since before the fourth Pleistocene glaciation have experienced the climatic changes associated with that period, which must have been considerable even in the south-west of England and of Ireland; while the subsequent Holocene colonists, then inhabiting what is now Continental Europe, could presumably withdraw from the advancing cold. Furthermore, the greater variation of the insects included in the earlier fauna must be due also to a considerable extent to the circumstance that they have in the British Isles been cut off in a number of isolated areas, while most of the Holocene arrivals have not; and it has already been shown that isolation can be an important factor in the adjustment of a species to its environment.

Thus it comes about that the collector of British butterflies has at his disposal material of unique value in the study of evolution. He may or may not use it to that end. Should he be inclined to do so, it would be a gain, for he would be adding to scientific knowledge; and in that work there would be no necessity for him to forgo his pleasure in the countryside nor need the beauty of the insects he examines be diminished in his eyes.

List of Scientific and English Names

Painted Lady *Vanessa cardui*
Pale Clouded Yellow *Colias hyale*
Peacock *Inachis io*
Pearl-bordered Fritillary
  Clossiana euphrosyne
Purple Emperor *Apatura iris*
Purple Hairstreak *Thecla quercus*

Queen of Spain Fritillary *Issoria
  lathonia*

Red Admiral *Vanessa atalanta*
Ringlet *Aphantopus hyperanthus*

Scotch Argus *Erebia aethiops*
Short-tailed Blue *Everes argiades*
Silver-spotted Skipper *Hesperia
  comma*
Silver-studded Blue *Plebejus argus*

Silver-washed Fritillary *Argynnis
  paphia*
Small Blue *Cupido minimus*
Small Copper *Lycaena phlaeas*
Small Heath *Coenonympha pam-
  philus*
Small Pearl-bordered Fritillary
  Clossiana selene
Small Skipper *Thymelicus syl-
  vestris*
Small Tortoiseshell *Aglais urticae*
Small White *Pieris rapae*
Speckled Wood *Pararge aegeria*
Swallow-tail *Papilio machaon*

Wall *Lasiommata megera*
White Admiral *Limenitis camilla*
White-letter Hairstreak *Strymoni-
  dia w-album*
Wood White *Leptidea sinapis*

SCIENTIFIC TO ENGLISH

Aglais urticae Small Tortoiseshell
Anthocharis cardamines Orange-
  tip
Apatura iris Purple Emperor
Aphantopus hyperanthus Ringlet
Aporia crataegi Black-veined
  White
Argynnis paphia Silver-washed
  Fritillary
Aricia agestis Brown Argus
A. artaxerxes Northern Brown
  Argus

Callophrys rubi Green Hairstreak
Carterocephalus palaemon
  Chequered Skipper
Celastrina argiolus Holly Blue
Clossiana euphrosyne Pearl-bor-
  dered Fritillary
C. selene Small Pearl-bordered
  Fritillary
Coenonympha pamphilus Small
  Heath

C. tullia Large Heath
Colias australis Berger's Clouded
  Yellow
C. crocea Clouded Yellow
C. hyale Pale Clouded Yellow
Cupido minimus Small Blue
Cyaniris semiargus Mazarine Blue

Danaus plexippus Monarch

Erebia aethiops Scotch Argus
E. epiphron Mountain Ringlet
Erynnis tages Dingy Skipper
Euphydryas aurinia Marsh Frit-
  illary
Everes argiades Short-tailed Blue

Gonepteryx rhamni Brimstone

Hamearis lucina Duke of Bur-
  gundy Fritillary
Hesperia comma Silver-spotted
  Skipper

Hipparchia semele Grayling

Inachis io Peacock
Issoria lathonia Queen of Spain Fritillary

Lampides boeticus Long-tailed Blue
Lasiommata megera Wall
Leptidea sinapis Wood White
Limenitis camilla White Admiral
Lycaena dispar Large Copper
L. phlaeas Small Copper
Lysandra bellargus Adonis Blue
L. coridon Chalkhill Blue

Maculinea arion Large Blue
Maniola jurtina Meadow Brown
M. tithonus Hedge Brown
Melanargia galathea Marbled White
Melitaea cinxia Glanville Fritillary
Mellicta athalia Heath Fritillary
Mesoacidalia adippe High Brown Fritillary
M. aglaia Dark Green Fritillary

Nymphalis antiopa Camberwell Beauty

N. polychloros Large Tortoiseshell
Ochlodes venatus Large Skipper

Papilio machaon Swallow-tail
Pararge aegeria Speckled Wood
Pieris brassicae Large White
P. napi Green-veined White
P. rapae Small White
Plebejus argus Silver-studded Blue
Polygonia c. album Comma
Polyommatus icarus Common Blue
Pontia daplidice Bath White
Pyrgus malvae Grizzled Skipper

Strymonidia pruni Black Hairstreak
S. w-album White Letter Hairstreak

Thecla betulae Brown Hairstreak
Thecla quercus Purple Hairstreak
Thymelicus acteon Lulworth Skipper
T. lineola Essex Skipper
T. sylvestris Small Skipper

Vanessa atalanta Red Admiral
V. cardui Painted Lady

Glossary

(All references to climate apply to the British Isles only)

Acheulean culture. One produced by men living in the earlier part of the Old Stone (Palaeolithic) Age, perhaps of a different genus (*Eoanthropus*) from ourselves.

Allelomorphs. A pair of genes controlling the same character, or set of characters. Their members are derived respectively from the two parents and segregate into separate reproductive cells.

Anal angle. The corner of the hind-wing nearest the posterior end of the body (*tornus* of hind-wing).

Androconia. Scales specialized for distributing the attractive scent of the male.

Antennae. The long pair of feelers on the head of a butterfly or moth. They are appendages and are sensory in function, especially scent receptors.

Aposematic. Possessing conspicuous 'warming' coloration, advertising toxic or distasteful qualities which protect from predators.

Appendages. Jointed limbs, originally one pair to each segment and used for walking. Some have later been modified to form jaws and other organs.

Atlantic climate. Moist; mild winters, and summers rather warmer than today. The woods were chiefly of mixed deciduous trees. Much peat was formed at this time, *c.* 5000–2500 BC.

Aurignacian culture. One belonging to the later part of the Old Stone (Palaeolithic) Age and immediately following the Mousterian culture. Produced by men of our own species, living in caves.

Autosome. Any chromosome other than a sex-chromosome.

Back-cross. A mating between a heterozygote and a homozygote. It leads to segregation in equality.

Boreal climate. Dry and 'continental': warm summers and cold winters. Aspen, elm, oak, and fir are found. About 6800–5000 BC.

Buffer. A substance which confers stability on a solution. (In physiology, one which prevents the reaction of a solution from changing on addition of acid or alkali).

Cells. Microscopic units into which protoplasm is divided.

Cells of wings. The central area of the wing surrounded, but not crossed, by nervures.

Chitin. Horn-like substance forming the external covering of insects.

Chlorophyll. The green pigment of plants.

Chromosomes. Rod-like structures present in pairs (called *homologous chromosomes*) in the nucleus of every cell of the body. There is usually a fixed number of them in each species, and they carry the genes.

Claspers (adult). Part of the male genital organs: a pair of modified appendages at the end of the body by which the female is held during copulation.

Claspers (larval). The pair of 'prolegs' at the hind-end of a caterpillar's body.

Cline. A character-gradient, in which the structure or physiology of an organism changes more or less gradually over a given area.

Cocoon. A case enclosing and protecting a pupa. It is made of silk, often strengthened with other materials.

Costa. The front edge of the fore- or hind-wings.

Cremaster. Arrangement of hooks at the end of the body by which a pupa is attached to its support. The hooks are entangled in a pad of silk spun by the larva.

Cryptic colours. Those which help to conceal an animal by making it resemble its surroundings.

Dominant. A character which is fully developed when the genes controlling it are in either the heterozygous or the homozygous state (compare *recessive*).

Ecdysis. The moulting of the chitinous cuticle of an insect.

Ecology. The relation of animals and plants to their environment.

Entomology. The study of insects.

F_1. The first filial generation.

F_2. The second filial generation.

Factors (hereditary). The hereditary units which control the development of definite characters. They are present in pairs, the members of which are separately called *genes* and, together, *allelomorphs* (or *alleles*).

First filial generation. The offspring of a given mating.

Flavones. Plant pigments lacking nitrogen and responsible for a range of colours from ivory to deep yellow.

Frenulum. A coupling apparatus uniting the fore- and hind-wings of moths, but not butterflies, during flight.

Ganglion. A swelling on a nerve due to the presence at one place of the nuclei of the nerve-cells.

Gene-complex. The interacting system produced by the whole of the hereditary factors of an organism.

Genes. The members of a pair of hereditary factors. They are responsible for the production of definite characters.

Genetics. The study of variation and heredity.

Genitalia. The external organs of reproduction.

Genotype. An individual judged by its genetic constitution.

Germ-cells. Those destined to produce the reproductive cells: the sperm and the egg.

Gland. An organ manufacturing substances of use to the body (secretions). They are normally passed down a tube (duct) to the place where they are required.

Gland, ductless. One which passes its secretions directly into the blood; these are hormones.

Gynandromorph. A sexual abnormality in which male and female parts develop simultaneously, due to an incorrect distribution of the X-chromosomes in the cells of certain tissues (compare *intersex*).

Hermaphrodite. Any individual in which the two sexes are combined.

Heterozygote. An individual in which the members of a given allelomorphic pair of genes are dissimilar.

Hibernation. A quiescent state in which some animals spend the winter.

Holocene period. Recent geological times, since the last ice-age.

Homozygote. An individual in which the members of a given pair of allelomorphs are alike.

Hormone. The product of a ductless gland which, when discharged into the blood, affects a distant part of the body.

Humeral lobe. A projection from the basal part of the costa of the hind-wings. It helps to keep the fore- and hind-wings together during flight by increasing the overlap between them.

Imago. The perfect insect, after emergence from the chrysalis.

Inner margin. The posterior edge of the fore- and hind-wings.

Instar. The form assumed by an insect between each ecdysis: the imago, the pupa, and the phase between each larval moult.

Intersex. A sexual abnormality in which an animal develops first as one sex and later as the other. It is due to an incorrect balance between the male and female-determining genes (compare *gynandromorph*).

Larva. A caterpillar.

Lepidoptera. Butterflies and moths.

Linkage. The tendency for genes to remain together, instead of segregating independently, because they are carried in the same chromosomes.

Magdalenian culture. The last of the Old Stone (Palaeolithic) Age cultures, produced by men of our own species who lived in caves.

Malpighian tubules. The excretory organs of insects. They open into the alimentary canal.

Mandibles. The jaws: present in the larva, atrophied in the imago.

Maxillae. In primitive insects, a second pair of jaw-like structures behind the mandibles. They are degenerate in butterfly larvae, and modified into the long sucking proboscis ('tongue') of the imago.

Melanin. Black, brownish, or dull red animal pigment containing nitrogen.

Mendelian heredity. Responsible for nearly all organic inheritance. The characters are determined by pairs of hereditary units (genes) received respectively from the two parents. The genes are very permanent, neither frequently changing (mutating) nor contaminating one another.

Mesothorax. The middle of the three segments of which an insect's chest (thorax) is formed. It bears a pair of legs and the fore-wings.

Metabolism. The life-processes of the body. Building up protoplasm from food, and breaking down compounds with release of energy.

Metamorphosis. A sudden alteration in form, without growth: the change from larva to pupa, or pupa to imago.

Metathorax. The last of the three segments of which an insect's chest is formed. It bears a pair of legs and the hind-wings.

Micropyle. The minute opening in the chitinous shell of the egg, through which the sperm enters.

Mousterian culture. That immediately following the Acheulean culture. It belongs to the middle part of the Old Stone (Palaeolithic) Age, and was produced by Neanderthal Man, a species different from ourselves.

Multifactorial characters. Those controlled by a number of genes having small, cumulative and similar effects; as with the genetic component of normal human height.

Mutation. The inception of a heritable variation, due to a change in a unit of inheritance.

Neolithic culture. That of the New Stone Age, *c.* 2500–2000 BC. The beginnings of material civilization, produced by men who grew corn and domesticated animals.

Nervures. The struts supporting the wings of insects.

Ocelli. Eyes of simple structure found in larvae and, rarely, on the top of the head in adult butterflies.

Oesophagus. The gullet, or first part of the alimentary canal, leading back from the mouth.

Outer margin. The edge of the fore- and hind-wings farthest from the body.

Ovipositor. The structure with which the eggs are laid.

Palpi. Pair of short sensory feelers belonging to the mouth-parts and attached below the head.

P₁ generation. The first parental generation, individuals of which are mated to produce a given cross.

Phenotype. An individual judged by its appearance or physical qualities (compare *Genotype*).

Pleistocene Period. Series of glacial and inter-glacial eras previous to recent (Holocene) times. The period of the great ice-ages.

Pliocene Period. The geological period immediately before the Pleistocene: one in which many of the fossils belong to forms still alive.

Polymorphism. The existence together in the same habitat of two or more distinct forms of a species none of which is relatively very rare.

Pre-boreal climate. Dry and cold. Pine, birch, and willow appear. About 8300–6800 BC.

Precostal nervure. That supporting the humeral lobe.

Prolegs. Legs belonging to the abdominal segments of the larva. They are absent from the imago.

Prothoracic legs. Those belonging to the first segment of the chest (thorax). They are degenerate in some families, fully-formed in others.

Protoplasm. The living substance of the body.

Pupa. A chrysalis.

Pupation. The formation of the pupa by metamorphosis.

Recessive. A character which is developed only when the genes controlling it are homozygous (compare *dominant*).

Recombination. The reassortment of genes, produced by segregation.

Scales. Flat microscopic structures of chitin covering the body and wings of butterflies and moths. They contain pigment and are responsible for the colours of these insects.

Second filial generation. The grandchildren of an original cross, produced by mating together brother and sister of the F₁ generation.

Secretions. Substances of use to the body, manufactured by glands.

Segregation. The separation from one another of the pairs of genes constituting the allelomorphs, and their passage respectively into different reproductive cells.

Setae. Structures resembling hairs, but formed of chitin.

Sex-chromosomes. The X- and Y-chromosomes.

Sex-controlled inheritance. That due to genes, situated in any chromosome, which produce their effects in one sex only, though transmitted by both.

Sex-linkage. The association of characters with sex or differently in the two sexes, because the genes controlling them are carried in the sex-chromosomes.

Specific modifiers. Genes which modify the effect produced by other genes. They may be without effect by themselves.

Sperms. The male reproductive cells.

Spiracles. Paired openings on the sides of insects, leading into the tracheal tubes.

Sub-boreal climate. Dry, with continental conditions: warm summers and cold winters. About 2500–1000 BC.

Tarsus. The foot; typically of five joints in butterflies, but it may be much reduced.

Tergum. The chitinous plate forming the dorsal side of each segment.

Thorax. The chest; composed of three segments. Each has a pair of legs, and the two last a pair of wings.

Tibia. The shin; it is immediately above the foot.

Tornus. The angle of the wings between the outer and inner margins; on the hind-wings often called the *anal angle.*

Tracheal tubes. The respiratory tubes of insects.

Tracheoles. The very fine ends of the tracheal tubes.

Variation, cyclic. The situation in which a quality is for several generations first at an advantage and then at a disadvantage, or the reverse. The two conditions succeed one another in a regular cycle.

Variation, endocyclic. The situation in which the effects of a gene change regularly from overall advantage to overall disadvantage, or the reverse, within the life of each individual.

Warning colours. Those which make an animal conspicuous, and advertise that it is protected by a nauseous taste or other means.

X-chromosomes. The chromosomes carrying the genes which in general control sex-determination; present as a pair in one sex, the partner of the Y-chromosome in the other.

Y-chromosome. The partner of the X-chromosome in one of the two sexes: the female in butterflies. It contains but few genes, and, in most organisms, does not control sex-determination, though it does so in Man.

Bibliography

Audcent, H. (1942). A Preliminary List of the Hosts of some British Tachinidae. *Transactions of the Society for British Entomology, 8,* 1–42.

Beirne, B. P. (1943). The Distribution and Origin of the British Lepidoptera. *Proceedings of the Royal Irish Academy, 49* (Sect. B), 27–59.

Brecher, L. (1921). Die Puppenfärbungen des Kohlweisslings, *Pieris brassicae* L. *Archiv für Entwicklungsmechanik der Organismen, 48,* 46–139.

Carpenter, G. D. H. (1937). Further Evidence that Birds do attack and eat Butterflies. *Proceedings of the Zoological Society of London,* A., *107* (Part 3), 223–47.

(1941). The relative Frequency of Beak-marks on Butterflies of different edibility to Birds. *Proceedings of the Zoological Society of London,* A., *111,* 223–231.

Carrick, R. (1936). Experiments to test the efficiency of protective adaptation in insects. *Transactions of the Royal Entomological Society of London, 85,* 131–40.

Committee for Protection of British Lepidoptera (1929). [Report on the Establishment of the Large Copper in the British Islands.] *Proceedings of the Entomological Society of London, 4.* 53–68.

Committee on Generic Nomenclature (1934). *The Generic Names of the British Rhopalocera with a Check List of the Species.* London: Royal Entomological Society.

Donovan, C. (1936). *A Catalogue of the Macrolepidoptera of Ireland.* Cheltenham: Burrow.

Dowdeswell, W. H., Fisher, R. A., and Ford, E. B. (1940). The Quantitative Study of Populations in the Lepidoptera. *Annals of Eugenics, 10,* 123–36.

Elton, C., and Nicholson, M. (1942). The ten-year Cycle in Numbers of the Lynx in Canada. *Journal of Animal Ecology, 11,* 215–44.

Eltringham, H. (1923). *Butterfly Lore.* Oxford.

(1930). *Histological and Illustrative Methods for Entomologists.* Oxford.

(1933). *The Senses of Insects.* London: Methuen.

Fisher, R. A. (1928). The Possible Modification of the Response of the Wild Type to Recurrent Mutations. *The American Naturalist, 62,* 115–26.

(1930). The Distribution of Gene Ratios for rare Mutations. *Proceedings of the Royal Society of Edinburgh*, 50, 204–19.

(1935). Dominance in Poultry. *Philosophical Transactions of the Royal Society*, B, 225, 197–226.

Fisher, R. A. (1941 *a*). The Average Excess and Average Effect of a Gene Substitution. *Annals of Genetics*, 11, 53–63.

(1941 *b*). *Statistical Methods for Research Workers* (8th edition). Edinburgh: Oliver & Boyd.

Ford, E. B. (1940 *a*). Polymorphism and Taxonomy. *The New Systematics* (Editor, Huxley, J. S.), Oxford.

(1940 *b*). Genetic Research in the Lepidoptera. *Annals of Eugenics*, 10, 227–52.

(1941). Studies on the Chemistry of Pigments in the Lepidoptera, with reference to their bearing on Systematics. (1) The Anthoxanthins. *Proceedings of the Royal Entomological Society of London*, A., 16, 65–90.

(1942 *a*). Ibid (2) Red Pigments in the Genus *Delias*, Hübner. Ibid. 17, 87–92.

(1942 *b*). The Proportion of the Pale Form of the Female in *Colias croceus*, Fourcroy. *The Entomologist*, 75, 1–6.

1950). *The Study of Heredity* (2nd Edition). Oxford: Home University Library.

(1965 *a*). *Mendelism and Evolution* (8th Edition). London: Methuen.

(1965 *b*). *Genetic Polymorphism*. All Souls Studies; Faber & Faber, London.

(1971). *Ecological Genetics* (3rd Edition). Chapman & Hall, London.

(1973). *Genetics for Medical Students* (7th Edition). Chapman & Hall, London.

Ford, H. D. (1920). On some Varieties of *Aphantopus hyperanthus*. *The Entomologist*, 53, 250–2.

Ford, H. D., and Ford, E. B. (1930). Fluctuation in Numbers and its Influence on Variation in *Melitaea aurinia*. *Transactions of the Entomological Society of London*, 78, 345–51.

Frohawk, F. W. (1924). *Natural History of British Butterflies* (2 vols). London: Hutchinson.

(1934). *The Complete Book of British Butterflies*. London: Ward Lock.

Gerould, J. H. (1921). Blue-green Caterpillars. *Journal of Experimental Zoology*, 34, 385–412.

Goldschmidt, R. (1933). Lymantria. *Bibliographia Genetica*, 11, 1–186.

Handford, P. T. (1973 *a*). Patterns of variation in a number of genetic systems in *Maniola jurtina*: the boundary region. *Proceedings of the Royal Society*, B., 183, 265–84.

(1973 *b*). Patterns of variation in a number of genetic systems in *Maniola jurtina*: the Isles of Scilly. *Proceedings of the Royal Society*, B., 183, 285–300.

Harrison, J. W. Heslop (1943). The Range of the Greasy Fritillary (*Euphydryas aurinia*) in the Hebrides and some possible Deductions therefrom. *Entomologist's Record, 55,* 27.

Higgins, L. G., and Riley, N. D. (1970). *A Field Guide to the Butterflies of Britain and Europe.* London : Collins.

Høegh-Guldberg, O. (1968). Evolutionary trends in the Genus *Aricia* (Lep.), *Natura Jutlandica, 14,* 3–76.

Huxley, J. S. (1942 & 1974). *Evolution: the Modern Synthesis.* London: George Allen & Unwin.

Ilse, D. (1928). Über den Farbensinn der Tagfalter. *Zeitschrift für Vergleichende Physiologie, 8,* 658–92.

Imms, A. D. (1937). *Recent Advances in Entomology* (2nd Edition). London: Churchill.
(1942). *A General Textbook of Entomology* (5th Edition). London: Methuen.

Kettlewell, H. B. D. (1944). Temperature Effects on the Pupae of *Panaxia dominula* L. *Proceedings of the South London Entomological and Natural History Society,* 1943–4, 79–81.

Klemann, P. (1933). Neues über Artbastarde. *Internationale entomologische Zeitschrift, Guben, 27,* 13–24.

McWhirter, K. G. (1969). Heritability of spot-number in Scillonian strains of the Meadow Brown Butterfly (*Maniola jurtina*). *Heredity, 24,* 314–18.

McWhirter, K. G., and Creed, R. E. (1971). The Analysis of Spot Placing in the Meadow Brown Butterfly (*Maniola jurtina*). In *Ecological Genetics and Evolution* (Editor, E. R. Creed), 275–88. Oxford: Blackwell.

Magnus, D. B. E. (1958). Experimental analysis of some 'over-optimal' sign-stimuli . . . *Proceedings of the 10th International Congress of Genetics, 2,* 405–18.

Mather, K. (1943). *Statistical Analysis in Biology.* London: Methuen.

Morley, C., and Rait-Smith, W. (1933). The Hymenopterous Parasites of the British Lepidoptera. *Transactions of the Royal Entomological Society of London, 81,* 133–83.

Moss, J. E. (1933). The Natural Control of the Cabbage Caterpillars, *Pieris* spp. *Journal of Animal Ecology, 2,* 210–31.

Neave, S. A., *et al.* (1933). *The History of the Entomological Society of London,* 1833–1933. London: Entomological Society.

Poulton, E. B. (1892). Further Experiments upon the colour-relation between certain lepidopterous larvae, pupae, cocoons, and imagines, and their surroundings. *Transactions of the Entomological Society of London,* 293–487.

Poulton, E. B., and Saunders, C. B. (1898). An Experimental Enquiry into the Struggle for Existence in certain common Insects. *Report of the British Association, Bristol,* 906–9.

Remington, C. L. (1954). The genetics of *Colias* (Lepidoptera). *Advances in Genetics*, 6, 403–50.

Sandars, E. (1939). *A Butterfly Book for the Pocket*. Oxford.

Scali, V. (1971). Spot Distribution in *Maniola jurtina* (L.) (Lepidoptera Satyridae): Tuscan Mainland 1967–1969. *Monitore Zoologia Italiana*, N.S., 5, 147–63.

Seitz, A., *et al.* (1906–10). *The Macrolepidoptera of the World:* (1) *The Palearctic Butterflies*, translated by K. Jordan; (vol. 1 text, vol. 2 plates). Stuttgart.

Shepherd, J. (1942). Breeding Experiments with the Irish Yellow Race of *Pieris napi*. *Entomologist*, 75, 233–5.

South, R. (1941). *The Butterflies of the British Isles* (3rd Edition). London: Frederick Warne.

Stokoe, W. J. (1944). *The Caterpillars of the British Butterflies*. London: Frederick Warne.

Süffert, F. (1924). Bestimmungsfaktoren des Zeichnungsmusters beim Saison-Dimorphismus von *Araschnia levana-prorsa*. *Biologisches Zentralblatt*, 44, 173–88.

Talbot, G. (1920). The Occurrence of *Strymon pruni* L. in Surrey. *Entomologist's Record*, 32, 40.

Warren, B. C. S. (1936). *Monograph of the Genus Erebia*. London: The British Museum.

Wigglesworth, V. B. (1938). *Insect Physiology* (2nd Edition). London: Methuen.

(1939). *The Principles of Insect Physiology*. London: Methuen.

Williams, C. B. (1930). *The Migration of Butterflies*. Edinburgh: Oliver & Boyd.

Bibliographical notes

The foregoing works provide detailed references for certain of the statements made in this book. In addition, a few of them may usefully be consulted by those who require a more extended treatment of some of the topics which have been discussed in it. However, the information on several others has never before been brought together, so that it is not possible to provide simple guides to the literature relating to every chapter.

Accordingly, I have selected a number of useful works of reference from the list in the previous section, where their full titles may be found, and have grouped them under the subjects with which they deal. These are arranged alphabetically.

As already explained, it has not been my purpose to give descriptions of British butterflies and their life-histories, as this has often been done before, but I have here listed a few of the books from which such information may be obtained. These will be found under the heading 'Textbooks of British Butterflies'.

Classification, structure and fundamental characters of Insects and of the chief groups into which they are divided
   Imms (1942); Imms (1937). See chapters 1 and 2 for insect structure.
Colours of Butterflies
   Ford (1941, 1942 *a*); Imms (1937), chapter 7.
Evolution
   Ford (1965*a*), chapters 4 and 5; Huxley (1974), a general survey of evolution, including a discussion of geographical races and clines.
Genetics
   Ford (1950), an elementary general text-book; Ford (1965b), special emphasis on genetic interactions; Ford (1971).
Migration
   Williams (1930).[1]
Nomenclature of British Butterflies
   Higgins and Riley (1970).
Physiology of Insects, giving an account of the working of the body and its chief organs
   Wigglesworth (1938 and 1939), the latter being the larger and more comprehensive work.

   [1] See also numerous articles by T. Dannreuther in *The Entomologist* from 1932 onwards.

Senses and Sense-organs of Butterflies
    Eltringham (1923 and 1933); Imms (1937), chapters 5 and 6.

Statistical Methods
    Fisher (1941 *b*), an extensive and authoritative treatment of the subject; Mather (1943), a smaller work.

Technical methods for making Microscopic Preparations of entomological material.
    Eltringham (1930).

Text-books of British Butterflies, with descriptions of adults and early stages, times of appearance, food-plants, and localities
    Frohawk (1924, 2 volumes, and 1934); Sandars (1939); Seitz (1906–10), standard work on butterflies of Europe, including Britain, and Asia (omitting the Oriental Region), many names of varieties and forms (with authors) are given; South (1941), first published, 1906; Higgins and Riley (1970). (Characteristics of genera may be obtained from Sandars and Seitz.)

Maps showing the distribution of certain butterflies in the British Isles

The following maps are selected to illustrate, in particular, the arguments advanced in Chapter 14 relating to the sequence in which various species of butterflies colonized Britain. They also demonstrate a variety of other phenomena, among which may especially be mentioned the following: clines (No. 6), discontinuous distribution (Nos. 2 and 28), the discontinuity of many English and Irish races (Nos. 7 and 27), the Irish affinities of the west coast of Scotland (Nos. 1 and 9), the limitation of various species to chalk or calcareous soil (Nos. 16, 17, 32), species with greatly restricted habitats (Nos. 23, 24, 31), and the recent increase in range of the Comma Butterfly and the White Admiral (Nos. 11 and 13).

These maps show approximately the present status of the species; that is to say, since 1910. The distributions are indicated by dots, but horizontal or perpendicular lines are used to distinguish sub-species or extensions of range. Areas in which a species has become extinct during the period 1860–1910 are marked by *diagonal* lines, but these are used only when the disappearance of a butterfly from some habitat is of special importance.

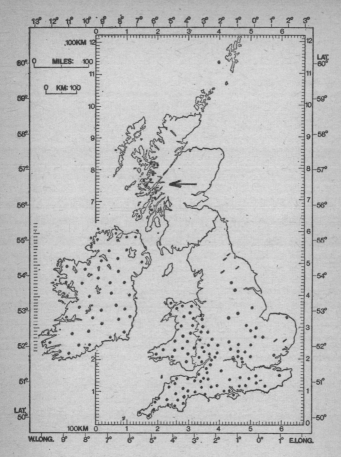

1. The Speckled Wood, *Pararge aegeria*

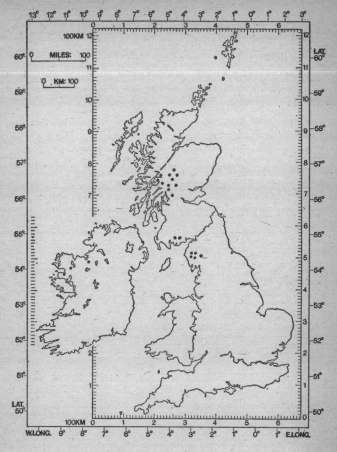

2. The Mountain Ringlet, *Erebia epiphron*

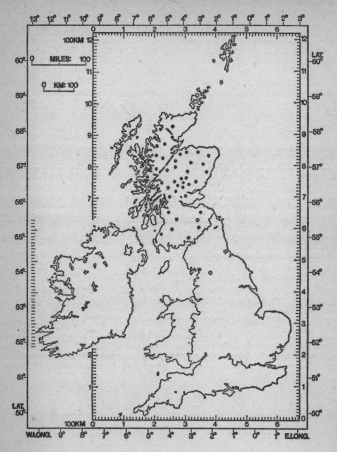

3. The Scotch Argus, *Erebia aethiops*

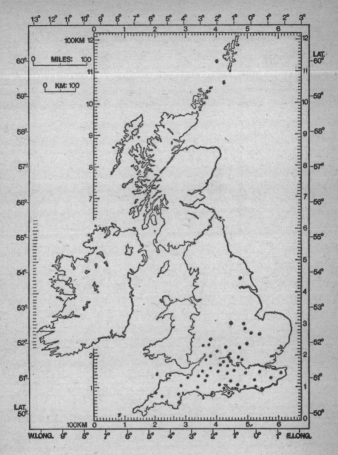

4. The Marbled White, *Melanargia galathea*

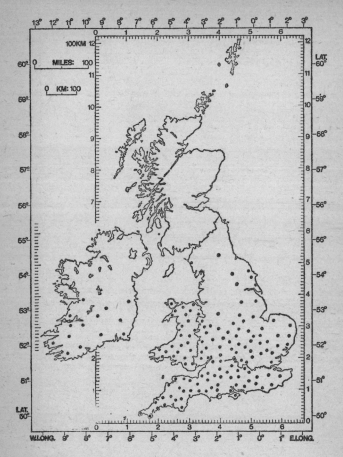

5. The Hedge Brown, *Maniola tithonus*

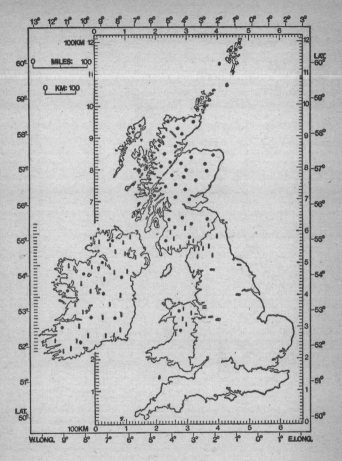

6. The Large Heath, *Coenonympha tullia*
● =sub-sp. *scotica*, ❙ =sub-sp. *tullia*, — =sub-sp. *philoxenus*

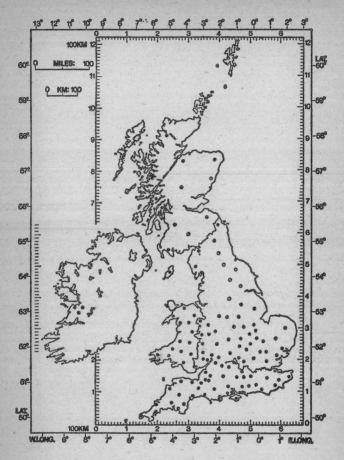

7. The Pearl-bordered Fritillary, *Clossiana euphrosyne*

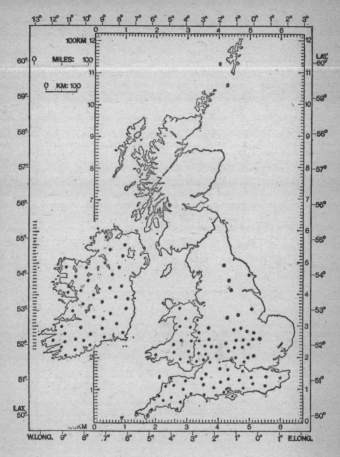

8. The Silver-washed Fritillary, *Argynnis paphia*
I = extinct

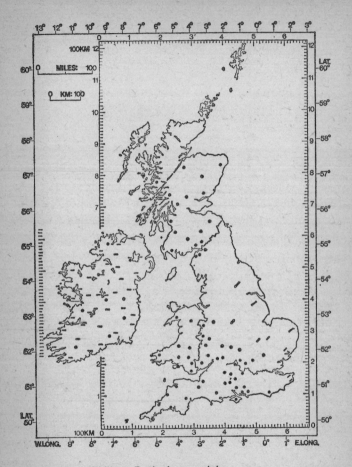

9. The Marsh Fritillary, *Euphydryas aurinia*
● =sub-sp. *aurinia*, — =sub-sp. *preaclara*
/=extinct

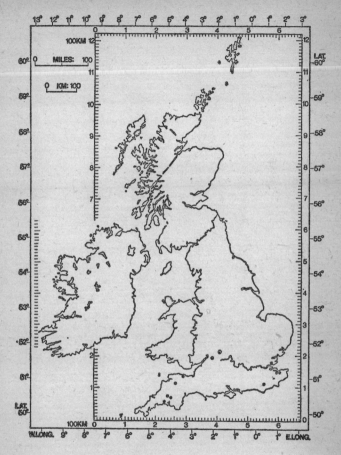

10. The Heath Fritillary, *Mellicta athalia*

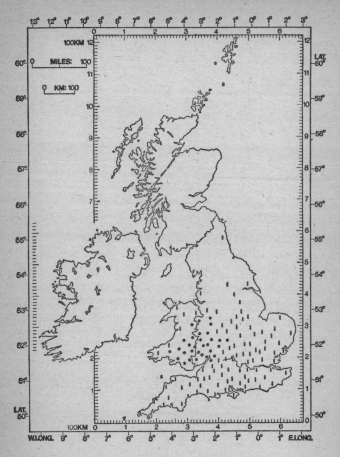

11. The Comma Butterfly, *Polygonia c-album*

❙ =extension of range since 1915
● =distribution prior to 1915

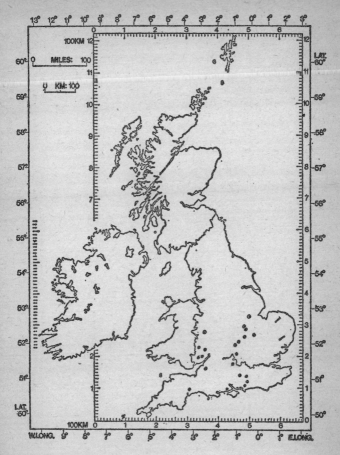

12. The Purple Emperor, *Apatura iris*
l = extinct

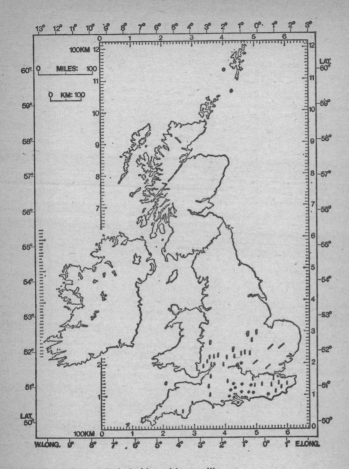

13. The White Admiral, *Limenitis camilla*
▌ = extension of range since 1920
● = distribution prior to 1920

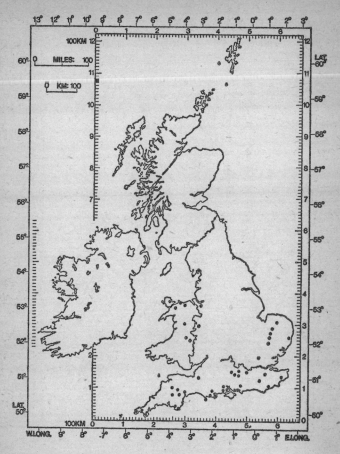

14. The Silver-studded Blue, *Plebejus argus*.

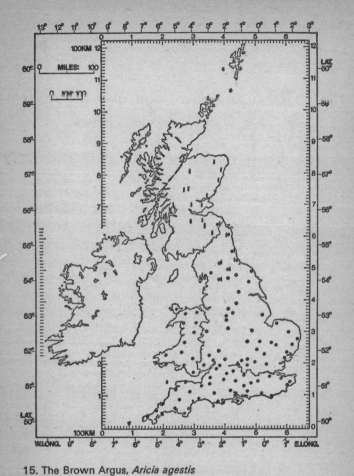

15. The Brown Argus, *Aricia agestis*
I = The Northern Brown Argus, *Aricia artaxerxes*
I● = The form of *A. artaxerxes* generally lacking the central white spot in the fore wings

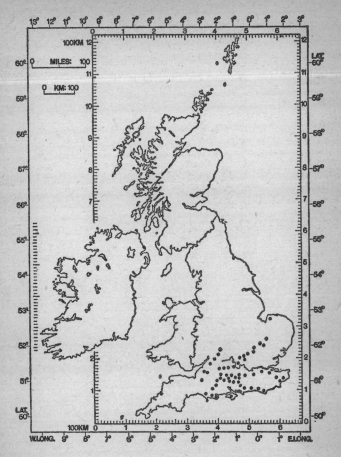

16. The Chalkhill Blue, *Lysandra coridon*

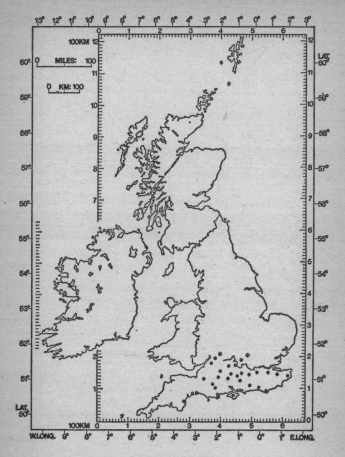

17. The Adonis Blue, *Lystandra bellargus*

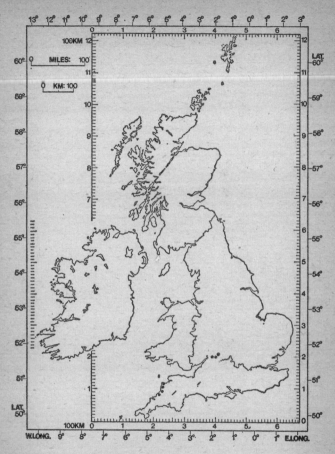

18. The Large Blue, *Maculinea arion*
/=extinct

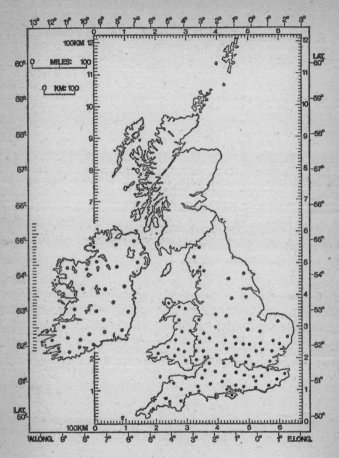

19. The Holly Blue, *Celastrina argiolus*

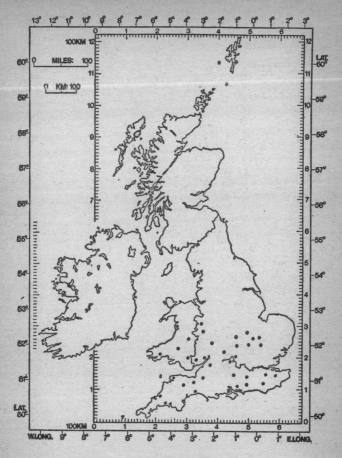

20. The Brown Hairstreak, *Thecla betulae*

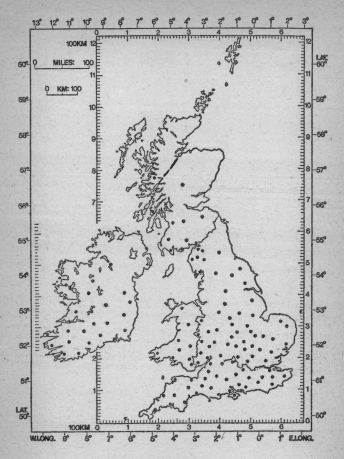

21. The Purple Hairstreak, *Thelca quercus*

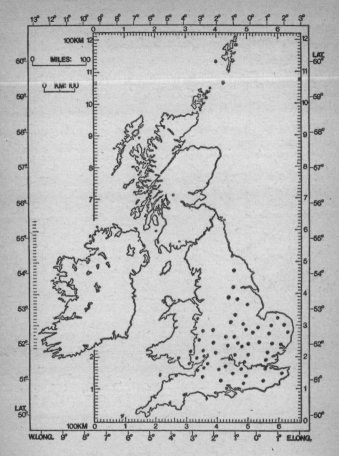

22. The White-letter Hairstreak, *Strymonidia w-album*

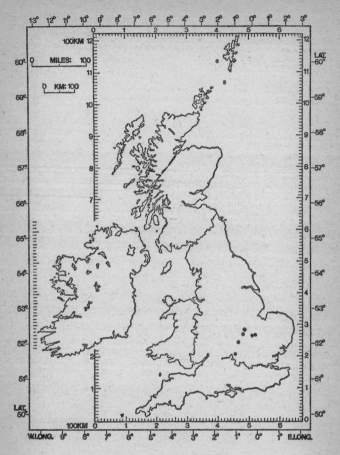

23. The Black Hairstreak, *Strymonidia pruni*

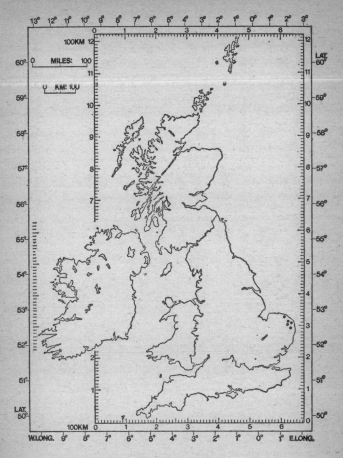

24. The Swallow-tail, *Papilio machaon*, sub-sp. *britannicus*

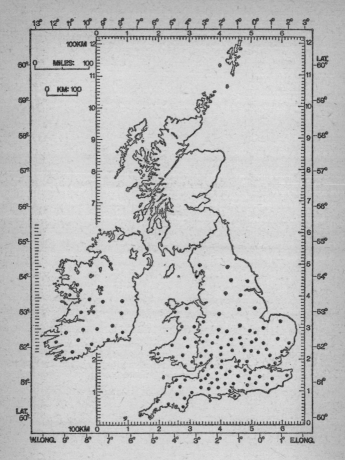

25. The Brimstone, *Gonepteryx rhamni*

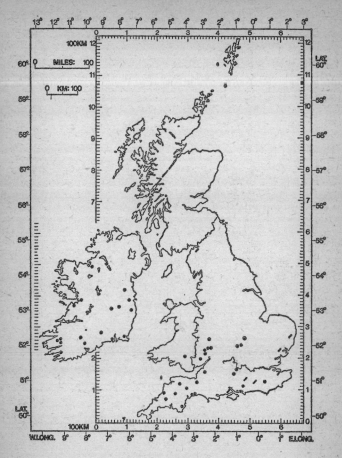

26. The Wood White, *Leptidea sinapis*
I = extinct

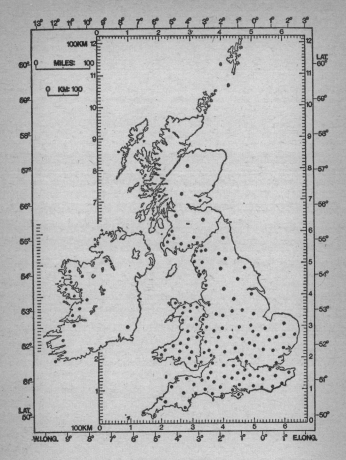

27. The Dingy Skipper, *Erynnis tages*

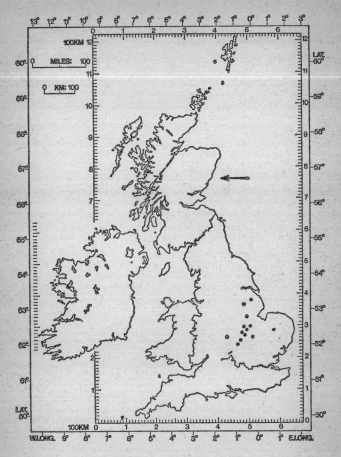

28. The Chequered Skipper, *Carterocephalus palaemon*

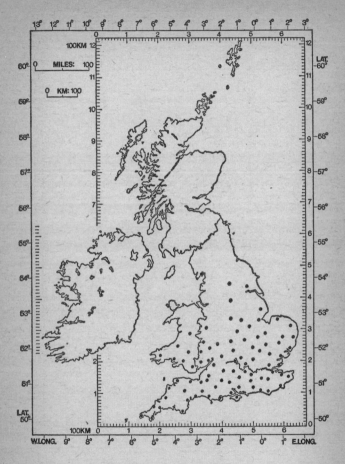

29. The Small Skipper, *Thymelicus sylvestris*

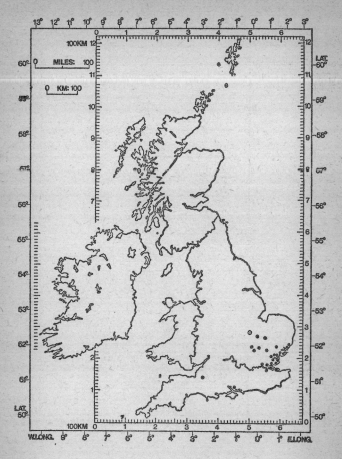

30. The Essex Skipper, *Thymelicus lineola*

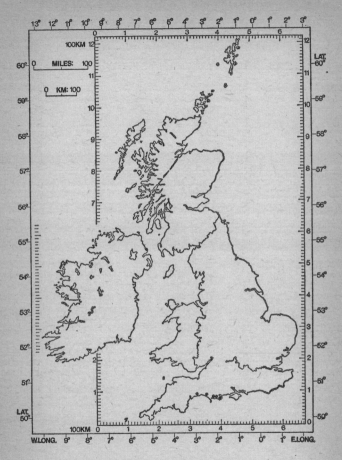

31. The Lulworth Skipper, *Thymelicus acteon*

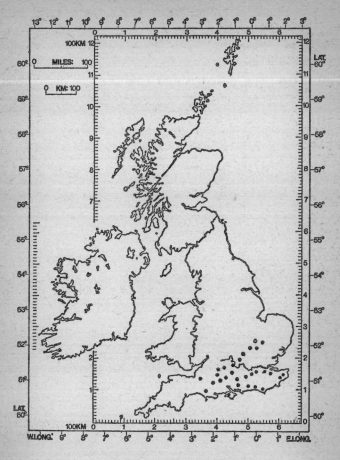

32. The Silver-spotted Skipper, *Hesperia comma*

Index

The plates are numbered *in heavy type*, from 1 to 24 in Arabic Numeration. Plates and maps are indexed immediately after the name of each species of butterfly, and before references to pages in the text, except when they apply to sub-headings, under which they are also entered before the pages.

Scientific names are used except for the species generally recognized as British, which are indexed under the English names employed in this book. The scientific equivalents for these are given on pp. 303–4

For Your Protection

Details of these attractive **C.I.S. PLANS** to protect You and your Family and your Home are yours for the asking—entirely without obligation. Fill in your name and address and post the card. Postage is paid.

CO-OPERATIVE INSURANCE SOCIETY LTD. MANCHESTER M60 0AL

Tick plan and post card today

Name _____

Address _____

_____

_____

Fire and Domestic Combined

Mortgage Security Plan

Motor Insurance Plan

Savings Plan For Young Men

Pension Annuity Plan

Savings Plan For Young Women

Special Endowment Plans

Ten Year Savings Plan

CFN